A Collection of Cases
in Marketing Management

SECOND EDITION

A Collection of Cases
in Marketing Management

SECOND EDITION

H. ROBERT DODGE
Youngstown State University

WILLIAM G. ZIKMUND
Oklahoma State University

WEST PUBLISHING COMPANY
St. Paul   New York   Los Angeles   San Francisco

Design Rick Chafian
Copyediting Bill Olson
Interior art Alice B. Thiede
Cover art and design Theresa Jensen

Library of Congress Cataloging-in-Publication Data

A Collection of cases in marketing management.

    Rev. ed. of: A Collection of outstanding cases in
marketing management. c1979.
    1. Marketing—United States—Management—Case studies.
I. Dodge, H. Robert, 1929–   . II. Zikmund, William G.
III. Collection of outstanding cases in marketing management.
HF5415.13.C64 1987   658.8'00973   87–6072 ∞
ISBN 0–314–85313–8

1st Reprint—1987

To the next generation of marketing managers

Contents

Preface

A Collection of Cases in Marketing Management is a select group of cases written by a number of authors with diverse experiences. A problem with many casebooks is that they contain three or four outstanding cases, because the author may have had recent consulting experience with three or four organizations, whereas the remainder of the cases tend to be of rather mediocre or poor quality. To minimize these extremes in case quality, we have gathered together this anthology of cases.

What makes a case outstanding for teaching and learning about marketing management? Selecting the best educational cases is not unlike choosing the winner of the Academy Awards or awarding the Nobel Prize. These are evaluative decisions that are, to an extent, subjective. Nevertheless, the editors have carefully attempted to make this selection as objective as possible.

Our major concern, in choosing cases, was the consideration: How much will the student learn about marketing management and strategy. To accomplish this broad goal, the cases selected for inclusion in this volume have been assessed on the basis of several criteria.

First, and of foremost concern, was whether or not a certain case could generate student involvement. Active participation is one of the most effective forms of learning. The case method is based on the principle of learning by doing. Each case in this volume meets this standard. A second factor, related to the first criterion, concerns the need to explore issues that are open to debate and criticism. Most of the cases included in this volume allow students to glean insights about the strengths and weaknesses of alternative solutions to the same problem. The world of marketing is not black and white, with clear-cut alternatives. Most solutions are found in that nebulous area of the real world.

The cases appearing in this book were evaluated so that the overall selection of cases would meet the criterion of diversity. The cases deal with products or services in both consumer and industrial markets. Some of the products are mundane, such as table salt, others are controversial, such as the Dungeons and Dragons brand, which adds an additional issue to discuss along with the organization's marketing management strategies and activities. The cases deal with diverse problems faced by large corporations and small businesses, business organizations and not-for-profit organizations, and domestic marketers and multinational organizations. But the one thing in common is each case in this book deals with a situation that actually occurred. Although each case meets the criterion of realism, in some instances the real names are disguised because the organizations involved prefer to remain anonymous. Nevertheless realism is a feature of every case in this collection of outstanding cases. An educational weakness of many cases is that they do not focus on a single problem area, such as pricing. While comprehensive cases have their purpose at the end of the semester, theory translated into action is best learned one step at a time. Although it was not always possible, we have attempted to include cases that address only one aspect of the marketing mix.

Another criterion was to include selections that allow the student to identify easily with the characters portrayed. The role-playing dimension of the case method has become an important factor in developing the young man's or woman's ability to respond to the old business curmudgeon playing the devil's advocate.

A final criterion was whether or not the case gives the students the opportunity to hone their analytical skills.

Using the above criteria, the editors undertook an extensive search of available cases to determine which of the many cases in marketing management should be included here. We are indebted to a number of colleagues for their help in compiling these cases; nevertheless, for the most part, the cases which have been selected reflect the editors' perceptions and biases about using the method.

The editors would like to acknowledge the help of numerous colleagues and universities in their allowing us to reproduce their cases. In particular, we would like to thank Moustafa H. Abdelsamad, Virginia Commonwealth University; Richard F. Beltramini, Arizona State University; Margaret L. Friedman, University of Wisconsin-Madison; H. Landis Gabel, INSEAD; Jon M. Hawes, University of Akron; Harry R. Knudson, University of Washington; Frederick B. Kraft, Wichita State University; Robert J. Listman, Valparaiso University; David Loudon, University of Rhode Island; Lester A. Neidell, University of Tulsa; James E. Nelson, University of Colorado; Stuart U. Rich, University of Oregon; Alain Sabathier, INSEAD-CEDEP; Jeffrey D. Schaffer, University of New Orleans; Donald Sciglimpaglia, San Diego State University; Nancy Stephens, Arizona State University; Patricia Stocker, University of Denver; W. Wayne Talarzyk, Ohio State University; Lester A. Thompson, California State University-Sacramento; Thomas L. Wheelen, University of South Florida; William R. Wooldridge, University of Massachusetts and William R. Wynd, Eastern Washington University.

We would also like to thank Decision Sciences Institute, Harvard University, INSEAD, University of Minnesota, Montana State University, and the University of Western Ontario.

The authors are most appreciative of the comments, suggestions and criticisms from the following individuals: James L. Brock, Montana State University; Randi S. Ellis, North Harris County College; Ron Hoverstad, Texas Christian University; Geoffrey Lantos, Bentley College; W. Glynn Mangold, Murray State University; Wayne Norvell, Kansas State University; Dillard B. Tinsley, Stephen F. Austin State University; and William R. Wynd, Eastern Washington University.

A special word of thanks goes to our editor, Molly Smith Weber, for her help in all the phases of the project. Peggy Adams carefully took control during the production of the book. Her concern for the quality of the book is deeply appreciated. Also, we thank Joan Kirkendall and Helen Costas, who have worked behind the scenes on permissions and performing the important word processing job. Ann Dyer served as an able graduate assistant. Finally, our appreciation is given to those members of our families who have had to adjust to grievances and short tempers that were directly attributable to bringing together this collection of cases.

The last we have to offer to the users of this anthology is the hope that you may find these cases as rewarding and useful in your instruction as we have found them in ours.

H. Robert Dodge
Youngstown State University

William G. Zikmund
Oklahoma State University

A Collection of Cases in Marketing Management

SECOND EDITION

The Case Method of Learning

"The essence of knowledge is having it to apply it." This old adage expresses the philosophy underlying the case method of learning. Although students accumulate a great deal of knowledge by reading textbooks, listening to lectures, and participating in classroom discussions, the accumulation of knowledge about facts and theories is not the true test of learning. The case method of learning is based on the idea that students must experience the situation to truly learn.[1]

A *case* (or *case study*) is a description of a situation, usually a specific organization, that will require you to identify a marketing problem and to make a decision concerning the best course of action. A case is like a short story, except that the events portrayed have actually occurred. The situation and story are real, not fictional. In some cases, the identity of the firm is readily apparent while in others it is disguised.

The typical situation portrayed in a case is a description of the circumstances that existed at a particular moment in time when an organization faced a problem or opportunity and had to come to a decision. The purpose of case analysis is not to learn what decision the managers actually made (they may have been quite wrong!), but to provide you with a realistic problem that allows you to apply "textbook knowledge." The historical aspects of the case method of learning will offer you the opportunity to add to your knowledge about marketing practices. Merely reading a case will provide you with some insights into the activities of various industries and organizations. More importantly, utilization of the case method provides the opportunity to develop the art of independent thought and critical judgment. You can enhance your ability to devise creative solutions in rigorous problem-solving situations.[2] The essence of the case method is that you apply what you have learned.

HOW TO PERFORM A CASE ANALYSIS

As much as we would like to tell you "The" best way to analyze a case, we cannot. Each case is unique. The cases in this book cover a broad spectrum of organizations and a diversity of problems. Further, and perhaps the main reason why we cannot, is that individual students will take different paths to develop logical ways to identify and solve the problems facing the decision makers identified in the case study. However, we may be able to offer some helpful hints and to suggest a standardized way of writing up a case analysis.

[1] Bruce Gunn, "The Competitive Case Presentation and Critique Training Method," *Journal of Marketing Education,* Spring 1983, p. 23.

[2] William F. O'Dell, "And Once Again ... The Case Method Revisited," *Collegiate News and Views,* Winter 1975, p. 17.

Remember, of course, that the specific nature and purpose of each case will place different demands upon you, and this outline should be altered to fit the situation. In general, you should prepare a case analysis by proceeding through the following stages:

1. Read the case thoroughly
2. Perform a situation analysis
3. Formulate a problem statement
4. Identify alternative decisions or courses of action
5. Identify the criteria for decision making
6. Choose an alternative and/or make recommendations for future company action

Read the Case Thoroughly

The purpose of reading the case is not only to familiarize oneself with the situation but also to comprehend its contents as efficiently as possible.[3] To get an accurate feel for the situation and to understand the pertinent information most students will have to read the case study more than once. Most students will find it useful to take notes summarizing key facts, symptoms of problems, constraints, and major issues. You may find it valuable to identify the role players in the situation and to ascertain their objectives that are not being met. For example, customers may not be assured of quality even though they pay higher than market price for the product or service.

Perform a Situation Analysis

The situation analysis is a systematic mapping of all the factors that focus on the case problem(s).[4] Many cases will be loaded with facts and descriptions about events, activities, and problems experienced or faced by the principal characters in the case. However, in many cases, as in the "real world," much of this data is superfluous. To do a good job in the situation analysis, you must be able to identify "red herrings," to distinguish miscellaneous facts, trends, opinions, and so forth from pertinent information that will be needed to make an intelligent decision. For example, a manager's opinion about what is causing a company's sales to drop may be stated in the case. In the situation analysis, you must determine if this is merely an "off-the-cuff" opinion by a "minor" character or pertinent information that is supported by quantitative data or other evidence presented in the case.

Some cases present an overabundance of accounting, survey research, or other data that may or may not be especially relevant to the problem. Your task is to analyze what information in the case is needed to adequately assess the situation. We warn you not to take everything at face value. A good starting point for a situational analysis is to ask questions about the case. This starts you thinking

[3] Robert Ronstadt, *The Art of Case Analysis: A Student's Guide* (Medham, Mass.: Lord Publishing, 1977), p. 7.
[4] Gunn, "The Competitive Case Presentation and Critical Training Method," p. 24.

about the various aspects of the case and their relative value to a solution of the problem. Questions also aid you in making sure that the analysis is complete.

Formulate a Problem Statement

The problem statement indicates a specific marketing decision area or problems that will be alleviated, or at least clarified, after a particular decision alternative is chosen. The old adage "a problem well defined is a problem half solved" is worth remembering because orderly definition of the problem gives a sense of direction to the case analysis. The problem statement should identify what you think are the key issues and what major hurdles must be overcome to achieve the organization's objectives.[5] In many situations you will not be able to discover the actual problem because you lack sufficiently detailed information. Under these circumstances it may be appropriate to make certain assumptions about the organization. However, a more typical difficulty is a situation in which the student confuses the symptoms for the real problem. Declining sales is of course a real "problem" in one sense but, in terms of the case analysis, it is merely a symptom that something is wrong. The problem may be the product, its pricing structure, or one or more of a host of happenings. Learning how to make the distinction between symptoms and problems is one of the goals of the case method. You can improve this skill with practice.

Identify Alternative Decisions or Courses of Action

Typically, you will be able to identify several courses of action. For example, introduction of the new product nationwide or the decision not to commercialize the product are two alternative courses of action that can be taken after a test market. In many situations, however, the listing of alternatives will require a great deal of imagination and creativity. Again, this is a situation where you may be leery about specifying alternatives. However, in coming to the best decision, you must avail yourself of the full range of possibilities.

The French philosopher, Emile Chartier, said: "Nothing is more dangerous than an idea when it is the only one you have." By presenting alternative solutions and different points of view at this stage, the case analyst can exercise better critical judgment at the decision-making stage.

Identify the Criteria for Decision Making

A criterion is a standard of judgment or an established rule for selecting the best alternative to solve a problem. The profit criterion, of course, is important in most case studies. However, other criteria such as maintaining professional ethics or making a decision consistent with the total company or organizational mission may be equally as important in some situations. Your job is to weigh the evidence provided in the case with respect to each criterion and evaluate each alternative while taking into account the relevant criteria.

[5] Ibid.

Choose an Alternative and/or Make Recommendations for Future Company Action

After the pros and cons of each alternative have been weighed, you must make a decision. You should also explain why your decision was made.

Making the decision is the "bottom line" of case analysis. Too often students will hem-and-haw and postpone making a true decision. Stating that there is not enough information in the case and that the decision maker should collect additional information is easy to do (and may be appropriate in some situations), but most case studies should not end on this tentative note. The purpose of this stage is to force students to make a critical judgment for the manager at that moment in time described in the case and based on the information currently available to the manager. This is not easy to do, but it is why the case method of learning is so enjoyable and effective.

Some Helpful Do's and Don'ts

Exhibit 1 is a checklist of do's and don'ts for case analysis that was written by two professors who utilize the case learning method in their classes.

Exhibit 1. Checklist of Do's and Don'ts in Case Analysis

Concept	Do	Don't
Finding the problems	Start with the firm's customers and their needs if you don't know where to begin.	Don't assume the problem is given. No problem is self-evident.
Problem reporting	List the two or three major problems in the company.	Don't mix minor and major problems together. Solving small problems usually is not enough.
Report direction	Provide direction to your written analysis. Address your report to a specific person or group.	Don't write without a particular person in mind. You have an audience to whom you are selling your ideas.
Report content	Cover the following areas: statement of the problem, proof you've found the problem. Recommendations. Prove your recommendations are worthwhile.	Don't cover the following areas: the firm's history or minor personality problems.
Financial data	Use the data given. Know how to compute basic financial ratios.	Don't skip over tables and charts. You should spend more time on these than you do with text space of similar size.
Recommendations	Make specific recommendations and prove why they should be adopted.	Don't be vague or call for a "re-evaluation." You have to be meaningful when offering improvements.
Plans	Offer the steps (method) that should be used to carry out your recommendations.	Don't assume a good recommendation is enough. The method of implementing your recommendation should be given in detail.
Organization	Use a format that has subheadings to ensure good organization of thoughts and a reader.	Don't write without breaks between major sections in your paper.
Imagination	Use outside material. Experts on the subject can be interviewed. You could even do your own market survey.	Don't begin writing without gathering all relevant data.

Note: Reprinted by permission from M. Wayne Delozier and Arch Woodside, *Marketing Management: Strategies and Cases* (Columbus, Ohio: Charles E. Merrill, 1978), p. 20.

One

Introduction

TSR HOBBIES, INC.

ST. PETER'S HOSPITAL

POTTY POSIES

TARGET STORES

THE STAMPLER COMPANY

ROCKWOOD MANOR

HOME PRODUCTS UNIVERSAL

TSR Hobbies, Inc.—
"Dungeons and Dragons" *

T SR (Tactical Studies Rules) Hobbies, Inc., had grown rapidly since its start in 1973 to sales of $27 million in fiscal 1983. TSR's star product responsible for this rapid growth was "Dungeons and Dragons," a unique fantasy/adventure game. The game was unique because it happened largely in the minds of its players. Its emphasis on cooperation among players and dependence upon their imaginative powers set it apart from traditional board games.

OVERVIEW

Company History

TSR Hobbies, Inc. was founded by E. Gary Gygax in a small Wisconsin resort town. Gygax never graduated from high school, but pursued his passion for fantasy in the forms of war games and science fiction books. When Gygax lost his job as an insurance underwriter in 1970, he started developing fantasy games almost full-time, while supporting his family with a shoe repair business in his basement. In 1973 Gygax persuaded a boyhood friend and fellow war game enthusiast, Donald Kaye, to borrow $1,000 against his life insurance and TSR Hobbies, Inc. was founded.

* This case was prepared by Margaret L. Friedman, University of Wisconsin. This case appeared originally in *Marketing Management: Knowledge and Skills,* J. Paul Peter and James H. Donnelly, Jr. Reprinted with permission of the author.

The two gamers published a popular set of war game rules for lead miniatures called "Cavaliers and Roundheads." In January of 1974 another inveterate gamer friend, Brian Blume, invested $2,000 in the company, and the three partners printed the first set of rules for "Dungeons and Dragons." The game was assembled in the Gygax home and was sold through an established network of professional gamers. In 1974, 1,000 sets of the "Dungeons and Dragons" game were sold. Eight years later it was selling at the rate of 750,000 per year. The sales history for the product is shown in Exhibit 1.

The rapid growth of TSR was not necessarily a reflection of keen and experienced management skill. The three top officers in the company all lacked formal management training, but felt they could remedy this deficiency by taking management courses and seminars. Although TSR wanted to attract older, experienced toy and game managers to their ranks, most of their recruits came from outside the toy/game/hobby industry.

Between 1977 and 1982 the TSR work force grew from 12 to more than 250 employees. Gygax's original partner, Donald Kaye, died of a heart attack in 1975, and so the partnership was assumed by Gygax and brothers Brian and Kevin Blume. Gygax was president of TSR, Kevin was chief executive, and Brian was executive vice president. All company decisions were directed through Kevin Blume, from major decisions down to authorization for a $12 desk calendar for a

Exhibit 1.　Hobbies Sales

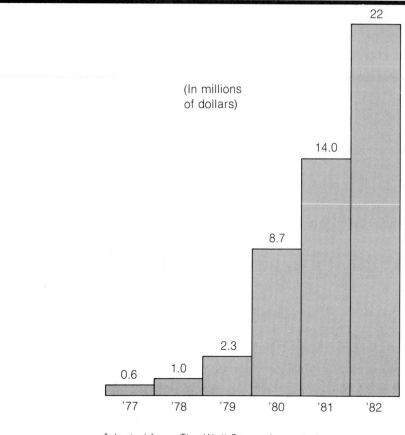

(In millions
of dollars)

22

14.0

8.7

2.3

0.6　1.0

'77　'78　'79　'80　'81　'82

Adapted from *The Wall Street Journal,* January 7, 1983.

secretary. There was some personnel turnover and evidence of employee dissatisfaction
due to nepotism in the company's hiring policies. It was reported that between 10 and 20
of Brian Blume's relatives were on the company's payroll.

The "Dungeons and Dragons" Game

"Dungeons and Dragons" represented a significant innovation in the game and hobby
industry. A basic set for a "Dungeons and
Dragons" game consisted of a lengthy instruction book, dice, and a wax pencil, all of
which sold for $12.

The game begins when each player gener-
ates a mythical character with a roll of the
dice. The personality profile for each character is determined according to rigorous
guidelines given in the instruction booklet.
For example, there is a Dungeon Master role
in each game. It is the Dungeon Master who
develops a map of the dungeon layout as
there is no game board. Each character has
particular spells and powers which are critical in negotiating the game's adventure. The
goal is to navigate through a treacherous
dungeon, arrive at a particular destination,
and depart alive with the treasure. The combination of mythical characters and adventure is why "Dungeons and Dragons" is
called a role-playing/fantasy/adventure
game. No two "Dungeons and Dragons"
games are alike since the way the game un-

folds depends upon the players' imaginations.

To survive, players must work together, rather than against one another, winding their way through a dangerous path to the treasure. Players are confronted with conquest after conquest involving ghouls, monsters, dragons, and other obstacles to finding the treasure and escaping with it. The instruction booklet describes the various powers and spells available to the different characters and general rules for behaving in the dungeon. The crayon is used to keep track of pathways taken and used-up spells. The game can last from two hours to weeks on end—it is all up to the imaginative powers of the players.

MARKETING STRATEGY

TSR's goal was to double sales every year. The strategy used to achieve this goal was based heavily on target market expansion, product line expansion, expansion of promotional activities, and more intensive distribution.

Expansion of Target Market

When "Dungeons and Dragons" was first introduced, it was targeted solely to experienced gamers. The first edition of the game came in a plain brown bag and the rules were so complex that only experienced gamers could decipher them. Word of the game spread to college campuses with the help of publicity involving a Michigan State University student who was rumored to be lost in the steam tunnels under the campus while playing a "live" "Dungeons and Dragons" game. This potentially negative publicity for "Dungeons and Dragons" turned into an advantage for the company since it created word-of-mouth advertising and interest among college students.

As the product matured, the median age of new buyers dropped from college age to the 10–14-year-old bracket. Typically, these consumers were boys described as introverted, intelligent, nonathletic, and very imaginative. The game provided an outlet for such boys to join in a group activity and helped bring them out of their shells. In fact, educators noted that "Dungeons and Dragons" welds a group of players into an ongoing joint project that teaches participation, assertiveness, and cooperation.

To further increase sales of the product, TSR targeted the product to new consumer groups. For example, at one point, women made up only 12 percent of the total number of purchasers. TSR conducted consumer research and found that women felt the game was created as a release for "macho" fantasies. Many women also stated that the lengthy instruction manual (63 pages) would take too long to read and be wasteful of their time. In response to such perceptions, TSR (1) publicized the fact that the game is not cutthroat and competitive, (2) reduced the length of the instruction manual, and (3) created a game which can be played in a limited amount of time. TSR also targeted downward to the younger children's market with a product that transferred the "Dungeons and Dragons" theme to a more conventional board game called "Dungeons!"

Expansion of Product Lines

Initially, the basic "Dungeons and Dragons" set was marketed as a hobby, rather than as a game. A hobby involves a starter toy which is enhanced with a myriad of add-ons. For example, a miniature train is considered a hobby since the engine and track form the basis for building an entire railroad system, including special cars, track, scenery, stations, and so on over time. Similarly, for each $12 basic "Dungeons and Dragons" set sold, retailers could expect an additional $150 in satellite or captive product purchases in the form of modules that provide supplemental adventures of varying complexity. There were at least 50 such satellite products on the market.

Since TSR management recognized that their short product line was vulnerable to competition from such toy and game giants as Mattel, Parker Brothers, Milton Bradley, and Ideal, several other new products were introduced to extend the line. Most of these new introductions followed the role-playing, fantasy theme. For example, since each fantasy world in a "Dungeons and Dragons" game has its own set of characters and monsters, a line of miniature lead figurines of these creatures was introduced. These included miniature dragons, wizards, and dwarves. Although these figurines are not necessary to play the game, it was hoped that a market of figurine collectors would develop.

TSR also marketed a number of other role-playing games, including "Top Secret," a spy adventure game; "Boot Hill," a western adventure game; "Gamma World," a futuristic game; and "Star Frontiers," a science fiction game, all of which were quite successful. Somewhat less successful have been TSR's other board game entrants, "Snit's Revenge," "The Awful Green Things from Outer Space," "Escape from New York," and "Dungeons!" These more conventional board games were intended to change the company's image from that of a producer of complex, esoteric games to a producer of a broader range of game products.

TSR also added new lines to their product mix. For example, they produced a feature-length film using a "Dungeons and Dragons" theme, as well as a successful Saturday morning cartoon program for children and an hour-long pilot for a radio-theater program. TSR's other ventures included purchase of *Amazing* magazine, the oldest science fiction magazine on the market (since 1926) and publishing *Dragon* magazine which was begun in 1976 and obtained a circulation of over 70,000 copies per issue. The Dragon Publishing division of TSR also produced calendars and anthologies of fiction, nonfiction, and humor. TSR's most popular publications included *Endless Quest* books. Young readers determine the plot of these stories by making choices for the main character. Depending on the choices made, the reader is directed to different pages in the book. Therefore, each book contains a number of different adventure stories. TSR also developed a line of books called *Heart Quest*, which are romance novels for teenagers in this same create-your-own-plot format. TSR had performed consulting services for a failing needlework company owned by a friend of Gygax. To further its diversification efforts TSR acquired this company briefly, realizing soon, however, that it was a poor investment.

TSR found licensing to be a profitable form of product line expansion. Arrangements were made to permit 14 companies to market products that displayed the TSR and "Dungeons and Dragons" name. For example, Mattel, Inc. was sold a license for an electronic version of "Dungeons and Dragons" and St. Regis Paper Company was sold a license for a line of notebooks and school supplies.

Expansion of Promotional Activities

In the beginning, TSR relied on word-of-mouth advertising among gamers to sell the "Dungeons and Dragons" game. As their markets expanded, TSR employed other promotional methods, including television commercials and four-color magazine ads. TSR's ad budget in 1981 was $1,194,879 which was divided as follows: 13 percent on trade magazines, 28 percent on consumer magazines, and 59 percent on spot television. During the Christmas season of 1982, $1 million was spent on a television campaign for the "Dungeon!" board game.

The company's logo and accompanying slogan were updated in 1982. Formerly, the logo showed a wizard next to the letters TSR and the slogan "The Game Wizards." The updated logo included a stylized version of the letters "TSR" and the slogan "Products of the Imagination." This updated logo and slogan were designed to convey an image with broader market appeal.

TSR sponsored an annual gamers convention which attracted dozens of manufacturers and thousands of attendees to Kenosha, Wisconsin. This became the largest role-playing convention in the world which included four days of movies, demonstrations, tournaments, seminars, and manufacturers' exhibits. The company also sponsored the Role Playing Game Association. This association offered newsletters and informational services and was responsible for calculating international scoring points to rate players in official tournaments. It also provided a gift catalog of premiums available only to RPGA members.

In the beginning, the printing and artwork needed for the "Dungeons and Dragons" instruction booklet were contracted with suppliers outside of TSR. The company has since engaged in backward vertical integration into the manufacturing process by hiring a staff of artists and purchasing its own printing facility.

Expansion of Distribution Channels

Retail distribution was originally concentrated in hobby stores, but expanded rapidly into department stores and bookstores, although some mass market retailers such as Sears, Penneys, and K Mart were reluctant to stock all of the satellite products generated by the basic "Dungeons and Dragons" set. This evolution from exclusive distribution through hobby stores to intensive distribution followed naturally from the concomitant expansion of target markets and product lines.

Over time TSR employed as many as 15 manufacturers' representatives who marketed the product through independent wholesalers in nine territories. One problem with this distribution system was that the company did not have close contact with its wholesalers, and hence, were not able to offer much merchandising assistance.

TSR opened its own retail hobby shop for a brief period. However, this outlet attracted a lot of mail order business, creating channel conflict among other retail hobby outlets, and the shop was closed in 1984.

EXPANSION PROBLEMS

TSR obviously grew quickly and expanded in many different directions which caused several problems. For example, TSR announced it would hire over 100 new employees and 50 new hires were actually made in June of 1983. However, by April of 1984, over 230 employees were laid off. The rapid loss of personnel resulted in coordination problems. For example, two different products were packaged in boxes with identical graphics on the covers. The layoffs also created morale problems.

In an effort to "tighten the reigns," Kevin Blume eliminated half of the company's 12 divisions to streamline accounting, reporting, and general decision making. TSR was then divided into four separate companies: TSR Inc. for publishing games and books, TSR Ventures Inc. for supervising trademark licensing, TSR Worldwide Ltd. for managing international sales, and Dungeons and Dragons Entertainment Corporation for producing cartoons. Each company functioned independently of the others, with its own stock and board of directors. Still, the three partners sat on all four boards in order to maintain tight control over the company.

TSR's full-fledged entry into the mass market also drained their cash reserves, creating cash flow problems for the company. Business practices in the mass market were different than what TSR was accustomed to in the specialized hobby market. For example, it is common to cater to mass retailers by allowing six months payment whereas 30 days or less is more usual for small hobby shops. Also, demand is relatively smooth in the hobby market unlike the mass market which experiences a Christmas buying rush. Thus, TSR was not prepared for the retail Christmas buying rush and many items ordered were out-of-stock.

TSR also faced an image problem in the mass market, illustrated in the positioning map shown in Exhibit 2. The early success of "Dungeons and Dragons" depended largely upon its image as a mysterious hobby that

Exhibit 2. Positioning Map

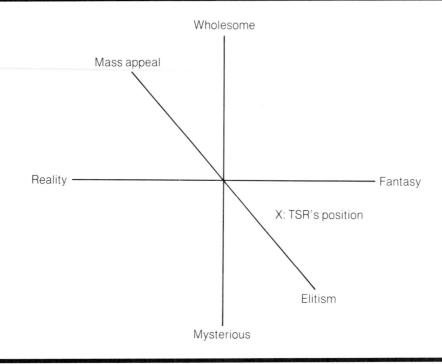

was not for just anyone, but only for an elite few. Because of this image, many consumers in the mass market were convinced that the "Dungeons and Dragons" game was "bad for the mind" because it involved hours and hours of make-believe. Dr. Joyce Brothers was engaged to endorse the product and to legitimize its role-playing format. In supporting the product she pointed to research results illustrating that children who played "Dungeons and Dragons" developed better reading skills, math skills, and basic logic and problem solving skills.

TSR faced formidable competition in the mass market. Large companies such as Milton Bradley, Mattel, and Parker Brothers spent more on advertising each year than TSR earned in profits. However, TSR's fantasy/role-playing concept was unique. Only Mattel's "He Man" and "Masters of the Universe" could be remotely compared to TSR's product concept. While the other traditional toy and game giants had no comparable fantasy/role-playing games, they dominated the northwest quadrant of the map in Exhibit 2, the market TSR wanted to enter. Though TSR was a market leader in fantasy/role-playing games in the hobby market, it remained to be seen whether this type of product could gain a respectable share of the mass market.

2

St. Peter's Hospital *

BACKGROUND

St. Peter's Hospital, a 200-bed acute care hospital in central Illinois, is owned and operated by an order of religious sisters. In 1978, the hospital's Board of Directors conducted a search to replace its retiring chief executive officer. Within six months, a successor was named: John Rowe, 40, who previously served in a similar institution as an assistant administrator. Mr. Rowe was selected for a variety of reasons, but primarily because of his reputation as an aggressive and innovative marketer of new health services. He was also considered an extremely diplomatic administrator with a proven track record in obtaining every *C.O.N.* he pursued. This was attributable to his skills in working with the regulatory agencies.

CURRENT DEVELOPMENTS

A Plan of Action. Within six months following Rowe's appointment to St. Peter's, he developed a priority plan for the hospital. Among the areas he hoped to develop were:

1. a home care dialysis center
2. an ambulatory care program (outpatient clinic)
3. expanded radiologic and laboratory facilities
4. the addition of 20 medical/surgical beds

5. recognition as an approved Trauma Center
6. remodeling of 90% of the existing facility
7. designation as a university teaching hospital

In a presentation which Rowe made to the hospital's Board of Directors he outlined his seven-point program. The Board was receptive to his assessment of needs; however, one member, an oncologist, stated the need to assign an eighth priority area, a hospice program. Dr. Bell, the oncologist, explained that,

Hospice is essentially an innovative program of palliative and supportive services to provide physical, psychological, social and spiritual care to the terminally ill and their families. St. Peter's is an ideal sponsor of a hospice program because of its already established acute care program.

Another board member, Sr. Marie Davis, noted that hospice care would be consistent with the healing mission of a Catholic health care apostolate. After minimal discussion, the Board overwhelmingly approved establishing hospice as the top priority area.

Determining Hospice Feasibility. The first action of the Board was to appoint a team to study the feasibility of implementing a hospice program. The in-house team proceeded to visit a variety of hospices around the U.S. and discovered several existing models. Included in these models were:

free-standing facilities
home care programs

* This case was prepared by Dr. Charles H. Patti and Debra Low. From *Cases in Advertising and Promotion Management* by C. Patti and J. Murphy, © 1983 John Wiley & Sons. Reproduced by permission.

combination home care/in-patient palliative care beds

multi-institutional arrangements

The team discovered that the pricing of
hospice programs was difficult to assess giv-
en the variety of existing hospice models, the
newness of the hospice concept, and the lack
of accurate cost data. They also discovered
that the Midland Illinois Health Systems
Agency which served the 12-county area en-
compassing St. Peter's service area would
recommend only one hospice per health systems area to the state's regulatory agency. It
was learned that three other hospitals within
the health systems area were also studying
the feasibility of launching a hospice program.

In speaking to hospice program directors,
the team learned that most persons in the
U.S. (including many physicians) have never
heard of hospice care. Although hospice care
had been featured in a number of television
news programs and was the subject of numerous newspaper and magazine articles, the
fact remained that the hospice movement
was suffering from a lack of sustained media
exposure.

Three months after its appointment, the
team reported its findings to the Board. Several conflicting points of view emerged at the
meeting. For example:

Four of the Board members proposed to
abandon the hospice program until additional information could be obtained on pricing
and reimbursement.

John Rowe stressed that he would like to
postpone commitment to the hospice program until the hospital achieved the other
seven priority areas.

Six nuns stressed that the Board already
made a commitment and should therefore
pursue the hospice program as the top priority.

Four persons believed the proposed St. Peter's Hospice should be a free-standing facility; four believed it should be a home care
program coordinated by the hospital's home

health department; and three others believed
it should be a combined home care/in-pa-
tient program.

Ultimately, all of this confusion led the
Board to decide to hire a marketing consultant to make recommendations. The consultant's mandate was to develop a complete
marketing plan for the proposed St. Peter's
Hospice. The plan was to focus on:

1. Service Development
   Major issues:
   a. determination of the most feasible
      hospice model to implement
   b. what needs exist among consumers?
   c. what services should be offered?

2. Pricing of Hospice Care
   Background facts:
   a. The room rate for an acute care bed in
      the oncology unit was priced at $140/
      patient day (semi private) and a nurs-
      ing home room was priced at $80 for a
      similar arrangement.
   b. Blue Cross/Blue Shield would not yet
      reimburse the costs of hospice care in
      the State of Illinois (see Exhibit 1).
   c. The availability of federal funds was
      limited due to a demonstration grant
      program awarded to 26 hospice pro-
      grams over a two-year period by
      DHHS (previously DHEW).

3. Distribution of Hospice Services
   Major questions to address:
   a. 24 hours a day or less?
   b. pain control medication as needed or
      on demand?
   c. who will refer to hospice?
   d. who should staff the hospice? who
      should direct it?
   e. should volunteers be used?

4. Promotion of Hospice Services
   Major questions to answer:
   a. who are the target market(s)?
   b. how to best create awareness among
      the target market(s)?
   c. how to stimulate ongoing patient re-
      ferrals?

d. what media are most effective in achieving communications goals?

Although the Board wanted to encourage maximum objectivity and creativity in the consultant's solutions, it decided to supply him with the information contained in Exhibits 1 through 4. The Board also told the consultant that:

1. The proposed hospice would service approximately 200 dying patients per year, based on the projections of anticipated cancer deaths in the hospital's service area.

2. The health care environment was extremely competitive.

3. The Board was reliant upon his recommendations due to their differing assessments of the situation.

4. He would have no more than three months to complete his analysis. He would also have up to $5,000 to spend on a suitable research project.

Exhibit 1. Summary of Promotion Studies *

Question 1:	"Have you heard of hospice care?"						
Results:	(1% of population responding "yes"):		Doctors:		88%		
			Nurses:		74%		
			General public:		18%		
Question 2:	"Indicate your level of knowledge about hospice care."						
Results:	General public	Very low	42%	28%	20%	8%	2%	Very high
	Doctors	Very low	0%	5%	8%	34%	53%	Very high
	Nurses	Very low	4%	12%	43%	23%	18%	Very high
Note:	Questions 1 and 2 were asked to a nationwide sample of doctors, nurses, and the general public.						
Question 3:	"How appealing is hospice care to you?"						
Results:	Very unappealing	21%	10%	32%	22%	15%	Very appealing
Question 4:	"How likely is it that you would prefer hospice care to conventional care?"						
Results:	Very unlikely	15%	20%	46%	11%	8%	Very likely
Note:	Questions 3 and 4 were asked only of the general public. Also, respondents were told to assume that they were in a position to consider hospice care.						
Question 5:	"If there was a hospice in your area, how likely is it that you would contribute your time as a member of a volunteer staff?"						
Results:	Very unlikely	8%	12%	62%	15%	3%	Very likely
Note:	Question 5 was asked to the general public only and they were told to assume that they had an appropriate amount of time available for volunteer work.						

Question 6:	"How likely is it that you would refer patients to a hospice?"						
Results:	Very unlikely	20%	30%	23%	12%	15%	Very likely

Question 7: "Rank order the following sources of information in terms of their importance in keeping you up-to-date on current trends in health care facilities. One (1) means the most important source of information and six (6) means the least important source of information."

Results:

Information source	Rank
talking with health care professionals	1
direct mail	2
tv, special topic tv programs	3
health care journals	4
health care columns in daily newspapers	5
medical journals	6

Question 8: "Rank order the following sources of information in terms of their importance to you as a source of general news."

Results:

Information source	Rank
newspapers	1
television	2
magazines	3
radio	4
direct mail	5

Note: Questions 6, 7, and 8 were asked of doctors only.

* During the past few years, several studies have been conducted among the various publics which are influential in the potential success/failure of the hospice movement. The above data have been extracted from some of the studies.

Exhibit 2. Summary of Distribution-Related Facts

- Population of the area which St. Peter's serves is 150,000.
- Population growth has averaged 5% during each of the past five years.
- There are no unusual demographic or economic characteristics of the geographic area in which St. Peter's is located. The city is one of the 10 largest in Illinois and is supported by agriculture, light manufacturing, service, and retailing.
- There is a rapid development of housing and shopping in areas away from the "downtown" district. Furthermore, there are no immediate plans for renewal of the "downtown" area.

Exhibit 3. Summary of Service-Related Information

Note: In early 1978, a government health agency conducted a nationwide survey on attitudes about hospice care. The following table has been taken from the final report.

Hospice care preferences: type of facility

Type of care	General public	Doctors	Hospital administrators
Home care	53%	5%	23%
In-patient	15%	82%	62%
Home care/in-patient combination	5%	10%	14%
No opinion	27%	3%	1%
	100%	100%	100%

Exhibit 4. Summary of Price-Related Information

1. The room rate for an acute care bed in the oncology unit was priced at $140/patient day (semi private) and a nursing home room was priced at $80 for a similar arrangement.
2. Blue Cross/Blue Shield would not yet reimburse the costs of "hospice care" in the State of Illinois. However, many hospice-type programs are reimbursed through other designations such as "acute care," "home health care," and "extended nursing care."
3. The availability of federal funds is limited due to a demonstration grant awarded to 26 hospice programs over a two-year period by DHHS (previously DHEW).
4. The general public does not consider pricing a highly relevant variable in the selection of the type of health care they can have because most health care is covered by third party reimbursement. This is particularly true when the health problem involves terminal illness. The cost of health care for terminally ill patients is relevant in the decision process only at the extremes of a cost continuum— that is, both "free" care and care costing $7,000–$10,000 per month are relevant decision variables.
5. Cost is more relevant to relatives of terminally ill patients than it is to the patient.
6. Hospice care *can* be a profitable unit for a hospital, but the nature of the service creates a comparatively low profit potential for doctors.

3

Potty Posies *

The New England Mop Company has been engaged in the development of a new style of toilet bowl deodorizer to be known as "Potty Posies." Ronald Felici, president of the company, must decide on the feasibility of the product and whether to launch it in the marketplace or abandon the idea.

COMPANY BACKGROUND

New England Mop is a small firm located in Rhode Island that manufactures wool dust mops. The company was taken over two years ago by new management, which changed several marketing policies and boosted mop sales. Peak sales revenue under the old management was $220,000 whereas under Mr. Felici's leadership the company has grown to over $400,000 in sales.

In addition to Mr. Felici, the company's management consists of a plant manager (a minority partner in the previous company) and a sales manager. The plant manager has developed machinery and techniques for manufacturing and has helped in the design of packaging for the mops. A staff of 9 to 17 report to the plant manager, depending on the amount of business at any time. The sales manager is responsible for generating and supervising the company's sales programs. Mr. Felici has worked most heavily in this area of the companies activities. He describes the company as being undercapitalized. Although the firm was purchased at a

price greater than the value of its assets, the new owners thought that with aggressive management this premium could be overcome with higher volume. The president describes the company's current situation as cash poor. "We are keeping our heads above water, with minimal profits being made," he said. "We don't have the physical resources to really run the company the way it should be," he commented, adding, "Any small company is at a disadvantage in human resources and good follow-through to really capitalize on all phases of their business."

CURRENT MARKETING ACTIVITIES

Product

New England Mop manufactures what it considers to be the "Cadillac" of the dust-mop market. The product is made of wool and has the brand name "Magnetic Mop," so named because wool creates static electricity as it is rubbed across a floor, and thus captures and holds dust particles. The company estimates its market share to be 75 percent of the wool mop sales made to the retail trade.

Most dust mops produced in the United States are made of acrylic fiber and are sold at low prices. Acrylic mops retail at $2 to $3 whereas the "Magnetic Mop" sells for $4.98. Some wool mops are even more expensive and sell for $9 when sold door-to-door. However, New England Mop considers the quality of their own product to be superior to even these higher priced products.

* This case was prepared by David Loudon of the University of Rhode Island. Used by permission.

Channels of Distribution

As of the late 1950s distribution of the mop was largely through hardware and department stores. This pattern has changed over time, away from the traditional hardware-houseware field toward large mass merchandisers and supermarkets. The company does no private branding. The process of shifting its emphasis from one channel to another has not been an easy one. Some resistance has been met on two fronts: (1) store buyers who never thought that top-quality mops would sell in mass outlets such as supermarkets and (2) consumers who were not used to buying high-quality dust mops in mass outlets. These resistances are being overcome and the company's penetration has been very successful.

New England Mop's sales force consists of 43 manufacturer's representatives who cover the United States. The representatives are paid 6 percent commissions on sales and carry complementary lines of other manufacturers.

Promotion

New England Mop offers an advertising allowance to its department store customers. The stores then advertise to final consumers. This program has been abused in the past and led to the shift to supermarkets and other mass merchandisers. The problem was that some stores exceeded their advertising allowance, which then had to be made up by New England Mop. For example, if a store ordered 100 mops, it would receive a $50 advertising allowance (at 50¢ per mop). However, their advertising for the mop might total $125. New England Mop would then have to pay the additional $75 expenditure. The difficulty in controlling these expenditures led the company to intentionally forgo much of the potentially profitable department-store business for other outlets. Despite this lost business, overall sales have risen substantially.

Pricing

The "Magnetic Mop" presently retails for $4.98 and wholesales for $2.36. Five years ago previous management raised retail prices from $3.95 to $4.49. As a result, sales to retailers dropped by one third. Two years ago, present management again raised prices, but only by 10 percent. However, costs of materials have gone up much more than 10 percent. For example, prices of corrugated cardboard for packaging have risen 50 percent in a year and a half. As a result of this particular increase, the company is designing a package to fit over only the mop's head, whereas previously the entire mop was placed in a box. Despite large and rapid cost increases, management did not think it could raise prices as fast as costs because of its desire to open up new retail outlets. It was feared that such price increases might alienate new customers. The firm decided instead to concentrate on higher volume to offset the higher costs. In retrospect, management thinks this decision was unwise. "We probably should have gone immediately to higher prices when increases were rampant, generally. Buyers would definitely have accepted the increases," Felici stated.

Price is determined by adding the cost of raw materials, labor, and manufacturing burden (directly related to fixed expenses of the business, expressed as a percentage of labor cost), together with allowance for poor products or rejects. Variable costs consisting of general and administrative expenses, selling commissions, cash discounts, freight, and other selling costs (e.g., advertising) are then added to yield total costs. A profit margin is then applied to determine a factory selling price.

NEW PRODUCT DEVELOPMENT ACTIVITIES

The increases in costs during the new management's first year of operation suggested that greater diversification was needed to generate additional profits. It was also thought that the company's channel of distribution was not being fully utilized with only one product. As Felici stated, however, "Getting into a new business without being experienced in this type of venture, and feeling as though we were amateurs in it, was not to be undertaken lightly."

The company decided to hire an industrial designer who had worked for some of the largest manufacturers in the country. The designer was given only one criterion for the work—to develop a product that would fit New England Mop's channel of distribution. The designer returned to the firm with the idea of a toilet bowl deodorizer made of colored cakes of paradichlorobenzene (better known as the material comprising moth balls) molded into the shape of flowers, which could hang in the toilet bowl, emitting a pleasant flower scent. The designer planned the product's shape, color, packaging, and merchandising display stand.

The coloring of toilet bowl deodorizers is not new; it was tried many years ago. However, it apparently created no great interest among consumers. The idea was discarded at the time because it also created manufacturing problems such as shorter production runs, downtime to clean machines, and so on.

Other minor changes which have been made in toilet bowl deodorizers in the past involve improved packaging and boxing of the product. However, there is currently no product on the market such as that suggested by the designer. All toilet bowl deodorizers presently on the market are simply round white cakes with rather antiseptic scents in basically the same form in which the product first appeared.

The industrial designer did not explicitly consider the market potential for the product in the development of the idea. The designer looked for a way to glamorize a product already on the market. Mr. Felici tried to estimate the market size for this item. He was unable to determine precise sales figures for toilet bowl deodorizers but did estimate the market for all paradichlorobenzene products (including moth balls, closet fresheners, and toilet bowl deodorizers) at between $10 to $15 million annually. This was based on estimated sales of some of the largest companies in the industry. Felici believed that toilet bowl deodorizers accounted for approximately one third of this total. He also determined that over a dozen large firms are active in the paradichlorobenzene market.

Although not being able to obtain a precise estimate of the size of the toilet bowl deodorizer market, two large associations of service merchandisers suggested that such products are the second largest selling item (behind panty hose) in the nonfood assortment in supermarkets. It is estimated that well over one half of all toilet bowl deodorizers are marketed through supermarkets. The only other important channel appears to be through mass merchandisers such as discount houses and variety chains.

Although the market potential appears sizable, Felici was somewhat uneasy over the fact that the item seems rather obscure to the average consumer. In talking with friends and acquaintances he has found that practically none of them uses this item. For this reason he suspects that the product is consumed mainly by lower income families who live in crowded housing and require deodorizing of the bathroom.

Based on the normal channels for this product, it appeared that New England Mop would not be able to capitalize on its distribution in the houseware-hardware field because they generally do not carry this item. Felici, however, was optimistic that they might be enticed to carry it because of the new item's special features.

New England Mop did not have facilities for production of toilet bowl deodorizers. Therefore, they would have to find a company to produce it for them. Mr. Felici knew his company could not be competitive on price with other companies in the business. He thought that the company, could, however, opt for a larger size cake with all its glamour and hit a price line not comparable with similar products, but still be in a price range the average consumer could afford. Felici decided that a reasonable retail price would be 69 cents for 5-oz Potty Posies. This compares favorably to the standard, white 3-oz cakes produced by other manufacturers which generally sell for 39 cents. Such products are advertised very little, and when they are, it is price-oriented; for example, a discount house may advertise a 39 cent toilet bowl deodorizer for 19 cents.

Mr. Felici saw no reason why sales of this item could not capture at least 5 percent of the toilet bowl deodorizer market of about $5 million. Thus, a realistic sales potential for this product would be $250,000 the first year. He estimated that the gross profit on the item should be 30 percent, with an expected return of 12 percent net profit on sales ($30,000 on sales of $250,000). This seemed to be an adequate return for not even touching the product.

Marketing research on other deodorizers (Tidy Bowl, Glade, etc.) was not considered by Felici. He believed his primary competition would come from other paradichlorobenzene cakes. Felici thought that the new product would reach a much different consumer from that reached by competitive toilet bowl deodorizers. He expected that it should attract not only about 5 percent of present buyers, but because of its unique qualities would also appeal to those who don't normally buy toilet bowl deodorizers. Those who buy aerosols should also be attracted because of the fear associated with inhaling such products. Penetration in the market might also be increased by offering it in new outlets such as hardware stores.

The product's prospects looked sufficiently promising for Mr. Felici to have some mock-ups made. The company spent $600 on handmade, plaster of paris toilet bowl deodorizers and a working model of a display merchandiser to be used in stores. These were taken to a large trade show in Chicago to test buyer reaction to the product. The display merchandiser and Potty Posies were also presented to two national groups of service merchandisers, and the reception by buyers was described by Felici as "great elation and enthusiasm."

4

Target Stores *

Target Stores is a division of Dayton-Hudson Corporation, one of the nation's largest and most diversified general merchandise retailing organizations. Dayton-Hudson is highly regarded in the retailing industry as an innovative and customer-oriented organization and is particularly well known as a firm that places great care on its strategic planning process.

The four main divisions of this multi-billion dollar retailing organization are organized around four principal business segments: Target low-margin stores, Mervyn's softlines stores, department stores (Hudson's, Dayton's, Diamond's, and John A. Brown), and specialty merchandisers (B. Dalton Bookseller, Lechmere).

Target is a low-margin discount store chain operating in more than 22 states located principally in the central and southwest sectors of the country. Target stores offer a merchandise mix of two-thirds convenience-oriented hardlines and one-third midrange fashion softlines. It was started in 1962 and has grown to become Dayton-Hudson's largest operating company and one of the country's largest chains.

TARGET MERCHANDISING STRATEGY

Target markets vast quantities of merchandise, accepting a lower profit per item in return for fast turnover. This simple retailing

* From: *Contemporary Cases in Consumer Behavior,* rev. ed., by Roger D. Blackwell, W. Wayne Talarzyk, and James F. Engel. Copyright © 1985 CBS College Publishing. Reprinted by permission of CBS College Publishing.

philosophy has generated a sales volume per Target store that is nearly twice the national average for discount stores.

In the typical 100,000-square-foot Target store, 65 percent of sales volume comes from convenience-oriented hardlines, from housewares to toys to white goods to toothpaste. Target management believes that Target has more of what the customer is looking for, including quality merchandise reinforced by brand names such as General Electric, Panasonic, Seiko, Norelco, Kodak, Polaroid, Coleman, Gillette, Michelin, Revlon, and many more. At the same time, Target taps the midrange fashion market, pressuring not only other discount stores but also department stores and softline giants such as J.C. Penney.

From its beginning, Target has employed first-rate data processing systems. It strives constantly for improvement in this area with electronic cash registers and in-store computers to aid in tight inventory control, timely markdowns, and quick trouble shooting. Target's Stock Status System gives buyers unprecedented information: complete sales histories plus current stock readouts for every store. Buyers can bring in key merchandise quickly to where it is selling the fastest.

MARKET TARGETS

Target describes itself as an upscale discounter, appealing to young families who are better educated, more affluent, and value conscious than other market segments. Target has traditionally been strong among mobile, fashion-conscious young families. Their active lifestyles require sporting goods, leisure clothes, and convenience appliances— all things Target stocks in abundance. A key to Target's growth has been its ability to recognize and react to a changing customer base, serving consumers of all ages and demographics who increasingly demand more for their money. Over 100 million customers visit Target stores each year.

Target attempts to hit its market segment with good merchandise at low cost. The needs of customers are met (1) by concentrating on the basic everyday merchandise families want most; (2) by selling less expensive versions of fashion-right merchandise; (3) by offering self-service shopping that saves the customer time and money; and (4) by selling quality imports that give customers more for their dollar.

Target researches trends early and moves fast to bring in new items that it believes are wanted by the target market. Target backs up this merchandise with substantial amounts of powerful advertising. Bold, colorful Target circulars reach over 13 million households almost every week of the year. Prepared at Target's Minneapolis headquarters, these circulars highlight such special events as Dollar Sale, Sight & Sound Sale, Birthday Sales, and many others. The company has documented that these circulars move tons of merchandise, producing dramatic sales increases.

TARGET: CONSUMER PROTECTOR

Target has taken an advanced position among retailers by formulating a corporate philosophy relating its assumptions about the contemporary consumer environment to its own plans for growth. Specifically, Target bases its plans and strategies on the assumption that its customers expect merchandise to last, to perform, and to be safe. Awareness of these concerns prompts Target to seek leadership in consumer satisfaction, but this awareness also has definite implications for management in many other areas of store operations and marketing.

The basis for many of Target's strategies and administrative and operating policies is contained in what the company describes as its "Guides for Growth." These guidelines, formulated by top management several years ago, have been central to almost every aspect of Target's policies during its period of rapid growth—growth that has occurred by both acquisition and internal growth. In recent months, management has begun to examine these guidelines, not because of any feeling of their inadequacy, but because of the firm's overall policy to keep all aspects finely tuned to the consumer environment.

The "Guides for Growth" that have been so central to Target's rapid growth and success are reprinted in Exhibit 1. Management is now discussing whether or not the guidelines need additions, deletions, or reprioritization to reflect current guidelines and values.

Exhibit 1.   Guidelines For Growth *

Target Is People

Target's growth plans will require a great many highly qualified people.

* This material is the property of Target Stores. A division of Dayton-Hudson Corporation and is reprinted with their permission. Reproduction without their written approval is forbidden.

Our objective is to put the most talented and the most experienced people in each job regardless of the source. We will favor our own people, training, developing and promoting the best qualified people from within. It is also expected that many well qualified people will be hired from outside.

We expect to develop and promote women and minorities because we believe such groups represent a valuable company resource which must be better utilized.

Target intends to pay salaries and to provide benefits which are equal to or better than those paid by other retail companies.

Target intends to manage the business unfettered by union organizations. This means that Target intends to satisfy employees' legitimate needs and concerns so well that union representation is not attractive to them.

Target is people.

Target Intends to Manage Its Growth

This statement says a lot.

It says we are not complacent. We are not satisfied. We are not as good as we want to be, nor are we as big as we intend to be.

It says we have a sense of urgency about the next decade. It speaks directly to how we intend to spend resources in pursuit of growth.

▪ First, we will refresh and maintain our present stores so they earn our customers' continued patronage. We recognize this as our number one obligation and our number one profit opportunity.

▪ Second, we will add stores where we already have stores, building back and filling in so profits and market share are improved.

▪ Third, we will grow into new markets. Our growth will be orderly and planned, in any area of the country where we can operate profitably.

Customers

Target Respects the People Who Shop Its Stores

We respect our customers' economic power and the fact that their decisions control our destiny.

We also respect customers as people, as individuals, with rights and with expectations.

▪ We respect their time. We try to lay out our stores so incoming people land immediately in merchandise and departing customers can do what they want most: get checked out and into their cars as fast as possible.

▪ We respect their dignity. In our contacts with customers we try to hear them as individuals, not as cash in the register. We try to look them in the eye. We try to smile a lot. We try to give the customer positive personal signals. This is hard and we fail often, but we try.

▪ We respect customers' desires to shop in a clean store. (And with that the desires of employees to be proud of the place they work.) This means all of the obvious things—clean floors, clean lots, fresh restrooms and much more.

▪ We respect customers' desires for honest communication. In ads, on signage, on hang tags, in personal contact. Any statement we make will be honest; totally, and without quibbling. We will not omit information of importance.

▪ We admit mistakes and correct them. In the normal course of a day, thousands of Target employees are in contact with tens of thousands of customers, who are buying hundreds of thousands of items of merchandise. Some mistakes will be made.

▪ Target's attitude on mistakes is clear. It is spelled out in our guarantee: we intend to correct. We intend to admit our mistakes, out loud. Customers have a right to know what is going on.

All of this adds up to respect for customers.

Target Is a Store for Young Families

I. Demographics

Target cannot be everywhere, serve all customer segments in the market, or sell all of the merchandise that everyone wants. We must choose whom we want to serve and what needs we will serve.

We will select locations, space departments, select and emphasize merchandise which appeals to families who are younger, have middle incomes and have younger children.

By emphasizing young families we recognize we will also be satisfying most of the needs of other age and economic groups. It is a conscious decision about who we intend to serve best in the future. It also recognizes Target is a chain, seeking uniformity of operations.

This statement carries with it the implications that merchandise which offers specific identification with the young family will be emphasized.

We intend to be meaningful, important, needed by young families.

II. Lifestyle

Target is a store for the young, the mobile, the active, the confident, the trend conscious. The customers that seek us out and whom we intend to serve have these lifestyle characteristics ...

- They are more active. Into leisure activities, sports, do-it-yourself, sportswear. Casual.

- They are more mobile. They move a lot. They buy merchandise associated with moving and with decorating new living quarters.

- They are confident about their own taste, able to discriminate. That is why they are in a self-service store.

- They appreciate value. They know quality. They know prices. Good quality merchandise at low prices is central to our offer and one of the key reasons they are in our store.

- They are up on trends. They know what's "right." They are at Target because they expect us to be a little ahead of some other stores.

These lifestyle indications help guide how we buy merchandise and how we run the stores.

III. A Special Rule of Common Sense

A rule of common sense applies to certain specific areas of merchandise which significant numbers of our customers find offensive in a family store setting.

Many of our customers have expressed themselves on the handling of "adult" magazines and we have responded by removing them. We have decided against handling merchandise in questionable taste. This is simply the application of common sense to our stores, the merchandise sold there and how it is sold.

We intend to be meaningful, important and needed by young families. We will be in keeping with the value systems of our young family-oriented customers.

Target Is an Honest-Dealing Store

This statement begins with society, with the customers whose needs we intend to meet better than anyone else. Very importantly, it begins with us— the management and employees of Target. It is what we—all of us at Target—want to be. It is what our customers want us to be—honest merchants of honest merchandise sold in an atmosphere of total honesty.

What do the words mean? A great deal . . .

- They mean our commitment to the idea that the customer has a right to expect us to act in his or her behalf, to choose merchandise carefully and to sell merchandise that performs as well as it looks. In a word—quality.

- They mean totally honest communications in advertising, in signage, in promotional techniques.

We explain our practices and policies, and meticulously avoid techniques which trick customers into the store, but lead to disappointment. When we advertise something, we have it in stock.

The concept of honesty continues to be one of the greatest opportunities we have to differentiate ourselves from the competitive alternatives our customers have available.

Being honest is good business. Being honest is the way we choose to operate.

Does that mean Target pays low salaries, or cuts corners on quality or service? No. It means very simply that all costs of operation are viewed in relation to their impact on our ability to deliver value as perceived by our customers.

Target Is a Self-Service Mass Merchant

Self-service means the presence of shopping carts in our stores. The carts say important things to our customers. They say "low prices." They say "don't expect merchandise you can't lift and put in the cart yourself."

Merchandise which requires sales help and product expertise is challenged as not consistent with customers' expectations of Target. Merchandise which cannot be handled conveniently by customers using shopping carts is suspect, and should be studied carefully before an exception is requested.

Target is a self-service store. Self-service means much to customers.

- It means low prices.

- It means fast and effective use of their time.

- It means "dress casually, come as you are, no need to dress up."

These customer expectations are the consequence of generations of experience with supermarkets and other self-service stores. They are not unique to Target, but perhaps we can be unique in living up to them better than other retailers.

Target is a self-service store. Our customers like it that way.

Target Matches Service to Customer Expectations

This statement speaks to the rare exceptions which will occur in our stores—the merchandise which does not meet the self-service criteria just laid down.

This is what it means . . .

- If an item of merchandise does not meet self-service criteria, it will be treated, examined and probed as an exception to our operating principles.
- Only Target's Chief Executive can authorize such exceptions. In the case of approved exceptions we are committed to providing whatever is called for to meet customers' service expectations—whether it be signs, technical information or added payroll.

Target Uses Management Systems and Computers to Keep Costs Down

Target has a record of accomplishments and leadership in its use of management systems and the computer. These systems are an important part of the traditions of Target, an integrating force in the business and a strong influence on the management style.

The systems we use are here to simplify our work, keep costs down, and expand our capacity to manage a larger chain.

- By helping us communicate the facts and the numbers of the business, continuously, to everyone who needs to know, when they need to know.
- By helping us maintain control of the many pieces of a business that gets far flung as it gets bigger.
- And by helping us perform tedious, repetitive, and expensive tasks more efficiently.

Target will be a leader in the early adoption of proven systems, techniques, and equipment. Since our business is retailing we do not intend to invest in the pioneering of new technology, but we do expect to be at the forefront of our industry using new technology when it is proven out. Since systems involve the whole Company, changes and improvements are only made with the involvement of all the affected parts of the Company.

This is one more way Target intends to serve its own and customers' interests in the future.

Target Is a Good Neighbor

Our stores are big. They are important to us; they are important to the neighborhoods where they are located, and their size places a special burden on us to be good neighbors.

We are committed to well designed exteriors, to parking lots that are maintained and kept clear, and to behavior and demeanor that makes us welcome in the communities where our stores are located.

That means . . .

- The exterior of our stores will be maintained to match the high housekeeping standards of the interior.
- Shopping carts will be picked up continuously.
- Special consideration for the handicapped including: parking spaces, restrooms, drinking fountains, telephones and checkout lanes.
- Outdoor signs will be maintained.
- Surfaces will be maintained, striping kept legible, lots kept free and clean.

It also means Target and its employees will be encouraged to be involved in community activities in meaningful ways.

Target is a good neighbor.

Target Will Keep the Cost of Moving Merchandise Down

This statement calls out a direction, the intent to create one of the most productive and efficient distribution systems in chain retailing. It is based on the belief that our present distribution systems are not good enough to support the growth we anticipate.

Target believes that "distribution" encompasses much of the cost of the business. It starts at the manufacturer's shipping dock and ends when goods have been checked out. It includes all of the ordering, receiving, moving, marking and recording of merchandise. Inherent in the direction are two thoughts about distribution technology . . .

- It must work to get merchandise to the store when needed.
- It must work to get distribution costs down and under rigorous control.

Getting and keeping distribution costs down is equally important to customers, employees and stockholders. It is a specific expression of the concept of keeping our costs low.

The Stampler Company *

The Stampler Company is a family-owned firm that supplies hardware to original equipment manufacturers (OEMs) in the automobile, recreational vehicle, and mobile home industries. In 1982 sales totaled some $200 million, about 5 percent more than in 1981, but only 20 percent higher than their best year in 1976. Profits before taxes were 11 percent of sales in 1982 compared to pre-tax profits in 1981 of 14 percent. The company operates three plants, two in the suburbs of Chicago and one in Rock Falls, Illinois, where the headquarters is located.

Tom Marks, the third in his family to hold the position of president and CEO, has regularly held staff planning meetings with his vice-presidents and designated staff officers for the last seven months. Worried about the progress of the company, Marks issued a confidential memo to those attending the meetings. Exerpts from the memo are as follows:

The question was raised at our last meeting about the purpose of these meetings, and it appears to be a good idea to hammer out the purpose of the meetings and define a procedure to follow to achieve that purpose. To start with, in a very naive state of mind, I would define the original purpose as follows:

Utilize a planning function approach (which could conceivably be a function of the staff organization if sold properly), to develop plans and procedures on a longer range basis (1–5 years) to achieve substantial growth in sales and profit for Stampler.

This purpose or goal is defined knowing that, although Stampler has shown growth over the

* This case was prepared by H. Robert Dodge.

years, the following factors detract from the assumption that significant growth will continue.

1. The growth we have had probably has been a result of the markets we were in rather than our own efforts. Increases in automobile production will not be as great because of increasing foreign car penetration.

2. Many new projects have aborted in the last few years for one reason or another. We seem preoccupied with the present.

3. Stampler already has a substantial share in each of our present markets.

4. We depend on too few customers. It is also possible that we may be in competition with our own customers.

A cursory investigation of the process of broadly establishing a corporate planning function to define how to achieve growth soon runs into a road block because the natural starting point seems to involve marketing and product planning, as well as research and development. In our organization, these functions are decentralized in both operating divisions, and there appears to be no way for staff to direct or influence the activities of these decentralized functions. The possibility of having a corporate staff marketing or R & D function is probably even more remote. Even financial planning or MIS (Management Information System) planning is largely dependent on the marketing and product plans of the operating divisions.

There is one factor, growth and diversification via acquisition, however, that appears potentially feasible for our staff activity. We already have a natural involvement in acquisition studies, as they may affect both operating divisions, and certainly if products and markets outside the operating divisions' interests could be identified, justified, and supported, our staff activity would probably be the only activity with that orientation.

Therefore, based on the above evaluation, our revised purpose for these meetings could probably be focused more sharply and be defined as follows:

Evaluate and define logical parameters for selecting acquisition candidates for Stampler, with the aim of establishing consistent and significant growth opportunities in sales and profit.

If we can mutually accept that purpose, then certain questions and concepts establish basic problems that have to be answered. At our last meeting on Friday, June 25, we were attempting to define possible products, markets, manufacturing processes, etc., as a natural step in the procedure to pursue the stated goal. (The results of that attempt are identified below.) It is now proposed that for our next meeting at 10 a.m., June 30th, we back up and mutually define the proper sequential procedure to follow, after we have agreed, of course, on the objective or purpose. This procedure, among other things, should probably include: (1) defining markets, products, and processes to be considered for acquisition; (2) zero in and define ways of evaluating the most logical products and markets and outline advantages and disadvantages to Stampler; (3) define methods of analyzing and evaluating markets and products for growth potential; (4) define alternative means of finding acquisition candidates—develop a shopping list; and (5) establish parameters for financial and risk evaluation of specific companies.

AUTOMOTIVE DIVISION

Stampler is divided into two operating divisions. In one, the Automotive Division, the company produces accessories, hardware, and components for all four automobile manufacturers. These items are made to the customer's specifications, and, for the last two years, Stampler has held the position of favored supplier because of its record on quality control. Braking systems have traditionally been a major product for the Automotive Division. Increasingly, however, the company has been receiving orders for automatic door-locking systems and brackets for air conditioning units.

The Automotive Division accounts for about 80 percent of total sales and contributes 60 percent of the pre-tax profits earned

by the company. No marketing or sales personnel are assigned to the automotive accounts. Initial contacts are made by their purchasing personnel with the top management of Stampler. Profits are low in the Automotive Division because of the extreme competitiveness in supplying the automotive industry. The two key questions for top management at Stampler are:

1. Do we want to make the product? and
2. Can we sell it for the price indicated by the automotive customer?

MOBILE PRODUCTS DIVISION

The other division, labeled the Mobile Products Division, makes jacks, couplers, brake systems, and various other accessories for makers of recreational vehicles RVs and motor homes MHs as well as water heaters and combination space/water heaters for RVs. The product lines in each of these areas is very complete. For example, twenty-three different jacks are manufactured, varying in capacity from one thousand to five thousand pounds. These jacks are safety engineered to give maximum support and resistance to any bending which may occur, even under the extremes of side loading. Unique features in side-wind and top-wind models are zinc iridite plating, welded cap construction, self-centering ball bearings, large mounting screws, lock washers, plastic handle sleeves, and operating ranges.

Manufacturers of RVs and MHs vary widely in size and are scattered all over the United States. As a consequence Stampler has developed brochures for its various products. All Stampler products from the Mobile Products Division are sold through manufacturers' representatives. A total of ten Stampler warehouses are located in the United States and Canada, and Stampler products can be serviced at over three hundred authorized service stations in the United States and Canada. The Stampler Company is so sure of its quality manufacturing that extended warranties are offered on all products. For example, brakes are warranted for twenty-five thousand miles and heaters for ten years.

RESULTS OF THE JUNE 30TH MEETING

At the staff planning meeting on June 30th, Marks was able to gain a consensus on several points.

1. Discussion was held and there was unanimous agreement that the planning meetings are potentially worthwhile.
2. The statement of purpose was reviewed and accepted.
3. The procedure to achieve the stated purpose was for Marks to present various candidates for acquisition to the committee. The committee would then screen the candidates and make assignments if candidates were judged viable. For example, engineering would be assigned the task of determining the compatibility of the acquisition from an engineering standpoint, manufacturing from their standpoint, and finance from their standpoint. In that the firm has no marketing department, Marks would be charged with this task. It was further suggested that he should retain a consultant to help with this task.
4. A list of potential products and markets was drawn up:
   (1) Related to present manufacturing and marketing organization:
      a. Automotive accessories
      b. Agricultural tractor and implement parts and accessories—contract and noncontract
      c. Automotive screw machine parts, fasteners, bolts, nuts, rivets, washers
   (2) Related only to present manufacturing:
      a. Automotive replacement parts
      b. Bolt hardware and accessories

      c. Truck trailer parts, suspensions, lights, air conditioning
      d. Job stamping and machining—nonautomotive
      e. Heat treating and plating
      f. Metal porch and lawn furniture
      g. Metal office furniture
      h. Metal shelving and lockers
      i. Steel parts and drums
      j. Furniture hardware
      k. Other hardware—casket hardware, fireplace hardware, hose, refrigerator, stove hardware
      l. Gas cylinders and metal tubes
      m. Sheet metal cornices, air conditioning ducts, elbows, shutters

  (3) Related only to present marketing organization:
      a. Plastic products for autos, recreational vehicles, and mobile homes
      b. Apparel and trimmings for automotive and mobile homes
      c. Other recreational and leisure time products

  (4) No obvious fit within present organization, but may have diversification and growth value, and may offset some disadvantages of our present orientation:
      a. Toys and school supplies
      b. Silos
      c. Irrigation equipment
      d. Fiberglass tubs and showers
      e. Bicycle and motorcycle parts
      f. Insulation
      g. Contractors' equipment
      h. Machine tool parts and components
      i. Household products, hand tools, plant food
      j. Burglar and fire alarms

See Exhibit 1 for a chart of the Stampler Company's organization.

Exhibit 1. Stampler Company Organization Chart

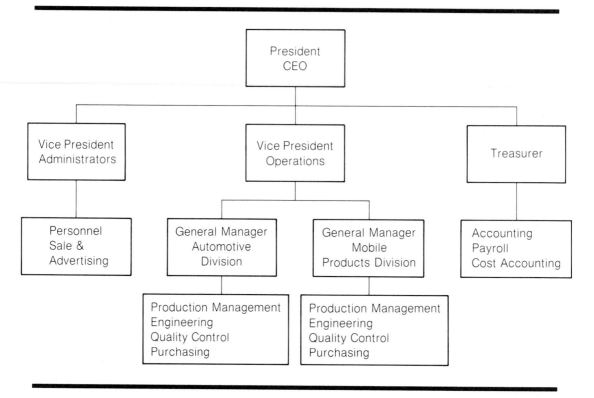

6

Rockwood Manor *

D an Chapman, administrator for Rockwood Manor retirement facility, sat in his Spokane, Washington, office contemplating a recommendation to his board of directors on how Rockwood could meet the apparent demand for housing to accommodate the active elderly in Spokane County. He knew the board would ask several important questions: What is the size of the market for retirement facilities? What kind of housing facilities do active elderly want? And how should those facilities be priced?

Dan had observed the increase in elderly both nationally and locally. Many of the newly retired were healthy, active people who looked forward to a physically active lifestyle. Although they did not wish to move into a dormitory-style facility, they did want to get out from under the burdens of maintaining a home. They wanted to be free to move about as they pleased, yet have a private secure place they could call home.

In his tenure at Rockwood, Mr. Chapman had also observed that seniors were concerned about financial matters. Some wanted to build an estate for their children while others felt they should spend their hard earned money on themselves. The current pricing schedule for rooms and health care at the manor accommodated both these two viewpoints. He was not sure how pricing would be handled in a different housing/ service configuration.

* This case was prepared by Professor William R. Wynd, Eastern Washington University. Used by permission.

NATIONAL TRENDS

The nation's population of the elderly is on the rise. According to *U.S. News and World Report,* "One of every five Americans is 55 years or older, and that figure will climb to one in every three and one-half over the next 40 years." [1] This increase is attributed to several factors. One is a decline in the death rate of 2 percent annually since 1970, due largely to improved public health care measures. A declining birth rate over the last decade has also contributed to a higher proportion of elderly in the population. Projections indicate that by the year 1990, 30 million people will be over age 65, accounting for 28 percent of the U.S. population.

Elderly households are increasingly well off financially when they reach retirement. Women currently account for an estimated 49 percent of the work force, and, with the increased number of women working, the income from a second pension is by far one of the most important factors in the maintenance of an upward trend in income among the elderly.

Business Week recently reported a study speculating that spending by the elderly since the mid-seventies may have been extensive enough to depress the national personal saving rate. [2] Those elderly currently 65 and older make up about 16 percent of all adults, but they received more than half of all interest income and close to one third of all capital gains reported to the IRS in 1982. Furthermore, while the average family held $18,695 in liquid assets in 1983, families headed by persons 65–74 averaged $30,666.

With an average age of 74, the nation's elderly can expect at least 10 more years of life. Common sense would indicate a tendency to spend their discretionary income. Most are in reasonably good health (though they hate to climb stairs), their spouse is still living and they have the time to enjoy a wide variety of leisure activities.

Indeed, the elderly are apparently spending more of their money on housing and transportation. The Department of Labor publishes three budgets for a retired couple made up of hypothetical lines of goods and services that were specified in the mid 1960s to portray three relative levels of living: lower, intermediate, and higher. The categories include food, housing, transportation, clothing, personal care, medical care, and other family consumption. In 1981 the percentage spent on housing, transportation, and clothing increased as income increased.

Although a growing elderly population constitutes a potential market for a wide variety of goods and services, the segment represented by active, affluent seniors is being increasingly cultivated by a wide variety of providers. A. T. Sutherland, advertising manager for *Modern Maturity,* indicates that the maturity market (50+) accounts for 25 percent of all consumer expenditures—purchasing 3 percent of all domestic cars, 30 percent of all food consumed at home, 25 percent of all cosmetics and bath products, 25 percent of all alcoholic beverages, 41 percent of all toaster ovens and food processors, 37 percent of all slenderizing treatments and health spa memberships, and 31 percent of all automobile tires.[3]

Contrary to the belief that many senior citizens are inclined to migrate to the sunbelt regions, evidence shows that many seniors prefer to live in the home they have lived in for years. Change becomes less appealing as time passes. Hence, many elderly wish to remain in familiar surroundings for as long as they can. According to the U.S. Department of Housing and Urban Development, 70 percent of the population 65 and over live in their own homes, 5–7 percent live in retirement homes, 18–20 percent live in apartments or government subsidized housing, and 5 percent live in institutions.[4]

Those elderly who opt to sell their homes have a wide variety of new concepts available to them, including condominium retirement settings, mobile home courts, and group homes as well as the traditional retirement center facilities. If they move to a new geographic location they are often drawn toward the less populous urban centers where the cost of living is usually more reasonable.

THE SETTING

Spokane, Washington, is one of the nation's most beautiful cities and has many attractions as a retirement community. Located in northeastern Washington state, Spokane was the site of the 1974 World's Fair. Conservative and rural in nature, the region is among the nation's most fertile wheat producing areas. Most of the urban population is employed in wholesale and retail trade, financial services, and health care servicing a number of sparsely populated counties in northeastern Washington and northern Idaho. Most Spokanites reaching retirement age stay in Spokane. Taxes, costs of maintaining a household, availability of doctors and sophisticated medical facilities, and low crime rate are among the attractions.

According to the 1970 census, 44,440 of the 287,487 total county population were aged 60 or over. The 1980 census counted 54,436 of the 341,058 total county population as aged 60 or over. The number of persons 60 or over increased by 9,996 in the 10 years between the censuses. Exhibit 1 is a bar chart showing the 1980 population in Spokane County with projections for 1985 and 1990. The population by age group and sex is shown in Exhibit 2.

ROCKWOOD MANOR

Rockwood Manor is a residential health facility that offers a full spectrum of services to meet the housing, nutrition, health, social,

Exhibit 1. 1980 CENSUS and Population Projections for Spokane County for 1985 and 1990

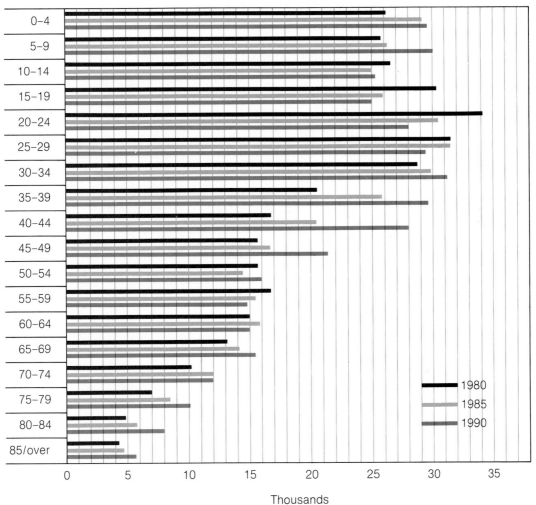

Spokane County
1980 Census and Population Projections for 1985 and 1990

Thousands

Source: Population, Enrollment, and Economic Studies
Division, Office of Financial Management
(November 1982)

and spiritual needs of older persons. It is operated by a nonprofit corporation related to the United Methodist Church but receives no financial assistance from the church or any other organization. Residents purchase the privilege of living in a unit of their choice. Prices are based upon the charge for a standard living unit of 300 square feet. Liv-

Exhibit 2. 1990 Population Projection for Spokane County

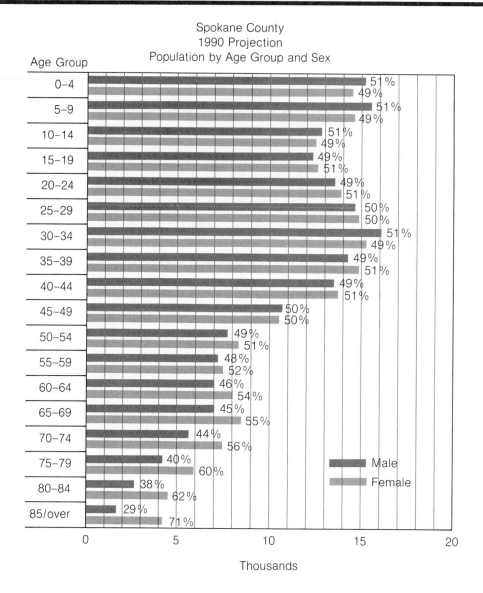

Source: Population, Enrollment, and Economic Studies
Division, Office of Financial Management
(November 1982)

ing units may be purchased for cash or under terms of a time payment contract. A minimum down payment is required for a living unit under terms of the contract. The balance, plus interest on the declining balance, is amortized for a term of 84 months. In addition, residents pay a monthly services fee.

Residents of Rockwood Manor must be

independently ambulatory and able to care for themselves at the time of admission. There is a per diem charge for infirmary care beginning with the eleventh day of confinement during any one month. The amount of this per diem charge is equal to the audited cost of a day's care in the infirmary. If a resident becomes a permanent patient in the infirmary, and his living unit is paid for in full, he may then surrender his living unit to the corporation, in which case he will then receive the infirmary care for the current monthly services fee of a standard living unit.

Rooms are also available for those residents who are not bed patients but who need assistance in the activities of daily living such as bathing and dressing. These rooms are attended by a special corps of aides under the supervision of the Director of Nursing Services. A per diem charge is made for this intermediate health care.

A resident may cancel his contract by giving sixty days notice in writing, except during illness. If the living unit has been paid for in full, the "unearned balance"[5] is refunded upon the resale of the unit. If the unit has been purchased under terms of a time payment contract, no refund is made. A time payment contract terminates with death.

Rockwood Manor enjoys a reputation of being one of the finest retirement homes in the region. Its physical plant is clean, neat, and well maintained. Its personnel are pleasant, helpful, and professional. The location is an exclusive residential area and relatively high fees project an "elite" image.

Rockwood owns enough land to develop a variety of housing configurations catering to the active elderly. Another high rise, condominiums, duplex units or cottages were all possibilities. Construction costs per square foot were greatest for cottages, least for a high rise apartment.

THE MARKET

An increasing elderly population represents a diverse market for a wide variety of retirement centers. Traditional retirement centers have almost always been operated by not-for-profit organizations, usually church affiliated. These centers normally sign a contract with the resident for lifetime care and promise that no one will be asked to leave due to financial problems.

According to a survey by the national accounting and consulting firm of Laventhol and Horvath, the future of the nation's life care/continuing care retirement industry is rapidly changing as entrepreneurs enter the expanding market.[6] These newer facilities, though still in the minority, offer a variety of possibilities. Some still offer the life care contract, but with totally or partially refundable entry fees. Others concentrate on renting units. They have no entry or endowment fees, and health care is usually provided strictly on a pay-as-needed basis.

Increasing costs and a growing market have brought together investors and not-for-profit organizers. An increasingly common partnership occurs when an investor group finances the development in return for the tax advantages. When these are exhausted, the not-for-profit organization purchases the development for fair market value.

Since 1975, marketing for the typical life-care center development usually precedes construction by a full year. Most developments presell half their units and achieve 66 percent occupancy within six months after completion and 95 percent within 18 months.

The results of a recent survey of the capacity of establishments listed in the Yellow Pages of the Spokane County Telephone Book under the heading "Retirement and Life Care Communities and Homes" is summarized in Exhibit 3.

Nearly half the retirement apartments and beds available in Spokane County are subsidized (beyond Medicare or Medicaid) by Federal or State Government. Occupancy of both apartments and beds is nearly 100 percent.

Competition in the current Spokane mar-

Exhibit 3. Capacity of Retirement and Life Care Facilities in Spokane County, 1985

	Apartments	Beds	Total	Percent of Total
Subsidized	832	551	1,383	44
Private	1,031	711	1,742	56
	1,863	1,262	3,125	100

ket to serve relatively high income retirees comes from two other not-for-profit organizations and one recently constructed for-profit condominium apartment complex with minimum health care. The retirement complex most similar to Rockwood Manor just announced a duplex/multifamily addition designed for the active elderly. Their existing and planned units are either apartments, condominiums, or duplex units. Although the existing facilities were full and often enjoyed a waiting list, what additional capacity would do to occupancy rates was a matter of conjecture. An estimated 250 new units would be added by the latest development.

PRICING/COST CONSIDERATIONS

Life care communities have an obligation to provide housing and health care for the life of their residents. This obligation can be separated into two financial cost components: housing and services. Costs in the housing component consist of debt service, maintence and periodic renovation. (See Exhibit 4.) Costs for monthly services cover such items as food service, laundry, recreation and utilities. But the largest single portion of the cost of services is health care.

Dan Chapman knew that setting a fee to fund the real estate portion of the obligation would be fairly straightforward. The fee would reflect the value of discounted cash flows for debt service, maintenance and renovation. Establishing a monthly fee for service, however, posed a problem because the

aging of the community affects the cost of health care. A young community would be relatively more healthy than a "maturing" group. As the average age of the community increases so does the largest single component of monthly service. Dan wanted to treat the residents fairly and at the same time keep the monthly service fee consistent with the "market" he was trying to reach. With this in mind he saw three possible pricing methodologies aimed at the new group of active elderly.[7]

PAY AS YOU GO

Under this methodology fees would be set annually on the basis of next years anticipated expenses and the revenue short fall or surplus of the current period. Fees would be low to start because the group would be young and healthy. As they matured health care costs and fees would increase. Although new entrants would moderate the aging of the community, the vagaries of inflation would insure inequity.

OPEN GROUP

This methodology dicates that discounted cash flows be anticipated for a relatively long period, say 20 years. Young entrants replace those deceased thus moderating health care costs. Overall fees set by this methodology are likely to be higher than pay as you go when the communities are young but lower as they mature. Insuring equity is difficult but not impossible.

Exhibit 4. Construction and Garage Costs Single Family Detached *

	House	Garage	Total Cash Costs	Total Value With Land
1,250 sq. ft.	$68,750	$10,368	$107,249	$112,249
1,000 sq. ft.	55,000	7,776	86,155	91,155
750 sq. ft.	41,250	5,184	65,060	70,060

* Construction costs for condominium units would average 12 percent less, including garages.

CLOSED GROUP

In the closed group method cash flows are anticipated for the actuarial life of residents in a cohort group (typically a group of new residents). This method differs from the open-group method because it centers on a specific cohort and requires that fees be self supporting without the benefit of new entrants. Fees are the highest when set by this pricing methodology but by definition they are most equitable to all residents.

Dan wasn't sure which pricing methodology to recommend in setting monthly service fees. He knew that any fee below what residents in the Manor were paying would likely anger them. On the other hand any fee above that would have to be justified to potential new residents.

REFERENCES

1. Mary Gallean, et al., "Life Begins at 55," *U.S. News and World Report,* September 1, 1980, pp. 51–60.
2. "Are the Elderly the Key to the Savings Puzzle?" *Business Week,* December 31, 1984, p. 17.
3. "Misdirected Advertising Prevents Marketers from Taking Bite from 'Golden Apple' of Maturity Market," *Maturity News,* October 26, 1984, p. 19.
4. U.S. Department of Housing and Urban Development, Office of Policy Development and Research, *Characteristics of the Elderly,* Washington, D.C.: Government Printing Office, February 1979, pp. 1–73.
5. Unearned balance is calculated by dividing the amount paid by the tenant by the number of months the tenant is expected to live as shown by actuarial tables in use by major life insurance companies. The quotient is multiplied by the number of months the tenant occupied his/her unit. This amount is kept by Rockwood, the remainder (unearned balance) is returned to the tenant.
6. Aaron M. Rose, "Entrepreneurs Reshaping Lifecare," *Modern Healthcare,* July 1984, pp. 148–153.
7. Howard E. Winklevoss and Alwyn V. Powell, *Continuing Care Retirement Communities: An Empirical, Financial, and Legal Analysis,* Irwin, 1984.

7

Home Products Universal *

Home Products Universal is a medium-sized Midwestern manufacturer of household cleaning and maintenance products. The company has managed to build market shares ranging from 5 to 25 percent for each of the seventeen products that it manufactures. It has successfully competed with the giants in the field through aggressive marketing, an insistence on quality products, and an imaginative program of cost cutting in warehousing, transportation, and production. Its president, Alfred Herbert Knutson, is the first grandson of founder, Eleazer Hudson, born to the founder's favorite child and only daughter, Sarah, in 1934. Knutson assumed the presidency on the retirement of the founder in 1971, after fifteen years' apprenticeship in all facets of the business.

Established in 1911 by Hudson, HPU is something of a phenomenon in the home cleaning and maintenance products industry: it is a successful regional operation. It has maintained its market position fundamentally because of its historic ability to produce products equal or superior to those marketed by the giants in the field. "Equal or superior to" means, according to HPU, product parity or superiority on critical laboratory characteristics and, in addition, a consumer preference of at least 55 percent in direct, blind paired comparison tests with consumers.

To this end, HPU has maintained an excellent product research and development program through its technical laboratory and

* Reprinted with permission of MacMillan Publishing Co., Inc., from *Marketing Management Cases,* 2nd edition, by William M. Weilbacher. Copyright © 1975, Arthur B. Kramer, Trustee.

has consistently recruited into this program superior graduate-degree holders in the physical and biological sciences. A very basic part of the product research and development program has been to establish critical performance factors for every product category manufactured by HPU and to evaluate each of its products on these performance factors and relative to the market leader or leaders. These competitive evaluations are made once every six months. This program keeps the company in constant touch with the technical characteristics of leading products in the market. As the key characteristics of the market leaders are changed, HPU knows it and can decide whether or not to change its own product to or beyond the level of performance achieved by the market leader. This program of testing has beneficial effects in keeping the HPU management in touch with its developed market and in ensuring that the necessary information to maintain the "equal or superior to" product quality policy of the company is continuously available. But it is fundamentally a defensive laboratory program and policy.

When Allen R. Scala was promoted to the job of director of product research and development in June of 1973, he also inherited this product evaluation program. He recognized the importance of the program in the overall scheme of HPU product research and development activities and appreciated the key role that it had played in the successful and profitable history of Home Products Universal. Nevertheless, he was certain that this program should not be the end of research and development activities. He noted that, in its history, HPU had been a follower in the development of new products rather than a leader. HPU had never, in its entire history, introduced a totally new product into the marketplace. It was not a matter of having tried and failed. To the contrary, it was a matter of never having tried at all. The HPU style had been to wait for others to innovate and then to follow, after basic consumer receptivity had been assured, with an equivalent or superior product developed in the HPU laboratories.

Scala recognized that this achievement was a very significant one. It was no mean trick to consistently duplicate or outperform the laboratory work of the leading "soapers" of the nation, and the success of HPU reflected an unusual level of competence among its laboratory people.

But the past success of this policy and its research and development program could not be depended upon to provide HPU with the base for successful and profitable operations in the second half of the 1970s, thought Allen Scala. There were three things wrong with it from his viewpoint.

First, the policy eliminated the possibility of developing totally new products. Of course, the odds against it were relatively high in new-product development work, but the opportunity for very significant new sales volume and profits was very high too, if one knew what he was about and if his laboratory and technical support were of the first order.

Second, the existing policy was tied to the regional operation of the company. Scala believed that the company should be a national operator and he believed that totally new products offered the easiest way to extend the operations of the company from regional to national. A hot new product could be handled through the HPU sales organization in that fraction of the country where the company was established and could be offered to brokers in the outside area. This would bring in extra sales and profits, with only marginal extra effort.

But the third effect of the traditional policy upset Scala the most. He was finding it increasingly difficult to attract talented people to his laboratories as employees. The fact that Home Products Universal's home office was situated in an Indiana town of modest size and crushing inelegance was problem enough. But the fun in product development work, the opportunity for fame, and the chance for fortune all came from working on totally new products. And if one could not offer this prospect to the potential employee, he had two strikes against him from the start. The clincher was that HPU was not a national company and had neither prospects nor intention of going national. Alfred Knutson was quite firm about this; he intended, apparently, to follow his grandfather's policies to the letter, at least until the old fellow passed on and was no longer looking over young Al's shoulder. Who, mused Scala, would want to come to central Indiana to work on old products that could be marketed only regionally? And how could he, Scala, do his job without a steady influx of new talent?

But Allen R. Scala was, after all, only the director of product research and development and it was apparent even to him that some of his thoughts were on a somewhat grander scale than he was entitled to by position alone. In theory, he reported directly to the president, Knutson himself. (See Exhibit 1.) For practical purposes he reported to two other men.

First of these was Arthur V. Pensa, vice-president and director of product marketing. Pensa was an old hand at HPU. He had been hired by Eleazer Hudson in 1955 and had been appointed to the directorship of product marketing in 1969, shortly before founder Hudson retired from active participation in the affairs of the company.

The second was Alphonso Caravelle, vice-president and director of manufacturing operations. Caravelle was a newcomer, having joined the company in 1970. But he was outspoken and important since everyone knew

Exhibit 1.   Excerpt of Home Products Universal Master Organization Chart as of October 1, 1974

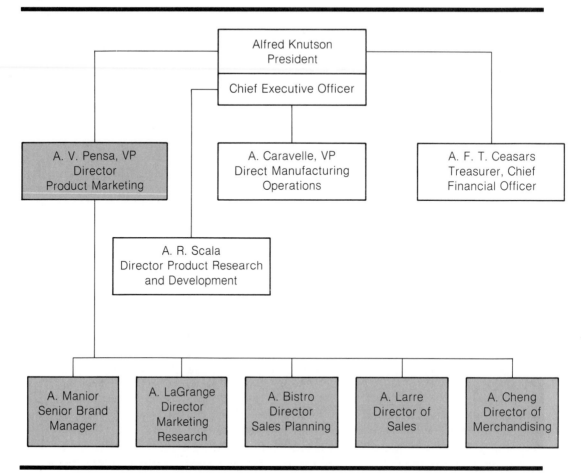

that Knutson himself knew nothing about the manufacturing side of the business.

As Scala was not a vice-president and as his slot on the organization chart was at a level below that of Pensa and Caravelle, he found it prudent, in practice, to make sure that both of these men supported any project or proposal that he intended to pursue or forward to President Knutson. So, before making any of his views about new products marketing public, Scala decided first to discuss them informally with Art Pensa. This was easier said than done because Scala had a lot of ground to cover and because Pensa seemed to have a congenitally short attention span. The appropriate moment arrived

when the two men set out on an air journey to the West Coast to attend a Chemical Specialities Manufacturers Association seminar. The airplane trip from Chicago to San Francisco provided Scala with just the opportunity he needed: there was, providentially, no in-flight movie, and dinner was served almost immediately after they boarded the aircraft.

So Scala introduced the topic of new product development and then proceeded to a discussion of national marketing and the problem of recruiting talented young people into the organization. Pensa listened to all of this with considerable patience at first, but as the presentation went on and on, he seemed to lose interest and toward the end appeared quite bored. Most of this was Scala's own fault: he had not mastered the art of organizing his ideas crisply and presenting them succinctly. But, anyway, he had delivered the viewpoint in its entirety to Pensa.

Pensa's response astonished Scala. He simply said, "Why do you tell me all of this?"

"Because I thought it was of interest and because you own a lot of our stock and want to see the company grow and prosper."

Pensa seemed to warm up a bit at this and smiled very slightly as he said, "All I want to do is cash in in six years and enjoy my retirement. So long-term plans and projects really don't interest me all that much. But I'll tell you this. I think you're dead right about new products. I don't know about national distribution. The only one that knows about that is Mr. Knutson and I wouldn't try to talk to him about it, if I were you, because it's not your job, it's my job, and if he asks me I'll tell him I advised you not to bother him about it. Maybe some other time, but not now. As far as your not being able to hire good guys, I don't think you sell hard enough. All it needs is a little determination and belief in our company—you've got to get that across, Scala. If you can't find good guys to work for Home Products Universal, there must be something wrong with your approach because the company's OK, solid as a rock." With this Pensa excused himself and wandered off in the general direction of the washroom.

Scala's next move, on returning home, was to solicit the support of Al Caravelle. In his approach to Caravelle, he decided to dispense with any talk of national expansion or his personnel recruitment problem and concentrate on the need for new products. Caravelle, as director of manufacturing operations, was the only man who could make new products become a physical fact, and without his ungrudging support, Scala's ambitions were doomed.

He talked to Caravelle over a hasty luncheon in the company cafeteria. "Al, I've been talking with Art Pensa about new products—I mean really new products, not just copies of other guys'—and he thinks we really ought to get into that kind of thing."

"Do you have people of that caliber in your R & D operation, Al?" asked Caravelle with a manner that made it difficult to judge whether he was inquiring innocently or putting Scala on a bit.

Scala assumed the best and responded, "My gang is OK—not P and G, but OK—and they won't come up with anything that's too tough to make, that's a sure thing."

Caravelle finished the conversation with a blunt response. "If you come up with anything we can make and Pensa thinks he can sell, we're with you. But I'm not going to waste any of my people's time with crackpot ideas that old Mrs. Consumer won't buy."

Scala chose to interpret this as an endorsement of his proposal. He was now left with the problem of coming up with products that could be made and would be bought by the consumer. The first issue that Scala faced was developing ideas for new products.

Where do such ideas come from? They come out of people's heads, and in one sense, one person's head is as good as another for generating new product ideas. Some people are more efficient at it than others because they are inherently smarter or have had more experience in juxtaposing different thought and experience fields to produce "creative" responses. Some people have greater technical knowledge of one field or another and can see solutions to obvious problems in terms of the technology that they have mastered. And some people have a greater innate sense of market opportunity because they are intuitively aware of both sales volume potential and the possibility of positive consumer response. But any consumer is a potential new product source.

Scala may have dimly perceived all of this, but he was in no position to seek out smart creative people, or a broad range of technologists, or consumer-market-oriented people. He had to make do with what was available to him, and this consisted, basically, of his staff of six and his wife. He described the problem to his staff in a special meeting called for this purpose. He rambled on about the need for new products, and the support of Pensa and Caravelle, and how they should be mindful that established company distribution systems would restrict the area of exploration to products sold in grocery stores, and that this work should not and could not impinge upon their regularly assigned tasks, and on and on.

After an hour and forty minutes Scala had exhausted both the subject and his listeners. But the staff had the point and it excited them and they went to work with enthusiasm, at least for the break in the routine of laboratory analyses that the quest for new products afforded them. And Scala's wife was duly briefed too, in even greater detail on the strength of a predinner cocktail, and she agreed enthusiastically to think and think hard, if for no other reason than to end Allen's lengthy exposition.

In three weeks' time Scala had accumulated a list of six new product possibilities. Three of these had come from his wife, one from the departmental secretary, and two from the newest professional employee in his group. Scala was embarrassed that he himself had drawn a complete blank.

The six products were these:

1. A liquid enzyme to break down and convert garbage to a harmless liquid
2. An electrically powered hand-held vegetable slicer
3. A powdered laundry bleach
4. A soft drink for dogs
5. A liquid detergent for dishwashing machines
6. A floor-sweeping compound for domestic use

Scala rejected all but two of these ideas. He believed that there was not adequate technology or understanding of enzyme activity available either in the literature or among his own staff to make the enzyme-garbage-product idea a good candidate for laboratory development. He suspected that a lot of time would be wasted on the project with relatively little hope of success. The vegetable chopper did not seem like a food store product to Scala, and again, none of his staff had any idea of how to put motors on chopping blades; they were chemists, not physicists. Scala thought that the idea of a soft drink for dogs might be promising but considered it off the HPU beaten track and one for which perhaps Pensa, and certainly Caravelle, would have little but ridicule. Finally, Scala rejected the liquid dishwashing product because it would, presumably, require an alteration in all those dishwashing machines that had been designed for and could only accommodate dishwashing powders.

This left the powdered bleach and the floor-sweeping compound for domestic use. Scala's next move was to go to Pensa and unveil these two ideas as potential new products. He asserted in this meeting that he believed that either could be formulated with relative ease by the research and development staff. Pensa seemed enthusiastic about both ideas but counseled that only one be forwarded to Knutson, because, after all, the very idea of the development of a totally new product was alien to HPU, and it seemed to him to make good sense to put a single best exploratory foot forward.

The two men talked at length about the two ideas. Scala was especially intrigued with the floor cleaner because he had swept out his basement only the preceding weekend and had had a severe allergic reaction to the dust that was raised in the sweeping process. But he believed that he could make a significantly safer and gentler powdered bleach with no sacrifice in product performance if he were to pursue the powdered bleach idea.

At length, Pensa interrupted Scala in the midst of a rather pointless soliloquy about dry bleach ingredients and said, "Work on the bleach product, Al. Our liquid bleach is just like the competition's and we don't get more than 5 or 6 percent of the business. But there's a big market sitting waiting for an innovation and we'll generate a lot of sales if you come up with something. The garage floor thing could be socko but I don't think Alfred [1] is allergic to anything and I know he's never swept out a cellar or a garage in his life—best to talk to him about something that he might vaguely understand."

The two gentlemen then went to Caravelle and outlined their thoughts to him. "We've got a carport and it doesn't ever need sweeping and our basement is hooked into the built-in suction vacuuming system so we wouldn't use that floor product, and I bet there are a lot of people like us," said Caravelle, and that was that. It was not clear that Caravelle endorsed the powdered bleach. It was only clear that he did not endorse the floor cleaner. This, Scala subsequently observed, was a characteristic of Caravelle.

Caravelle often spoke out against a proposal, but he rarely endorsed anything. In this way he was rarely responsible for failure and could often point out that he had personally opposed a course of action in the event that it did not pan out. Scala was, in due course, to learn how this tactic worked out in practice, to his annoyance and chagrin, but for the moment all was blue skies and clear sailing.

At this point the professionals took over. The job of actually exploring the ways in which a superior powdered bleach might be formulated was turned over to Robert J. Johnson, one of the senior lab technicians employed under Scala. In previous assignments, Johnson had shown a sophisticated knowledge of chemical brighteners and phosphorus derivatives that might be expected to produce the effect of bright whiteners in clothing. In addition, he had a very impressive general background in inorganic

chemistry and had specialized in developing methods and concepts to ensure that HPU products were both safe to humans and nondestructive of natural and man-made materials and fibers.

Johnson immersed himself in the relevant literature for a period of six weeks. Toward the end of this period he began to experiment with various combinations of dry ingredients that, although they technically were not bleaches at all, did accomplish what liquid bleaches are supposed to accomplish, only better and with total fabric and color safety.

Another four weeks passed, and finally, Johnson had assured himself that one of his formulae passed all of his tests and satisfied each of his developmental criteria. This formula—the laboratory designation of the product was DB–14—had the following characteristics:

1. It was concentrated. A packet weighing three tenths of an ounce was sufficient to bleach a fully loaded automatic washer.

2. It outperformed regular bleach: tests show that it produced 20 per cent greater brightness (reflected light) on white sheets than did the leading liquid bleach when used as directed on full washing machine loads.

3. It would not bleach out colors under any circumstances: it was totally color safe.

4. It had a pleasant perfume—a pine-scent odor rather than the harsh acrid scent of typical liquid bleaches.

5. It was mild to fabrics and hands. Fabric deterioration due to bleaching was reduced by a full 38 percent on extended-use tests of white sheets using identical washing machines with all other factors held constant.

6. Although this product was somewhat more expensive to produce than liquid bleach, some of this extra could be recaptured through lower transportation costs, and it was anticipated that it could be marketed at a price about one third higher

---

[1] It was understood within HPU that the first name Alfred, in conversation, referred to Mr. Knutson and that all other names that could be shortened to Al were shortened to Al. This created considerable confusion because either a malevolent god or a perverse personnel department had stocked the company richly in names that could become Al. See Exhibit 1.

than liquid bleach on a completed-washload basis.

Johnson was immensely pleased with his accomplishment. He had produced a superior product on all counts, and he had done it in a relatively short period of time. But even more important was the opinion of Home Products Universal's legal counsel that the particular combination of ingredients and the method of combining them was, in fact, protectable by patent.

Scala was ecstatic. He seemed to have struck oil on his very first new product enterprise. His first step was to deliver the wonderful news to his president, Alfred Knutson.

Scala, Pensa, and Caravelle agreed that the proper way for this communication to take place was in the form of a formal stand-up/chart presentation by Scala to Knutson. They settled on this device as a succinct way to summarize all of the steps leading to the final product development. Knutson had not been informed that the project was afoot and thus a heavy dose of background was in order for him. A chart presentation seemed a feasible way to discipline Scala's descriptions and conserve Knutson's valuable time. And so the presentation was made. Scala got through it all in about forty minutes and at the conclusion he waited with bated breath for Knutson's reaction.

It was short and to the point. "Have any housewives used the stuff in their homes?" asked Knutson. Scala said, "No." Knutson said, "Let's get the consumers' reaction before we go any further."

"Well, Allen," said Pensa, "maybe the old man makes a point. You know this product is better than anything else on the market, and I know it's better, too. But maybe the consumer won't feel the same way. I can't imagine any consumer not preferring this new bleach, but we don't know that she will, and now we've got to prove it, whether we want to or not."

At this point, Scala called upon Aloysius LaGrange, director of marketing research for Home Products Universal. LaGrange specialized in two kinds of marketing research: sales analyses to determine where and under what conditions HPU sales were favorable or not; and blind product-testing to establish consumer reactions to products.

Scala took LaGrange through the same presentation that he had just given to Knutson and said at its conclusion, "Alfred wants the product tested by consumers. Can you do it?" LaGrange said that he would be delighted to take a crack at it, but he emphasized that research work on a new product might involve considerably different and more sophisticated procedures than those used in the standard Home Products Universal blind comparison test of established and known products.

First of all, LaGrange proposed that samples of the product be distributed to two hundred housewives who were regular users of liquid bleach. Each of these housewives would receive, in addition to the bleach samples, a brief *factual* description of exactly what the product was and its unique characteristics. Then these consumers would be asked to use the new powdered bleach in their next regular wash. In a callback interview they would then be questioned concerning their overall reaction to the product; their views of its strengths and weaknesses; their evaluation of its performance relative to the liquid bleach they usually used; an appraisal of the likelihood they would purchase it; and a projection of what price they would expect to pay for the product.

At the same time, LaGrange suggested that a basic study of consumer attitudes toward and usage of bleach products should be undertaken to determine demographic patterns of bleach usage and basic knowledge about the kinds of wash items that were regularly bleached; the frequency with which they were bleached; consumer attitudes about what bleach actually accomplished; the major shortcomings of available liquid bleaches; and the major advantages of available bleach products.

**Exhibit 2. Cost Estimates for Market Research Job 27–347
(In-Home Placement DB–14)**

	Bid 1 *	Bid 2 *	Bid 3 *	Final Estimate
Internal time	–	–	–	$ 1,700
Field work	$4,000	$4,250	$3,650†	4,000
Tabulation	800	1,000	1,275	800
				$ 6,500

* Supporting documents in MR File 27–347–001.
† Required fourteen weeks for completion at this cost.

LaGrange pointed out that the second study might well have been undertaken before the laboratory had started development so that the development of the new product, once initiated, would respond insofar as possible to expressed consumer needs and to the shortcomings perceived by consumers in the existing products in the marketplace. But LaGrange still believed that the results of such research work would be helpful in appraising the market potential of the new bleach product. LaGrange prepared formal research proposals for these two projects. These proposals described in some detail just how the research work would be carried out, how much time it would take,

and how much money would be involved in the recommended studies.

The estimated cost of the first, the home placement study, was $6,500. It was anticipated that the work would require approximately ten weeks to complete, although a preliminary or top-line report could be expected in approximately seven weeks from the date of authorization. The attitude and usage study would also take approximately ten weeks to complete, with top-line results again in about seven weeks, and the estimated cost was $26,300.

Scala was disturbed by two factors about these proposals: their cost and the amount of time that they were expected to take. He

**Exhibit 3. Cost Estimates for Market Research Job 27–349
(Consumer Bleach Attitude DB–14)**

	Bid 1 *	Bid 2 *	Bid 3 *	Estimate
Internal time	–	–	–	$ 4,900
Field work	$20,000	$18,500	$21,500	18,500
Tabulation	2,000	2,900	4,000	2,900
				$26,300

* Supporting documents in MR File 27–349–003.
 (All bids were solicited for field work and tabulation together, as a "package," because of the size and complexity of the job.)

asked LaGrange to prepare a brief memorandum justifying the time and cost requirements. LaGrange relished this request, because he knew that his time and cost estimates were reasonable and because he knew that Scala had no choice but to accept them.

His memorandum is below.

Scala immediately authorized the research work to proceed but entreated LaGrange to do everything in his power to speed it up while minimizing the cost. The inconsistency of these wishes amused LaGrange. He delivered the research reports exactly when he said that he would and within 7 percent of the estimated costs.

LaGrange presented the results of the two studies when they became available. These presentations were made to all of those who had been either interested or involved in the

development of DB–14, but Mr. Knutson was not invited. When Scala had first proposed that Knutson be included in the group receiving first exposure to the research reports, Pensa exploded.

"You really don't get it, do you, Al? We are hired to provide solutions for Alfred, not to give him an opportunity to share our problems. Let's take a look at these studies and then we'll figure out what to do. Maybe we'll even let him see them, but let's keep control, huh, Al? Let's not give him, or the old man, a shot at providing an afternoon's entertainment at our expense."

But it was not to be. Knutson had been in the organization for fifteen years. He knew it like the back of his hand and he had developed excellent informal sources of information about what went on within its walls. More often than not, he "knew" what went

---

HPU INTERNAL COMMUNICATION

September 18, 1974

From: A. LaGrange

To: A. Scala

You have asked me to explain in some detail our estimates of time and cost supplied to you in connection with two research proposals for product DB–14.

As you know, it is the policy of the Marketing Research Department to farm out all field work and tabulation for such studies, reserving to ourselves only the functions of study planning, data analysis, and interpretation of results. Thus, the major elements in our cost and time estimates are developed for us by the outside suppliers who are always subjected to the discipline of competitive bidding. Our internal time estimates are relatively modest, and our costs are computed on the basis of standard-work-grade hourly rates supplied to us by the central accounting office.

The attached exhibits detail these factors for the studies in question.

You have also asked for a draft of the factual description of product DB–14 that would be given to consumers in the home placement test. Here it is.

Dry Bleach

This product is to be used in the same way as liquid bleach: one packet to each automatic washer load. The product is an extremely effective bleach as you will see, and it is very mild to hands and to fabric fibers. It is guaranteed safe for colored fabrics: it will absolutely not cause color fading or bleeding. The product delivers full power performance with total mildness and safety.

Your approval of the research plans and of this description of the product is awaited.

on because he had a superb memory for detail as well as an excellent intuitive understanding of how his key people worked and how they were likely to respond in a particular situation. Knutson either sensed or overheard or was told that the new product research on the bleach was available, and he advised LaGrange, upon finding this out, that he would be pleased to review it in his office the next morning at 8:45 A.M.

LaGrange informed his superior, Pensa, of this development, Pensa informed Scala and Caravelle, and these latter three appeared uninvited and without joint consultation in Knutson's office for his "review" of the consumer research work.

The material seen by Knutson is summarized in Exhibits 4 through 9 (the product-placement study) and in Exhibits 10 through 16 (the usage-and-attitude study).

When the material had been presented by LaGrange and discussed by the group, Knutson said, "Al, have you reached any conclusions about where we should go from here?" When Knutson could be referring to more than one Al, the company custom was for the senior man to respond.

And so Pensa said, with a rather indicative quietness, "No, Alfred, these studies have only just become available, and we haven't had a real opportunity to explore all the ramifications of them. We'll be back with

Exhibit 4. DB–14 Placement Study Specimen Data: Overall Reaction to Product (5-point scale supplied to testers)

Base: All testers	
Number	206
Percent	*100*
DB–14 is	
Excellent	12%
Good—above average	4
Average	38
Not so good—below average	30
Poor	16

Exhibit 5. DB–14 Placement Study Specimen Data: Reported Advantages of Product DB–14

Base: All testers		
Number	206	
Percent	*100*	
Product has an advantage *	37%	
Mild to hands		21
Pleasant odor		7
Safe for colors		7
Safe for fabrics		6
Convenient		4
All other responses		1
Product has no advantage	63	

* Some testers gave more than one advantage.

Exhibit 6. DB–14 Placement Study Specimen Data: Redorted Disadvantages of Product DB–14

Base: All testers		
Number	206	
Percent	*100*	
Product has a disadvantage *	74%	
Doesn't get clothes whiter		51
Not strong enough, too mild		47
I don't bleach colors		8
Packet is too small		2
Doesn't smell strong enough		1
All other responses		6
Product has no disadvantages	26	

* Some testers gave more than one disadvantage.

Exhibit 7. DB–14 Placement Study Specimen Data: DB Performance Relative to Liquid Bleach Regularly Used

Base: All testers	
Number	206
Percent	*100*
Liquid bleach better	72%
DB–14	18
No choice	10
Reasons liquid bleach better	
Base: Liquid bleach preferrers *	
Number	148
Percent	*100*
Gets clothes whiter	72%
Is stronger	64
Best for me	31
The powder is too mild	10
All other responses	6
Reasons DB–14 better	
Base: DB preferrers *	
Number	37
Percent	†
Good odor	(12)
Mild to hands	(11)
Mild to fabrics	(10)
All other responses	(8)

* Some respondents gave more than one reason.

† Small base: only absolute numbers are reported.

Exhibit 8. DB–14 Placement Study Specimen Data:
Purchase Intention for Product DB–14 (5-point scale supplied to testers)

Base: All testers	
Number	206
Percent	*100*
Definitely will purchase	6%
May purchase	7
Not sure	21
Probably won't purchase	12
Definitely will not purchase	54

Exhibit 9. DB–14 Placement Study Specimen Data:
Price Testers Expect to Pay for DB–14

Base: All testers		
Number	206	
Percent	*100*	
Expect to pay more than liquid bleach	13%	
1–5¢ more		10
6–10¢ more		3
11¢–or more		–
Expect to pay the same as liquid bleach	12	
Expect to pay less than liquid bleach	75	
1–5¢ less		21
6–10¢ less		42
11¢–or less		12

Exhibit 10. DB–14 Usage and Attitude Study Specimen Data:
Bleach Usage and Intensity of Bleach Usage

Base: All households		
Number	1,479	
Percent	*100*	
Use bleach	78%	
Heavy bleach users (more than 1 quart a month)		20
Light bleach users (less than 1 quart a month)		58
Do not use bleach	22	

Exhibit 11. DB–14 Usage and Attitude Study Specimen Data: Bleach Usage and Intensity of Bleach Usage by Standard Demographic Characteristics *

	Use Bleach	Heavy Bleach Usage†	Light Bleach Usage‡
All households	78%	20%	58%
Income			
Under $5,000	88%	34%	54%
$5,000–$7,999	84	21	58
$8,000–$9,999	78	16	62
$10,000–$14,999	64	6	58
$15,000–$24,999	58	4	54
$25,000 and over	50	4	46
Education of household head			
Grade school or less	85%	33%	52%
Some high school	82	24	58
Graduated high school	78	16	62
Some college	60	4	56
Graduated college	49	2	47
Age of household head			
24 and younger	56%	4%	52%
25–34	68	10	58
35–49	78	18	60
50–64	98	42	56
65 and older	96	42	54
Geographic area			
Northeast	72%	18%	54%
Central	76	20	56
South	88	24	64
West	78	20	58

* The percentages are based on the number of households falling in each demographic category.

† A heavy-bleach-using household consumes more than 1 quart of bleach a month.

‡ A light-bleach-using household consumes less than 1 quart of bleach a month.

Exhibit 12.   DB–14 Usage and Attitude Study Specimen Data: Items Most Frequently Bleached and Estimated Bleaching Frequency *

Base: All households using bleach
  Number   1,154
  Percent   *100*

Items Bleached †		Estimated Bleaching Frequency ‡
White fabrics	100%	1.00
Sheets, pillowcases	97	1.00
Towels, bathroom linen	94	1.00
Undergarments	42	.25
Outer garments	77	.62
Shirts	82	.76
Others	36	.31
Colored fabrics	12	.10
Delicate fabrics	6	.05
Synthetic fabrics	2	.05

* Respondents were asked to mention the three or four kinds of fabrics they bleached "most often."

† There is duplication in this classification. A white nylon undergarment would show up as a white undergarment, a delicate fabric, and a synthetic fabric, for example. If a garment could be classified in more than one category, it was so classified.

‡ The proportion of washes out of total washings in which bleach is used, as estimated by respondents. White undergarments are bleached, for example, in .25 washings, or one in four.

Exhibit 13.   DB–14 Usage and Attitude Study Specimen Data: What Consumers Think Bleach Accomplishes for Them *

Base: All bleach-using households
  Number   1,154
  Percent   *100*

Gets clothes whiter, brighter	98%
Gets clothes cleaner	96
Gets colored clothes brighter	14
Saves work in getting out dirt	10
All other mentions	6

* Some respondents gave more than one answer.

Exhibit 14. DB–14 Usage and Attitude Study Specimen Data: Major Advantages of Liquid Bleaches *

Base: All bleach-using households	
Number	1,154
Percent	*100*
Does the job, gets clothes whiter, cleaner, brighter	100%
Strong	85
Economical	76
Chlorine ingredient does the job	40
Odor denotes cleanliness	26
Flexible—easy to measure and works better	21

* Some respondents gave more than one answer.

Exhibit 15. DB–14 Usage and Attitude Study Specimen Data: Major Shortcomings of Liquid Bleaches *

Base: All bleach-using households		
Number	1,154	
Percent	*100*	
Harsh, too harsh	52%	
Too harsh on fabrics		32
Too harsh on hands		26
Ruins colors	26	
Can't use on synthetic fabrics	24	
Clumsy and heavy to carry around	22	
No shortcomings	41	

* Some respondents gave more than one answer.

Exhibit 16. DB–14 Usage and Attitude Study Specimen Data: Characteristics of an Ideal Bleach *

Base: All bleach-using households	
Number	1,154
Percent	*100*
Gets clothes totally white and bright	98%
Gets clothes totally clean	94
Same price as liquids	82
Safe for colored clothes	22
Safe for synthetic fabrics	16
Safe for skin	8
Light and easy to carry	6

* Some respondents gave more than one answer.

our joint recommendation early next week if that's OK."

But it was not OK with Knutson: "I'll tell you what, Al; this is kind of a new venture for us, right? And none of us has had much experience with this kind of information [his left hand jerked spasmodically in the direction of LaGrange's reports], and if we are going to do more of it, I'd like the chance to see how each of you goes at it as an individual. Why doesn't each of you write me a private note telling me where you come out on DB–14 and why, if that's OK."

And this second proposal was OK, whether anyone except Knutson liked it or not. Here are the three memoranda received by Knutson:

HPU INTERNAL COMMUNICATION

December 5, 1974

From: A. Scala

To: Alfred Knutson

It is clear from the consumer research that DB–14 should not be introduced into the market place. Good as it is, it is not what the consumer wants. The research results are simply too negative and too conclusive.

The research results suggest that the product should be reformulated:

a Liquids are the preferred form and seem to suggest strength.

b DB–14 smells too mild.

c DB–14 should have all of its current performance attributes but should not appear in any way to be mild, or lacking in effectiveness.

The research results suggest even more strongly that we should change our description of the product:

a The reformulated DB–14 should only be described in terms denoting strength, cleaning power, whitening power.

b All mention of gentleness and safety should be omitted.

In order to get some idea about the importance of the words in describing the product, I would like to recommend that a second home placement test be run with DB–14, unchanged, but with a new description along these lines:

Powerful Dry Bleach

This powerful dry bleach should be used in the same way as liquid bleaches—one packet will clean and whiten a normal automatic-washer load.

For loads containing deep soil or stains, use a second packet.

This powerful product is extremely effective in whitening and cleaning clothes—its bleaching agents surround individual fabric fibers and wrench dirt and grime away. You'll be amazed at the difference.

My second recommendation is that I immediately be authorized to develop a new form of bleach that is totally consistent with consumers' expectations in this product category. This new product may be a liquid—if we can find ways of stabilizing our active ingredients in solution. But it may be a powder if the recommended new consumer research indicates that the proper product positioning will strip away consumer resistance to dry bleaches.

HPU INTERNAL COMMUNICATION

December 5, 1974

From: A. Pensa

To: Alfred Knutson

The DB–14 research poses a real dilemma for us.

The research indicates that the consumer does not want a bleach product that has the characteristics of DB–14. DB–14 apparently doesn't do the job as far as consumers are concerned. We know, from our own laboratory tests, that it *will* do the job for them. Somehow we have gotten the consumers off on the wrong track. Maybe it's because we emphasize the safety of the product rather than its performance. But we know the product is a good one.

If a competitor came along with this product, and it was patented, we would have a devil of a time equaling or surpassing the formulation. And yet the consumers say they don't like it. I know all about the science of sampling and all, but I really wonder if we should take the word of a few hundred women and run off the end of the dock with it. I believe the best bet is to introduce the product as it stands into a test market and try to develop advertising that will overcome the consumer negatives that have been uncovered by the research. It could be that the research is wrong, but maybe by developing a new positioning for the product, we can convince the consumer.

I recommend that we introduce the product into two medium-sized test markets as soon as we see advertising copy that we like.

HPU INTERNAL COMMUNICATION

December 5, 1974

From: A. Caravelle

To: Alfred Knutson

We can make DB–14 and we can make it profitably, under the proposed pricing structure. As far as the product itself is concerned, it's a beauty. It really does all of the things that Johnson in R & D says that it will. I have to conclude that we have an important breakthrough in technology. To achieve a result of this importance on our very first try in new product development strikes me as extraordinarily lucky and all I can say is I'm glad we're the ones that have this product to put on the store shelves under the HPU name.

But, my question has always been whether we should be developing any new products at all. This way, we have to shoot dice with consumers, and we all know how fickle they are—LaGrange's research proves that, if nothing more. Before we got into new product development, we let our competitors spend their money trying to please the consumer, and while they blithely threw money away, we profited by their errors.

I say let the other guys make the mistakes for us. I say let's not throw any more good money after bad with this bleach product, good as it may be, that consumers won't buy.

I recommend we forget the whole thing.

Two

Evaluating and Assessing Consumer and Market Opportunities

VOLKSWAGEN OF AMERICA

SEB

NORTH BRANCH PAPER

METROPOLITAN CABLE TV

HAMILTON POWER TOOLS (A)

HAMILTON POWER TOOLS (B)

SUNCOAST NATIONAL BANK

HAMPTON MAYORAL SURVEY

Volkswagen of America *

In 1981 Volkswagen introduced what was hoped to be the company's flagship for the 1980s—the Quantum. Called Passat in Europe, the Quantum replaced the Dasher which was originally brought to the United States in 1974. However, initial sales of the Quantum were disappointing and Volkswagen management wondered why customer acceptance was not stronger. One issue that divided Volkswagen management was whether the name Quantum provided the right image for their new car. Management also wondered what consumer behavior concepts they should consider to help Volkswagen appeal to new car buyers. Some executives felt that a better understanding of the consumer decision-making process would lead to more Quantum sales.

BACKGROUND

The Volkswagen concept was developed in the 1920s by a young automobile designer, Ferdinand Porsche. Porsche intended the car to be a completely practical vehicle. At first his plans for an unconventional, small, inexpensive automobile were rejected by European automobile manufacturers. The rise of Hitler and his pledge to the German people that every man would own his own car, "The Volkswagen," made Porsche's dream a reality, and manufacture of the Volkswagen

got underway. The car's production, however, was disrupted by World War II.

After the war British Occupational Forces controlled the Volkswagen factory until 1949. The factory was then turned over to Heinz Nordoff, who faced the major task of rebuilding the Volkswagen organization. The basic design of the car, however, was not altered, and engineering emphasis was directed toward internal improvements of the automobile. Gradually a global sales and service organization developed. At present, Volkswagen A.G., located in Wolfsburg, is West Germany's largest industrial enterprise with factories located throughout the world.

In its early years, the Beetle, which had become the car's "nickname," had problems gaining acceptance in the American market. To gain initial sales, a foreign-car dealer who had been appointed exclusive importer and agent east of the Mississippi for Volkswagen advocated that dealers who wanted the more popular foreign cars should also purchase a few of the unconventional Beetles. His suggestion was accepted. From this rather humble beginning in the early 1950s, interest in and sales of Volkswagens began to increase rapidly.

Volkswagen sales peaked in 1970 at 582,500 cars, accounting for almost 7 percent of total sales in the United States. While imports expanded their share of the market as the 1970s continued, Volkswagen began to decline in market share and absolute sales. This decline came about because of the obvious increase in foreign-car competition and the step-up of smaller car production by major U.S. manufacturers.

* This case was prepared by W. Wayne Talarzyk of the Ohio State University. From *Contemporary Cases in Consumer Behavior*, rev. ed. by Roger D. Blackwell, W. Wayne Talarzyk, and James F. Engel. Copyright © 1985 by CBS College Publishing. Reprinted by permission of the Dryden Press, CBS College Publishing.

THE QUANTUM

The information in Exhibit 1 is from the media package used to introduce the Quantum to the United States. Exhibit 2 provides a description of the rationale behind using the name Quantum in the United States. As originally introduced the Quantum was available in three versions: coupe, four-door, and station wagon. The following information provides a description of the Quantum as "top-of-the-line Volkswagen":

Exhibit 1. Promotional Material Used to Introduce the Quantum

Englewood Cliffs, N.J.—Volkswagen today announced the introduction of the all-new Quantum—the most technologically advanced and elegantly executed line of cars ever to wear a VW logo.

Conceived as Volkswagen's flagship line for the '80s, the Quantum comes in three body styles—a sporty Coupe, 4-door Wagon and 4-door Sedan. (The latter does not go on sale until Spring '82.) All three models are completely equipped, full five-passenger vehicles possessing the sophisticated road manners, functional-yet-handsome European styling and interior spaciousness and appointments of cars costing half again as much.

The technological superiority of the Quantum is most evident in two areas: aerodynamics and chassis design. The sleek, almost fluid silhouettes of the three cars are a result of extensive development work in VW's climatic wind tunnel in Wolfsburg, West Germany. The two-door hatchback Coupe, which features an integrated front air dam and rear deck lid spoiler, has a drag coefficient (c_d) of only 0.39, the lowest of the three and one of the best to be found on a vehicle of this size.

For improved ride comfort and stability, the frontwheel drive chassis of the new Quantum features a longer 100-inch wheelbase and wider track than the Dasher it replaces. In addition a completely new "twist-beam" with trailing arms and coil spring struts is being used for the first time on a vehicle as large as a Quantum.

This new "track-correcting" axle, as VW engineers call it, utilizes unique asymmetrical rubber-metal bushings at the pivot points to reduce the natural tendency for the rear wheels to "steer" under high lateral loads.

Not only is this new rear suspension fully independent, it is extremely light, and so compact that a 15.8 gallon fuel tank is located between the rear wheels underneath a low trunk floor.

To provide the best possible combination of space and comfort, the external dimensions of the top-of-the-line car are slightly larger than those of the Dasher. However, through exhaustive computer-aided analysis of the Quantum's components and material makeup by Research & Development at Wolfsburg, it has been kept lean and trim. In fact, the Quantum weighs only about 120 pounds more than the smaller Dasher.

Fuel Mileage Improved

Low curb weight, a clean, wind-cheating shape and an efficient powertrain are responsible for the Quantum's impressive fuel mileage. The Federal Environmental Protection Agency rates the manual transmission Quantum at 28 miles per gallon in the city and 41 miles per gallon on the highway—a four-percent improvement over the gas used by the Dasher.

Power for the Quantums comes from a 1.7-liter overhead cam fuel-injected gasoline engine mounted longitudinally under the hood and mated to a Formula E 5-speed gearbox. This new wide-ratio transmission features long-legged fourth and fifth gear ratios for economical, relaxed highway cruising, and shorter first through third gears for brisk acceleration and passing.

Power assisted rack and pinion steering is standard on all Quantums, as is a Formula E. Upshift Indicator Light that tells the driver how to increase fuel economy at no expense in performance by shifting up the next higher gear.

Luxury Interior

The well-planned cockpit of the Quantum features fully reclining front seats with a height-adjustment lever on the driver's side, cut pile carpeting, padded four-spoke steering wheel, a passenger reading lamp and an electric rear window defroster. Both the sporty Coupe and Wagon come with fold-down ½– ⅔ split rear seat backs for increased luggage capacity. The Wagon also has a rear wiper/washer system and bins in the cargo area so that small items such as a camera can be hidden from view. Befitting its sporting nature, the Coupe comes with a tachometer, LCD quartz digital clock and black exterior window trim and black front and rear spoilers.

Streamline remote-control outside mirrors, 5½ × 13-inch alloy wheels and 185/70–13 steel radials are standard on all models. Black accented 6 × 14-inch light alloy wheels fitted with low-profile 195/60– 14 high-performance radials are optional.

Quantums can be specified with a GL package consisting of cruise control, power windows, central door locking, electrically operated outside mirrors, illuminated vanity mirror, adjustable rear seat head-rests and "GL" identification on the rear deck lid.

Other options include a new push-button air conditioning and heating system, automatic transmission, sliding steel sunroof with tilt feature, AM/FM stereo with electronic tuning, auto-reverse cassette, auto-matic antenna and four-speaker sound system.

Efficient aerodynamic design, an advanced suspension system together with the intelligent size of the Quantum reaffirm Volkswagen's technological leadership in automotive development. The Quantum is backed by a 12-month, 20,000-mile limited warranty that is honored by over 1000 authorized VW dealers nationwide.

Exhibit 2. Rationale for the Name Quantum

The 1981 Quantum will be Volkswagen's new top-of-the-line model, replacing the phased-out Dasher.

As a basic positioning statement (final statement forthcoming) it would be safe and fitting to describe it as a family car, available in notchback sedan, hatchback wagon and two-door coupe body styles. With a Turbo-diesel engine, the new model joins a select group of higher-priced imports in the luxury category.

Name criteria for this new model must convey characteristics and attributes that are consistent with the car's marketing image, that is, top-of-line, sophisticated technology, superior engineering.

The name *quantum* directly relates to mathematics and physics. In scientific usage, it means an abrupt transition. The new model is a *quantum* leap above the Dasher on several styling, engineering and marketing levels. It is VW's entry into a higher class of automobile. The word has strong scientific connotations all of which are positive, important and, to the layperson, high-sounding.

Also important, the name must make a strong visual impression (look good on the printed page or nameplate on car) as well as sound good to the ear. It must also work well for all three body styles, that is, fit the character of the various configurations.

Further, like all Volkswagens past and present, it must stand out from the pack, be unique but also very much to the point. Not different just to be different, but different because it portrays all of the special meaning inherent in the car. Lastly, the name should at once combine dignity with personality, the latter especially important for advertising/merchandising consideration.

In the name Quantum, we believe there is the embodiment of all the name criteria that are important. Moreover, since the new model will be priced higher than previous top line Volkswagens, the proposed name supports the price/value relationship in a very effective manner.

Among the scores of names that were considered, Quantum best measured up to the high standards that were set for Volkswagen's new top line automobile.

Styling Characteristics

- All steel unit body construction
- Dual rectangular halogen headlights
- Turn signals integrated in headlights and taillights
- Wrap-around side markers, front and rear
- Radiator grille, black and bright edge

Price

$10,400 Coupe, $10,700 Four-Door, and $11,000 Station Wagon

Model Versions

- Body styles: 2-door Coupe, 4-door hatchback, and 4-door station wagon
- Engine: 1715 cc with CIS injection system (5 cylinder is proposed with automatic transmissions, on all models; turbo diesel will be an option on automatic or 5-speed models)
- Transmission: 5-speed manual (standard)
- Trim level: Deluxe

Interior Design

The interior design objective was

- To provide harmony with the overall character of the vehicle
- To establish continuity between exterior and interior appearance
- To promote the VW top-of-the-line image

Engineering

Progressive: A large number of components are used from other VW models in line with the modular unit principle. The new models are larger and may give better fuel economy than the previous model. There has been no change in the transmission and engine; it is identical to the 1980 model.

Automobile Market Segmentation

The United States automotive market is often divided into three broad categories: family cars, luxury cars, and sports or sporty cars. Volkswagen positioned the Quantum to compete in two of these categories: (1) a coupe in the sporty car group and (2) a four-door sedan and station wagon in the family group. Exhibit 3 shows how Volkswagen perceived the competition and consumer characteristics in the various segments of the family group. Exhibit 4 indicates how

Exhibit 3. Family Car Market Segments

Automobile Makes

Segment 1: *High priced:*
               Audi 5000   Cadillac   Mercedes-Benz
               BMW   Lincoln

Segment 2: *Medium priced:*

	2a. Four-Door Sedans:	2b. Station Wagons:
	VW Quantum	VW Quantum
	Audi 4000	Datsun 810/Maxima
	Datsun 810/Maxima	Renault 18i
	Renault 18i	Toyota Cressida
	Toyota Cressida	Volvo DL
	Volvo DL	

Segment 3: *Low priced:*
               Volkswagen Jetta   Ford Fairmont   Mazda 626
               Chrysler "K" Car   GM "X" Body
               Fiat Brava   Honda Accord

Exhibit 3. (Continued)

Customer Types

Segment 1:   *Married, males*
        30–55 years old
        Income—$35,000+
        College Educated

Segment 2a: *Married, males*
        25–50 years old
        Income—$20,000+
        Attended College
        Family size: 2.7
        Occupation—sales work,
        engineers and proprietors

Segment 2b: *Married, slightly female*
        30–60 years old
        Income—$25,000+
        College Educated
        Family size: 3.1
        Occupation—retired, sales work,
        proprietor, farmers, skilled trade

Segment 3:   *Married, males*
        25–44 years old
        Income—$20,000+
        College Educated

Exhibit 4. **Sporty Car Market Segments**

Automobile Makes

Segment 1:   *Very high-priced, superluxurious, ultrahigh-performance, sports cars:*

Porsche 928	Ferrari	Maserati
Porsche 911	Lamborghini	Mercedes-Benz 380SL
Audi Quattro	Lotus	

Segment 2:   *High-priced, sleek, high-performance, sports cars:*

Porsche 924	Corvette	* Mazda RX–7
Porsche 924T	Datsun 280ZX/T	* Triumph TR7/8
Alfa GTV6	DeLorean	

Segment 3:   *Moderately priced, sporty cars, with some performance characteristics:*

VW Scirocco	Chrysler TC3/024	Honda Accord/Prelude
Audi Coupe	Datsun 200SX	Plymouth Sapporo
VW Quantum Coupe	Ford Mustang	Toyota Celica/Supra

Segment 4:   *Lower-priced, sporty type cars, with some performance:*

VW Rabbit	GM "J" Body Coupe	Toyota Corolla—SR5
Datsun GX	Honda Civic	
Ford Escort	Mazda GLC	

Customer Types

Segment 1:   *Strongly male, married*
        30–54 years old
        Income—$50,000+
        Education—Post Graduate

Segment 3:   *Slightly male, married*
        25–40 years old
        Income—$20,000+
        Education—Some College

Segment 2:   *Mainly male, married*
        25–49 years old
        Income—$35,000+
        Education—College Degree

Segment 4:   *Slightly male, married*
        20–40 years old
        Income—$17,000+
        Education—Some College

---

* Lower price, but sleek; definite competition.

Volkswagen perceived the competition and consumer characteristics in the segments of the sporty car market.

Quantum's Position

The basic positioning statement for Quantum was stated as "Volkswagen's flagship cars for the 1980s. Built with advanced German technology, European styling, and sophisticated aerodynamic design and collectively offering superior performance, handling, and fuel economy without sacrificing spaciousness and comfort."

The following characteristics were used as aids in executing the positioning function.

- Quantum's high price: Appeal to emotion and self-image
- Quantum's high resale value: A way to counteract the original high price reaction ... an intelligent investment
- Quantum's gas economy: The key selling advantage ... still a leader in this segment
- Quantum's Corporate Umbrella: Utilize the VW image strengths that are high on the consumers' desired list, namely:
  - Well-built car
  - Reliable/trouble free operation
- Advertising: A new sophisticated approach; elegance rather than humor—a possibility "Quantum—by Volkswagen."

Consumer Research

Rogers National Research of Toledo, Ohio, conducts an annual survey among second quarter (January, February, and March) new car buyers. The Quantum portion of the 1982 study can be summarized as follows.

- Quantum owners' overall satisfaction with their new car is on a par with Subaru, but below Cressida, Audi and Maxima. "Excellent/very good" ratings are

Vehicle	Percent rating
Toyota Cressida	94
Audi 4000	93
Datsun Maxima	93
VW Quantum	86
Subaru	86

- Dasher was behind these three vehicles in 1981; no upward movement by Quantum.
- Basically, the same order applies for delivery condition ratings, with Subaru third and Datsun and VW dropping down one place.
- While the overall opinion rating is comparable to Dasher's 1979/1980 level, the Quantum's delivery condition rating has slightly surpassed any of the Dasher's previous ratings. Quantum shows significantly higher owner satisfaction ratings than Dasher for overall quietness, overall front seat comfort, overall interior roominess, overall exterior styling, riding comfort, overall ease of handling, overall power and pickup, smoothness of engine idle, ease of starting, absence of wind noise, and absence of water leaks.
- Quantum, Maxima, and Cressida buyers list quality of workmanship, durability/reliability and ease of handling as their primary purchase motivators. The remainder, that is, Audi 4000, Renault 18i, Subaru, Dodge Aries, Plymouth Reliant, and Oldsmobile Ciera supplant handling with fuel economy.
- Before purchasing their car, more Quantum and competitive owners considered a GM product than any other vehicle. Subaru buyers are the exception, staying within the Japanese family of products. Few buyers seriously considered a Quantum.
- Honda and Toyota are capturing a large number of previous Dasher owners. Quantum/Dasher owner loyalty is a very low 4 percent.

- Many Quantum buyers disposed of a Volkswagen, with GM disposals a poor second. Some VW owners have apparently upgraded to the 4000. Renault, Datsun and Toyota are making heavy inroads in the domestic market. Dasher was capturing more of the domestic market than the Quantum is.
- The Quantum buyer is a married male, about 44 years of age. He is a college graduate, earning approximately $41,000 per annum. This profile closely resembles that of the Dasher buyer.

Exhibit 5 shows the trends in how Quantum (Dasher) purchasers rate automobiles on various attributes. The importance of certain aspects of the automobiles and the purchase decision are shown in Exhibit 6. Exhibit 7 presents trend information about automobiles replaced as a result of the purchase of a Quantum (Dasher) from 1979 through 1982. Trends in consumer characteristics are presented in Exhibit 8.

Exhibit 9 provides selected sales data for various imported cars for the years 1980 through 1982. In Exhibit 10, share of market statistics for imports and the leading brands of automobiles are given.

Exhibit 5. Owner Satisfaction Trend (excellent/very good ratings)

| | New Quantum/Dasher purchased in | | | |
	1982	1981	1980	1979
Overall, How Do You Rate Your Car on These Features?				
Average MPG city	26%	37%	36%	31%
Average MPG highway	32	42	42	38
Overall average MPG	28	40	39	35
Overall opinion	86	74	85	87
Delivery condition	84	74	81	79
Value for the money	56	47	54	66
Overall quietness	65	26	42	—
Overall quality of workmanship	84	60	81	83
Overall front seat comfort	88	81	74	—
Overall interior roominess	84	45	48	58
Overall interior styling	83	76	74	79
Overall exterior styling	86	80	78	78
Mileage (fuel economy)	75	93	91	94
Riding comfort	84	67	70	79
Overall ease of handling	97	77	83	89
Overall power and pickup	58	10	25	—
Smoothness of engine idle	74	48	51	63
Ease of starting	90	83	81	82
Absence of engine stalling	96	97	92	88
Proper fit of doors	92	82	93	89
Fit of other body panels	94	87	90	—
Absence of wind noise	84	70	73	74
Absence of water leaks	91	65	83	80
Fit of exterior chrome and molding	84	79	88	84
Lack of squeaks and rattles	71	59	75	59
Appearance of paint job	91	81	89	81

Exhibit 6. Important Reasons for Purchase Decision Trend

	New Quantum/Dasher purchased in			
	1982	1981	1980	1979
How Important Was Each of the Following in Your Purchase Decision?				
Mileage/fuel economy	87%	100%	100%	98%
Fun to drive	56	31	—	—
Power and pickup	48	10	16	34
Ease of handling	92	72	—	—
Durability/reliability	95	97	—	—
Quality of workmanship	98	92	93	93
Technical innovations	57	56	—	—
Exterior styling	48	30	31	36
Interior styling	52	31	32	41
Riding comfort	82	66	56	63
Passenger seating capacity	57	43	—	—
Quietness	59	31	—	—
Safety features	76	63	—	—
Luggage capacity	77	60	50	51
Value for the money	75	83	70	83
Prestige	19	9	11	7
Resale or trade-in value	64	64	68	60
Cost of maintenance	54	49	53	81
Price or deal offered	58	57	39	57
Quality of dealer service	72	62	65	62
Warranty coverage	57	59	—	—
Dealer's finance plan	12	8	—	—

Exhibit 7. Source of Sales Trend

	New Quantum/Dasher purchased in			
	1982	1981	1980	1979
If You Disposed of a Vehicle at the Time of Purchase, What Was the Make?				
Did not own a vehicle	2	—	—	3
Did not dispose of a vehicle	15	17	22	18
Vehicle disposed of				
General Motors	17	25	26	21
Ford Motor Company	7	13	14	14
Chrysler Corporation	5	5	7	6
American Motors	2	1	1	1
Domestic Trucks/Vans	5	11	—	—
Total Domestic Disposals	36	55	48	50
Volkswagen	32	13	14	14
Audi	2	—	1	1
Honda	1	4	1	1
Toyota	1	2	2	2
Datsun/Nissan	2	2	2	2
Other Imports	9	8	10	9
Total Import Disposals	47	29	30	29

Exhibit 8. Demographics Trend

About yourself	Owners of a Quantum/Dasher that was purchased in							
	1982	1981	1980	1979	1978	1977	1976	1975
Sex: Male	68	73	77	73	62	73	69	77
Married	86	95	86	85	73	82	80	87
Age: Under 20	—	—	—	1	1	1	—	1
20–24	1	—	1	4	7	10	8	4
25–29	10	6	9	13	23	21	19	25
30–34	14	18	13	14	17	18	20	16
35–39	15	23	17	12	5	9	11	14
40–44	11	18	10	10	8	8	10	10
45–49	10	9	8	9	10	10	8	12
50–54	10	6	10	10	8	11	9	8
55–59	7	7	10	13	9	10	7	4
60–64	12	5	11	6	5	8	6	4
65 and over	9	8	11	9	6	6	4	2
Median age (years)	44	41	45	43	37	42	36	36
Education:								
High school or less	17	21	20	33	24	20	25	19
Some college	16	22	21	23	19	22	20	23
College graduate	23	18	20	19	18	20	19	20
Post grad. study/degree	44	38	37	35	39	35	37	38
Total family income								
Under $10,000	—	1	2	2	5	7	10	6
$10,000–$14,999	5	1	3	6	16	14	17	21
$15,000–$19,999	5	7	8	11	19	19	22	26
$20,000–$24,999	5	7	10	18	13	15	13	14
$25,000–$29,999	7	13	9	12	10	12	14	9
$30,000–$39,999	22	27	21	22	21	17	12	11
$40,000 Plus	46	36	35	29	17	13	11	13
Median Income	41,000	36,700	35,600	29,400	24,000	22,900	20,400	19,300
Occupation								
Professional/Technical	25	22	30	30	32	31	44	41
Manager/Proprietor	18	16	15	13	12	7	10	10

Exhibit 9. Sales of Selected Imported Cars

	1980	1981	1982
Celica	140,934	103,879	115,330
Cressida	11,627	29,583	36,977
Supra	21,542	16,146	34,045
Maxima	9,440	35,495	54,502
200SX	92,514	76,024	48,340
Accord	185,977	172,557	194,233
Prelude	50,676	43,450	38,931
Alfa	10,967	27,972	20,462
Scirocco	22,456	17,042	13,207
Dasher	30,958	13,660	645
Quantum	—	515	11,281
Audi 4000	14,683	18,647	13,120
Audi 5000	16,004	17,611	16,659
Audi Coupe	—	2,553	4,264
Total Import Sales	2,392,794	2,319,560	2,214,888

Source: Ward's Automotive Reports.

Exhibit 10. Market Shares for Imports by Brand

Year	Total U.S. registrations	Foreign imports % of U.S.	Toyota % of U.S.	Nissan % of U.S.	Honda % of U.S.	Volks [a] % of U.S.	VW as % of car imports
1981	8,443,919	28.8%	6.7%	5.4%	4.3%	2.7%	9.5%
1980	8,760,937	28.2	6.4	5.8	4.0	2.9	10.3
1979	10,356,695	22.7	4.5	4.3	3.3	2.8	12.2
1978	10,946,104	17.8	3.9	3.1	2.3	2.2	12.3

[a] R.L. Polk continued to count all VW models as imports in 1979–1981 although a sizable portion were made in the United States.
Source: Ward's Automotive Yearbook, 1982.

9

SEB *

Early in 1980, the marketing department of the Société Européenne de Brasseries (SEB) was considering the launch of a new product, a bottled shandy.[1] In April 1979, one of SEB's main competitors, l'Union des Brasseries (U.B.), had launched the first bottled shandy–PANACH'—with great success. SEB, if it is going to enter this market in 1980, will have to move quickly. The factory would have to start production of the shandy around March 15 in order to get the product on the market in time for the peak consumption period which begins around May.

THE COMPANY

SEB ranks second among French breweries with sales exceeding one billion francs. Its 1979 production was 5.3 million hectoliters and its products had about a 22 percent share of the beer market. Following two years of large losses, SEB made a net profit of 29.6 million francs due to favorable market conditions and also because staff was reduced. SEB's head office is located at Sévres, near Paris.

SEB was created in 1966 when several French breweries merged. In 1970, BSN-Gervais Danone took over SEB and Kronenbourg at the same time. Kronenbourg is the best-

selling beer in France (1.8 billion francs sales) and its head office is located in Strasbourg. BSN-Gervais Danone is a diversified multinational company. Its divisions have leading positions in industries such as beverages, dairy products, pasta, and glass manufacturing. Its 1979 sales amounted to 16.5 billion francs. SEB and Kronenbourg are managed as separate divisions with independent marketing, sales, and production operations.

SALES AND MARKETING

SEB's sales go through two channels: food (two thirds of sales) and cafe-hotel-restaurant (C.H.R.) outlets. SEB has an excellent sales network, particularly in the Paris area and in Western France. Its sales force is divided into food and C.H.R. teams and there are six sales regions, each headed by a regional sales director.

Marketing is managed by a general product director who supervises product group managers who in turn direct the individual product managers. Market studies are performed by outside companies. A product manager would work with the SEB-Kronenbourg Market Research Department (which centralizes both companies' studies) in order to define the study's objectives and choose the contractor.

THE BEER MARKET

In France, the overall volume of beer produced has remained stationary at around 22 million hectoliters (hl) per year. The only exception was 1976 when the summer was

* This case was prepared by Alain Sabathier under the supervision of Reinhard Angelmar, associate professor, INSEAD–CEDEP. Copyright © 1984 by CEDEP (Centre Européen d'Education Permanente). Reproduced by permission.

[1] Shandy is a mixture of beer and lemonade. The percentage of beer may vary between 10 and 50 percent.

extremely hot. Since 1973, the percentage of the French adult population (over 15 years old) drinking beer has remained stable at around 56 percent. There are four basic varieties of beer with different alcohol levels: nonalcoholic beers; table beers; luxury beers; and special beers. Retail prices per liter are as follows: about Fr 4 for nonalcoholic beers, Fr 2.20 for table beers, Fr 4 for luxury beers, and Fr 5.80 for special beers.

Underneath the overall market stability, the French are radically changing their beer-drinking habits. Since 1960, French beer drinkers have gradually turned away from table beers and have begun drinking more and more luxury and special brews. At the same time, large packs (1 liter) have sold less and are being replaced by smaller packs (250 ml). SEB is the market leader for beer sold in large packs (table and luxury beer in 1 liter packs) and in the off-the-tap market. It ranks second in the small pack market (see Exhibit 1).

NONALCOHOLIC BEVERAGES

The French consumed 3.4 million hl of lemonade in 1979, and the percentage of adults

Exhibit 1.   Trends in the French Beer Market and Market Shares

A.   Trends in the Beer Market

Year	Table (% of total)	Luxury and Special (% of total)	Total (in millions of hl)
1970	30	67.3	20.25
1976	19	80.1	23.87
1977	16.4	82.8	22.77
1978	14.9	84.4	22.39
1979	12	86 (70% Luxury + 16% Special Brews)	22.40

B.   Brands on the Market in 1979 and Their Market Shares in Food Outlets

Type	SEB	Kronenbourg	UB	Others
Nonalcoholic	Tourtel	—	Panther	
Table	Valstar (57%)	—	—	Many brands
Luxury				
25 cl	Kanterbrau (16.5%)	Kronenbourg (39%)	33 Export (12.5%)	
litre	Kanterpils +Super Valstar (25%)	Kronenpils (17%)	33 Export (23%)	
Special	Gold (12.6%)	1664 (28.6%)	—	Killians (15.3%) Heineken (13.5%)

Source: SEB

drinking lemonade has been increasing noticeably: 35 percent in 1979 compared with 23 percent in 1973. The same trend is true for soft drinks: 27 percent in 1979 compared with 22 percent in 1973. The 1979 consumption of soft drinks amounted to 2.9 million hl.

Lemonade retails at around Fr 1.50 per liter in France. Soft drinks are considerably more expensive. For example, Canada Dry retails at Fr 5.90 per liter and Coca-Cola at Fr 6.30 per liter. SEB is the lemonade market leader with its Sic and Valstar brands. Sales of its soft drink Canada Dry are growing and reached 175,000 hl in 1979.

THE SHANDY MARKET

Before bottled shandy was launched, shandy was drunk in two different ways. One way was in cafés in half-liter glasses of tap beer mixed with lemonade to the customer's taste ("lighter" or "darker" depending on how much beer the customer wanted). A second way was at home where beer and lemonade were mixed by consumers themselves.

A consumer focus group study in the summer of 1978 had supplied SEB with the following information. All adults had heard of shandy ("It's old hat—it's been around for ages"). However, very few young people had heard of shandy and this latter group thought that shandy was much the same thing as beer ("It tastes like beer, smells like it too ... The froth's the same. So is the color"). However, shandy was far less alcoholic than beer ("not as strong"; "milder"; "it's not as alcoholic; I can drink more"; "when it's hot a drink of beer makes me tired ... a write-off ... shandy doesn't do that to me!"), less bubbly, less bitter-sweet. For those who had tried shandy, it was above all a drink which was thirst-quenching ("when you're really thirsty, nothing quenches your thirst better") and a pleasant drink even for people who did not like beer.

People found bottled shandy more convenient (easier to carry and prepare and keep cold) than making shandy at home. However, some consumers did not like the taste ("it's too bland") or the strength ("I can't make it weaker or stronger according to what I feel like drinking") and felt that it was a pity not to make shandy at home. Others preferred going out to a café where they liked the atmosphere ("I meet my friends at a café; it's more fun than staying at home") and found this the most important aspect. However, for those who liked going out to a café, café shandy was not always as they would have liked it ("café shandy isn't always mixed how you like it; they don't always make it the way you asked"). Overall, the information had not been encouraging enough to make SEB enthusiastic about launching a bottled shandy.

The Launching of PANACH'

In April 1979, Union de Brasseries launched the first bottled shandy on the French market with the name PANACH'.[2] U.B. is the third largest French brewery and has a 15 percent share of the market. Its biggest seller is its luxury beer 33 EXPORT.

PANACH' is a mixture of 50 percent beer and 50 percent lemonade and is sold in 250 ml bottles in the beer section of food stores. The type of bottle used is the same as for luxury beer. The bottles are sold in packs of 6 × 250 ml and 10 × 250 ml. The retail price is about Fr 4.20 per liter.

Advertising emphasizes the similarity between PANACH' and shandy drunk in cafés: "PANACH': Shandy which is like café shandy"; "with PANACH' in small bottles, you can drink real shandy at home" (Exhibit 2). PANACH's advertising budget is estimated at about Fr 6 million, divided into 54 percent for radio and 46 percent for outdoor advertising.

Available data on PANACH's sales show that it is a great success. In its first year on the market, PANACH' sold 140,000 hl. This volume was similar to that of Canada Dry and greater than of some well-established

---

[2] The French word for "shandy" is *panache.*

Exhbit 2. PANACH' Radio Ad, 1979

---

30 second theme song

Sung	*Spoken*
Panach', shandy,	With Panach' in small bottles
the real McCoy	You can have a real shandy at home.
Drink PANACH',	Panach', a mild shandy you have.
drink shandy at home	
Panach' is great and cool,	Panach', shandy,
It's a real shandy	Panach', made by Union de Brasseries.
in a small bottle	Panach', shandy.
open one, pour it and drink it . . .	

Source: SECODIP

---

special beers (e.g., Kanterbrau's GOLD). Sales are highly seasonal, with the peak during the summer months. Sixty percent of sales are made south of the Loire river. PANACH' does not sell very well in the C.H.R. sector but sells extremely well in food outlets. Fifty percent of these sales are through hypermarkets, and 30 percent are through supermarkets. The 10 × 250 ml pack is by far the bigger seller of the two pack sizes. It was responsible for 80 percent of food sales.

Shandy Consumers

A national survey conducted at the end of 1979 of 2006 French adults showed that 25 percent of the French population drinks Shandy and of those who consume it, at least 28 percent drink it "quite often." In 1973, a similar survey showed that 14 percent of the French adult population over 16 years of age drank Shandy.[3]

In 1979, shandy drinkers were mostly young with 33 percent of shandy drinkers in the 16–24 year age bracket and 29 percent were workers (Exhibit 3).

A focus group study conducted in September 1979 drew the following conclusions concerning shandy drinkers' reasons for drinking shandy.

The shandy drinker is attracted to beer

- but doesn't like beer's bitterness and alcohol
- or is scared of the effects of alcohol
- or for some reason cannot drink beer (when driving for instance)
- or submits to group pressure when in fact he would prefer soft drinks

To conclude, the shandy drinker wants to be recognized as a beer drinker.

Competition

Beer is a vital ingredient in shandy. Its manufacturing requires experience and large-scale industrial investment. Potential shandy manufacturers, therefore, are to be found among brewers. For a brewer who decides to make shandy, the additional investment in production plant is estimated at Fr 6 to 7 million spread over three years. Anyone who is not a brewer would have to buy a brewery or buy beer from a brewer. In the first case, the investment costs would be very high. For the second case, production costs would be likely to be much higher than those of a brewer who made shandy.

---

[3] Penetration was measured as follows: the percentage of persons interviewed who cited shandy when asked "among the drinks on this list, which ones do you yourself drink, even merely occasionally?"

Exhibit 3. Shandy's Market Penetration, 1979

Demographics	French population (>15 years)	Shandy's penetration index in the survey (France = 25% = 100)
Gender		
Men	48%	112
Women	52	86
	100%	
Age		
15–24	20%	134
25–34	19	107
35–44	15	98
45–54	14	77
55–64	14	56
	82%	
Socioprofessional categories		
A (owners of small companies, managers, professional people)	15%	95
B (white-collar employees)	22	95
C (workers)	30	116
D (inactive)	26	91
	93%	
Total	36 million	2006 (sample)

Source: "Etude d'Usages et d'Attitudes 1979," Direction des Etudes Commerciales.

SEB's managers believe that, apart from the three biggest French breweries (Kronenbourg, SEB, and U.B.), no other French competitor has the necessary financial and distribution strength to market a shandy. Moreover, no foreign brand appears to be well-placed enough to try such an operation in France, with the possible exception of Stella-Artois. This is a Belgian brewer, but it is presently faced with serious financial problems. Imported drinks play a small role in this price range, as transportation costs are disproportionately high.

SEB'S PROJECTS

Market research studies and PANACH's results suggest that people would like to drink a beverage which resembles beer but is lighter than beer. SEB has not given top priority to shandy, believing that low-calorie beer would have greater potential. Although PANACH' has proven to be a success, SEB could still go ahead with its plans to produce a low-calorie beer which could be ready for launching early in 1980. Fischer Breweries has already put a low-calorie beer ("Fischerlei") on the market, and this beer appears to be a flop. Other low-calorie beers (notably OBERNAI, manufactured by Kronenbourg) are also being introduced, but these beers too seem to be meeting with a lukewarm response from consumers. One alternative for SEB, therefore, is to follow U.B. into the shandy market.

Segmentation and Positioning

The major strategic decision concerns the shandy's target segment and its positioning. The national survey provided information about the demographic and social class characteristics of shandy drinkers (Exhibit 3), but other segmentation variables might be more relevant. A focus group study conducted in September 1979 was designed to gather data for positioning decisions. The main recommendations resulting from this study are shown in Exhibit 4.

Exhibit 4. Extracts from a Shandy Positioning Study

Reasons

What Should Not be Said About Shandy

- That it's sweet
- That it should fall into the soft-drink category
- That it's alcoholic
  That it's bitter
- That it's a traditional drink
- That it comes from a particular country
- Sweetness is antibitterness and, therefore, antibeer
- It would lose its image as a beer-related drink

- It would meet with criticism from those who are against beer drinking
- It's a drink which is on a new expanding market rather than a revamped old drink
- Its cosmopolitan dimension is a very strong point

The Following Perceptions Should be Avoided

- The idea of being alone
- Authority, the law, prohibitedness
- A static situation, dullness
- A gloomy, unhappy atmosphere
- It's a product which lends itself to being drunk by groups

- Shandy represents freedom from the imposing beer world
- Shandy is movement and bubbliness
- Shandy is lively and happy

How and When Shandy is Consumed

Shandy is light enough to be drunk at any time. However, symbolically, as shandy drinking is associated with activity, it is more likely to be consumed during periods of activity—this is its "lively" image.

At home, shandy drinking has a more utilitarian aspect. When drunk at home, shandy no longer has the romantic or emotional impact which it had when it was invented in cafés.

Shandy, being a mixture of two drinks and two different worlds, lends itself to becoming a means of communication based on two concepts: birth—getting together.

The Shandy Drinker's Image

Shandy's image is dynamic—for busy people of action with healthy bodies. The shandy drinker:

- Is dynamic—he doesn't need the alcoholic stimulus which beer provides.
- Is well-balanced: being a moderate drinker of alcohol, he fits in with society's norms.
- Is young: he likes his youthfulness and makes it last through his mature age.
- Is sensitive and up-to-date: he's one of the *new breed.*

Exhibit 4. (continued)

How Shandy is Related to Other Beverage Concepts

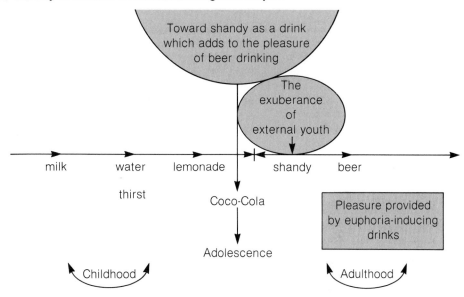

Source: *Le Panaché: Recherche de Positionnement et Axes de Communication,* Créargie, September 1979.

Communication

Communication decisions involve the brand name, the bottle, packaging (label and pack), advertising copy, media, and budgets. Three *brand names* have been preselected after analyzing results of creativity sessions conducted by specialized contractors: CHOPP [4], PANCHO, and PANCHA. Reactions to these names were tested in 150 people (64 percent men, 61 percent under 35 years of age, 50 percent beer drinkers, B, C, and D socioprofessional status). Data concerning memorization, image induction, and suitability of these three names for shandy are given in Exhibit 5.

For the *bottle*, SEB has to decide whether to

[4] "CHOPP" (which is pronounced like "shop") sounds similar to "chope," which is the French word for beer mug.

use a small or large bottle. The designing of a special bottle is out of the question as there is not enough time available. SEB, therefore, must choose between the liter bottle used for table beer and the 250 ml bottle used for luxury beer. The bottle size does not significantly affect variable costs.

Packaging projects have to wait until positioning decisions are made. The briefing session with the advertising agency which will produce the *copy* will take place after the positioning decision. Given how little time is left to get the product onto the market, it is possible that neither the packaging nor the copy will be ready in time to be tested in the usual manner.

Advertising for shandy might involve radio, cinema, the press, or outdoors. A problem exists regarding television advertising. According to television authorities, shandy is

Exhibit 5.   Extracts from a Brand Name Test

Memorizing of Names

Each person interviewed was shown (for about 10 seconds) a card on which six names were marked. The interviewer then removed the card and asked the person being interviewed to cite all of the names which he had remembered.

	Pancha	Pancho	Chopp
% of persons interviewed citing the name			
■ first	13	18	17
■ second	11	17	12
■ *total*	<u>52</u>	<u>50</u>	<u>41</u>

Name Image

Replies to the question: "Which of these names seems the most ordinary (up-to-date, etc. . . .)?"

	Pancha	Pancho	Chopp
■ the most ordinary	37	24	37
■ the most up-to-date	12	23	61
■ the saddest	27	23	35
■ the bubbliest	22	28	43
■ the most conventional	46	27	24
■ the dullest	28	27	34
■ the happiest	26	37	35
■ the oldest	55	29	9
■ the most authentic	25	29	24
■ the youngest	16	24	44
■ the least natural	23	21	32
■ the most original	19	32	37

Spontaneous Association: Names—Types of Drink

The interviewed persons were asked of what drink each of the three names reminded them.

	Pancha	Pancho	Chopp
■ Coca-cola type soft drinks, soda, tonics	8	13	20
■ Appetizers, liqueurs, cocktails	36	26	3
■ Fruit drinks	23	39	5
■ Beer	3	1	58
■ Lemonade	3	5	3
■ Shandy	—	1	—
■ Other drinks	18	12	6
■ No drink at all	11	3	5

Suitability for a Bottled Shandy

This name is

	Pancha	Pancho	Chopp
■ Highly suitable	8	4	15
■ Well-suited	31	33	53
■ Not very well-suited	41	47	20
■ Not at all suitable	19	15	11
■ No opinion	—	1	—
Which name is the best-suited?	24	19	56

Source: "Test de 3 Noms envisageables pour un Panaché," TMO, January 1980.

an alcoholic beverage, and advertising of such drinks on French television is illegal.

SEB's previous experience has shown that radio advertising produces a strong impact on brand name memorization and is also an excellent means of conveying the context in which a drink is consumed. Combined with its ability to reach only a small percentage of the target audience the high cost of making a cinema ad (at least Fr 300,000) appears to be prohibitive. Advertising in the press and outdoors is usually designed to enable customers to visualize the product in its packaging so they can then recognize it on store shelves. Outdoor ads can be seen by all potential consumers. The press, however, is perceived as the best medium for directing advertising at specific target groups. When launching a product as a follower, SEB normally bases its *advertising budget* on the media plan of the market leader.

The Product

The main decision concerning the product is, What proportion of beer and of lemonade should be used? The main, *mixture alternatives* considered by SEB were: 50 percent beer and 50 percent lemonade (like PANACH') or 30 percent beer and 70 percent lemonade.

To help make this decision, the Market Research Department set up blind pairwise tasting sessions in November 1979. Two hundred shandy drinkers, aged 20 to 35, were asked to indicate which of two shandies they preferred: One was a 30–70 mixture, and the other was PANACH'. The tasters were not told the name of either shandy. The results of this blind taste test are shown in Exhibit 6.

The composition of the shandy does not in any way affect production facilities, as the factory has excess capacity for beer and lemonade. Variable production cost is the same whatever composition is chosen. Although beer is normally much more expensive than lemonade, the high-quality lemonade destined for use in SEB's shandy costs the same as beer.

Price

SEB's shandy can be priced identically to, above, or below PANACH'. In SEB's experience, retail prices in the food channel are typically 30 percent higher than selling prices to the trade. The ex-factory variable production cost is estimated at Fr 2 per liter. Promotional costs are estimated at 6 percent of sales, and sales forces expenses would be around 15 percent.

Exhibit 6. Extracts from a Blind Taste Study

Product Preference

	Preferred 30–70	Preferred 50–50 (PANACH')	Number of consumers
Overall preference	51%	49%	196
Preference according to			
■ Paris	43%	57%	99
■ Marseilles	60%	40%	97
Preference according to			
■ Men	57%	43%	97
■ Women	46%	54%	99

Exhibit 6. (continued)

Overall Liking of Products

	Overall rating of 30–70 Shandy by consumers who ...		Overall rating of 50–50 Shandy (PANACH') by consumers who ...	
	Prefer it	Prefer 50–50	Prefer it	Prefer 30–70
Very good	16%	—	5%	—
Good	72	2%	69	9%
Not bad	12	31	24	38
Nothing exciting	—	46	2	45
Awful	—	21	—	8
No opinion	—			
Total	100%	100%	100%	100%
n	101	95	95	101

How the Preferred Product is Perceived

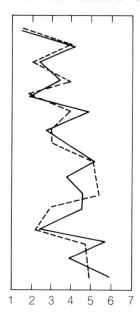

Pleasant taste	Unpleasant taste
Too sweet	Too bitter
Thirst-quenching	Not thirst-quenching
Too much like lemonade	Too much like beer
Pleasant odor	Unpleasant odor
For men	For women
Bubbly	Flat
Similar to café shandy	Not like café shandy
Insignificant color	Pleasant color
Not bitter enough	Too bitter
Fruity taste	No fruity taste
Froths nicely	Froth doesn't last
Refreshing	Not refreshing
Acidic	Sweet
Not enough beer	Too much beer
Highly alcoholic	Mildly alcoholic

1 2 3 4 5 6 7

———— How 30–70 shandy was rated by the 101 consumers who had indicated that this was their preferred shandy.

– – – – How 50–50 (PANACH') shandy was rated by 95 consumers who had indicated that this was their preferred shandy.

Exhibit 6. (continued)

How the Rejected Product is Perceived

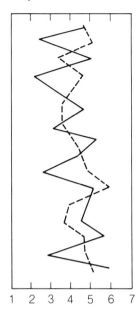

Pleasant taste	Unpleasant taste
Too sweet	Too bitter
Thirst-quenching	Not thirst-quenching
Too much like lemonade	Too much like beer
Pleasant odor	Unpleasant odor
For men	For women
Bubbly	Flat
Similar to café shandy	Not like café shandy
Insignificant color	Pleasant color
Not bitter enough	Too bitter
Fruity taste	No fruity taste
Froths nicely	Froth doesn't last
Refreshing	Not refreshing
Acidic	Sweet
Not enough beer	Too much beer
Highly alcoholic	Mildly alcoholic

1 2 3 4 5 6 7

————— How 30–70 shandy was rated by 95 consumers who
has indicated that they preferred 50–50 shandy (PANACH')

– – – – – How 50–50 (PANACH') shandy was rated by the 101 consumers
who had indicated that they preferred 30–70 shandy.

Source: "Test de Produit Aveugle Panaché," Direction des Etudes Commerciales, January 1980.

Distribution

To check out the CHR sector's opinion, a meeting with about 10 cafe managers was held in November 1979 to find out what they thought about bottled shandy. Overall, those present were not particularly enthusiastic. Their main argument against bottled shandy was that they could not adjust the strength of the shandy to serve. They argued that their customers' preferences varied enormously. They also added that bottled shandy might turn out to be more expensive than their own shandy.

Food retailers were far more enthusiastic about bottled shandy. During its first year on the market, PANACH' proved to be an excellent seller and obtained a distribution coverage of 65 percent, the same as that of EXPORT 33. According to SEB's sales force, a second brand of shandy would be welcomed by the food retailers.

DECISIONS

Early in 1980, SEB faced three main options.

1. Launch a shandy nationally in 1980.

2. Launch a shandy on a test market.

3. Go ahead with the low-calorie beer project.

Forecasts predict a bright future for the shandy market: Sales will rise from 140,000 hl in 1979 to about 300,000 hl in 1980 and will then double to 600,000 hl in 1981 before leveling off to increase gradually in 1982 and 1983: 700,000 hl and 800,000 hl respectively.

The main area of uncertainty was SEB's shandy potential market share. Also it would be impossible to fully test the launch campaign. SEB usually performs quantitative tests in order to develop a five-year brand plan. In addition, SEB normally tests every aspect of its communication mix. Judging by past experience with follower products, SEB estimates that arriving second on the shandy market could mean shandy sales of 110,000 hl for a 1980 national launch.

The second option is to launch the shandy in a test market with one formula, one type of packaging, and one communication strategy. Results would then be analyzed at the end of the season and the marketing mix could be adapted according to market reactions. This trial would provide the basis for a nationwide launch which would take place the following year. The test market launch requires the same decisions as a nationwide launch since a complete marketing mix would have to be used.

A third option is to give up all idea of launching a shandy and to go ahead with the low-calorie beer project. This product is almost ready for launching, and communication is the only part of the product which remains to be finished.

10

North Branch Paper *

In 1978 a small regional producer of industrial and consumer paper products, North Branch Paper Mills, Inc., was purchased by American Food Products Corporation (AFP). AFP produced and marketed several nationally known brands of canned fruits and vegetables, prepared frozen foods, and snack items. Sales in 1977 were over $275 million, and the net profit margin was 3.5 percent. Industry observers considered this profit margin adequate, but it certainly was not outstanding. In order to improve profits, the firm decided to seek acquisitions that would allow it to sell high margin, nonfood items through established marketing channels. It was this strategy that led to the acquisition of North Branch Paper Mills, Inc., in 1978.

North Branch Paper Mills, Inc., had grown from a small producer of newsprint, groundwood paper, and unbleached kraft paper to a middle-sized, but relatively unknown, company. Major products included a wide range of industrial paper products and a somewhat smaller number of consumer items, including bathroom and facial tissues, paper napkins, and paper towels. Consumer products either carried distributor's labels or were sold under the company's Countess label. Sales of North Branch consumer products were well over $1 million in 1977, though very little effort had been made by the company to promote the Countess label.

North Branch Paper was operated as a separate division by AFP. AFP grouped related

* This case was prepared by Frederic B. Kraft of Wichita State University. Demographic data were collected by John A. Miller. Copyright © Frederic B. Kraft. Reproduced by permission.

products in separate divisions and brand managers were made responsible for individual brands. Staff functions, such as marketing research and advertising, were centralized at the AFP corporate level.

The North Branch Paper Division had four brand groups and the responsibility for the Countess brand of paper towels was given to Dan Orr. Orr had been an assistant brand manager for a major consumer products company, and AFP had hired him to develop and test a marketing program for the Countess brand. Orr was asked to build sales of Countess in the Midwest as a prelude to a large-scale national marketing effort. When he began this task in early 1977, Orr was aware that brand managers at AFP were usually given no more than 18 to 24 months to develop a profitable product. The AFP president had made it clear that he did not intend to "waste dollars propping up dead products."

PAPER TOWEL INDUSTRY

Rapid increases in sales, and intense competition marked the paper towel industry in the 1970s. In 1971, two major competitors (Laddy and Vera) accounted for over 76 percent of total market sales of $144 million. By 1978 the paper towel market was shared by eight producers and totaled $418 million, a sizable increase over the 1968 figure. Although industry analysts projected annual increases in paper towel consumption of 10 percent, some paper towel producers were having difficulty maintaining their market share. Laddy, for example, failed to meet the growing competitive emphasis on coupons, price deals, and increased advertising and suffered serious erosion of its market position.

The entry of new competitors in the national market was prompted by the traditional high profits of paper products. The newcomers included small regional firms, such as the maker of Conserve, who first established its product in one region and then began to enter other regional markets. A second type of competitor was the large established consumer products company, such as the maker of Bouquet. These companies purchased regional paper producers to acquire trade names and production capacity and then rapidly introduced their brands nationally through established marketing channels.

Product and promotional appeals also changed during the 1970s. In the early 1970s advertising stressed absorbency, with conflicting claims made by each of the two larger competitors. In order to increase the absorbency of its product, Vera introduced the first two-ply towel nationally during 1971 and 1972 using a vigorous mail coupon campaign. An East Coast regional brand (Swan) followed with a regional introduction of a three-ply towel it claimed was more absorbent than the two ply.

Later in the 1970s towel strength became an important advertising theme. The maker of Tuffi introduced the ultimate durability with a nylon reinforced four-ply towel. When Tuffi's initial sales were somewhat lower than expected, its maker considered stressing the reusability of the product. By late 1979, it was rumored that the makers of Laddy were about to test a four-ply product.

Another trend in the paper towel market was the introduction of colors and patterns. Originally a white commodity, the paper towel became available in "decorator," colors, bright patterns, and border strips. The makers of Laddy successfully tested a four-pattern, four-color towel in the western states, while the makers of Regal introduced a "color-on-color" towel with daisies imprinted on a colored background.

CURRENT SITUATION

In January 1980, Dan Orr asked his assistant, Ann Ballinger, to help him review the progress made by Countess paper towels. "I'm afraid we're going to have to improve these reports if headquarters is going to let us go national," Orr said, as he handed Ballinger the report on market shares for the last three months of 1979 (Exhibit 1). Ballinger was aware that Countess paper towels had not made much progress despite fairly extensive promotional efforts aimed at establishing Countess as a colorful new towel. She suggested that an in-depth study of their product and of the paper towel market was in order.

Orr agreed, stating, "We've got to come up with some more facts. For one thing, Nielsen data are expensive and usually consistent, but here's a report from Compusamp showing that Vera is outselling Bouquet by 10 percent, the direct opposite of the Nielsen figures. Besides, I'd like to have more detail so we can really analyze our customers! The Nielsen figures show we're in sixth place in our region, with 6 percent of the market. Unless we can get that up to at least 8 or 9 percent, I don't think we'll get the go-ahead. However, the market share figures don't tell us what the consumer is thinking. If we spend some money and find out what's going on out there, maybe we can make some adjustments and get things moving." Orr telephoned the marketing research manager to set up a meeting to discuss a research plan for Countess towels.

CONSUMER RESEARCH PLAN

When Orr met with the corporate research manager, O.C. Thomas, he outlined his needs for a thorough analysis of the paper towel consumer. He was concerned with the success of the recent couponing campaign which featured a 7¢ offer. Orr was also interested in determining the level of awareness of Countess and other brands, the relative brand preferences, the perceived

Exhibit 1. Average Market Shares for Paper Towels in the Midwestern States (fourth quarter, 1978)

Brand	Percentage
Bouquet	25
Laddy	22
Vera	16
Regal	12
Softex	9
Countess	6
Old South	4
Tuffi	2
Conserve	2
Others	2
	100

importance of product features, and the ratings of available brands on these features. Thomas suggested that demographic data be collected to determine whether the competing brands appealed more to one group of consumers than another.

"Why not just ask consumers what they usually buy, or maybe even see what brands are on hand?" asked Ballinger. Orr responded, "I want to know more than simply the most recent purchase because the purchase could be an exception to the usual buying pattern. I think the biggest differences among consumers are shown by their purchasers over a period of time. For example, we could determine which buyers were heavy users and which were light users and then compare their preferences to determine who responds best to our brand."

Thomas agreed, and he suggested that a fairly small panel study would be appropriate. "If we draw a sample from just one town, say Fort Wayne, Indiana, where we feel that buying habits are representative, we can get useful information and keep costs down." Although research funds for the study were limited, enough money was allocated to permit an 18-week longitudinal panel study. Furthermore, the panel study of paper towel purchases was to be preceded by

interviews with housewives to determine their attitudes toward the available brands.

RESULTS OF THE STUDY

Professional interviewers were hired by AFP to collect the data and in February they interviewed 500 Fort Wayne consumers. Of these, 217 agreed to fill out the questionnaire, and to record their purchases for the duration of the 18-week study. At the end of the 18 weeks, 132 of the participants had made one or more towel purchases. Persons who claimed to be paper towel users but who did not purchase during this time were not retained for the final analysis.

The questionnaires completed at the beginning of the study were designed to collect six types of information: (1) the first brand of paper towels the person could mention, (2) a statement of favorite brand of paper towels, (3) recall of the brand most recently purchased, (4) perception of the importance of four paper-towel attributes (absorbency, strength, color, and economy) in her choice of brands, (5) evaluation of each of the nine leading brands on these attributes, and (6) the categorization of each family on 11 demographic variables.

The average ratings of the importance of

Exhibit 2. Perceived Importance of Attributes Used in Selecting a Brand of Paper Towels

Attribute	Average rating [a]	Standard deviation
Absorbency	4.50	.75
Strength	4.20	.96
Color	2.41	1.34
Economy	4.07	1.03

[a] Each individual rated the perceived importance of each attribute on a five-point scale on which 1 signified "not at all important" and 5 signified "very important."

the four attributes in brand choice (Exhibit 2) and the average rating of each brand on these attributes (Exhibit 3) were combined to give a special "summated index" of the consumer's evaluation of each brand. This index was calculated for each person by multiplying satisfaction ratings of the four attributes of each brand times perceived importance of each attribute, and then adding together the four scores. The summated scores were then converted into index form by dividing by the highest summated rating made by the con-sumers. Thus, the highest evaluation had an index value of 100, and lower rated brands were some fraction of 100. The summated indexes, first brand mentioned, stated favorite brand, and most recently purchased brand were key-punched along with the purchase information recorded by each person in the 18 weeks following the completion of the questionnaire. Information was also collected at the time of the February interviews on the average selling prices in Fort Wayne grocery stores for the nine lead-

Exhibit 3. Average Ratings of Towel Attributes by Brand

Brand [a]	Absorbency		Strength		Color		Economy	
	Rating [b]	Rank	Rating	Rank	Rating	Rank	Rating	Rank
Bouquet	4.01	(2)	3.84	(3)	4.07	(1)	3.39	(3)
Laddy	3.92	(4)	3.86	(2)	3.91	(5)	3.46	(2)
Regal	3.78	(6)	3.67	(5)	3.97	(3)	3.31	(5)
Vera	3.66	(7)	3.70	(4)	3.73	(6)	3.14	(8)
Softex	3.00	(9)	2.82	(9)	3.46	(9)	3.57	(1)
Countess	3.80	(5)	3.66	(6)	3.94	(4)	3.23	(7)
Old South	3.53	(8)	3.35	(7)	3.64	(7)	3.30	(6)
Tuffi	4.24	(1)	4.17	(1)	3.97	(2)	2.93	(9)
Conserve	3.99	(3)	3.13	(8)	3.62	(8)	3.34	(4)

[a] Brands are presented in order of the number of purchases during the study.

[b] Each individual rated her satisfaction on a five-point scale on which 1 signified "very unsatisfactory" and 5 signi-fied "very satisfactory."

ing brands of towels. Thomas had suggested that these data might aid in interpreting consumers' brand evaluations.

DATA ANALYSIS

When the data collection was completed in May, Orr and Ballinger met with Thomas to discuss the analysis plan. Orr was anxious to analyze the data as soon as possible, since competitive brands were becoming more aggressive. He was particularly concerned with Laddy, who was beginning a new promotional program stressing economy. Furthermore, a new three-ply towel was being test-

ed in several markets, including some in which Countess was sold. Also, it had recently been rumored that the price of Tuffi would be reduced in all markets to bring it in line with competitive brands. The need to develop a coherent marketing strategy was clear. Heavy competitive advertising, such as Bouquet with its liquid absorption test, had been very successful. Countess had developed no particular strategy other than using a promotional theme based on Countess's colorful new towel designs. Orr began his analysis by examining the prices and package sizes of his competitors (Exhibit 4).

Exhibit 4. Prices of Paper Towels in Fort Wayne Stores, February 1980

Brand number	Brand name	Average price per roll (cents)	Roll length (feet)
1	Bouquet	87.5	100
7	Laddy	87.6	120
10	Vera	87.4	100
3	Regal	86.0	100
11	Softex	81.2	100
5	Countess	87.3	110
6	Old South	82.5	100
8	Tuffi	95.5	50
4	Conserve	84.4	100

Format for Data Analysis—Countess Paper Towel Study [a]

APPENDIX A

Card 1		Variable	Variable number
Column	1–4	Questionnaire identification number	
		(Number of purchases in first month—cols. 5–22)	
Column	5–6	Number of purchases of brand 1 in first month	1
	7–8	Number of purchases of brand 3 in first month	2
	9–10	Number of purchases of brand 4 in first month	3
	11–12	Number of purchases of brand 5 in first month	4
	13–14	Number of purchases of brand 6 in first month	5
	15–16	Number of purchases of brand 7 in first month	6
	17–18	Number of purchases of brand 8 in first month	7
	19–20	Number of purchases of brand 10 in first month	8
	21–22	Number of purchases of brand 11 in first month	9
		(Number of purchases in second month—cols. 23–40)	
Column	23–24	Number of purchases of brand 1 in second month	10
	25–26	Number of purchases of brand 3 in second month	11
	27–28	Number of purchases of brand 4 in second month	12
	29–30	Number of purchases of brand 5 in second month	13
	31–32	Number of purchases of brand 6 in second month	14
	33–34	Number of purchases of brand 7 in second month	15
	35–36	Number of purchases of brand 8 in second month	16
	37–38	Number of purchases of brand 10 in second month	17
	39–40	Number of purchases of brand 11 in second month	18
		(Number of purchases in third month—cols. 41–58)	
Column	41–42	Number of purchases of brand 1 in third month	19
	43–44	Number of purchases of brand 3 in third month	20
	45–46	Number of purchases of brand 4 in third month	21
	47–48	Number of purchases of brand 5 in third month	22
	49–50	Number of purchases of brand 6 in third month	23
	51–52	Number of purchases of brand 7 in third month	24
	53–54	Number of purchases of brand 8 in third month	25
	55–56	Number of purchases of brand 10 in third month	26
	57–58	Number of purchases of brand 11 in third month	27
		(Number of purchases in fourth month—cols. 59–76)	
Column	59–60	Number of purchases of brand 1 in fourth month	28
	61–62	Number of purchases of brand 3 in fourth month	29
	63–64	Number of purchases of brand 4 in fourth month	30
	65–66	Number of purchases of brand 5 in fourth month	31
	67–68	Number of purchases of brand 6 in fourth month	32
	69–70	Number of purchases of brand 7 in fourth month	33
	71–72	Number of purchases of brand 8 in fourth month	34
	73–74	Number of purchases of brand 10 in fourth month	35
	75–76	Number of purchases of brand 11 in fourth month	36

APPENDIX A (continued)

Card 1		Variable	Variable number
Column	1–4	Questionnaire identification number	
	19–20	First brand mentioned	37
		Code	
		0 Respondent couldn't answer	
		12 Brand number 12 (IGA) named	
	21–22	State favorite brand	38
		Code	
		0 Respondent couldn't answer	
		98 Don't know (although claimed to have favorite brand)	
		99 Don't care, or no preference	
	23–24	Most recent brand purchased (prior to start of study)	39
		Code	
		0 Respondent couldn't or wouldn't answer	
		15 Brand number 15 (Scot Lad)	
		98 Don't know (although claimed to have made a recent purchase)	
		Summated attitude index of 9 brands. 100 represents highest score given by subject. Lower numbers represent a proportion of 100. Cols. 25–51.	
Column	25–27	Attitude rating on brand 1	40
	28–30	Attitude rating on brand 3	41
	31–33	Attitude rating on brand 4	42
	34–36	Attitude rating on brand 5	43
	37–39	Attitude rating on brand 6	44
	40–42	Attitude rating on brand 7	45
	43–45	Attitude rating on brand 8	46
	46–48	Attitude rating on brand 10	47
	49–51	Attitude rating on brand 11	48
	52	Marital status	49
	53–54	Wife's age	50
	55–56	Husband's age	51
	57	Number of children	52
	58–59	Age of youngest child	53
	60–61	Total number of persons in household	54
	62–63	Total years of schooling—wife	55
	64–65	Total years of schooling—husband	56
	66	Wife work?	57
	67	Husband's occupation	58
	68	Income	59

[a] Brands 2 and 9 are not included in the study as no purchases were made of these brands.

APPENDIX B

Codes for Demographic Data

Variable number				
49	Marital status:	1 = married 2 = single	3 = widow 4 = divorced	
50	Wife's age:	01 = <20 02 = 20–24 03 = 25–29 04 = 30–34	05 = 35–39 06 = 40–44 07 = 45–49 08 = 50–54	09 = 55–59 10 = 60–64 11 = <64
51	Husband's age:	01 = <20 02 = 20–24 03 = 25–29 04 = 30–34	05 = 35–39 06 = 40–44 07 = 45–49 08 = 50–54	09 = 55–59 10 = 60–64 11 = <64
52	Number of children: 1 = 1, 2 = 2 ... 9 = 9 or more			
53	Age of youngest child: 01 = 1, 02 = 2 ... to 99 years			
54	Total number of persons in household: 01 to 99 persons			
55	Total years of schooling, wife: 01 to 20 is same as the number of years 21 = 21 or more years			
56	Total years of schooling, husband: 01 to 20 is same as the number of years 21 = 21 or more years			
57	Does the wife work? 1 = yes 2 = no			
58	Husband's occupation: 1 = Professional, technical 2 = Proprietor, manager, official, wholesale/retail dealer 3 = Clerical or sales 4 = Craftsman, skilled worker, foreman 5 = Semiskilled worker, operatives		6 = Unskilled worker 7 = Student, military 8 = Retired, disabled 9 = Unemployed Blank = not reported	
59	Total family income 1 = $ 0–2,999 2 = 3,000–4,999 3 = 5,000–7,499	4 = $ 7,500–9,999 5 = 10,000–12,499 6 = 12,500–14,999	7 = $ 15,000–19,999 8 = 20,000–24,999 9 = 25,000 and over	

APPENDIX C

Data Listing—Countess Paper Towel Study

```
     3    6   10   14   18   22   26   30   34   38   42   46   50   54   58   62   66   70   74   76
 1   0 0 0 0 0 0 0 1 0 0 0 0 0 0 0 0 0 1 0 0 0 0 0 0 0 0 1 0 0 0 0 0 0 0 0 0 0 0
 1   0 0 0 0 0 0 0101010 60 50 71100 80 69 65100 69110110   021608283
 2   1 0 0 0 0 0 0 0 0 1 0 0 0 0 0 0 0 0 0 0 2 2 0 0 0 0 0 0 0 1 0 0 0 0 0 0 0 0 0 0
 2   0 0 0 0 0 0 0039998 54 64 76 86 86100    0   0   010607306041719117
 3   2 0 0 0 0 0 0 0 0 0 0 0 0 0 0 0 0 0 0 1 0 0 0 0 0 0 0 1 0 0 0 0 0 0 0 0 0 0 0 0
 3   0 0 0 1 0 0 0010101100   0  0100  0100   0   0   010607210041419219
 4   0 0 0 0 0 0 2 0 0 0 0 0 0 0 4 0 0 0 0 0 0 0 3 0 0 0 0 0 0 0 0 0 2 0 0 0 0 0
 4   0 0 0 0 0 0 0070707 60  0  0 80   0100   0 80   010606304051721219
 5   3 0 0 0 0 0 0 0 0 1 0 0 0 0 0 0 0 0 4 0 0 0 0 0 0 0 3 0 0 0 0 0 0 0 0 0 1 0
 5   0 0 0 0 0 0 0010101100   0  0 38  0 38  0   0   010507509071820217
 6   2 0 0 0 0 0 0 0 1 0 0 0 0 0 0 0 0 0 0 0 1 0 0 0 0 0 0 1 0 0 0 0 0 0 0 0 0 0
 6   0 0 0 0 0 0 0010101100 88   0 73 64 64 97 80   010504102031720218
 7   0 0 0 0 0 0 0 0 1 0 0 0 0 0 0 0 0 1 0 0 0 0 0 0 0 1 0 0 0 0 0 0 1 0 0 0
 7   0 0 0 0 0 0 0079907   0 87 84   0 0100   0 97 84104040   021821118
 8   0 0 0 0 0 0 0 0 0 0 0 0 0 0 0 0 0 0 0 0 0 0 0 0 0 0 0 0 0 0 0 0 0 0 0 0
 8   0 0 0 0 0 0 0100710100 98100 93100 93  0100   0110100   031510286
 9   0 0 0 0 0 0 1 0 0 0 0 0 0 0 0 0 0 1 0 0 0 0 0 0 0 0 0 1 0 0 0 0 0 0
 9   0 0 0 0 0 0 0100810  0 91  0  0  0 91100 91   010404502081216214
10   0 0 0 0 0 0 0 0 0 1 0 0 0 0 0 0 0 0 1 0 0 0 0 0 0 1 0 0 0 0 1 0 0 0 0 0
10   0 0 0 0 0 0 0080809100   0  0  0  0 0100   0   010909616041312145
11   0 0 0 0 0 0 0 0 1 0 0 0 0 0 0 0 0 0 0 0 0 0 0 0 0 0 0 1 0 0 0 0 0 0 0 0
11   0 0 0 0 0 0 0079998   0  0  0  0 87100   0   0   0103030   022121172
12   0 0 0 0 0 0 0 0 0 0 0 0 0 0 1 0 0 0 0 0 0 0 0 0 0 0 0 0 0 0 0 0 0 0 0 0
12   0 0 0 0 0 0 0079907100100100100100100100  0100   010406209021821119
13   0 0 0 0 0 0 0 1 0 0 0 0 0 0 0 0 0 0 0 0 0 0 0 0 0 0 0 0 0 0 0 0 0 0 0 0
13   0 0 0 0 0 0 0010808100   0  0100  0100100  0   0109080   02  12156
14   0 0 0 0 0 0 0 0 0 0 0 0 0 0 0 0 1 0 0 0 0 0 0 0 0 0 0 0 0 0 0 0 0 0
14   0 0 0 0 0 0 0079805100   0  0 89 75 63  0   0   0102020   021618173
15   0 0 0 0 0 0 0 0 1 0 0 0 0 0 0 0 0 0 0 0 0 0 0 0 0 0 0 0 0 0 0 1 0 0 0
15   0 0 0 0 0 0 0070715 89 85 89 96  0 89  0 85   0103030   022021113
16   0 0 0 0 0 0 1 0 0 0 0 0 0 0 0 0 0 0 0 0 0 0 0 0 0 0 0 0 0 0 0 0 0 0
16   0 0 0 0 0 0 0070707   0 77  0 87 87 90100   0   0109091320022112135
17   0 0 0 0 0 0 0 0 0 1 0 0 0 0 0 0 0 0 0 0 0 0 0 0 0 0 0 0 0 0 0 2 0 0 0
17   0 0 0 0 0 0 0070707 82 82   0 82 82100 99100   010303203041212244
18   2 0 0 0 0 0 0 0 0 0 4 0 0 0 0 0 0 0 0 0 0 0 0 0 0 0 3 0 0 0 0 0 0 0
18   0 0 0 0 0 0 0010107100 57 75 55 86 77 57 77 63109114270412084164
19   1 0 0 0 0 0 0 0 1 0 0 0 0 0 0 0 2 0 0 0 0 0 0 2 1 0 0 0 0 0 0 0 0 0
19   0 0 0 0 0 0 0079907100100100100100100100   0   010506506071009155
20   2 0 1 1 0 0 0 0 0 1 0 0 0 2 0 0 1 0 1 0 1 0 0 0 1 0 0 0 3 0 0 0 0 0
20   0 0 0 0 0 0 0050105100 87 91 87 97 99 80 74   010406310051112155
21   0 0 0 0 0 0 0 0 2 0 1 0 0 0 0 0 2 0 0 0 0 1 0 0 0 0 0 1 0 0 1 0 0
21   0 0 0 0 0 0 0079907 58 61   0 45  0 84 35 0100105063050512   244
22   0 0 0 0 0 0 0 1 0 0 0 0 0 0 0 0 1 0 0 0 0 0 0 1 0 0 0 0 0 0 0 1 0 0 0
22   0 0 0 0 0 0 0101010 58 63 60 60 60 69 69100   010809315041010281
23   0 0 0 0 0 1 0 0 0 0 0 0 0 0 0 0 0 0 0 0 0 0 0 0 0 0 0 0 0 0 0 0 0 0
23   0 0 0 0 0 0 0079907100   0 58  0100100 90  0   010505306041712126
24   1 1 0 0 0 0 0 0 0 0 0 0 0 0 1 0 0 0 0 0 0 0 0 0 0 0 0 0 0 1 0 0
24   0 0 0 0 0 0 0070101100 64   0  0  0  0 0100   010202101031519171
25   0 0 0 0 0 0 0 0 0 0 1 0 0 0 0 0 0 0 0 0 0 0 0 0 0 0 0 0 0 0 0 0 0 0
25   0 0 0 0 0 0 0129912 91 98   0100 76 98 98 98   0102030   021417272
26   0 0 0 1 0 2 0 0 0 1 0 0 1 0 0 0 0 0 0 0 0 1 0 0 3 0 0 0 0 0 0 0
26   0 0 0 0 0 0 0070808   0  0  0100  9100100   010807203041313135
27   0 0 0 0 4 0 0 0 0 0 0 0 4 0 0 0 0 0 0 2 0 0 0 0 0 0 0 0 2 0 0 0 0
27   0 0 0 0 0 0 0070707   0  0   0  0100   0 90   010303207041212146
28   2 0 0 0 0 0 0 1 0 0 0 0 0 0 0 0 1 0 0 0 0 0 0 0 0 0 0 0 0 0 0 0
28   0 0 0 0 0 0 0030303100100 63 58 63100 46  0   010707217031214115
29   0 0 0 0 0 0 0 0 0 0 0 0 0 0 0 0 0 0 0 0 0 1 0 0 0 0 0 0 0 0 0 0
29   0 0 0 0 0 0 0010101 57  0 33100  0100  0   0   01111124003080828
30   1 0 0 0 0 0 0 0 1 0 0 0 0 0 0 0 0 0 0 0 0 0 1 0 0 0 0 0 0 0 0 0
30   0 0 0 0 0 0 0079901100   0  0 91  0 91   0100   0102030   021721215
31   0 0 0 0 0 0 0 1 0 0 0 0 0 0 0 0 0 0 0 0 0 0 0 0 0 0 0 0 0 0 0 0
31   0 0 0 0 0 0 0071010   0 85  0 87 77100   0100   0105060   021821117
32   0 1 0 0 1 0 0 0 0 0 0 0 0 0 1 0 0 0 0 0 1 0 0 0 0 0 0 0 0 1 0 0
32   0 0 0 0 0 0 0070708 59 67  0 88  0 91100 64   010404407061212155
33   2 0 0 0 0 0 0 0 0 2 0 0 0 0 0 0 0 2 0 0 0 0 0 2 0 0 0 0 0 0 0 0
33   0 0 0 0 0 0 0010101100 78  0  0  0 77  0  0   0104040   021716225
```

APPENDIX C (continued)

```
34   0 0 0 0 0 0 0 0 0 0 0 0 0 1 0 0 0 0 0 0 0 0 0 0 0 0 0 0 0 0 0 0 0 0 1 0 0
34   0 0 0 0 0 0 0070810 95 95   0 95 95 95100 95    010405307051216226
35   0 0 0 1 0 0 0 0 0 0 0 0 0 0 0 0 0 0 0 0 3 0 0 0 0 0 0 0 0 3 0 0 0 0 0 1 0
35   0 0 0 0 0 0 0050501100 92  0100  0  0  0  0    010909231021213145
36   0 0 0 0 0 0 0 0 0 0 0 0 0 1 0 0 0 0 1 0 0 0 0 0 0 0 0 0 0 0 0 0 0 0 0 0 0
36   0 0 0 0 0 0 0019901 97 84 89100 85 79 77 82   0309  4200215  1 3
37   0 0 0 0 0 0 0 0 0 0 0 0 0 0 0 0 0 0 0 0 0 0 0 0 0 0 0 0 0 0 1 0 0 0 0 0 0
37   0 0 0 0 0 0 0100505  0  0  0100  0  0 96 81   0104042010417142 17
38   0 0 0 0 0 0 0 0 0 0 0 0 0 0 0 0 0 0 0 0 0 0 0 0 0 1 0 0 0 0 0 0 0 3 0 0
38   0 0 0 0 0 0 2039903 67100  0  0 67100  0 85   010405405061416214
39   0 0 0 0 0 0 0 1 0 0 1 0 0 0 0 0 0 0 1 1 0 0 0 0 0 0 0 1 0 0 0 0 0 0 0 0
39   0 0 0 0 0 0 0050303 60100 54 81  0 76  0 66   010202102031516253
40   0 2 0 0 0 0 0 0 0 0 0 0 0 0 0 0 0 0 0 0 0 0 0 0 0 1 0 0 0 0 0 0 0 0 0 0
40   0 0 0 0 0 0 0039901 83100  0 92  0  0 0103   01110913202161522
41   0 0 0 1 0 0 0 0 0 0 0 0 0 0 0 0 0 0 0 0 0 0 0 0 0 1 0 0 0 0 0 0 0 0 0 0
41   0 0 0 0 0 0 0070505 94 73 67100 94100  0 59   010908227021021217
42   0 0 0 0 0 0 0 0 0 0 0 0 0 1 0 0 0 0 0 0 0 0 0 0 0 0 0 0 0 1 0 0 0 0 0 0
42   0 0 0 0 0 0 0070707  0  0  0 75 75100  0  0   010909320021620217
43   0 0 0 0 0 0 0 0 0 0 0 0 0 0 0 0 0 0 0 0 0 0 0 0 0 0 0 0 0 0 0 1 0 0 0
43   0 0 0 0 0 0 0         0 89  0  0  0 79 79100   010404405061619117
44   0 0 0 0 0 1 0 0 0 0 0 0 1 0 0 0 0 0 0 0 0 0 1 0 0 0 0 0 0 0 0 0 0 0 0
44   0 0 0 0 0 0 0101008 89100  0 89 89 97 97100   010505205041221216
45   0 0 0 0 0 0 0 0 0 0 0 0 1 0 0 0 0 0 0 0 0 0 0 0 0 0 0 0 0 0 0 0 0 0
45   0 0 0 0 0 0 0070707 93 82 75100 82 91  0  0   01080831804151821
46   0 0 0 0 0 0 0 0 0 0 0 0 0 0 0 0 0 0 0 0 0 0 0 0 0 0 0 0 0 0 1 0 0 0
46   0 0 0 0 0 0 0070707 78 82 78 85 78100  0100   0102030  021516153
47   0 0 0 0 0 0 0 0 0 0 0 0 0 0 0 2 0 0 0 0 0 0 0 0 0 0 0 0 0 0 0 0 0 0
47   0 0 0 0 0 0 0010101100 75 58 48 69 85 82 79   011111443020808283
48   0 0 0 0 0 0 0 0 0 0 1 0 0 0 0 0 0 0 0 0 0 0 0 0 0 0 0 0 0 0 1 0 0 0 0
48   0 0 0 0 0 0 0030803 57 92  0 66  0 0100 66   010505111031212144
49   4 0 0 0 0 0 0 0 0 0 0 0 0 0 0 0 0 3 0 0 0 0 0 0 0 0 0 0 0 0 0 0 1 0
49   0 0 0 0 0 0 0010101100  0 74 74 74 67 84  0   010505305051212244
50   0 0 0 0 0 0 0 0 0 0 0 0 0 0 0 0 0 0 0 0 0 0 0 1 0 0 0 0 0 0 0 0 0 0
50   0 0 0 0 0 0 0050101 98 98 80 94 82  0 0100   8210708316031008156
51   0 1 0 0 1 0 0 0 0 0 0 0 0 0 0 0 0 0 0 0 0 0 0 0 0 0 0 0 0 0 0 0 0 0
51   0 0 0 0 0 0 0069906100  0 0100100 86 88  0   010811317041314145
52   0 0 0 0 0 1 0 0 0 0 0 0 0 0 2 0 0 0 0 0 0 0 0 0 0 0 0 0 0 2 0 0 0
52   0 0 0 0 0 0 0101010 85 85 85100 85 92 51 92   010506511061618118
53   0 0 0 2 0 0 0 0 0 0 0 1 0 0 0 0 0 1 0 0 0 1 0 0 0 0 0 0 0 0 0 0 0 0
53   0 0 0 0 0 0 0080103 97  0 0100 69 74100  0   01091023102121214
54   0 0 0 0 0 0 0 0 0 0 1 0 0 0 0 0 0 0 0 0 0 0 1 0 0 0 0 0 0 0 0 0 0 0
54   0 0 0 0 0 0 0070598100 85 85100 89 89 94  0   010404203041921217
55   1 0 0 0 0 0 0 0 0 0 0 0 1 0 0 0 0 0 0 0 0 0 0 1 0 0 0 0 0 0 0 0 0 0
55   0 0 0 0 0 0 0070707 87  0  0 87 87 87100  0   0109091280216202 17
56   0 0 0 1 0 0 0 0 0 0 0 0 0 2 0 0 0 0 0 0 0 2 0 0 0 0 0 0 1 0 0 0 0
56   0 0 0 0 0 0 0089808 74 74 74 64 74 64100 74   7410404301051620126
57   0 0 0 0 0 0 0 0 0 0 0 0 0 0 0 0 0 0 0 0 0 0 0 0 0 0 0 0 0 1 0 0 0 0
57   0 0 0 0 0 0 0       100  0100100100100  0  0   010606312051720117
58   0 0 0 0 1 0 0 0 0 0 0 0 0 0 0 0 0 0 0 0 0 0 0 0 0 3 0 0 0 0 0 0 1 0 0
58   0 0 0 0 0 0 0100707100100 88 60100100  0 86   010404304051414245
59   0 0 0 0 0 0 0 1 1 0 0 0 0 0 0 0 0 0 0 0 0 0 0 1 1 0 0 0 0 0 0 0 0
59   0 0 0 0 0 0 0010111100 76  0 83 59 80  0 56   011011233021516136
60   0 0 0 0 0 0 0 0 0 0 0 0 0 0 0 0 0 1 0 0 0 0 0 0 0 0 0 0 0 0 0 0 0 0
60   0 0 0 0 0 0 0079910  0 89 0100 89 89  0 91   0105075160712 14228
61   0 0 0 0 0 2 0 0 0 0 0 0 0 0 0 0 0 0 1 0 0 0 0 0 0 0 0 0 0 0 0 0 0
61   0 0 0 0 0 0 0050598 74100 86 79 74 89 33  0   010809210041316137
62   0 0 0 0 1 1 0 0 0 0 0 0 0 1 0 0 1 0 0 0 0 0 0 0 0 0 0 0 0 1 0 0 0 0
62   0 0 0 0 0 0 0070507  0  0  0 89100100  0 91   010404205042020219
63   0 0 0 0 0 0 0 0 0 0 0 0 0 0 0 0 0 0 0 0 0 0 0 1 0 0 0 0 0 0 1 0 0 0
63   0 0 0 0 0 0 0101010 94 94 94 88 88100 0100   010608413061820119
64   0 0 0 0 0 0 0 1 0 0 0 0 0 0 0 0 0 0 0 0 0 0 0 0 0 0 0 0 0 0 0 0 0 0
64   0 0 0 0 0 0 0050505 71 71100100100100100 94   9410808510051420219
65   0 0 0 0 0 0 0 0 0 0 0 0 1 0 0 1 0 0 0 0 0 0 0 0 0 0 0 0 0 0 0 0 0 0
65   0 0 0 0 0 0 0010101100  0  0 48  0 69  0  0   010304203041516117
66   0 0 0 0 0 0 0 2 0 0 0 0 0 0 0 0 1 0 0 0 0 0 0 0 0 0 0 0 0 0 1 0 0 0 0
66   0 0 0 0 0 0 0070798100 93  0 71 64100  0100   83103020  021518115
```

APPENDIX C (continued)

```
57  2 0 0 0 0 0 0 0 1 0 0 0 0 0 0 0 0 2 0 0 0 0 0 0 0 0 0 2 0 0 0 0 0 0 0 0 0 0
67  0 0 0 0 0 0 0 0010101100 31 41 66 60 69 69 26 2611010325021210115
68  0 1 0 0 0 0 0 0 0 0 0 0 0 0 0 1 0 0 0 0 0 0 0 0 0 0 0 1 0 0 0 0 0 0 0 0 0 0
68  0 0 0 0 0 0 0 0030303 0100 0 84 0 84 0 0 0110100 021011216
69  0 0 0 0 0 2 0 0 0 0 0 0 0 0 0 0 0 0 0 1 0 0 0 0 0 0 0 0 0 0 0 0 1 0 0 0 0 0
59  0 0 0 0 0 0 0 0079907 94 94 89 89 89100 89 89 0104031010 31417272
70  0 4 0 0 0 0 0 0 0 3 0 0 0 0 0 0 0 0 0 3 0 0 0 0 0 0 0 3 0 0 0 0 0 0 0 0 0 1
70  0 0 0 0 0 0 0 0030303 77100 0 83 60 60 0 50 0102021020 31212132
71  0 0 0 0 0 0 0 0 0 1 0 0 0 0 0 0 0 0 0 0 0 0 0 0 0 0 0 0 0 0 0 0 0 0 0 0 0 0
71  0 0 0 0 0 0 0 0010101100 0 0 0 0 0 0 0 0102030 0213181 2
72  0 1 0 0 0 0 0 0 0 0 0 4 0 0 0 0 0 0 0 2 0 0 0 0 0 0 0 2 0 0 0 0 0 0 0 0 0 0
72  0 0 0 0 0 0 0 0030303100 92 0 75 0 0 0 53 0403031020 31415242
73  1 0 0 0 0 0 0 0 0 1 0 0 0 0 0 0 0 0 0 0 0 0 0 0 0 0 0 0 0 0 0 0 0 0 0 0 0 0
73  0 0 0 0 0 0 0 0010101100 91 0 0 0 0 0 0 0103030 021620174
74  0 0 0 0 1 1 0 0 0 0 0 0 0 2 0 0 0 0 0 0 0 2 0 0 0 0 0 0 0 0 0 0 0 0 0 0 0 0
74  0 0 0 0 0 0 0070707 73 73 0 0 0100 0 0 0111112270 31919219
75  0 0 0 0 0 0 0 0 1 0 1 0 0 0 0 0 0 0 0 0 0 0 0 0 0 0 0 0 0 0 0 0 0 0 0 0 0 0
75  0 0 0 0 0 0 0 0019901100 0 0 0 0 0 89 0 0103041010 31818215
76  0 0 0 1 0 0 0 1 0 0 0 0 0 0 0 0 0 0 0 2 0 0 0 0 0 0 0 0 1 0 0 0 0 0 0 0 0 0
76  0 0 0 0 0 0 0101010 0 0 0100 82 88 0100 0109090 022119219
77  0 1 0 0 0 0 0 0 0 0 0 0 0 0 0 0 0 0 0 0 0 0 0 0 0 0 0 0 0 0 0 0 0 0 0 0 0 0
77  0 0 0 0 0 0 0059898 0 0 0 0 0 0 0 0 0104042070 41720216
78  0 0 0 0 0 0 1 0 0 0 0 0 0 0 0 0 0 0 0 0 0 0 0 0 0 0 0 0 0 0 0 0 0 0 0 0 0 0
78  0 0 0 0 0 0 0070798 0 0 0 91 91100 91 85 0104052010 61716216
79  0 0 0 0 0 1 0 0 0 0 0 0 0 1 0 0 0 0 0 0 0 0 0 0 0 0 0 0 0 0 0 0 0 0 0 0 0 0
79  0 0 0 0 0 0 0070701 47 0 0 0 0100 92 0 0103042010 41717227
80  0 0 0 1 0 0 0 0 0 0 0 0 1 0 0 0 0 1 0 0 0 0 0 0 0 0 0 0 0 0 0 0 0 0 0 0 0 0
80  0 0 0 0 0 0 0050505 0 0 0100 0 93 95 0 0105053030 51619218
81  1 0 0 0 0 0 0 0 0 0 0 0 0 0 0 0 0 0 0 0 0 0 0 0 0 0 0 1 0 0 0 0 0 0 0 0 0 0
81  0 0 0 0 0 0 0070707100 82 82 82 88100 0 0 0107072160 41314227
82  0 1 0 0 0 0 0 0 0 0 0 1 0 0 0 0 0 0 0 0 0 0 0 0 0 0 0 2 0 0 0 0 0 0 0 0 0 0
82  0 0 0 0 0 0 0100707 88 96 0 96 88 96100 88 0102021020 31413233
83  1 0 0 0 0 0 0 0 0 1 2 0 0 0 0 1 0 0 0 2 0 0 0 0 0 0 0 4 0 0 0 0 0 0 0 0 0 0
83  0 0 0 0 0 0 0070707100 76 58 67 94100 69 60 0109100 021313244
84  0 0 0 0 0 0 0 0 0 0 0 0 0 1 0 0 0 0 0 0 0 0 0 0 0 0 0 0 0 0 0 0 0 0 0 0 0 0
84  0 0 0 0 0 0 0070505 0 0100 93100 93 0 0 0107077060 61616225
85  0 0 0 0 0 0 0 0 0 0 0 0 0 0 0 0 0 0 2 0 0 0 0 0 0 0 0 0 0 0 0 0 1 0 1 0 0 0
85  0 0 0 0 0 0 0079907 0 0 0 0100100 0 80 0106061180 32021118
86  1 0 0 0 0 0 0 0 0 2 0 0 0 0 0 0 0 9 1 0 0 0 0 0 0 0 0 1 0 0 0 0 1 0 0 0 0 0
86  0 0 0 0 0 0 0010101100 0 0100 0100 0 0 0105073180 31212243
87  1 0 0 0 0 0 0 0 1 3 0 0 0 0 0 0 0 0 1 0 0 0 0 0 0 0 0 0 0 0 0 0 1 0 1 0 0 0
87  0 0 0 0 0 0 0010101100 60 0 60 60 66 0 0 0103032030 41212246
88  0 0 0 0 0 0 0 0 0 0 0 0 0 0 0 0 0 0 0 0 0 0 0 1 0 0 0 0 0 0 0 0 1 0 0 0 0 0
88  0 0 0 0 0 0 0010101100 95 29 79 79 90 98 55 0104044070 61212145
89  1 0 0 0 0 0 0 0 0 1 0 0 0 0 0 0 0 0 0 0 0 0 0 0 0 0 0 1 0 0 0 0 0 0 0 0 0 0
89  0 0 0 0 0 0 0059905 79100 53 93 63 63 86 79 0104054020 61321217
90  0 0 0 0 0 1 0 0 1 0 1 0 2 0 0 0 0 0 0 0 0 0 0 0 0 0 0 2 0 0 0 0 0 0 0 0 0 0
90  0 0 0 0 0 0 0010303 94100 81 60 81 81 81 92 0106063130 51216127
91  0 0 0 0 0 0 0 0 0 0 0 0 0 1 0 0 0 0 0 0 0 0 0 0 0 0 0 0 0 0 0 0 0 0 0 0 0 0
91  0 0 0 0 0 0 0050505 82 84 71100 82 73 93 44 0110113350 21411281
92  0 0 0 2 0 0 0 0 1 0 0 0 0 0 0 0 1 0 0 0 1 0 0 0 0 0 0 0 0 0 0 0 0 0 0 0 0 0
92  0 0 0 0 0 0 0070101100100 0100100100100 0 0107083140 31112146
93  0 0 0 0 0 0 0 0 1 0 0 0 0 0 0 0 0 1 0 0 0 0 0 0 0 0 2 0 0 0 0 0 0 0 0 0 0 0
93  0 0 0 0 0 0 0010101100 84 0 81 0 73 84 91 0109112310 21208182
94  0 0 0 1 0 0 0 0 1 0 0 0 0 0 0 0 2 0 0 0 0 0 0 0 1 0 0 0 0 0 0 0 0 0 0 0 0 0
94  0 0 0 0 0 0 0199998 0 0 0100 0 0 0 0 0111112430 20812253
95  3 0 0 0 0 0 0 0 3 0 0 0 0 1 0 0 4 0 0 0 0 0 0 0 0 0 0 0 0 0 0 0 0 0 0 0 0 0
95  0 0 0 0 0 0 0030303100100 65100130 55100100 8210606512 05121622
96  1 0 0 0 0 0 0 0 1 0 0 0 0 0 0 0 0 0 0 0 0 0 0 0 1 0 0 0 0 0 0 0 0 0 0 0 0 0
96  0 0 0 0 0 0 0010101100 0 0 0 0 0 86 36 0110090 021408253
97  0 0 0 0 2 0 0 0 0 2 0 0 0 0 0 0 0 1 0 0 0 0 0 0 0 0 0 0 0 0 0 0 0 0 0 0 0 0
97  0 0 0 0 0 0 0060806 73 73 73 77 84 67100 57 0108073210 41210146
98  3 0 0 0 0 0 0 0 0 1 0 0 0 0 0 0 0 1 1 0 0 0 0 0 0 0 0 0 1 0 1 0 0 0 0 0 0 0
98  0 0 0 0 0 0 0010801 79 77 0 0 0 77100 84 0106075010 61012224
99  0 0 0 0 0 0 0 0 0 0 0 0 0 0 0 0 0 0 0 0 0 0 0 0 0 0 0 1 0 0 0 0 0 0 0 0 0 0
99  0 0 0 0 0 0 0100110100100 0 82 52 74 77 85 0103032060 41213205
```

APPENDIX C (continued)

```
100  0 0 0 0 0 0 0 0 0 0 0 1 0 0 0 0 0 0 0 0 0 0 0 0 0 0 0 0 0 0 0 0 0 0 0 0 0 0
130  0 0 0 0 0 0 0 0101010 96 94 86 86 86100 89 86 8010506601081314245
101  0 0 0 0 0 0 0 0 0 0 1 0 0 0 0 0 0 0 0 0 0 0 0 0 0 0 0 0 0 0 0 0 0 0 0 0 0 0
101  0 0 0 0 0 0 0 0010103100 80 55 60 60 55 83 55   01080822203131 2247
102  1 0 0 0 0 0 0 0 0 0 1 1 0 0 0 0 0 0 0 0 0 0 0 0 0 0 0 0 0 0 1 0 0 0 0 0 0 0
102  0 0 0 0 0 0 0 0010101 99100 83 88 88 94 83  0   0107082220412 12129
103  1 0 0 1 0 0 0 0 0 1 0 0 1 0 0 0 0 0 1 1 0 0 0 0 0 0 0 0 2 0 0 0 0 0 0 0 0 0
103  0 0 0 0 0 0 0 0010501 88 88 76100 88 88100 76 641060721603121 2244
104  0 0 0 1 0 0 0 0 0 0 0 0 0 1 0 0 0 0 0 0 0 0 0 0 0 0 0.0 1 0 0 0 0 0 0 0 0 0
104  0 0 0 0 0 0 0 0059998  0 93  0100 21100100  0   0111113350214 08253
105  0 0 0 0 0 0 0 0 0 0 0 1 0 0 1 0 0 0 0 0 0 0 0 0 0 0 0 0 0 0 0 0 0 0 0 0 0 0
105  0 0 0 0 0 0 0070711 81100 76 87 88 87 87 89 65108093290212 14215
106  0 0 0 0 0 3 0 0 0 0 0 0 0 2 0 0 0 0 0 0 0 0 0 0 4 0 0 0 0 0 0 0 2 0 0 0 0 0
106  0 0 0 0 0 0 0070707  0  0  0  0   0100  0  0  010404103031920215
107  0 1 0 0 0 0 0 0 0 0 0 0 0 0 0 0 0 0 0 0 0 0 0 0 0 0 0 0 0 0 0 0 0 0 0 0 0 0
107  0 0 0 0 0 0 0070808 55 75 65 65 65 72100 55 6510304302051 212117
108  1 0 0 0 0 0 0 0 0 1 0 0 0 0 0 0 0 0 0 1 0 0 0 0 0 0 0 1 0 0 0 0 0 0 0 0 0 0
108  0 0 0 0 0 0 0050505  0  0  0100  0  0  0  0   0111112410217 13224
109  0 0 0 0 0 0 0 0 1 0 0 0 0 0 0 0 0 1 0 0 0 0 0 0 0 0 1 0 0 0 0 0 0 0 1 0 0 0
109  0 0 0 0 0 0 0079915  0 86  0 86 86 86 93  0   0105063080518 19116
110  0 1 0 0 0 0 0 1 0 0 1 0 0 0 0 0 0 0 0 0 0 0 0 0 0 0 0 0 0 0 0 0 0 0 0 0 0 0
110  0 0 0 0 0 0 0039903  0100 80 80 80 80  0  0   01070910803192 1218
111  0 0 0 0 0 3 0 0 0 0 1 1 0 0 0 0 0 0 0 0 0 0 2 0 0 0 0 0 0 0 0 0 2 0 0 0 0 0
111  0 0 0 0 0 0 0079910 85 95100 85 85 90  0100  01080911803121223
112  0 0 0 0 0 0 0 0 0 0 0 0 0 0 0 0 0 0 0 0 0 0 0 0 0 0 0 0 0 0 0 0 3 0 0 0 0 0
112  0 0 0 0 0 0 0079907  0  0  0  0  0100  0100  010404201041621218
113  0 0 0 0 0 0 0 0 0 0 0 0 0 0 0 0 0 0 0 0 0 0 1 0 0 0 0 0 0 0 0 0 0 0 0 0 0 0
113  0 0 0 0 0 0 0050505 75 75 75100 75 75  0  0   01050520804162 1116
114  0 0 0 0 0 2 0 1 0 0 0 0 0 0 1 0 2 3 0 0 0 0 0 3 0 0 0 0 0 0 0 1 0 0 0 0 0 0
114  0 0 0 0 0 0 0070707 42  0 42 46 40100 40 75  0106053040519 21118
115  0 0 0 0 0 0 0 0 0 0 0 0 0 0 0 0 0 1 0 0 0 0 0 0 0 0 0 0 0 0 0 0 0 0 1 0 0 0
115  0 0 0 0 0 0 0100111100100 75 75 75 75 75 83 83110100  021721219
116  0 0 0 0 0 0 0 0 0 0 0 0 0 0 0 0 0 0 1 0 0 0 0 0 0 0 0 0 0 0 0 0 0 0 0 0 0 0
116  0 0 0 0 0 0 0019901100  0  0100  0100  0  0   01071120904182 1218
117  0 0 0 0 0 2 0 0 0 0 0 1 0 0 0 0 0 0 0 0 0 0 0 1 0 0 0 0 0 0 1 0 0 0 0 0 0 0
117  0 0 0 0 0 0 0070707  0 87  0  0 60100  0  0   010809315031612227
118  0 0 0 0 0 0 0 0 0 0 0 0 0 0 0 0 0 0 0 0 0 0 0 0 0 0 0 0 0 0 0 0 0 1 0 0 0 0
118  0 0 0 0 0 0 0061010 87 95  0 95  0  0 91100  010505312041518229
119  0 0 0 0 0 0 0 0 0 0 0 0 0 0 0 0 0 0 0 0 1 0 0 0 0 0 0 1 0 0 0 0 0 0 0 0 0 0
119  0 0 0 0 0 0 0079905  0  0  0100  0100  0 96  0102030  021621218
120  0 0 0 0 0 0 0 0 0 0 0 0 0 2 1 0 0 0 0 0 0 0 0 0 0 0 0 0 0 0 0 0 0 1 0 0 0 0
120  0 0 0 0 0 0 0059998  0  0  0  0  0  0100 91 911040821304  19117
121  0 0 0 0 0 0 0 0 0 0 0 0 0 0 0 0 0 0 0 1 0 1 0 0 0 0 0 0 0 0 0 0 0 0 1 0 0 0
121  0 0 0 0 0 0 0070707 73  0 68 62  0100 95 89 63308  2150318  1 6
122  0 0 0 0 0 0 0 0 0 0 0 0 0 1 0 0 0 0 0 0 0 0 1 0 0 0 0 0 0 0 0 0 0 0 0 0 0 0
122  0 0 0 0 0 0 0050707 80  0 80 80 73100 87  0   0107074100616 16217
123  0 0 0 1 0 0 0 0 0 0 0 2 0 0 0 0 0 0 0 0 0 0 0 0 0 0 0 0 1 1 0 0 0 0 0 0 0 0
123  0 0 0 0 0 0 0050505 75 88 91100 91 57 84  0   0106070  021214115
124  0 0 0 0 0 1 0 0 0 0 0 0 0 0 0 0 0 0 0 0 0 0 1 0 0 0 0 0 0 0 0 0 0 0 0 0 0 0
124  0 0 0 0 0 0 0070707  0  0 85 85  0100  0  0   0308  1170213  1 8
125  0 0 0 0 0 0 0 0 1 0 0 0 0 0 0 0 0 0 0 1 0 0 0 0 0 0 0 0 0 0 1 0 0 1 0 0 0 0
125  0 0 0 0 0 0 0 0   0  0  0  0  0  0  0  0   010707311041719217
126  0 0 0 0 0 0 0 0 0 0 0 0 0 0 0 0 0 0 0 0 0 0 0 0 0 0 0 0 0 0 1 0 0 0 0 0 0 0
126  0 0 0 0 0 0 0060707 67 67  0  0 83100  0  0   01050730505121621
127  1 0 0 0 0 0 0 0 0 0 0 0 0 0 0 0 0 0 0 0 0 0 0 0 0 0 0 1 0 0 0 0 0 0 0 0 0 0
127  0 0 0 0 0 0 0010901100 92  0  0 76  0100  0   01050760508121 2245
128  0 0 0 0 0 0 0 2 0 0 0 0 0 0 0 1 0 0 0 0 0 0 0 2 1 0 0 0 0 0 0 0 0 0 0 0 0 0
128  0 0 0 0 0 0 0019905100 94 59 83 76 65 94 94 01030420204161 2244
129  1 1 0 0 0 0 0 1 1 0 1 0 0 0 0 0 1 0 1 0 0 0 0 0 0 0 1 0 0 0 0 0 0 0 0 0 0 0
129  0 0 0 0 0 0 0010101100100  0 88  0 88  0 94 01080831506131 4117
130  0 0 0 0 0 1 0 0 0 0 0 0 0 1 0 0 0 1 0 0 0 0 0 0 0 0 0 0 0 0 0 0 0 0 0 0 0 0
130  0 0 0 0 0 0 0069906 91 91  0  0100 94  0  0   01040530705131 8216
131  0 0 0 0 0 1 0 0 0 0 0 0 0 0 0 0 0 0 0 0 0 0 0 0 0 0 0 0 0 0 0 0 0 0 0 0 0 0
131  0 0 0 0 0 0 0030808 79 84 79 79 79 79100 84 791020330405090 91 4
132  0 0 0 0 0 0 0 0 0 0 0 0 0 0 0 0 0 0 0 0 0 0 0 0 0 0 0 0 0 0 0 0 0 1 0 0 0 0
132  0 0 0 0 0 0 0070501 87 82 82 97 89 82 85100  0109090  031712129
```

11

Metropolitan Cable Television Company *

Metropolitan Cable Television Company (MetroCable) is a medium-sized cable television company serving a combination of communities and suburban areas in Orange County, California. Located immediately south of Los Angeles, this sprawling area is actually part of the greater L.A. metropolitan area, even though some areas served by MetroCable were nearly 100 miles from downtown Los Angeles. Although each year had seen increasing revenues, and total sales were now nearly $25 million, the management of MetroCable was becoming increasingly concerned as to whether or not this growth trend could be sustained. Indeed, a cursory analysis of customer data indicated that this year's revenues were not increasing at the rate seen in recent years. Management recognized that it was necessary to begin to be concerned about some things that previously had been only given lip service—namely, marketing research and marketing planning.

CABLE TELEVISION INDUSTRY

The cable television industry, which today is a multibillion dollar business, began in a rather inauspicious manner. From the early days of television broadcasting, many areas of the country suffered from poor reception due to characteristics of the terrain (mountains, valleys, etc.) which interfered with the TV signal. In the mid-1950s, a frustrated television viewer who lived in such an area mounted a television antenna on a nearby mountain and ran a cable to his home in the valley. The experiment worked and soon the homes of his friends and neighbors were hooked up to this common lead from the mountain-top antenna. Soon other people who saw the dramatically improved television reception agreed to pay a fee to have their homes hooked up as well. Thus, the first cable television system was born.

Most of the early growth in the cable television industry was generated by similar installations. In areas of poor television reception, due to terrain problems or due to distance from the broadcast signal, independent operators mounted a large centralized antenna and proceeded to establish a network of home subscribers. Many of the original cable operations were best described as "wire-stringers," an industry term referring to what they knew best how to do—lay wire or cable. From a business standpoint, many were small, underfinanced and relatively unsophisticated.

In spite of this lack of sophistication, the industry grew rapidly during the 1960s and 1970s. Cable systems became available in many large metropolitan areas as well as in more remote locations. By 1980, roughly 16.6 million homes in the U.S. (22 percent of all households with TV sets) were subscribers to some sort of cable system. Individual cable operators also grew rapidly. For instance, Mission Cable in San Diego, California, the nation's largest single operator, has 210,000 subscribers (about 50 percent of the market area's homes).

This growth period also saw profound technological and business changes in the industry. Some of the technological advances included the use of microwave and communications satellites to beam signals to cable operators. These signals included the broadcast of regular programming by so-called "super-stations" (such as WTBS in Atlanta) which could now be received throughout the country. Also broadcast by these new technologies were specialty programming such as Home Box Office (movies and entertainment specials), Cable News Network (twenty-four-hour news and special events) and ESPN (twenty-four-hour sports and entertainment programming). Another change in technology allowed some cable operators to offer two-way, interactive communications to subscribers (such as QUBE in Columbus, Ohio). Still another allowed operators to offer service without using cable by broadcasting an electronically scrambled signal which was decoded by a receiving device at the subscriber's home.

At the same time, more and more local operators were either branching into new geographical markets or were being acquired by bigger cable operators to form "multiple system operators" (MSOs). Many of these MSOs, in turn, were being acquired by large, sophisticated, marketing-oriented firms such as Warner Communications and Westinghouse Corporation. So, too, was the market changing; subscribers, particularly in metropolitan areas where reception of local signals was not such a problem, were demanding more varied and more sophisticated program offerings.

METROCABLE

MetroCable was founded in 1958 by Ross Hall, whose previous experience was as a technician at an early cable operation on the East Coast. Hall built MetroCable from a system having less than 1,000 subscribers in

1960 to one having over 100,000 in 1980. Much of this growth came from Hall's innate business sense (he made more right decisions than wrong), the rapid growth of the Orange County area, and some much-needed capital which was supplied by outside investors along the way. For all his success, Hall was primarily a "wire-stringer." He liked what he knew best, the technical side of the business, and gave little attention to marketing or business development, areas which he never thought were very important. By 1976 Hall had settled into semiretirement in a small beach community and became increasingly concerned with sailing, fine wines and modern art.

The marketing area at Metro was headed by Dave Chambers. Dave started with the firm while he was a student in business at the University of Southern California. He now had primary responsibility for advertising, sales and customer service. Much of his time and efforts were directed toward managing the twelve-person sales force that was used for customer contact. Dave's principal approach toward marketing was to generate enough leads for his sales force to try to close. Some were easily obtained, such as new apartment residents who could not use an outside antenna, while other leads were generated by more creative marketing strategies, such as seasonal special promotions or price incentives.

Service Offerings of MetroCable

MetroCable offered three types of services to subscribers: (1) regular broadcasts of stations transmitting from Los Angeles and San Diego which were rebroadcast over cable; (2) specialty programming which was available to cable subscribers as part of the service fee, and (3) Home Box Office (HBO) which was offered on an optional basis for an extra monthly fee. MetroCable program offerings are listed in Exhibit 1.

The basic cable service was priced at $9.00 per month for a single outlet after a $15.00 one-time installation charge. Multiple con-

Exhibit 1. MetroCable Program Offerings

Channel	Program Service
1	Metro-TV, movies, Madison Square Garden sports
2	KNXT (CBS) Los Angeles
3	KCST (NBC) San Diego
4	KNBC (NBC) Los Angeles
5	KTLA (independent) Los Angeles
6	XETV (independent) Tijuana/San Diego
7	KABC (ABC) Los Angeles
8	KFMB (CBS) San Diego
9	KHJ (independent) Los Angeles
10	KGTV (ABC) San Diego
11	KTTV (independent) Los Angeles
12	KPBS (PBS) San Diego
13	KCOP (independent) Los Angeles
14	KMEX (independent) Los Angeles (Spanish)
15	KCET (PBS) Los Angeles
16	XEWT (independent) Tijuana (Spanish)
17	Associated Press, financial news, NYSE quotes
18	TV program guide
19	Weather information
20	Home Box Office (optional)
21	Educational Community Services
22	Public access
23	Consumer shopping guide
24	C-SPAN, line coverage of U.S. Congress proceedings
25	ESPN, entertainment and sports programming
26	CNN, Cable News Network
27	Christian Communications, religious broadcasts

nections at a household were slightly higher (and about 43 percent of subscribers had more than one service connection). HBO was priced at $7.95 per month for a single set. Roughly 20 percent of MetroCable's customers subscribed to HBO. Average annual revenue per household derived from cable service was nearly $200 per subscriber in 1980. The remainder of Metro's revenue base was generated from advertising sales on its own Channel 1 and from other business.

Metrocable's Market

Dave Chambers was aware of a number of things that were occurring in Metro's market area. While the last decade had seen ever-increasing growth in new subscribers and in revenues, the customer base appeared to be leveling off at around 105,000 subscribers. While this was happening, Metro's market penetration was steadily declining. It now serviced about 32 percent of all households in its service area, down from nearly 40 percent in 1975. In addition, the customer turnover rate had been accelerating. Chambers' sales efforts were barely sufficient to keep up with the number of customers who left the system, for whatever reason.

MetroCable enjoyed a virtual monopoly on cable service in its market area. No one else could string cable in the areas serviced since Metro had been awarded exclusive service rights by the local governing agencies.

However, two new subscriber broadcast systems were now available to households in the MetroCable area. Both of these (ON–TV and Omega) broadcast specialty programming, mainly sports and movies, which could be received only by paid subscribers. These program offerings competed directly with MetroCable's HBO service and indirectly with its other specialty programming.

Research Problem at MetroCable

Since MetroCable had no formal marketing research position, most previous consumer research was normally commissioned and directed by the marketing manager. Chambers recognized that he needed some information to help him assess the effectiveness of the marketing program and the programming offered by MetroCable. He decided that it would be important to generate information regarding the following:

1. Customer evaluation of MetroCable program offerings
2. Effectiveness of MetroCable advertising
3. Effectiveness of sales activities
4. Attitudes toward Home Box Office
5. Demographic and household information

Chambers thought that it would be relatively simple to draw a sample of customers using the firm's computerized accounting system. He could have the computer select, for example, every one-hundredth account and print out that list. Or, it would be possible to have the computer use a random number generator and select the accounts at random. Although it would be more difficult, Chambers could have a data processing person write a short program which could select accounts by such variables as average monthly billing, area of residence, length of service or type of service used.

Chambers thought that he would like to gather information from about 500 customers, since this was a number frequently used in past studies. It would be important to have included in that figure roughly 100 HBO subscribers so that they could be analyzed separately. Chambers thought that he could do either a mail or telephone survey to collect the data. If the survey were to be done by phone, it would be possible to use MetroCable personnel which would hold expenses down, even though this would still be more costly than mail.

Chambers began to wonder about the pros and cons of using mail versus telephone to conduct the survey. For example, he knew that mail would probably have a higher nonresponse rate. This might not only affect survey accuracy but would also affect the number of accounts that would have to be generated by the computer for the initial mailing.

Once he settled on a choice between mail or telephone, Chambers needed a way to estimate the number of accounts to select in order to yield his desired sample size. In addition, he also needed to determine how the sample of accounts should be selected.

12

Hamilton Power Tools (A) *

BACKGROUND INFORMATION

On July 13, 1983, Mr. Campagna, the marketing manager for Hamilton Tools, was anxiously awaiting his meeting with the marketing research firm. He felt the findings from the marketing research would change Hamilton Tools from a sales-oriented company to a firm that would adopt the consumer-oriented philosophy of the marketing concept.

For more than thirty years, Hamilton Power Tools had been marketing industrial products by catering to the construction and industrial tool markets. Their construction product lines included tools such as power trowels, concrete vibrators, generators, and power-actuated tools. Their industrial lines were primarily pneumatic tools: drills, screwdrivers, etc. One of their products, the gasoline-powered chain saw, was somewhat different from traditional construction and industrial tools. The chain saw line had been added in 1949, when John Hamilton, Sr., had had the opportunity to acquire a small chain saw manufacturer. Mr. Hamilton believed that construction workers would have a need for gasoline-powered chain saws. He had acquired the business in order to diversify the company into other markets.

During the 1970s, and early 1980s, the chain saw market was changing rapidly, and Hamilton Tool executives began to realize they needed some expert advice. Mr. Campagna, marketing manager, felt a major

change in Hamilton's corporate direction was on the horizon.

Mr. Campagna had been in the chain saw business for fifteen years. Reports from trade publications, statistics from the chain saw manufacturers association, and personal experience had led him to believe that the state of the chain saw industry in the last few years was composed of roughly the following markets: professionals (lumberjacks), farmers, institutions, and casual users (home or estate owners with many trees on their lots). The casual user segment was considered to be the future growth market. Campagna wished to ensure that Hamilton would not make any mistakes marketing to this segment of "weekend woodcutters," who once or twice a year used a chain saw to cut firewood or to prune trees in the backyard.

In March 1983, when chain saw sales began to slow down because of the seasonal nature of the business, Mr. Campagna and Ray Johnson, the chain saw sales manager, had a meeting with John Hamilton, Sr. Although Mr. Hamilton believed they had been doing well enough in chain saw sales over the past decade, Mr. Campagna and Mr. Johnson were able to persuade the aging executive that some consumer research was necessary. After talking with several marketing research firms, Hamilton Tools hired Consumer Metrics of Chicago to perform two research projects.

The TAT (Thematic Apperception Test) research was completed the first week in July. Mr. Campagna arranged for a meeting with the marketing research firm the following week.

* All names are fictitious to protect confidentiality. This case is copyright 1978 by William G. Zikmund.

As Dale Conway and Frank Baggins of Consumer Metrics made their presentation of the results of the survey of chain saw users, Bill Campagna, the marketing manager, thought back to the day Consumer Metrics had originally suggested the idea of a TAT to Hamilton. Dale Conway had sold him on the idea with his argument that motivational research was widely used in consumer studies to uncover people's buying motives. Conway had mentioned that Consumer Metrics had recently hired a bright young M.B.A. The young M.B.A.—Baggins, as it turned out—had specialized in consumer psychology and marketing research at a major state university. Conway had thought that Frank Baggins was one of the best qualified people to work on this type of project. Since Hamilton Power Tools had had no previous experience in consumer research, Campagna had been eager to proceed with the in-depth Thematic Apperception Test.

Mr. Conway told Mr. Campagna, Mr. Hamilton, the owner, and Mr. Johnson, the sales manager, that, in the TAT, respondents are shown a series of pictures and are asked to tell their feelings concerning the people in these photographs. He told Mr. Campagna that, while the present study was exploratory, it could be used to gain insights into the reasons people buy. He also suggested that the test would be a means for gaining the flavor of the language people use in talking about chain saws, and it could be a source of new ideas for writing advertising copy.

Mr. Campagna remembered that he had not thought this project would be very worthwhile; however, he realized he did not know that much about the consumer market. During the initial meeting with the research firm, it had been proposed that an exploratory research project be conducted in the states of Illinois and Wisconsin to obtain some indication of the attitudes of potential casual users toward chain saws. The researcher had suggested a TAT. Mr. Campagna did not know much about this type of research, and he needed time to think. After a week's de-liberation, he called Mr. Conway and told the researchers to go ahead with the project.

At the meeting, Mr. Conway and Mr. Baggins carefully presented the research results. (See Exhibits 1 through 4 for the TAT used by the researchers.) They pointed out that, in the TAT study, several screening questions were asked at the beginning of the interview. The findings of this study are based on those respondents who either planned to purchase a chain saw in the next twelve months, owned a chain saw, or had used a chain saw in the past. The presentation closely followed the written report submitted to Mr. Campagna. The findings were as follows.

RESEARCH FINDINGS

The first photograph (Exhibit 1) shown to the respondent was a picture of a man standing looking at a tree. The interviewer asked the respondent the following question:

I have a problem which you may find interesting. Here's a picture of a man who is thinking about the purchase of a chain saw. Suppose that such a man is your neighbor. What do you suppose he is thinking about?

After the respondent's initial answer, the following probing question was asked:

Now, if he came to you for advice and you really wanted to help him, what would you tell him to do? Why do you think this would be the best thing for him to do?

Initial responses seemed to center around what the man would do with the tree. Many respondents were concerned with saving the tree because they had interest in the tree. It seemed there was some pride in having a tree that beautified the owner's property. Some of the typical responses given are as follows:

He's thinking about cutting the tree down.

Why cut a whole tree when you can save part of it.

He could trim out part of those trees and save some of them.

We lose trees due to disease and storm damage.

Trees beautify property and make it more valuable.

I don't like to destroy trees.

Considering the alternatives to buying a chain saw was the next step many of the respondents took. Basically, the ultimate consumer sees the alternatives to the purchase of a chain saw as:

1. Using a hand saw
2. Hiring a tree surgeon
3. Renting or borrowing a chain saw

These alternatives were in the respondents' minds partly because they were concerned about the cost of doing the job. They seemed to be worried about the investment in a chain saw, about whether it paid to buy one for a small, single-application job. (Another reason for the alternatives came out in responses to a later picture.) Some quotations illustrating these points are as follows:

He's thinking how to go about it. He will use his hand saw.

He doesn't have to invest in a chain saw for only one tree.

He's thinking about how to get the tree down—the cost of doing it himself versus having someone else do it. Have him cut it down himself, it's not too big a tree. He'll save money.

He's thinking whether it pays for a couple of trees. If it would be worth it. How much longer with an axe.

He's thinking whether he should do it himself or get someone else to do it for him. Get someone who knows what he is doing.

He's thinking he'll rent a chain saw for a small area and would buy one for a large area.

The best way to get a job done. A chain saw is faster but a hand saw is cheaper. Depends on how much work he has to do.

An interesting comment made by two respondents was, "He's thinking about Dutch elm disease." The area had recently been hit by the disease. The respondents were projecting their situation into the TAT picture.

Other statements were made concerning the ease and speed of using a chain saw.

Some questions regarding the characteristic performance of a chain saw were raised in responses to this question; however, the second picture covers this area more adequately.

The second picture (Exhibit 2) showed two men in a store looking at a chain saw. The question asked went as follows:

Here is a picture of the same man in a store selling chain saws. Suppose he's a friend of yours—your next-door neighbor perhaps. Tell me what you think he will talk about with the clerk.

The issue most frequently raised was how the chain saw worked. An equal number of respondents wanted to know first how much it cost. Weight (lightness) was the next most frequently raised issue. Horsepower was of concern among many of the respondents. Other subjects they thought the man would talk about with the clerk were maintenance and the availability of repair, performance (what size tree the chain saw would cut), durability and expected life, safety (what safety features the chain saw has), and ease of starting the chain saw. In relation to price, the following comments were made:

Well, price is the most important, of course.

He's wondering how he will pay for it.

He's not considering price; price means nothing in regard to safety.

One individual was concerned whether the chain would come off the "blade." Individuals referred to the guide bar as a "blade" rather than a "guide bar." Various other issues were raised by respondents, such as:

■ Ease of handling
■ Length of blade
■ Which was the best brand
■ Whether it had direct drive
■ Whether it had a gas protector
■ Self-lubrication
■ The warranty (guarantee)
■ Ease of controls
■ Specifications

- Availability of credit
- Possibility of mixing oil and gas

The third picture (Exhibit 3) showed a man cutting a felled tree with the chain saw. The question asked was as follows:

The man in the picture is the same man as in the last picture. He purchased the chain saw he was looking at in the store. Knowing that he purchased the chain saw, what can you tell me about him? Can you tell me anything about the character and personality of this man? A following probe was, "What do you suppose this man is thinking about while he's using his chain saw?"

A common response to the first part of the question was that the man was satisfied. Typical responses were: "He's pleased." "He's happy he bought the chain saw." "Lots of time saved." "He's happy with the chain saw; he made the right decision." Many favorable responses to the man actually using a chain saw were given, such as:

Sure beats bucking with an axe.

He's thinking about speed of getting through, time saved.

How much easier it is to cut a tree down with a chain saw over a hand saw.

He seems to be saying, "Why didn't I buy a chain saw sooner?"

Respondents in general seemed to think the man was using the chain saw for the first time. Very prominent in many respondents' answers was the fear of using a chain saw. It seems to be a major reason why people do not purchase one. Some additional comments were:

He's a little frightened. He doesn't know how to go about it, but he's willing to learn.

If he gets caught in that blade ...

He's watching what he's doing—he could lose a limb.

He might be somewhat apprehensive about the use of it.

He looks scared of it.

He better think safety.

In general, as the test is designed to do, it made the respondents project their own personalities and backgrounds onto the character of the man. A wide variety of responses were given describing the man. He was described as a blue-collar working man, an office worker laboring after hours and on weekends, a somewhat wealthy man able to afford a chain saw, and a homeowner. A number of responses indicated that he was a "do-it-yourselfer," a man who liked to do things for himself, somebody who liked to "do his own thing." "Farmer" also received more than scattered response. Associations with an outdoorsman, a man who liked to keep in shape, were also indicated. He liked the out-of-doors. One quotation seems to sum it all up:

This seems to be his first job. He seems to be happy about it. He seems to think the chain saw will lighten his workload. He looks like he has not owned many power tools. He looks excited. He seems like he will be able to do a lot of cleanup work that he would not have been able to do without the chain saw. The chain saw is sure an improvement over the hand saw. It's faster, easier to use.

The fourth picture (Exhibit 4) showed a man and woman seated before a fireplace. The question read as follows:

Here's a picture of the same man [as] in the previous pictures, sitting and talking with a woman; what do you suppose they're talking about?

An analysis of the fourth picture in the projection test shows that respondents feel the man and woman in the picture are happy, content, cozy, enjoying the fireplace. The man is "enjoying the fruits of his labor." It comes out very strongly that the man who uses a chain saw is proud of himself after he cuts the wood. He thinks his cutting wood with a chain saw is a job well done. Some typical comments concerning this were:

He's very happy to cut his own wood for his fireplace—real proud of himself.

He's telling her how much he saved by cutting it himself.

They're talking about the logs; how pleased he is with himself.

He's thinking about the beauty of the fire, fire logs he, *himself*, sawed from their property.

The people projecting onto the picture seem to think that, because it is a job well done, purchasing a chain saw is worthwhile. Some additional comments were:

The man in the picture is saying, "The chain saw pays for itself. There's a $200 job and you will be able to use the chain saw afterwards."

Work's done and there's enough for winter and he has trees for winters to come.

What a good buy that chain saw was. Cut wood costs, save money.

The woman in the picture is also very happy; she's satisfied. Probably thinking about the future. But most of all she is very proud of her husband. This comes out very strongly. Some responses included:

The woman is looking to the enjoyment of the fireside and of the money saved because they cut their own wood. She might have questioned the investment before this, before sitting in front of the fireplace.

She is proud of her husband.

She is pleased the tree is down.

The woman is probably proud of the fireplace and starting the fire. He's probably thinking about the wood he sawed.

The man and woman are congratulating each other on finally getting around to buying a chain saw and cutting firewood.

She is complimenting him on his ability and on how handy it is to have a man around the house. She is also thinking that possibly it was easier for her husband to use a chain saw.

The woman doesn't care about the chain saw but she's satisfied.

A husband's concern over his wife's approval of this investment was also brought out by this picture. Evidently, men are worried that their wives will not see the value of a chain saw purchase. Also, there are implications that the man should be tired after using the chain saw.

After the presentation, Mr. Campagna was reasonably impressed. He asked John Hamilton what his opinion was. Mr. Hamilton said, "This is all very interesting, but I don't see how it can lead to greater profits in our chain saw division."

Exhibit 1

Exhibit 2

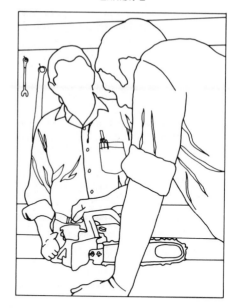

Exhibit 3

Exhibit 4

13

Hamilton Power Tools (B) *

BACKGROUND

Prior to 1949, Hamilton Power Tools had been engaged in the manufacture and sale of industrial power tools to the construction industry. In 1949, John Hamilton, Sr., had acquired a small chain saw producer to broaden the product line offered to Hamilton Tool's existing customers. Some of the industrial buyers had found the Hamilton chain saw to be well designed and had begun using it around their own homes. From this simple beginning, Hamilton chain saws had been "pushed" into the consumer market without the company having prior knowledge of its customers.

Over the years, chain saws grew to be a sizable portion of Hamilton's business. In 1982, when the chain saw's marketing manager of twelve years retired and moved to Florida, Bill Campagna was promoted to executive status. When he took the job, he vowed he would change the Hamilton chain saw division from its sales orientation to a consumer orientation.

Shortly after his promotion, the new marketing executive included a short questionnaire on the warranty cards that purchasers returned after buying a Hamilton chain saw. On the basis of the warranty card "survey," the fastest growth in the chain saw market was in the homeowner or casual-user market segment. This market consisted of the "weekend woodcutter," who once or twice a year used a chain saw to cut firewood or to prune trees in the back yard.

* *Note:* All names are fictitious to ensure confidentiality. Copyright © 1978 by Dr. William G. Zikmund.

In 1984, at Bill Campagna's urging, Consumer Metrics had been brought in to conduct Hamilton's first effort in consumer research. Their initial study was a consumer survey on chain saw users, followed by a Thematic Apperception Test (TAT) study of buyer motives.

A meeting was arranged with Consumer Metrics when the survey results had been tabulated. Dale Conway, vice-president of the research corporation, and Frank Baggins, a young research assistant, were to make the presentation for Consumer Metrics.

Mr. Conway began, "As you gentlemen know, the nonprofessional user has been a growing factor in the chain saw market. This user is a weekend woodcutter or a casual user, who once or a few times a year uses a chain saw to cut firewood or prune trees in the back yard. Beginning in March of this year, we conducted two research projects. The first was a survey of chain saw consumers, and the second was a Thematic Apperception Test (TAT). Today, Frank will give the results of the survey."

Frank stood up, thanked Mr. Conway, and began his presentation.

The West Coast is one of the faster growing markets for Hamilton chain saws. The number of retail outlets and servicing distributors in this area is in line with Hamilton marketing strategies. From a distribution standpoint, it is an excellent market. Therefore, we felt it would be best to sample people in California who purchased Hamilton chain saws between 1983 and 1984. Warranty cards that listed the purchasers during those years were used as a sampling frame. Cards that gave only institutional names and no individuals' names were omitted, as the purpose of the study was to learn about the behavior of the ultimate chain saw consumer rather than about the use of chain saws in private or public institutions. Of the 463 questionnaires mailed, 201 (43.4 percent) were returned and eighteen (3.9 percent) were not delivered.

The slides that Mr. Baggins showed are reproduced in Exhibits 1 through 15.

CONSUMER PROFILE

In Exhibit 1, the breakdown of age of Hamilton chain saw purchasers, we find that almost all purchasers of Hamilton chain saws are twenty-five years or older. The median age of a Hamilton chain saw owner is fifty.

More than two-thirds of the respondents had combined family incomes above $28,000 per year, and 59 percent were above $50,000 per year. Exhibit 2 shows the actual family income dispersion of the California chain saw owner.

Almost 70 percent of the respondents had graduated from high school, and 41 percent had attended college. Exhibit 3 shows the educational dispersion of chain saw customers.

Of all the people owning Hamilton chain saws in the California market, only 5.5 percent use a chain saw professionally. Twenty percent use chain saws on their farms. More than 70 percent of the respondents to the survey can be classified as casual users, as seen in Exhibit 4.[1]

Significant categories among the casual-user segment of the California market were:

1. Workers, handicrafts workers, and skilled workers (16.5 percent)
2. Professional and technical workers (12.0 percent)
3. Operative workers and laborers (9.5 percent).

Almost as significant were:

4. Managerial, official, and proprietary (including rental) personnel (12 percent)

[1] Institutions, such as universities, municipalities, etc., were not sampled. However, this segment is estimated at less than 5 percent of the market.

5. Government workers (9 percent)
6. Retired persons (10 percent).

As Exhibit 5 shows, the quality of Hamilton chain saws is considered to be good or excellent by more than 85 percent of the respondents. Slightly more than one-third of the respondents have had their chain saws repaired, and 75 percent of these people were satisfied with the repair work.

RETAIL ACTIVITY

Exhibit 6 shows Hamilton receives 35 percent of its retail sales from chain saw specialty stores, 20.5 percent from equipment or tool stores, and 9.5 percent from hardware stores. Only 7 percent of the respondents mentioned purchasing their chain saws from farm stores and only 5 percent from sports stores.

Exhibits 7 and 8 show the number of times Hamilton chain saw purchasers visited a chain saw dealer and the number of different chain saw dealers they visited before purchasing their first chain saw. More than 60 percent of the respondents visited two or more *different* chain saw dealers before purchasing a Hamilton chain saw. Two, three, four, or more trips to chain saw dealers were the general rule for potential buyers.

BUYING BEHAVIOR

More than one-half of all respondents thought for three months or more about purchasing a chain saw (see Exhibit 9).

Exhibit 10 shows that only 32 percent of the respondents rating their familiarity with chain saws said they were completely familiar with them when they first visited a dealer. "Somewhat familiar" (44 percent) was the most common response, and 19.5 percent stated they were unfamiliar with chain saws when they first visited a dealer. Therefore, it can be concluded that at least 63.5 percent of potential chain saw purchasers could use more knowledge about (familiarity with) chain saws.

Exhibit 1. Age of Hamilton Chain Saw Owners

Age Group	Total		1983		1984	
	No.	%	No.	%	No.	%
Under 25	4	2.0	1	1.0	3	3.1
25–34	26	13.0	16	15.4	10	10.4
35–44	48	24.0	24	23.0	24	25.0
45–54	65	32.5	37	35.6	28	29.2
55–64	38	19.0	18	17.3	20	20.8
65 and over	18	9.0	7	6.7	11	11.4
No answer	1	0.5	1	1.0	—	—
Base	200	100.0	104	100.0	96	100.0

Almost two-thirds of the respondents had a specific brand or brands of chain saw in mind when they first visited a dealer. Only 20 percent of all respondents had planned to buy Hamilton (Exhibits 11 and 12).

An important finding from this question is that all these people purchased Hamilton chain saws even though more than 50 percent had another brand name in mind before they first visited a chain saw dealer. Although we have no measurement of name brand preference, we can conclude that it is possible to sway some people who have preconceived purchasing plans. The other side of the coin is that 30 percent of the people planned to purchase a Hamilton and actually did. However, perhaps even more significant, we do not know how many people who had planned to purchase other leading brands actually did purchase one of these competitive saws.

The amount of influence a chain saw dealer's recommendation had on the purchasing decision of the consumer is given in Exhibit 13.

We can see that in 45 percent of the cases the dealer had considerable influence on the purchasing decision. In at least 16 percent more cases, the dealer exerted some influence. Thus, the dealer can be an important part of the marketing of chain saws. But we see that there are other influencing factors involved, as 26.5 percent of the respondents mentioned that the dealer had no influence

Exhibit 2. Income of Hamilton Chain Saw Owners

Income	Total		1983		1984	
	No.	%	No.	%	No.	%
Under 15M	7	3.5	3	2.9	4	4.2
15M–27,999	35	17.5	17	16.4	18	18.8
28M–49,999	34	17.0	21	20.2	13	13.5
50M–54,999	64	32.0	33	31.7	31	32.3
55M and over	54	27.0	28	26.9	26	27.0
No answer	6	3.0	2	1.9	4	4.2
Base	200	100.0	104	100.0	96	100.0

Exhibit 3. Education of Hamilton Chain Saw Owners

Education	Total		1983		1984	
	No.	%	No.	%	No.	%
Attended grade school	8	4.0	4	3.8	4	4.2
Graduated grade school	26	13.0	12	11.5	14	14.6
Attended high school	28	14.0	14	13.5	14	14.6
Graduated high school	51	25.5	27	26.0	24	25.0
Attended college	44	22.0	21	20.2	23	24.0
Graduated college	42	21.0	25	24.0	17	17.6
No answer	1	0.5	1	1.0	—	—
Base	200	100.0	104	100.0	96	100.0

on their decision, 16 percent said only some influence, and 6.5 percent said the dealer hardly influenced their decision.

What happened when the respondents first visited a chain saw dealer? Exhibit 14 shows the activities respondents stated happened. When analyzing the information, it appears significant to look at what did *not* happen at the dealer level. More than one-third of all respondents did not *talk* to a dealer the *first* time they visited. Only 21.5 percent saw the chain saw demonstrated

and only 28.5 percent learned the proper model of chain saw for their needs. In most cases, it looks as if the first visit was a *passive* buying visit to a chain saw dealer. The responses indicate that most potential customers talked to a salesperson rather than looked at chain saws. Thus, with some non-stocking dealers a customer would have to go to another store to see a chain saw.

Finally, Exhibit 15 shows how Hamilton purchasers first learned of the stores where they purchased their chain saws.

Exhibit 4. Occupations of Hamilton Chain Saw Owners

Occupation	Total		1983		1984	
	No.	%	No.	%	No.	%
Professional, technical	24	12.0	11	10.6	13	13.5
Managerial, official, proprietary	24	12.0	17	16.3	7	7.3
Clerical/sales	8	4.0	6	5.7	2	2.1
Worker, handicrafts, skilled	33	16.5	19	18.3	14	14.6
Operative workers and labor	19	9.5	14	13.5	5	5.2
Government	18	9.0	9	8.7	9	9.4
Farmer or rancher	40	20.0	16	15.4	24	25.0
Retired	20	10.0	7	6.7	13	13.5
Student	2	1.0	—	—	2	2.1
Tree surgeon/professional cutter	11	5.5	4	3.8	7	7.3
No answer	1	0.5	1	1.0	—	—
Base	200	100.0	104	100.0	96	100.0

Exhibit 5. Opinion of Owners of Quality of Hamilton Chain Saws

Quality	No.	%
Excellent	81	40.5
Good	90	45.0
Fair	15	7.5
Poor	7	3.5
No answer	7	3.5
Base	200	100.0

Exhibit 6. Retail Outlets Where Hamilton Chain Saws Are Purchased

Outlet	No.	%
Chain saw specialty	70	35.0
Equipment/tools	41	20.5
Hardware	19	9.5
Department	16	8.0
Farm	14	7.0
Sports	10	5.0
Catalog	8	4.0
Marine	2	1.0
Other	15	7.5
No answer	5	2.5
Base	200	100.0

Exhibit 7. Number of Times Visited Chain Saw Dealer

Times Visited	No.	%
0	7	3.5
1	53	26.5
2	40	20.0
3	39	19.5
4	16	8.0
5	7	3.5
6 or more	25	12.5
No answer	13	6.5
Base	200	100.0

Exhibit 8. Number of Different Chain Saw Dealers Visited

Number of Dealers	No.	%
0	9	4.5
1	50	25.0
2	51	25.5
3	47	23.5
4 or more	28	14.0
No answer	15	7.5
Base	200	100.0

Exhibit 9. Time Respondents Had Been Thinking About Chain Saw Purchase

Length of Time	No.	%
Less than 1 week	7	3.5
1 week to 1 month	25	12.5
Over 1 to 3 months	24	12.0
Over 3 to 6 months	37	18.5
Over 6 months to 1 year	35	17.5
Over 1 year	33	16.5
Owned chain saw previously	20	10.0
Don't know/no answer	14	7.0
Part of inventory	2	1.0
Not long	3	1.5
Base	200	100.0

Exhibit 10. Respondents' Ratings of Familiarity With Chain Saws

Response	No.	%
Completely familiar	64	32.0
Somewhat familiar	88	44.0
Unfamiliar	39	19.5
No answer/don't know	9	4.5
Base	200	100.0

Exhibit 11.   Respondents Had Specific Brand in Mind on First Visit to Chain Saw Dealer

Response	No.	%
Yes	129	64.5
No	67	33.5
No answer	4	2.0
Base	200	100.0

Exhibit 12.   Brand of Chain Saw Planned to Purchase

Brand	No.	%
Homelite	59	45.7
Hamilton	41	31.8
McCulloch	41	31.8
Stihl	2	1.5
Pioneer	1	0.8
Other	5	3.9
Base	129	*

* Multiple answers possible; base exceeds 100 percent.

Exhibit 13.   Dealer Influence

Amount of Influence	No.	%
Great	54	27.0
Quite a bit	36	18.0
Some	32	16.0
Hardly any	13	6.5
None	53	26.5
No answer	12	6.0
Base	200	100.0

Exhibit 14. Activities on First Visit to Chain Saw Dealer

Activity That Took Place	No.	%
Talked to salesperson or owner about chain saws	123	61.5
Looked at chain saws	116	58.0
Learned the price of the chain saws	114	57.0
Picked up information about chain saws	71	35.5
Learned proper model of saw for own needs	57	28.5
Watched chain saw demonstrated	43	21.5
Rented or borrowed a chain saw	11	5.5
No answer	13	6.5
Base	200	*

* Multiple mentions; base exceeds 100 percent.

Exhibit 15. How Purchaser Learned Store Carried Chain Saws

Response	No.	%
Previous visit	101	50.5
Friend/relative recommended	18	9.0
Magazine/newspaper advertising	14	7.0
Yellow pages	12	6.0
Radio/TV	6	3.0
Outside store identification/driving by	6	3.0
Other	24	12.0
No answer	19	9.5
Base	200	100.0

14

Suncoast National Bank *

Suncoast National Bank maintains its headquarters and twenty-three branch offices in the San Diego metropolitan area. As such, Suncoast National is one of the largest locally headquartered banks in the region. Most of the other major financial institutions located in the San Diego area (such as Bank of America and Security Pacific Bank) are headquartered in either Los Angeles or San Francisco.

The San Diego metropolitan area presently has a population of about 1.8 million persons. It is the second largest city in California and is the eighth largest metropolitan area in the United States. Figures from the U.S. Census show that the San Diego area grew roughly 35 percent in population between 1970 and 1979. Estimates indicate further growth of about 20 percent by 1985.

NEWCOMER PROJECT

Steven Bennett, the marketing research analyst for Suncoast National, was impressed with these population growth figures. In recent years Suncoast had been losing market share to other banks and its management was looking to the marketing area to help retain its place in the market. Bennett's direct superior, Bob Redmund, had asked him to give some thought to any research that could be conducted to help him formulate Suncoast National's marketing strategy.

Bennett was aware of programs used by banks in other cities which targeted new people moving into the area. In particular, he

was familiar with one such "newcomer" program conducted by a bank in Atlanta which was so successful that it had earned the bank an award from the Bank Marketing Association. No doubt, Bennett thought, it probably also earned its originator a substantial raise in salary.

As he understood it, the Atlanta program worked this way. The bank accumulated the names of persons about to move to Atlanta from elsewhere and names of persons who had moved there within a very short time. The names were obtained through Atlanta employers, the Chamber of Commerce, realtors and welcoming services such as Welcome Wagon and Hospitality Hostess. The bank offered each person a complete kit to help make their transition a little easier. Included in the kit were such things as maps, city guides, guides to services, bus schedules and discount coupons. Each person contacted was sent an engraved invitation which entitled him or her to receive a newcomer kit at one of the bank's branch offices. Reportedly, the Atlanta bank had been successful in converting into new customers many of those who accepted the invitation.

Since San Diego is a high-growth and highly mobile community, Bennett thought that such a program should be investigated by Suncoast National. Accordingly, he wrote the memo seen in Exhibit 1 to Redmund.

NEWCOMER FOCUS GROUP STUDIES

Bennett received approval to proceed with the project. He knew that, in addition to information that would be available from industry

Exhibit 1. Suncoast National Bank—Interdepartmental Communication

---

TO: Robert R. Redmund, Vice President, Marketing
FROM: Steven R. Bennett, Marketing Research Analyst
DATE: July 21, 1981
SUBJECT: NEWCOMER RESEARCH PROPOSAL

Purpose and Background: That we live in a highly mobile society is reflected by the fact that approximately one out of five U.S. citizens changes residence every year.

As people relocate, their life styles are temporarily disrupted and certain "needs" become self-evident at their new locale. Among those needs are services provided by financial institutions.

The match between newcomers and financial institutions seems to be a natural one; however, many feel that the difficulty in reaching prospective newcomers outweighs the advantages of designing a newcomer program. Contrary to this belief, the newcomer is one of the best retail markets available to the bank. Rather than expand an entire marketing effort to redistribute the existing market, we should develop a program to tap this newcomer segment with the advantage being that we would have little or no competition from other institutions.

The newcomer program will have to be based upon information. In order for us to identify, locate, and capture this market segment, we must understand the key issues of the newcomer segment, their needs as newcomers to San Diego, and what it will take to attract them to our bank. We must understand how newcomers learn about banks (and savings and loans), who in a family will make the banking decision, at what point do they decide on a bank, and what their profile is.

Research must be undertaken to provide us with the necessary information to design and effectively market a newcomer program.

Methodology: A survey instrument will be designed to gather the above information via mail questionnaire of prospective San Diego residents and newcomers to San Diego. Address lists will be generated by the San Diego Chamber of Commerce and from San Diego Hospitality Hostess. The survey will be conducted of those persons most responsible in a household for the banking activities and it will be designed to gather the necessary attitudinal and demographic information in order to maximize the success of a future newcomer program.

Focus Groups: To better understand the problems that newcomers experience, we need to conduct some focus group research. This research will result in our being better able to design a survey instrument which relates to the needs of this segment. I think that two or three group sessions should be sufficient.

Time Schedule:	*Completed By:*
Focus groups	*August 21*
Questionnaire design	*September 7*
Pre-test questionnaire	*September 12*
Survey	*September 29*
Data Analysis	*October 5*

---

sources, he needed to know more about the feelings and experiences of newcomers. This would assist him in designing a better survey questionnaire for the mail study. Bennett was especially interested in knowing about the problems that were encountered in moving, how newcomers selected a new bank and what kinds of information newcomers thought would be useful to them. All of this would be thoroughly evaluated in the survey.

Bennett selected Professional Interviewing to conduct two focus groups to help find out more about problems experienced by newcomers. That firm, a local field interviewing company, was instructed to recruit twelve persons who had moved into San Diego within the last month for each of two group interview sessions. Bennett prepared the outline seen in Exhibit 2 for the interviews.

Paula Jackson, the owner of Professional Interviewing, was to be the group moderator. For the first group session, seven participants, six women and one man, attended. The transcript of that session is seen in Exhibit 3.

Exhibit 2. Newcomers Study Focus Group Outline

General Purpose: 1) to determine problems and inconveniences experienced in moving to San Diego or shortly after arrival, 2) to understand how initial banks were selected, 3) to determine problems associated with banking transactions.
Topics

1. Reasons for moving to San Diego
2. Problems in *planning* the move
3. Problems *during* the move
4. Problems *after* the move
5. How problems could have been corrected
6. Problems related to banking
7. How participants learned about various banks available in the city
8. How they selected initial bank
9. What banks could do to make move less inconvenient
10. What other groups or organizations could do to make the move easier

Exhibit 3. Newcomers Study Focus Group

MODERATOR I'm Paula from Professional Interviewing and I really appreciate your participation in this group session. As you can see, we are taping this session because after the end of this it would be impossible to remember what has transpired. First of all, we are here tonight to talk about your reasons for moving to San Diego. Let's start out by having each of you introduce yourself and state how you came about coming to San Diego ... how you got here and where you're from.

MARY My name is Mary—and we came to San Diego because my husband works here, and I came from New York.

BRENDA Brenda Cole from Maine—was headed for Arizona but came to San Diego by chance. Came west because of the weather.

MARIAN Marian from Kansas City—came here because my husband took a job here.

LISA Lisa, Pacific Northwest, read in a magazine that San Diego had the most perfect climate and wanted to get away from Redlands where it was all smog. Came alone by bus.

ANNA I'm Anna, from Sacramento area and I came to go to San Diego State, pre-med student.

CAROLYN Carolyn, from Virginia. My husband took a job in San Diego.

ROGER Roger from Los Angeles, came because of a transfer in the company and liked a smaller city.

MODERATOR Undoubtedly, some of you had situations that arose when you got ready to come here, inconveniences that happened to you. They may have been major things or minor things, but no matter what, they were still problems that came about when you got ready to move. I'd like to talk about the problems and inconveniences you had in getting ready to come to San Diego.

BRENDA What do you mean by inconveniences?

MARIAN Like changes of addresses in banks or your subscriptions?

MODERATOR Things that disrupted your living the way you were living.

MARIAN Taking my daughter, who is a senior in high school, away and leaving all her friends. She despises it. That is an inconvenience. The move itself. The movers were late naturally. The furniture was broken. The claim is still not settled.

MODERATOR You mentioned banking, was that a problem?

MARIAN I've changed banks since I've been here. I don't like the banking hours here. In Kansas City, the banks were open just like department stores, day and night. So the banking was very easy. Here I started with Bank of America, but they were never open so I switched real quick.

MODERATOR What do you mean they were never open?

MARIAN They didn't open early, the one near me didn't open until 10:00 in the morning and is only open until 3:00 and we're used to 7:00 to 7:00 hours. I'm surprised by the banks. In such a big place, why not open longer and on Saturdays. I found a bank that is open Saturdays for my checking account. I've never seen such long lines in my whole life. With so many working in such a large population you would think they would accommodate more. You could wait an hour just to get a check cashed. I'm trying to get my account going, just to add a name. The drive-up is open, but they can't pass the card. I have to go inside and stand in the hour-long lines to do that, and I'm not willing to do that. I learned a long time ago that anything you open up, use the word *or* not *and*. Like Marty *or* Marian—not *and*. Then you don't have any trouble.

MODERATOR Brenda, how about you?

BRENDA Trying to weed out what to bring or throw away. We brought only what we could take in the car. We have a few things in storage but not much. Like everyone, I feel the banks out here are

the most horrendous situations I've ever seen. I've never found it so hard to get a check cashed. My husband, in his own bank, has to show his drivers license, and if you don't have a picture ID, you're out of luck. They are too untrusting, it's outrageous. I've been in many cities in many states and have never run into anything so outrageous in my entire life.

MODERATOR Then your difficulty in cashing a check is your main difficulty in banking?

BRENDA Just everything ... people's attitudes. Out here it's like everyone is for themselves, no one wants to help anyone else. Everybody is on their own. The last place I lived was a small town and the people were more willing to help you out. Most people I've run into out here are not willing to be helpful, especially the banks. I haven't been here long enough for firsthand evidence, but from what I've heard, even the residents have trouble. The lady I'm staying near has had to change banks three times in the last year.

MODERATOR Lisa, what problems have you encountered?

LISA Well, not really very much. I take life as it comes, living day-to-day. I don't have any money in banks. I would never put money in a bank. Why? Because I don't like the way they do business. I don't like what they do with the money while it's in there. I don't like the interest they give you and I don't like the waiting in lines. I don't like anything about it. The banks aren't interested in us, they just want the money so they can use it.

MODERATOR Carolyn?

CAROLYN The moving van gave us the most problems. Many of our things were damaged and many stolen. I don't know how to claim these items. We were delayed one day because the vans won't move less than five tons and we only had two. We paid for five. Also the banks ... cashing out-of-state checks in your own bank. My husband applied for a VISA card here. Our credit is fantastic but we were denied the credit because they say they have no record of our credit rating. We could not transfer it out here, so fine, they won't use our money, we'll just keep sending it back to Virginia. The service charge out here is outrageous. I had a totally free checking account. No service charge, no minimum balance, everything was free. The checks were free. We figured it will cost about $40 a year to maintain a checking account.

LISA So she has the right idea not to put money in the bank, put everything in cash. Also your records are not closed. The government can get your records. They can come in and construct a whole lifestyle by your transactions, so if you want the whole world to know about you, where you bank, where you buy, where you borrow, what church you donate or go to, then just use a bank!

CAROLYN Another thing that surprised me is that when you buy a money order, even in the city, the banks won't cash it. That's wrong. This is just like cash. It was bought and paid for. Where can you cash them? You have to open an account and leave them there for so many days ... in the city a couple of days, out of the city probably two weeks, and out of state up to eighteen to twenty days. A cashier's check is the same. Nobody trusts nobody. It took a friend about thirty days to cash a cashier's check. It was for $1,000 from Las Vegas so they couldn't cash it. The money is there so why can't they cash it? Travelers checks are not acceptable everywhere. Some stores and gas stations will not accept them.

MODERATOR Anna, tell us about your problems.

ANNA You wouldn't believe it. Being a student, I have no credit cards, no credit. I have a driver's license and a military ID and it's impossible to cash a check without a credit card. Also, trying to find a place to live. I'm not twenty-one so they won't let you rent an apartment. They would not take my signature. I had to call my Dad and have him fly down, which is $50 one-way, and sign for me to get the apartment, and then fly back home. My parents send me money each month in a cashier's check, but I go through the problem all the time to cash it. I could get my parents to put me on their VISA card as a signer.

ROGER Couldn't you go to a bank and get a check guarantee card?

ANNA I've heard of it, but I don't have one. I have a military ID and a driver's license. I feel those two should be sufficient.

MODERATOR Did you experience any other problems as you were planning the move?

ANNA Yes, getting into school. They sent my application to San Jose instead of San Diego State, so by the time I got it back it was too late to register and I had to go contract register and it cost me $40 more per unit. At the time I was taking fifteen units, so I dropped all but ten units. I paid $400 instead of $100 and after moving down here and everything, I couldn't move back home.

MODERATOR Roger, how about you? When you were planning to move from Los Angeles?

ROGER I had no problems moving down as I moved all my own stuff so if anything was broken, it was no one's fault but my own. As far as banking, you just go down and open an account and hope the bank has interest in other personal accounts in California. Most banks don't. I don't feel San Diego is any different than Los Angeles. In transferring down here, Bank of America would not give me a check guarantee card here, even though my account was with them in L.A., because they say I have not established my record with them. I closed my account with them. I switched. Of course, I had the same problem, but I'd rather give them the chance and build my record than a bank that didn't consider my past twelve-year record where I held two existing loans. I think it's like a franchise, you should get the same service here that you did in the other place if it's the same bank.

MODERATOR What bank do you bank with now?

ROGER Security Pacific Bank.

MODERATOR Do you notice any difference?

ROGER No. No difference. They all have the same policy. Their cause is not for you. You put a large sum of money into their savings account, you don't ask them their life history, they just take your money and put it in there. Just try to borrow money or try to get your own money out ... it seems to be a different story. The interest they pay you is nothing. They're using that to invest at a much higher rate. You're donating to their cause when you have money in the bank, but yet they're a necessary evil. I wouldn't feel safe with that money at home. I think you need a bank. It's a must! They need some of the starch taken out of them. There are exceptions, some managers are nice but they're very few. Most are VIPs and we are the peons.

LISA If we could figure some other way to handle our money that would put them down to size and then they wouldn't be VIPs anymore. They would be human beings and maybe they would treat us better.

ROGER   Credit unions are an alternative to banks if you have one; they are good.

LISA   Why do you feel credit unions are better than banks?

ROGER   I think they are more concerned with the people that are in that organization. They make loans to people in their organizations. They come first, not just someone who comes in off the street. If you're not a member, you don't get a loan. They deal more with people who are willing to invest some of their savings with them. They in turn give priority to that person. When you borrow money from a bank, they decide whether it's a good investment or not. What is a good investment to one person may not be to another. If he has a past record of paying back money, they should give him the same responsibility. The money is there to lend. And money should be there to lend when they hold "X" amount of money in savings accounts. When they have money to build new branches and furnish them quite lavishly, then I think they've got money. The bank manager shouldn't feel like the money is coming out of his own personal checking account. Their business is making loans. They don't make it on checking accounts. Even if checking accounts aren't free, that $2 or $3 a month isn't paying the salaries, it's the loans. As an example, we took out a loan for $125,000 for constructing apartments in L.A. through a savings and loan. We were putting $25,000 of our own money into the S & L when they OK'd the loan. We then sold the land prior to construction, never used one penny out of the account, but it cost us for that loan ... $10,000—it was never used. Not only the cost for the loan but there was the prepayment penalty on the construction loan. Now in personal loans, if I was to borrow that amount of money from someone here, they would not be allowed to do that.

LISA   What makes a bank an exception? I don't understand, but there is nothing you can do. It's in the fine print, they are above the law.

MODERATOR   Let's talk about immediately after you all moved here ... what situations you came up against and what inconveniences.

MARIAN   Finding the shopping areas and schools. It's pretty hard to find out which schools are for which districts ... and which ones are good. We have found that the schools here are a little behind in their teaching. Getting your children to feel as though they belong in the new school ... everyone is in their little cliques and no one wants new people.

CAROLYN   I find the people here very unfriendly. It seems that it's each to themselves. The drivers here are wild. I need to get a new driver's license and, I think, California plates. I'm not sure.

MODERATOR   Brenda, how about you?

BRENDA   Finding an apartment was hard. Knowing what area is good or not. Getting the apartment is hard. They need your life history even though you have the first month's rent and the deposit. They expect you to take a motel for awhile. They feel their apartments are worth gold and you are going to destroy them or something.

CAROLYN   They don't want to rent to people with children. I have only an infant but they don't want to rent to me. I think the best thing going on now are the people that are trying to stop these apartment owners from not renting to families.

BRENDA   Oh yea ... and I'd bet that some of you had trouble finding out where to pay your utility deposits for gas and electricity and for the telephone. I had to go to four separate places. We had to wait two weeks for our phone to be installed.

MODERATOR   If you had it to do over again, can you come up with any suggestions or other ways you may have handled the move to prevent some of these problems?

BRENDA   I don't think I would move here. The weather is great, but that's about it. I've lived in a lot of big and little cities, all over, and the people around here are the hardest to get to know of anyplace I've lived. There is a housing shortage here for renting and buying.

ROGER   There is no way to solve the problems of housing since it is a bureaucracy. If you could get the bureaucracy out of it, then private enterprises would take over and meet the demands of the people, but it can't be done.

MODERATOR   Well, thanks very much for coming in to participate. You've been very helpful.

15

Hampton Mayoral Survey *

THE PROBLEM

In the early weeks of the 1983 mayoral campaign, most party leaders felt that Frank Wagner's many accomplishments as mayor of Hampton virtually assured his election as a second term Democratic mayor. By early October of that year, John Adams, Wagner's campaign manager, was not as confident due to what he believed was a subtle but observable shift in voter preferences towards the Republican candidate and past mayor, Bill Lucking. Adams was bothered by the number of Democratic precinct workers who had reported residents' caustic comments concerning Mayor Wagner's integrity and leadership style. He partially attributed these remarks to a series of damaging editorials and political advertisements which accused Mayor Wagner of being a dictatorial administrator. Reporters frequently labeled Wagner's leadership style as autocratic although the majority of the city administrators viewed him as an impatient man who too frequently lacked tack when dealing with controversial issues. Nevertheless, his rather direct manner did convey an image of rigidity to the press, and this conveyed image was not improving his reelection chances.

Bill Lucking's public image was the opposite of Wagner's because of his relaxed laidback approach to city governance. Former Mayor Lucking avoided politically sensitive issues and gave the county and city branches

of government almost complete autonomy over their operations. This lack of centralized planning caused frequent coordination problems among city and county officials and often resulted in delayed and unfinished projects. Even though Lucking was a congenial individual and a popular politician in Hampton, his lack of accomplishments did lead to his defeat by Frank Wagner, who ran on a reform platform. Wagner delivered his campaign promises and was successful in obtaining many civic improvements for Hampton residents. His principal accomplishments were: installing storm and flood control sewers in the low-lying areas of Hampton; securing new equipment for the fire department; obtaining passage of a controversial tax referendum for improvement of the city parks; enlarging the city ambulance fleet; installing curbs and sidewalks in older areas of the city; improving county and city roads; and facilitating the selection of Hampton as the location of the state-funded job training facility and the site of the North County Hospital Annex. Unfortunately, these accomplishments did not come without political conflict, and Wagner was frequently involved in political infighting with other county and local administrators. His terse manner and tenacious approach to these problems made him a favorite target of reporters in spite of his many successes.

Approximately five weeks before the election, a minority faction of the opposing Republican party strategically leaked to the *Hampton Chronicle* the accusation that Wagner owned the land upon which the proposed North County Hospital Annex was to be

* Prepared by Dr. Robert J. Listman of Valparaiso University as basis for class discussion rather than to illustrate effective or ineffective research practice. Copyright © 1985 by Dr. Robert J. Listman. Used by permission.

built. The paper published the accusation, which was later proved to be false, but it did hurt Wagner's image because he had publicly fought for the location of the Hospital Annex at this site. The newspaper printed a retraction, but, in spite of this, most party leaders felt that Wagner's image was severely damaged. Wagner himself was greatly disheartened over this latest turn of events, because he felt that the people of Hampton should see through what he termed a "shabby political assault."

After weighing Wagner's many accomplishments against his further tarnished image, Adams had to conclude that the election was going to be a lot closer than originally had been predicted. Lucking was an astute politician, and he was quite adept at publicly exaggerating Wagner's seemingly autocratic manner. However, the real concern was what did the voters believe and how would these beliefs affect their voting behavior? Adams felt that marketing research could help in assessing Mayor Wagner's image and in determining his reelection chances. Therefore, he asked for and received authorization to commission a political poll.

THE STUDY

Upon authorization by the reelection committee, Adams was able to divert $3,200 from the promotional budget to fund the needed research. Penton Research Associates, a local marketing research firm, was commissioned to complete the survey. After thoroughly reviewing the problem with the reelection committee, Joe Meyers, the Penton Account Executive, concluded that answers were needed to three key questions:

1. How do potential voters evaluate Frank Wagner as opposed to Bill Lucking on the dimensions of (a) job performance as mayor, (b) success in obtaining civic improvements, (c) honesty and integrity, and (d) overall concern for the welfare of Hampton residents?

2. Would Wagner or Lucking win the elec-

tion and, specifically, which precincts would each carry?

3. What factors would influence the way in which Hampton residents would vote in this election?

For issue number three, Adams hypothesized that the key vote determinants would be the critical factors of political affiliation, candidates' stands on community issues, their previous performances in office, and the voters' perceptions concerning the honesty and integrity of the candidates. Adams reasoned that since there had been many controversial community issues over the past four years, respondents should not be given a lengthy list from which to select. Both Adams and Meyers concluded that a response bias might likely occur if the respondents were asked to select issues from a list because they might frequently select issues which were not key determinants to them, but merely remembered issues. It was, therefore, agreed that if respondents identified the category, local issues, as a primary factor affecting their vote, then they would be directed to state the issue(s). Later a frequency distribution could be developed, and the most influencing issues could be easily identified.

Adams believed answers to these three questions would allow him to predict the results of the election on a city-wide and precinct basis and also to access the present image of Mayor Wagner. If a reelection problem did exist, then an intensified "promotional blitz" in selected precincts would be undertaken with the intent of changing voters' preferences in the remaining three weeks of the campaign.

RESEARCH METHODOLOGY

Both Adams and Meyers believed the answers to the three research questions could be more effectively obtained by conducting a large telephone survey rather than by conducting time consuming and expensive personal interviews. Their rationale was based upon the advantages of telephone surveys which included an obvious cost efficiency, specific control over selection of the sample, speed in completing the survey, and a higher degree of supervisory control over the actual interviewing. Meyers felt this last point was extremely important, because if interviewers varied on the phrasing of key questions, then a substantial but unquantifiable response bias could occur.

After discussing how to control interviewer bias, Joe Meyers raised the issue of sampling error. In explaining sampling error to Adams, Meyers stated, "The precision of data obtained through survey research is directly related to the size of the sample because the larger the sample, the more likely you are to reduce sampling error. In practice, however, a sample size is a compromise between some acceptable level of precision and restricting budgetary constraints. So, John, you have to evaluate precision against increased costs in selecting sampling parameters which are used to determine the actual sample size. Precision could be increased and sampling error reduced by selecting more statistically stringent parameters, such as a 99% versus a 90% confidence level, and/or by stipulating a smaller error range, such as $+2$ versus $+5$ percentage points from any given survey mean or percentage. This increased precision would result in a large and, therefore, more expensive sample."

Meyers interrupted and said, "Joe, is there any relationship between cost and precision?"

Meyers replied, "As a rule of thumb, doubling the sample size for surveys like this one would increase cost by 60%, but if you cut the sample size in half, costs would only decrease 25–35% due to high fixed expenses."

Adams looked somewhat confused and asked, "Does this mean that if I double the sample size, I will cut the sampling error in half?"

"Unfortunately, no," replied Meyers. "Precision increases in proportion to the square root of the increase in sample size.

Let's look at a standard error of a proportion table, Joe, and you can see what I mean. (Refer to Exhibit 1.) Assume we have a 50/50 proportional split and a stipulated error range of 5.8% at the 90% confidence level. This gives us a calculated sample size of 200. Doubling the sample size to 400 will only reduce the error range from $+5.8\%$ to $+4.1\%$. It would require a sample size four times as large, or 800, to cut error in half to 2.9%. This would result in a cost increase of 250–300% higher than the original survey of 200."

Adams appeared to be satisfied with this response, although he was getting impatient because of all these "scientific uncertainties" as he labeled them. He wanted to begin the survey immediately and cut back upon the time spent in drawing a sample by employing the local telephone directory as the sampling frame. He believed he could reduce both time and cost with this approach. Meyers disagreed and strongly recommended that the sampling frame be registered voters and be proportionately stratified by the percentage of registered voters within each political precinct. Although, he did agree that approximately 150 fewer calls could be made for the projected five hours of time it would take to select about 900 respondents, Joe Meyers projected that the actual sample size would be between 400–500, but he felt they should obtain 900 phone numbers to obtain double the sample size ratio needed for political polls. Meyers eventually obtained agreement to adopt his sampling frame, but he knew Adams believed that the result of this selection was a net loss of 150 calls!

In order to minimize further conflict, Meyers cautiously raised the last sampling issue. "John, I am glad that you approved the sampling frame of registered voters, but there still remains an additional source of sampling error which we must discuss."

Adams's reaction was immediate and abrupt. "Listen, Joe, if you are trying to sell me on a larger or more expensive survey, forget it."

Meyers was rather surprised by Adams's autocratic response, so he cautiously added,

Exhibit 1. Standard Error of Proportion Table— Sampling Error Parameter at 90% Confidence Level

	1% OR 99%	2% OR 98%	3% OR 97%	4% OR 96%	5% OR 95%	6% OR 94%	8% OR 92%	10% OR 90%	12% OR 88%	15% OR 85%	20% OR 80%	25% OR 75%	30% OR 70%	35% OR 65%	40% OR 60%	45% OR 55%	50%
25	3.3	4.6	5.6	6.5	7.2	7.8	9.0	9.9	10.7	11.8	13.2	14.3	15.1	15.7	16.2	16.4	16.5
50	2.3	3.3	4.0	4.6	5.1	5.5	6.3	7.0	7.6	8.3	9.3	10.1	10.7	11.1	11.4	11.6	11.7
75	1.9	2.7	3.3	3.7	4.2	4.5	5.2	5.7	6.2	6.8	7.6	8.3	8.7	9.1	9.3	9.5	9.5
100	1.6	2.3	2.8	3.2	3.6	3.9	4.5	4.9	5.4	5.9	6.6	7.1	7.6	7.9	8.1	8.2	8.3
150	1.3	1.9	2.3	2.6	2.9	3.2	3.7	4.0	4.4	4.8	5.4	5.8	6.2	6.4	6.6	6.7	6.7
200	1.2	1.6	2.0	2.3	2.5	2.8	3.2	3.5	3.8	4.2	4.7	5.1	5.3	5.6	5.7	5.8	5.8
250	1.0	1.5	1.8	2.0	2.3	2.5	2.8	3.1	3.4	3.7	4.2	4.5	4.8	5.0	5.1	5.2	5.2
300	0.9	1.3	1.6	1.9	2.1	2.3	2.6	2.9	3.1	3.4	3.8	4.1	4.4	4.5	4.7	4.7	4.8
400	0.8	1.2	1.4	1.6	1.8	2.0	2.2	2.5	2.7	2.9	3.3	3.6	3.8	3.9	4.0	4.1	4.1
500	0.7	1.0	1.3	1.4	1.6	1.8	2.0	2.2	2.4	2.6	3.0	3.2	3.4	3.5	3.6	3.7	3.7
600	0.7	0.9	1.1	1.3	1.5	1.6	1.8	2.0	2.2	2.4	2.7	2.9	3.1	3.2	3.3	3.4	3.4
800	0.6	0.8	1.0	1.1	1.3	1.4	1.6	1.8	1.9	2.1	2.3	2.5	2.7	2.8	2.9	2.9	2.9
1000	0.5	0.7	0.9	1.0	1.1	1.2	1.4	1.6	1.7	1.9	2.1	2.3	2.4	2.5	2.6	2.6	2.6
1200	0.5	0.7	0.8	0.9	1.0	1.1	1.3	1.4	1.5	1.7	1.9	2.1	2.2	2.3	2.3	2.4	2.4
1500	0.4	0.6	0.7	0.8	0.9	1.0	1.2	1.3	1.4	1.5	1.7	1.8	2.0	2.0	2.1	2.1	2.1
2000	0.4	0.5	0.6	0.7	0.8	0.9	1.0	1.1	1.2	1.3	1.5	1.6	1.7	1.8	1.8	1.8	1.8
2500	0.3	0.5	0.6	0.6	0.7	0.8	0.9	1.0	1.1	1.2	1.3	1.4	1.5	1.6	1.6	1.6	1.6
3000	0.3	0.4	0.5	0.6	0.7	0.7	0.8	0.9	1.0	1.1	1.2	1.3	1.4	1.4	1.5	1.5	1.5
4000	0.3	0.4	0.4	0.5	0.6	0.6	0.7	0.8	0.8	0.9	1.0	1.1	1.2	1.2	1.3	1.3	1.3
5000	0.2	0.3	0.4	0.5	0.5	0.6	0.6	0.7	0.8	0.8	0.9	1.0	1.1	1.1	1.1	1.2	1.2
7500	0.2	0.3	0.3	0.4	0.4	0.5	0.5	0.6	0.6	0.7	0.8	0.8	0.9	0.9	0.9	0.9	1.0
10000	0.2	0.2	0.3	0.3	0.4	0.4	0.4	0.5	0.5	0.6	0.7	0.7	0.8	0.8	0.8	0.8	0.8

"Well, John, we both know that customarily only 60% of eligible voters actually vote in local elections which gives us a built-in sampling error. What we need is a way of subdividing our survey respondents into homogeneous groups representing their probability of voting in this election. We could easily accomplish this by including filtering questions in the questionnaire which would assess respondents' interests in local politics, their interest in this campaign, and their past frequency of voting in local elections. After completing the interviews, we can weight and score each question, create an index of anticipated voter behavior, and, based upon composite scores, group the respondents.

"OK, Joe, you have my interest. What would you do then?" replied Adams.

"Well, assume we end up with three groups which have a high, moderate, and low probability of voting in this election. By analyzing the grouped responses, we could more precisely predict the results of the election and more accurately identify the campaign issues of greatest importance to those individuals most likely to vote."

Adams responded: "How much is this going to cost?"

Meyers replied: "Assume an extra two and one-half minutes for each questionnaire times approximately 400 questions gives us almost 17 additional hours of survey time. To this product, we should add the cost of six hours of account executive time in formulating the filtering questions, calculating the index, and interpreting the results. In total, this should add approximately $950 to the research bill."

Adams started shaking his head and emphatically said: "Well, you lost my interest with that $950 projection, Joe, but maybe we can still reach an agreement. Adopt my original sampling frame, which will give us 150 additional respondents, and I think I can convince the election board to add the $950.00 to the survey costs."

Joe Meyers quickly responded: "No, John, I can't support that approach because all we will accomplish is to reintroduce our original sampling problem."

"OK, Joe, you are the expert," replied Adams, "but it is my money, and I don't think it is worth $950 merely to break down our findings into three additional categories of responses, so I am going to say no!"

After fifteen minutes of further discussion, Joe Meyers was unable to persuade John Adams to approve the addition of filtering questions. Since Adams was becoming progressively more agitated, Meyers reluctantly concluded that the issue was a stalemate which would not be resolved in an amicable fashion.

Therefore, Adams left this issue and moved to the problem of determining a specific sample size. The sampling parameters of $\pm 4\%$ at the 90% confidence level, with an assumed voter split of 45/55 in favor of Wagner were agreed upon. This resulted in a calculated sample size of 400 which was possible to obtain for a cost of $3,000. However, Meyers believed that if the election was going to be that close (45/55 split), then a more statistically stringent and, therefore, larger sample was warranted. However, the subject was quickly dropped when Adams, who was obviously agitated, said, "Look, if you need a larger sample, then adopt my sampling approach and we will be able to survey one hundred and fifty more people." Since Meyers did not wish another confrontation at this stage of the project, he dropped the issue.

The next day Penton personnel started the research project. Joe Meyers developed, pretested, and refined the telephone questionnaire while other Penton employees randomly selected a pool of 800 respondents from the precinct listings. Exhibit 2 contains a copy of the survey instrument used in the study. The actual selection process did not attempt to further stratify the sample by political affiliation even though most registered voters declared their political affiliation in the primaries as either Democratic or Republican. In fact, only 60% of the registered voters even voted in past mayoral elections, and the majority of these voted a straight party ticket.

Penton personnel were instructed to select twice the number of needed calls for each precinct. All numbers were randomly selected from precinct listings so any biasing periodicities in the alphabetized listings were eliminated.

Interviewers were directed to speak to only the registered voters within the surveyed households, and all interviews were conducted between the hours of 6:30 and 9:30 P.M. over a three-day period. Interviewers were assigned specific precincts and a supervisor was present to monitor the quality of the phone interviewers. If a phone number was busy or there was no answer, then repeated callbacks were made in an effort to reach that household.

RESULTS OF THE STUDY

In total, 629 calls had to be made in order to obtain the requisite sample size of 400. In several precincts, the number of nonrespondents (those who refused to participate in the survey) approximated the needed quota of calls in that precinct. Of the 402 completed interviews, approximately 43% (171) were males while 57% (231) were females. Exhibits 3–5 contain these and other descriptive statistics concerning the sampling distributions.

The findings indicate that the primary reasons affecting voters' preferences, Exhibit 6, were voters' perceptions of the candidates' integrity/honesty and the candidates' past performances as mayor. The data also suggests that candidates' political affiliation and

Exhibit 2.

Precinct ID Number: _____   Telephone Number: _____

Good Evening, this is Penton Research Associates and we are conducting a very brief *randomized survey* of Hampton residents to determine their opinions of the two candidates running for mayor of Hampton. May I speak to (*insert name*)? All responses are, of course, treated anonymously and confidentially. Thank you. (Check space below.)

_____ Participated   _____ Male   _____ Female   _____ Did not participate

Question One: I will read four reasons which could likely affect the way people will vote in this election. *After* I state all four reasons, select the *one primary* reason which will influence your vote the *most*. (Interviewers: Mark 1 after that response and if they identify another primary factor, describe it below.)

_____ Candidate's political affiliation   Other _____
_____ Candidate's personal integrity and honesty
_____ Candidate's previous performance as mayor
_____ Local community issues (ask following question)

Of the remaining three reasons (read again), please identify any *secondary reasons* which will *significantly influence* your vote. (Interviewers: Code 2 (secondary) after each choice. If none, leave blank.)

Question Two: Please describe the *community issues* which you believe will influence your vote in this election. (Describe below)

_____
_____

Question Three: In your opinion, who do you believe has done the best job as mayor?

_____ A   the present mayor, Frank Wagner
_____ B   the previous mayor, Bill Lucking
_____ C   there is no difference between the two
_____ D   don't know or no opinion (do not give as an option)

Question Four: How do you believe Bill Lucking compares to Frank Wagner on the following points? *After* I read each point, indicate which candidate is superior to the other *by stating* the *name* of the candidate *you prefer.* If you have no preference, respond *no preference.* (Interviewers: If respondents are unable to make a decision, check the don't know column.)

(1) Lucking	(2) Wagner	(3) No Preference	(4) Don't Know	Qualifications
_____	_____	_____	_____	1. Successful in obtaining community improvements for Hampton residents
_____	_____	_____	_____	2. Personal integrity and honesty
_____	_____	_____	_____	3. Concern for welfare of Hampton residents
_____	_____	_____	_____	4. Candidate's overall performance as mayor of Hampton

Question Five: If the vote were tomorrow, would you vote for (check one):
_____ Bill Lucking or _____ Frank Wagner _____ Undecided (Interviewers: Do not give as an option but check if they can't decide.)

Question Six: Would you classify your political affiliation as:
_____ Democratic _____ Republican or _____ Independent

community issues were not as important in this election as the preceding two reasons. Approximately 18% of the surveyed voters indicated that local community issues were a primary factor and 27% indicated they were a secondary factor. Exhibit 7 contains a listing of these identified community issues.

Exhibit 3. Precinct Sampling Statistics

Precinct	Sample size	Completed calls	Would not participate in survey	Total contacts
2	24	24	8	32
3	24	24	14	48
5	20	20	19	39
6	16	16	8	24
7	28	28	10	38
8	20	20	7	27
9	24	25	13	39
12	13	13	9	22
13	16	16	13	29
14	20	20	9	29
17	17	17	7	24
18	20	20	12	32
* 20	20	16	18	34
21	29	29	13	42
22	20	21	13	34
23	16	16	6	22
24	20	21	8	24
25	20	20	13	33
26	20	22	18	40
27	13	13	9	22
Totals	400	402	227	629

* Fifty numbers were supplied; however, after repeated callbacks, only thirty-four out of the fifty could be reached.

Exhibit 4. Breakdown of Political Affiliation and Gender

Political Affiliation *	Count	Percentage
Democratic	128	31.84%
Republican	72	17.91%
Independent	198	49.25%
Would not respond	4	1.00%

* Note: Many respondents register in primaries as Democratic or Republican but vote the issues or person. Consequently, they classify themselves as independent even though they may have registered as a member of a political party.

Breakdown by Gender:

Males: 171 surveys   Females: 231 surveys
42.54%   57.46%

Total: 402 surveys

Exhibit 5. Cross-tabulation—Political Affiliation by Precinct

Political affiliation of respondents:

Precinct	Democratic	Republican	Independent	Would not respond	Total
2	8 33.33%	5 20.83%	9 37.50%	2 8.33%	24 5.97%
3	9 37.50%	3 12.50%	12 50.00%	0 0.00%	24 5.97%
5	5 25.00%	2 10.00%	13 65.00%	0 0.00%	20 4.98%
6	6 37.50%	5 31.25%	5 31.25%	0 0.00%	16 3.98%
7	8 28.57%	3 10.71%	17 60.71%	0 0.00%	28 6.97%
8	7 35.00%	1 5.00%	12 60.00%	0 0.00%	20 4.98%
9	7 26.92%	8 30.77%	11 42.31%	0 0.00%	26 6.47%
12	1 7.69%	3 23.08%	9 69.23%	0 0.00%	13 3.23%
13	4 25.00%	2 12.50%	10 62.50%	0 0.00%	16 3.98%
14	4 20%	3 15.00%	12 60.00%	1 5.00%	20 4.98%
17	9 52.94%	4 23.53%	4 23.53%	0 0.00%	17 4.23%
18	10 50.00%	1 5.00%	9 45.00%	0 0.00%	20 4.98%
20	5 31.25%	3 18.75%	7 43.75%	1 6.75%	16 3.98%
21	5 17.24%	7 24.14%	17 58.62%	0 0.00%	29 7.21%
22	6 28.57%	5 23.81%	10 47.62%	0 0.00%	21 5.22%
23	6 37.50%	0 0.00%	10 62.50%	0 0.00%	16 3.98%
24	8 38.10%	4 19.05%	9 42.86%	0 0.00%	21 5.22%
25	10 50.00%	3 15.00%	7 35.00%	0 0.00%	20 4.98%
26	6 27.27%	8 36.36%	8 36.36%	0 0.00%	22 5.47%
27	4 30.77%	2 15.38%	7 53.85%	0 0.00%	13 3.23%
TOTALS	128 31.84%	72 17.91%	198 49.25%	4 1.00%	402 100.00%

Exhibit 6. Primary/Secondary Reasons Affecting Vote

Voter preference by the primary reason affecting vote

Reason	Bill Lucking	Frank Wagner	Undecided	Would not respond	Total
Political Affiliation	6 26.09%	13 56.52%	2 8.70%	2 8.70%	23 5.72%
Personal Integrity/ Honesty of Candidate	64 42.11%	52 34.21%	30 19.74%	6 3.95%	152 37.81%
Previous Perform- ance as Mayor	52 35.62%	71 48.63%	18 12.33%	5 3.42%	146 36.32%
Local Issues	28 39.44%	24 33.80%	14 19.72%	5 7.04%	71 17.66%
Could not Identify any Primary Reason	2 20.00%	5 50.00%	1 10.00%	2 20.00%	10 2.49%
TOTALS	152 37.81%	165 41.04%	65 16.17%	20 4.98%	402 100.00%

Frequency Distributions of the Secondary Reasons Affecting Voting Decision:

Question	Count	Percentage
Political affiliation	42	10.45%
Personal integrity and honesty	76	18.91%
Previous performance as mayor	109	27.11%
Local community issues	107	26.62%
Could not identify any secondary reason	68	16.92%

*** Summary Results of Voter Preference and Question Five ***

Choice	Count	Percentage
Bill Lucking	152	37.81%
Frank Wagner	165	41.04%
Undecided	65	16.17%
Would not respond	20	4.98%

The summary results of voters' preferences contained in Exhibit 6 suggest that Frank Wagner is slightly preferred over Bill Lucking. However, 21% of the registered voters classified their preference as still undecided. Exhibits 8–11 contain summaries of cross-tabulations of registered voters' preferences by (1) candidates' qualifications, (2) gender, (3) precinct, (4) political affiliation, and (5) candidates' past performance as mayor.

Exhibit 7. Breakdown of Primary/Secondary Community Issues Affecting Voter Behavior *

1. Need for sidewalks and curbs—29
2. Need for hospital in community—17
3. Drainage and/or flood control—15
4. Controversy over hospital land issue—10
5. Police point system—6
6. Firehouse equipment needs—5
7. Frank Wagner's autocratic image—2
8. Examples of other reasons:

    Improved management—3

    Cleaner city—3

    School busing program—2

    Job training facility and attracting business to Hampton—3

    Nepotism—3

    Park/tax increases—10

    City/road improvements—6

    Ambulance—5

    Miscellaneous—4
9. Would not state any specific community issue—40

* Some respondents cited more than one reason so the tallies do not represent number of respondents.

INTERPRETING THE FINDINGS

In reviewing all of this data, Adams concluded that the election would be very close but that Wagner would win by a narrow margin. He based this conclusion upon the assumption that the undecideds would vote in approximately the same proportion as those who were able to state their preference. He saw no data refuting this conclusion; therefore, he felt it was a valid assumption to make.

On the other hand, Meyers felt that the results were not very conclusive because he believed the high undecided factor could easily reverse the narrow margin Wagner presently enjoyed. He was also bothered by the fact that a large percentage of area voters would not respond to the poll. John Adams listened to Meyers's concerns but said, "Joe,

don't be so pessimistic; your people did a good job and your worries are really unwarranted. After all, the calculated sample size was obtained and the respondents were selected at random." Therefore, Adams saw no reason to assume that the opinions of the nonrespondents or undecideds would deviate significantly from the findings of the survey. He was further encouraged by the fact that Wagner appeared to carry twelve of the twenty precincts and was slightly trailing or equal to Lucking in two, while clearly losing in only six. Exhibit 10 contains a summary of voters' preferences by precinct.

John Adams did realize that the election was not a "shoo-in" for Wagner, but he felt that concentrating the promotional blitz in precincts 5, 9, 12, 13, 14, 21, 22, and 26 would help to increase Wagner's narrow

Exhibit 8. Breakdown of Opinion of Best Job as Mayor Question Three

Preference	Count	Percentage
Frank Wagner	129	32.09%
Bill Lucking	101	25.12%
No difference between the two	94	23.38%
Don't know or no opinion	78	19.40%

Exhibit 9. Candidates' Qualifications Question Four

1. Comparison of success in obtaining community civic improvements for Hampton residents

Preference	Count	Percentage
Bill Lucking	81	20.15%
Frank Wagner	158	39.30%
No preference	114	28.36%
Don't know	49	12.19%

2. Comparison of personal integrity and honesty

Preference	Count	Percentage
Bill Lucking	130	32.34%
Frank Wagner	97	24.13%
No preference	136	33.83%
Don't know	39	9.70%

3. Comparison of concern for welfare of Hampton residents

Preference	Count	Percentage
Bill Lucking	117	29.10%
Frank Wagner	122	30.35%
No preference	122	30.35%
Don't know	41	10.20%

4. Comparison of candidates' previous performance as mayor of Hampton

Preference	Count	Percentage
Bill Lucking	115	28.61%
Frank Wagner	133	33.08%
No preference	104	25.87%
Don't know	50	12.44%

Exhibit 10. Cross-tabulation—Voter Preference by Precinct

Precinct	Bill Lucking	Frank Wagner	Presently Undecided	Would not Respond to Question	Precinct Total
2	9 37.50%	11 45.83%	3 12.50%	1 4.17%	24 5.97%
3	8 33.33%	10 41.67%	6 25.00%	0 0.00%	24 5.97%
5	10 50.00%	6 30.00%	1 5.00%	3 15.00%	19 4.98%
6	4 25.00%	6 37.50%	3 18.75%	3 18.75%	16 3.98%
7	7 25.00%	13 46.43%	7 25.00%	1 3.57%	28 6.97%
8	4 20.00%	11 55.00%	4 20.00%	1 5.00%	20 4.98%
9	15 57.69%	7 26.92%	3 11.54%	1 3.85%	26 6.47%
12	6 46.15%	3 23.08%	2 15.38%	2 15.38%	13 3.23%
13	7 43.75%	3 18.75%	6 37.50%	0 0.00%	16 3.98%
14	8 40.00%	6 30.00%	5 25.00%	1 5.00%	20 4.98%
17	7 41.18%	8 47.06%	2 11.76%	0 0.00%	17 4.23%
18	6 30.00%	13 65.00%	1 5.00%	0 0.00%	20 4.23%
20	3 18.75%	6 37.50%	6 37.50%	1 6.25%	16 3.98%
21	17 58.62%	8 27.59%	3 10.34%	1 3.45%	29 7.21%
22	12 57.14%	7 33.33%	2 9.52%	0 0.00%	21 5.22%
23	3 18.75%	10 62.50%	2 12.50%	1 6.25%	16 3.89%
24	5 23.81%	12 57.14%	2 9.52%	2 9.52%	21 5.22%
25	7 35.00%	10 50.00%	3 15.00%	0 0.00%	20 4.98%
26	9 40.91%	9 40.91%	2 9.09%	2 9.09%	22 5.47%
27	5 38.46%	6 46.15%	2 15.38%	0 0.00%	13 3.23%
TOTALS:	152 37.81%	165 41.04%	65 16.17%	20 4.98%	402 100.00%

Exhibit 11. Cross-tabulations—Voter Preference by Political Affiliation/Past Performance as Mayor/and Gender

Voter preference by political affiliation:

Political Affiliation	Bill Lucking	Frank Wagner	Undecided	Would not respond	Total
Democratic	21	85	16	6	128
	16.41%	66.41%	12.50%	4.69%	31.84%
Republican	52	12	7	1	72
	72.22%	16.67%	9.72%	1.39%	17.91%
Independent	78	67	40	12	198
	39.39%	34.34%	20.20%	6.06%	49.25%
Would not respond	1	0	2	1	4
	25.00%	0.00%	50.00%	25.00%	1.00%
Totals	152	165	65	20	402
	37.81%	41.04%	16.17%	4.98%	100.00%

Voter preference by past performance as mayor:

Prefer	Bill Lucking	Frank Wagner	Undecided	Would not respond	Total
Frank Wagner	5	112	10	2	129
	3.88%	86.82%	7.75%	1.55%	32.09%
Bill Lucking	95	2	2	2	101
	94.06%	1.98%	1.98%	1.98%	25.12%
No Difference	31	21	31	11	94
	32.98%	22.34%	32.98%	11.70%	23.38%
No Opinion	21	30	22	5	78
	26.92%	38.46%	28.21%	6.41%	19.40%
Totals	152	165	65	20	402
	37.81%	41.04%	16.17%	4.98%	100.00%

Voter preference by gender:

Sex	Bill Lucking	Frank Wagner	Undecided	Would not respond	Total
Male	65	67	23	16	171
	38.01%	39.18%	13.45%	9.36%	42.54%
Female	87	98	42	4	231
	37.66%	42.42%	18.18%	1.73%	57.46%
Totals	152	165	65	20	402
	37.81%	41.04%	16.17%	4.98%	100.00%

margin because these were the precincts Wagner was losing or trailing in. Joe Meyers felt intimidated by Adams's optimistic interpretation of the findings. He believed that Penton provided the Democratic Party with a scientific poll free from biased questions, and he did not wish to conclude the engagement by discrediting the findings and the efforts of his staff. Maybe his concerns were unwarranted, but he believed that Adams's interpretation of the findings was not entirely valid and that the election could go either way. He wondered if he was professionally justified in accepting the commission for this study when he had reservations concerning what he felt was a built-in sampling problem. Meyers knew that he informed the client about this problem and repeatedly tried to convince Adams of the need for the filtering questions. There was personal conflict in this engagement, and Meyers further believed that Adams did not fully understand the technical justification for his suggestions, but he did not want to admit this to Joe or take the time to listen to Joe's rationale. Meyers sadly concluded that this was a classic example of a line decision maker not understanding the technical reasons underpinning a "staff" person's suggestions. Unfortunately, as is often the case, this resulted in study findings which could be interpreted in a variety of ways, depending upon one's perspective.

Three

Product

BODINE COMPANY

THE TRENTEN CORPORATION, MIDCRON DIVISION

RAKCO CORPORATION

16

The Bodine Company *

The Bodine Company, located in Collierville, Tennessee, just outside of Memphis, is a relatively small assembler of electronic components. Last year annual sales were approximately $5 million. The major product of the Bodine Company is a fluorescent emergency lighting ballast which converts fluorescent fixtures into emergency lights. The market for the ballast consists of commercial/industrial lighting contractors and industrial construction companies. Other products marketed by the Bodine Company include DC inverter ballasts, electronic controls, and custom electronic equipment. The company has a SIC code of 3648 (lighting equipment n.e.c.).

David Crippen, Bodine's marketing manager, needs to develop a marketing plan for a recently developed new product, the photoelectric registration control often called an eye-mark control.

PRODUCT DESCRIPTION

The Bodine W–20 photoelectric registration control maintains the alignment of the final wrap (e.g., a package of frozen foods is wrapped with paper designating the product, brand name, and sundry information) by regulating the feed of the wrapping material. This is accomplished by monitoring a registration mark (the black mark you see on frozen foods wrappings) each cutting cycle and automatically controlling the coil on the machine which advances or retards the roll-fed wrapper a preset distance. In this way, labels

or what should be on the top of the package, such as brand name and product description, are displayed on the top of the package. Thus, an eye-mark control is essential in packaging operations of most every type.

The control has flexibility in that it can be used with most wrapping materials including kraft and waxed paper, reinforced foils, and opaque or transparent films, such as cellophane. Solid state electronics and plug-in circuity combine to give the W–20 dependability which in turn eliminates downtime, a crucial consideration in any packaging operation.

The W–20 operates by sensing the coincidence of the edge of the register mark and the closure of a set of contacts on the wrapping machine that operate once each cycle. When the proper positioning of the mark and the contact closure occur at the same time, the W–20 control supplies 220 DC to a coil on the packaging machine that causes the roll-fed wrap to be adjusted backward or forward a predetermined amount. Since the wrap is being slightly overfed or underfed, it slowly drifts back to where the W–20 again detects the coincidence of the contract closure and the edge of the register mark, repeating the adjustment.

The W–20 Control comprises a control panel, a scanner, and three plug-in circuit boards. The control panel contains the circuit boards, transformer, setup switch, cable assemblies, and terminal block for connecting the required 110 AC input. The scanner includes the light source and the photocell. The three plug-in circuit boards contain the electronic circuitry.

* This case was prepared by H. Robert Dodge.

A HISTORY OF THE INTRODUCTION STAGE OF THE PRODUCT LIFE CYCLE

The W–20 photoelectric registration control device was developed by the Bodine engineering department in response to problems encountered at two packaging operations in the immediate area. One of these was Tennessee Foods (Winter Garden) in Rossville, Tennessee, and the other was General Foods (Birdseye) in Searcy, Arkansas. Both customers were highly enthusiastic about the control device, but isolated attempts to sell the control to other packagers had not met with any success. In fact, Bodine had been unsuccessful in its attempts to sell the control to other plants of General Foods or receive any kind of corporate approval from the parent organization.

It was decided to use those manufacturers' reps specializing in electrical equipment and supplies and who already sell Bodine products to introduce the control to other customers. The basis for this decision was that manufacturers' reps are useful to small companies such as Bodine in that they already call on potential customers for a new product and can add the new product at a relatively low cost. After a period of six months; however, these manufacturers' reps reported little success for the W–20. One reason for this failure was that the purchase of a W–20 is not planned, but is one occasioned by the failure of existing equipment. Replacement must be immediate and, because most manufacturers' reps do not inventory products, immediate delivery and service were not possible.

MARKET STUDY

The year after W–20 was developed, a market study was conducted by a professional market research firm for the Bodine Company. The first part of the study consisted of discussions with management and engineering personnel from Tennessee Foods and General Foods. Trade association personnel from the packaging industry were also interviewed. The information gained from these interviews (i.e., need, specification, and installation of product) was used in designing a questionnaire. The mailing list of potential users was extracted from trade association materials.

A questionnaire together with a cover letter (see Appendix) was mailed to the maintenance engineer in plants designated as possessing an overwrap-packaging operation. The following SIC code designations were utilized in identifying potential customers that might use the control:

2034— Dried and dehydrated fruits, vegetables, and soup mixes

2035— Pickled fruits and vegetables, vegetables, vegetable sauces and seasonings, and salad dressing

2037— Frozen fruits, fruit juices, and vegetables

2047— Dog, cat, and other pet food

2051— Bread and other bakery products

2052— Cookies and crackers

2065— Candy and other confectionery products

2066— Chocolate and cocoa products

2067— Chewing gum

2092— Fresh or frozen packaged fish and seafoods

2099— Food preparations not elsewhere classified

2647— Sanitary paper products

A total of 303 questionnaires were mailed. Of this total, 7 questionnaires were returned as undeliverable and 57, or 19 percent, were completed and returned as usable responses. Visits were also made to several other packaging operations, and the maintenance engineers at these installations were interviewed.

RESULTS OF THE STUDY

The significant findings and appropriate support data developed from the personal interviews and mail survey can be summarized as follows:

1. The primary and perhaps the only market for the W–20 is the replacement market. The reasons for this are that (1) packaging machinery is not readily replaced; and (2) even with the two maintenance engineers who truly supported the product, there was serious doubt that the W–20 would be specified as part of a new machine when ordered. When asked to explain, both maintenance engineers gave answers to the effect that they thought it would be easier to replace low-cost auxiliary equipment than to include the W–20 in initial specifications. One maintenance engineer professed no knowledge of who made the processing machinery in his plant.

2. Product interest, as witnessed by the extent of response to the mailing, indicated three types of accounts classified on the basis of potential—key (highest potential), secondary (next highest potential), and marginal. The key and secondary account types are listed in Exhibit 1. The marginal accounts are: 2013—Prepared meat products; 2035—Sauces and seasonings; 2038—Frozen specialties; and 2051—Bread and other bakery products.

3. The most popular brands of control are Dietz and General Electric (Exhibit 2). There are a total of fifteen brands on the market.

4. Packagers have a tendency to own more than one brand of control. Exhibit 3 shows that over one-half of the packagers name more than one brand of control. For example, almost 75 percent of the users of Dietz controls name at least one other brand. The brands most often found with Dietz are General Electric and Photoswitch. Only three of the twelve packagers using General Electric use it alone. Three packagers use only Tri-Tronics, two only Microswitch, while only one reported singular usage of Bartelt, Photoswitch, or Erwin.

5. Of the thirty-four packagers where information was available on number of brands owned, six own only one brand while the other eighteen have purchased at least two different brands (Exhibit 3).

6. The two most frequently mentioned problems with controls were readjustment and downtime caused by control failure (Exhibit 4). Six of the 34 respondents indicated few if any problems with controls. By plotting the four most troublesome problems, it can be seen that downtime and readjustment affected small users as well as large users.

7. Some unique problems were as follows:

   a. A dairy using the W–20 for packaging butter reported a problem with water getting into photocells and bad relays.

   b. In a Del Monte packaging operation, the problem was heat burning the bottom of photocells.

   c. A contract packager had a problem with dirt getting into the cells.

   d. A packager in Connecticut encountered trouble in getting repair service and parts for Dietz controls.

   e. A packager of licorice in St. Louis attributed most of his downtime to bulb burn-out, relays wearing out, and occasionally defects in condensers, resistors, and the like. He uses four brands of control—Dietz, General Electric, Electronics Corporation of America, and Tri-Tronics.

8. Maintenance engineers seemed to live with their problems. About the only reaction when further repair was impractical was to buy another brand and see if it worked better.

9. Slightly more than one-half of the respondents (54 percent) mentioned more than one problem with controls. The most common was downtime caused by readjustment.

10. A clustering of problems such as shown in Exhibit 5 shows that servicing of the

Exhibit 1. Customer Targets

Key Accounts
    2034— Dried and dehydrated fruits, vegetables, and soup mixes
    2037— Frozen fruits and vegetables
    2065— Candy and other confectionery products
    2067— Chewing gum
    2647— Sanitary paper products (towels and tissue)
       — Contract packagers (food)

Secondary Accounts
    2021— Creamery butter
    2022— Natural and process cheese
    2052— Cookies and crackers
    2092— Frozen packaged fish and seafoods
    2098— Macaroni and related products
    2099— Potato chips only

---

control (readjustment and replacement) is generally associated with downtime rather than with difficulties in service and getting parts. A possible explanation for this is that plant personnel can handle most if not all servicing of the control. Exhibit 5 also shows that frequent readjustment is more of a problem than frequent replacement.

11. The more controls a packager has, the greater the incidence of problems and the number of different types of problems.

12. There is not a lot of difference in the popularity of desired improvements (Exhibit 6). As expected, sensitivity control is important. One packager (Pepperidge) feels that controls should be as simple as possible, with plug-in solid state electronics and easy to understand electromechanical devices.

13. A matchup of problems with improvements shows the following:

   ■ frequent readjustment—sensitivity control

Exhibit 2. Brands of Controls Mentioned by Users

Dietz	19	(56%)
General Electric	12	(35%)
Photoswitch	8	(24%)
Farmer Electric	6	(18%)
Westinghouse	4	(12%)
Tri-Tronics	3	
Microswitch	2	
Autotron	2	
Electronics Corporation of America	2	
Bodine, EPI, Dolan-Jenner, Warner, Bartelt, Erwin	1	
Did not identify	2	

Exhibit 3. Brand Ownership for Packagers

Number of Brands	Number of Packagers	Average Number of Lines
1	6	9
2	8	12
3	8	20
4	2	13
Totals	34	12

- frequent change of photocells—one photocell
- difficulties in obtaining service and parts—plug-in circuitry

PROPOSED MARKETING PROGRAM

Crippen reviewed the findings of the study and made the following notes in preparation for development of a marketing plan.

1. The customer target is the packager (replacement).

2. The decision to purchase is made by the maintenance engineer.

3. Manufacturing representatives are not the appropriate middleman because of the need for localized inventory.

4. Seeing the product in actual operation would seem to be a powerful selling inducement.

5. A set of three circuit boards should be included with the product.

6. The package as envisioned using the normal markup for Bodine would have a price of $304. With seemingly no price resistance and higher prices for the competition, the package price would be raised to $350 or $400.

7. Discussions with engineers indicate that the W–20 does not require adjustment for sensitivity as machine temperatures increase. It is also insensitive to humidity or temperature changes.

8. The W–20 has one photocell for all colormarks or lettering except yellow.

Exhibit 4. Problems With Controls

Problem Experienced	Total	Packagers Responding		
		1–4 Lines	5–10 Lines	11 or more Lines
Frequent readjustment of eye sensitivity	18	7	5	6
Downtime due to control failure	17	3	6	8
Service and parts difficulties	9	4	—	5
Frequent change of photocells	8	3	2	3
Water in photocell	2	1	1	—
Bad relays	2	—	—	2
Heat burning bottom of photocell	2	—	2	—
Dirt in control	1	—	—	1
Relays and other parts burning out	1	—	1	—

Exhibit 5.   Association of Problems

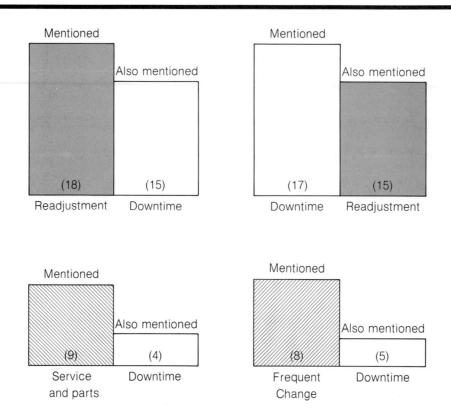

Exhibit 6.   Desired Improvements

Improvement	Number of Packagers
Sensitivity control	15
Plug-in circuitry	15
One photocell	10

APPENDIX

BODINE INDUSTRIAL RESEARCH ASSOCIATES
P.O. DRAWER "B"
COLLIERVILLE, TN 38017

Dear Maintenance Engineer:

We would like your answers to a few questions about PHOTOELECTRIC REGISTER (Eye Mark) CONTROLS for overwrap packaging machines. Your time is worth more than 25 cents, but please accept this new quarter with our thanks.

The questionnaire is short, simple, and easy to complete. We would like to know about your actual operational experiences with PHOTOELECTRIC REGISTER (Eye Mark) CONTROLS. Please take a few minutes to answer the questions. A postage paid, self-addressed envelope is provided for your convenience.

Please be assured that your answers will not be identified with you or your company. There is no way we can tell who is responding to our survey.

Sincerely,

BODINE INDUSTRIAL RESEARCH
ASSOCIATES

Don Roberts
Research Associate

HRD/gs
encls.

MARKET SURVEY

1. Do you use a PHOTOELECTRIC REGISTER (Eye Mark) CONTROL in adjusting roll print (either paper or plastic) or polyethylene bags in your packaging operation?
   ☐ YES   ☐ NO   (If no, THANK YOU and please return the questionnaire).
2. Check the make(s) or brand(s) of PHOTOELECTRIC REGISTER (Eye Mark) CONTROLS on your packaging or wrapping machines.
   ☐ DIETZ
   ☐ GENERAL ELECTRIC
   ☐ WESTINGHOUSE
   ☐ OTHER (please name) _____
3. How many packaging lines with controls do you operate? _____
4. Check the problems you have experienced with PHOTOELECTRIC REGISTER (Eye Mark) CONTROLS.
   ☐ FREQUENT CHANGE OF PHOTOCELLS TO PICK UP DIFFERENT COLOR MARKS
   ☐ DOWN TIME DUE TO FAILURE OF CONTROL
   ☐ DIFFICULTIES IN OBTAINING REPAIR SERVICE AND PARTS
   ☐ FREQUENT READJUSTMENT OF THE SENSITIVITY OF THE EYE
   ☐ OTHER (please describe) _____
   _____
   _____
5. Check any of the following improvements that would be helpful to you in working with PHOTOELECTRIC REGISTER CONTROLS.

☐ ONE PHOTOCELL (Eye) FOR ALL COLORS EXCEPT YELLOW
☐ PLUG–IN CIRCUITRY TO SPEED UP CONTROL REPAIR
☐ SENSITIVITY CONTROL THAT DOES NOT HAVE TO BE READJUSTED AS
MACHINE HEATS UP DURING THE DAY

6. If there are any other changes or comments you would like to make relative to PHOTO-ELECTRIC REGISTER CONTROLS, please do so below. _____

_____

_____

_____

_____

THANK YOU

17

The Trenten Corporation, Midcron Division *

INTRODUCTION

The Trenten Corporation, headquartered in Cleveland, Ohio, is a highly diversified manufacturer of industrial products. Total sales in 1981 were $520 million with a return on sales of slightly less than 10 percent (actually 9.87 percent) after taxes. During the last ten years, sales have doubled and profits, after taxes, have tripled. Much of the growth of Trenten during this period of time has come from the purchase of small companies making industrial products. One of these companies was Midcron, which now operates as a division.

The Trenten Corporation is organized into four major groups that, in turn, are divided into fifteen operating divisions or companies. As part of the Electronics Group, Midcron manufactures a general line of precision electronic switch products. Total sales volume in 1981 was $19.7 million, with profits after taxes of over $1.8 million. In terms of sales, Midcron would place fifteenth among some four hundred manufacturers who make essentially the same type of products and compete for the same customers. Cutler-Hammer, Micro-Switch, Allen Bradley, and Square "D" are the industry leaders. The largest firm is Cutler-Hammer with sales in excess of $250 million and a market share of somewhere near 10 percent.

* This case was prepared by H. Robert Dodge.

COMPETITIVE STATUS OF MIDCRON

When asked the question "what business do we want to be in?" top management at Trenten answered "high tech and high growth." The Midcron division is in the forefront of this strategic issue. Midcron by the very nature of its product line has had to market many products in markets that could be labeled high tech and high growth. For example, Midcron is already selling components to firms such as IBM.

According to Allen Stansky, Operating Manager of Midcron, the biggest question for Midcron is how to compete in their product-market segments. In framing this question for his marketing staff, he summarized what he feels are the strengths and weaknesses of Midcron.

Strengths

1. Positioned in high-growth markets such as computer/process control and office/retail/medical;
2. Competition is fragmented;
3. Larger competitors, with the exception of Micro-Switch, concentrate on "industrial" type switches;
4. Small share in all product types and all user segments affords the opportunities for growth without the risk of high expo-

sure and possible retaliatory actions by larger competitors; and

5. Appliance and automotive controls are moving toward low-current designs, providing opportunities for Midcron products.

Weaknesses

1. Reliance on labor-intensive, relatively high-cost assembly capability;

2. Insufficient R & D;

3. Vulnerability to pricing tactics of competitors who are capable of volume runs using low-cost, automated production; and

4. Technological threats to the mechanical switch from such advancements as solid-state switching, sensors, and membrane switching.

DEVELOPMENT OF A MARKETING PROGRAM

Steve Hovey, Marketing Manager at Midcron, has the job of setting up the marketing program for the division. The basis of his plan is the fastest growth of the business deemed possible in a multi-product, multi-market environment. This will result in a return on sales (ROS) roughly comparable to the company's historical performance. He also expects, through a restatement of Midcron's primary objectives and a reassessment and reclassification of its previous goals, strategies, and tactics, to provide a more focused look at the business. Further, the action plan should be clearer, and simpler and company priorities should be obvious.

Two of the products covered in the marketing program are the BA switch and the HD switch. Both are well established and mature products sold to essentially the same market segments through the same marketing channels. The BA switch is a single-break, snap-action type of switch with a broad range of applications. It is sold to manufacturers of major appliances, transpor-

tation equipment, industrial equipment, materials-handling equipment, and valve indicators. A good example of the use of a BA switch is with a fork lift truck where the switch is used to initiate different mechanical movements.

The HD switch is a heavy-duty, industrial-limit switch that can be used anywhere one has a motor control and the need to turn a motor on and off. Limit is a catchall term for an on-and-off switch for actions or current. As the name implies, the HD switch is a heavy-duty switch that holds at a particular limit of power generation. Uses of the HD switch can be found with industrial equipment, farm machinery, and metal-working machines.

Market Segments

Total sales for the BA and HD switches in 1981 were $535,000 and $175,000 respectively (Exhibit 1). The average price for the BA switch was $4.90 while the average for the HD was $5.70. The major use of the BA switch is in industrial controls. For the HD switch, automotive and transportation represents the most important segment.

Marketing Channels

Both switches are sold to the original equipment manufacturer (OEM) market and the aftermath or replacement market. The OEM purchases a switch for incorporation into the product it is building. For the typical purchaser, the function of the switch is essential to the operation of the product initiating or regulating current or action. Orders from OEMs are usually large and may cover a period of a model year or more. For example, a computer manufacturer such as IBM may buy a BA switch as a system unit switch for turning the power on or off. The term of the contract will probably run at least a year and could possibly run the product life of the particular IBM computer model.

In contrast, the aftermarket consumer purchases switches to replace any that have

Exhibit 1. 1981 Sales of BA and HD

Major Market Segments	Sales in Thousands	
	BA	HD
Industrial Controls	$ 203	$ 35
Office, Retail, Medical	107	31
Automotive & Transportation	54	75
Communications	43	7
Test Equipment	37	4
Computer & Process Control	27	2
Appliances	21	2
Aircraft & Military	—	18
Other	43	1
Totals	$ 535	$ 175
Average Price	$4.70	$5.70

failed or worn out through usage. Order size is necessarily small and the consumer will want quick delivery. Midcron, following industry practice, markets both switches directly through its own sales force as well as indirectly through sales reps and electronic wholesalers.

In both markets, about the only differentiation between sellers is in terms of quality. Midcron's experience has been that their BA and HD switches are more dependable and have a longer product life than those produced by competitors. The OEM purchaser initiates the sale, usually by asking for price information. Neither Midcron nor any of its competitors do any direct promotion of these two types of switches.

Sales and Financial Information

After Hovey analyzed the last ten years of sales for both the BA and HD switches, he came to the conclusion that both were in the maturity stage and perhaps very near the decline stage of their product life cycles (see Exhibit 2). He also noted that demand tended to be inelastic. Therefore, price increases seemed to have no effect on demand. The result of raising prices has been increased dollar sales.

The financial data provided Hovey (Exhibit 3) shows that Midcron has improved its financial position in the last four years. At the present time about sixty cents out of every dollar is spent on making the product. Another twenty cents or so goes to operating expenses. The commission paid to manufacturing reps and electronic distributors is 5 percent. This rate is more or less uniform in the industry.

Manufacturing Information

In meeting with John Jacobs, head of manufacturing for Midcron, Hovey learned that the cost of making both switches has averaged about 70 percent of the sales dollar. The reasons for the higher-than-normal cost were, in the opinion of Jacobs, the inability to get quantity discounts on materials used in the switch and the fact that small-batch production does not allow learning curve economies. Jacobs added that most of the materials used in producing the switches are not used with the other switches. Also, orders for both switches are placed on an irregular basis. Not wanting to stockpile switches, this has resulted in small-batch scheduling.

Using the information provided by manu-

Exhibit 2. Sales of BA and HD Switches

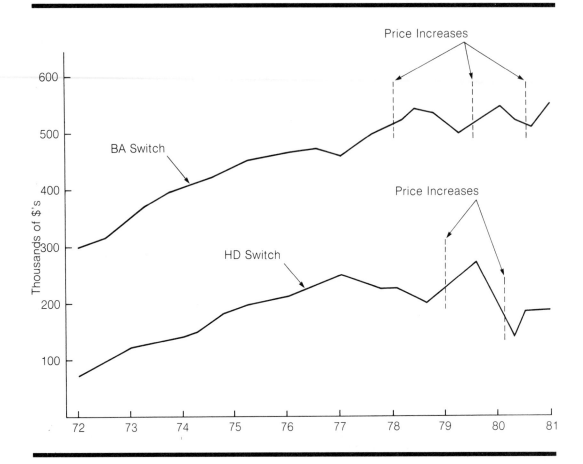

facturing, Hovey developed cost structures for the two products (see Exhibit 4).

At this point Hovey asked for a meeting with Stansky. He also asked that Jacobs be present along with Beverly Turner, Director of Marketing for the Electronics Group, and Howard McGill, National Sales Manager for Midcron.

Marketing Alternatives

At the meeting Hovey presented all the information he had assembled on the BA and HD switches. As part of his introduction, he stated that his goals for the next three to four years were to increase sales by a yearly rate of 8 percent without a parallel increase

in costs and to extend the viable product life of both switches.

Turner commented at this point that both switches are in the latter part of the maturity stage of the product life cycle, maybe in decline. She wondered how Hovey could hope to achieve sales growth from what looked like "dead horses." In replying to Turner, Hovey pointed out that Midcron had to adopt a more aggressive selling approach and work harder, particularly in the aftermath or replacement market. Hovey said he would be delighted to work with Midcron's sales people as well as their reps and distributors. He believed that advertising would also be helpful in securing more sales in both markets.

When asked his opinion by Stansky, Ja-

Exhibit 3. Financial Summary Midcron

			Revenue and Cost Figures in Thousands of $'s		
Category	*1977*	*1978*	*1979*	*1980*	*1981*
Sales	9,535	11,080	13,296	16,700	19,739
Cost of Goods Sold	5,578	6,637	7,855	9,653	11,843
Gross Profit	3,957	4,443	5,441	7,047	7,896
	41.5%	40.1%	41.0%	42.2%	40.0%
Expenses					
Marketing	1,068	1,165	1,412	1,526	1,933
Product Engineering	572	499	706	724	861
Administrative	257	313	363	365	382
Trenten Overhead	400	444	532	668	718
Product Development	315	372	397	3	252
Total	2,612	2,793	3,410	3,286	4,146
Operating Income (Before Taxes)	1,345	1,650	2,031	3,761	3,750
	14.1%	14.9%	15.3%	22.5%	19.0%
Operating Income (After Taxes)	667	809	997	1,870	1,875
	7.0%	7.3%	7.5%	11.2%	9.5%

cobs said he would opt for the phasing out of both products from the Midcron line. The only advice Beverly Turner had was that Hovey should consider some of the other strategies that offer the hope of lengthening the maturity stage, or better yet, start a new growth phase. She listed three possibilities: product modification, market modification, and marketing mix modification.

Product modification would involve redesign of the switches so that they would have a broader base of application. The only drawback here, other than engineering costs and some manufacturing changes, would be that the switches might cut into the markets for other Midcron switches. Market modification would seem more promising in that Midcron would direct itself exclusively to those segments holding forth the greatest potential for the switches. Modifying the marketing mix would be a good idea, but one that may not bring in any more sales. It would mean spending promotion dollars more effectively.

Stansky told Hovey that a plan should be finalized for presentation to Group management in three weeks. In the meantime, all those present are available to him for consultation.

Exhibit 4. Cost Structures for BA and HD Switches

	BA		*HD*	
Selling Price	$4.90		$5.85	
Manufacturing Cost	3.43		4.10	
Gross Profit	$1.47		$1.75	
Operating Cost	1.03		1.23	
Profit	$ .44	8.9% of sales	$ .52	8.88% of sales

18

RAKCO Corporation *

The RAKCO Corporation, with headquarters in Fort Wayne, Indiana, had sales in 1984 of nearly $300 million. This represented an increase of 2 percent over 1983. Profits, however, fell over 5 percent compared to two years ago. RAKCO could be called a conglomerate of parts manufacturers. In addition to the headquarters and plant in Fort Wayne, Indiana, the corporation operates eighteen plants scattered throughout the United States. Most of the expansion of RAKCO has come from buying out small manufacturers of parts or components. The corporation is made up of ten fairly autonomous manufacturing divisions. Marketing and sales are centralized, with the sales force handling all the products of the corporation. Also centralized at the Fort Wayne headquarters are finance and accounting along with R & D.

At RAKCO, a maker of a wide range of industrial components, the marketing philosophy is tied very closely to quality high-performance products priced above the market. Basic to company policy is the statement from the last annual report that superior product performance is the key to success in marketing and a major contributor to overall company growth. Indeed, the marketing philosophy is that RAKCO sells "quality functioning." At the various production facilities an extraordinary amount of time and talent is assigned the task of making sure that only parts of the highest quality are shipped to customers. Quality assurance at RAKCO is

* This case was prepared by H. Robert Dodge.

estimated to cost over $7 million a year, or more than 2 percent of sales.

A question some members of top management are raising is, "Why does any business that places so much emphasis on quality and spends a disproportionate amount of money on ensuring quality products have major problems relating specifically to quality?" In bringing this to the attention of other executives, three examples were presented in a position paper by the vice-president of operations with a view to establishing quality policies.

PROBLEM SITUATION—INLET WATER VALVES

On January 21, 1984, Jim Rice, Southwest regional sales manager, obtained a copy of the letter that had been circulated internally among members of management of the Moasby Company located in Dallas, Texas. Moasby is the biggest customer for valves from RAKCO's Turnmore Division and one of the largest consumers of valves in the market. The letter related the results of a comparison life test of the RAKCO and Monarco Company products. Monarco is the market leader in the valve industry. The results showed that RAKCO's inlet water valve had a failure rate of 30 percent, whereas the Monarco inlet water valve had a failure rate of only 7.5 percent, or some 75 percent less. This is all the more crucial in that valves from Monarco are priced about 15 percent below comparable products from RAKCO. The memo concluded by stating that in all probability RAKCO's 15 percent share of the total valves purchased by Moasby should be decreased in light of poor quality. Upon reading the memo the regional sales manager obtained samples of the failed valves from Moasby and urged the Engineering and Manufacturing Department to analyze immediately the samples of the failed valves to determine the cause of failure and suggest a program for correction.

Seven days later, on January 28, samples of the valves were received by RAKCO's Meridian, Mississippi, plant that produced the valves. With a sense of urgency, Gordon Willmark, the quality control manager, along with the quality control engineer, Elwood Barnes, went about the task of finding the cause for the failures. Since approximately 14,000 valves representing nearly $64,000 were being held up in Moasby's Receiving Inspection Department until positive identification of the problem and a corrective action plan was proposed by RAKCO, obviously, time was of the essence,

Investigation of the Problem

The first step the Quality Control Section initiated was to take the failed samples and put them through the same test that Moasby had run in order to duplicate and verify their results. In this test the failed inlet water valves are put into a life-test chamber. This chamber simulates actual field use and yields fairly conclusive data as to what the life of the product can be expected to be in actual field use. The results of the life test indicated that, indeed, a significant rate of failure was occurring. The next step was to test the inlet water valves on the final tester that is used after assembly and prior to shipment. This "leak tester" is used as a 100 percent check to see that the valves meet the customers specifications and no defective valves are shipped to a customer. The results of the leak test were negative. That is, all of the failed valves passed the leak test, indicating the leaking of liquid between the plastic molded body and the fabricated steel bracket, the most common cause of failure, was

not the cause of the failures with the valves shipped to Moasby.

Proceeding further with the investigation, members of the Quality Control Section broke down ten of the failed units to see if there were any internal problems that might be causing the failures. At this time, they uncovered a problem with the flow-control diaphragm. It seemed that the diaphragms were oversized and thus were sticking, with no pattern of regularity, in both the "on" and "off" positions. The problem was defined as either the assembly of the diaphragm into the plastic molded body or physical aspects of the diaphragm itself. With the aid of the Manufacturing and Engineering Department, the assembly of fixtures and processes related to manufacturing were reviewed. Still, no solution was apparent.

When the diaphragm itself was examined, it was found that the outside diameter was oversized and that this caused the sticking problem. Measurements of all the rejected valves indicated the presence of an oversized diaphragm. Since a review of specifications sent to the supplier showed the correct size, the next step was to contact the vendor.

RAKCO buys all of its diaphragms from the Wilkins Corporation of Fremont, Ohio. Gordon Willmark called his counterpart at Wilkins to explain the problem. He said the problem would be checked out and he would get back to Willmark the next day. Meanwhile, the plant manager for RAKCO called the regional sales manager and told him that the problem had been identified and that a course of corrective action would be forthcoming within two weeks. The regional sales manager, in turn, relayed the information to the director of quality control at Moasby.

Solution of the Problem

The next day, February 14, the quality control manager at Wilkins called and stated that they had traced the problem to the injection mold used to make the diaphragm. It seems that one of the sections of the mold was running out of specification, with the result that about one in every four parts was defective in size. The quality control manager from Wilkins said that the mold would be pulled and fixed immediately. In the meantime, RAKCO was to hold all existing diaphragms that were in stock until Wilkins could send a team over to sort through the stock. The following day, three people from Wilkins flew to the RAKCO facility and started going through the diaphragms in stock. In all, 10,000 of 55,000 parts, about 18 percent, were found to be "out-of-print" as a defect in size is called in the industry.

Customer Relations

Wayne Dastoli, regional marketing manager for RAKCO, took it upon himself to arrange a meeting with individuals from Moasby to discuss the problem. The meeting was set for February 20, a month after the firm was alerted to the possible loss of business. Dastoli, along with the quality control people from Meridian, Mississippi, went to the Moasby Company to explain what happened. Moasby was represented at the meeting by their purchasing manager and the quality control people. The purchasing manager for Moasby stated that the high level of failure for the valves has necessitated his company altering its purchasing relationship with RAKCO. Henceforth all items, including the 14,000 now on hand, must be subjected to the life test before shipment to Moasby. Any failures in those presently held in stock will be sent back to RAKCO for reworking. He added that because of this incident the vendor rating of RAKCO would be dropped from excellent to unsatisfactory and that if this unsatisfactory rating did not improve within four months the 15 percent share of valves supplied by RAKCO would be cut to 5 percent.

The total cost of retesting, reworking, and shipping was estimated by Dastoli to run about $70,000 out-of-pocket plus undetermined goodwill. Two weeks later negotiations were completed with Wilkins (1) to re-

place any out-of-print parts found in stock at the Wilkins Corporation at no cost to RAKCO; (2) to replace at no cost the 10,000 out-of-print parts in stock at RAKCO; and (3) to pay 50 percent of the rework costs associated with failed units returned to RAKCO by Moasby. In addition, the purchasing manager at RAKCO made it clear that until the problem was solved, the incoming inspection of Wilkins' parts would be beefed-up and Wilkins must make significant improvements over the next six months. As for RAKCO, policies were modified and the sampling of valves that are subjected to the life test was increased to 50 percent.

PROBLEM SITUATION—DRAIN VALVE

Another quality problem of serious marketing proportions involved noise with a drain valve RAKCO sold to the Haleck Corporation. Total sales to Haleck amounted to $500,000 last year, making them one of the firm's largest customers. The problem originated in October of 1983. On October 18, the RAKCO sales representative, Tom Porter, calling on the Haleck Corporation, was given rejected samples of drain valves shipped to them by RAKCO and was told that approximately 30,000 valves were being held in rejection until the cause of the failures was identified and corrective action instituted. Porter took ten samples of the valve to the Division Engineering Department for analysis and also sent ten samples to the plant where they were made in Lima, Ohio.

Solution of the Problem

On October 20, a design engineer assigned to drain valves wrote a memo that was sent to Peter Kaegel, regional marketing manager for the Northeastern part of the country, to Porter, and to Neil Broden, manager of the plant making the valves. The memo stated that when the drain valves were tested with water at thirty to forty pounds per square inch, which is the flow pressure the product is meant to operate at, a high-pitched flow noise was indeed emitted. The design engineer added that inspection of the noise diffuser for each valve revealed a degraded diffuser. Inspection also showed a slurry-like material packed solidly around the noise diffusers. When the slurry-like substance dried, it turned out to be fine, metal-like particles. The particles were then tested and found to be a magnetic concentration of iron and iron oxide particles. When the engineer replaced the noise diffusers and tested the drain valves, the noise problem was no longer evident. It was the test engineer's conclusion that the noise diffusers with the slurry-like material were incapable of handling the contaminated water that the Haleck Corporation personnel used in their testing facility. The engineer stated that the contaminated water is not typical of actual field use and competitors' valves would probably react the same way if subjected to the same conditions.

Steve Paluski, the quality control manager at the Lima manufacturing facility, stated that he thought that someone should be sent to Haleck's facility to explain why they were experiencing the problems with the drain valves. On the first of November, Porter, who regularly calls on Haleck, attended a meeting with their purchasing and quality control people. At the meeting the results of RAKCO's engineering analysis were reported. The director of purchasing, Miles Dotson, responded to the analysis by stating that the contaminated water was used purposely to simulate conditions in rural areas where filtered water was not always available. He also said that it was up to RAKCO to upgrade the noise diffusers to meet Haleck's quality standards.

On November 3, Porter reported the results of the meeting with Haleck to Marketing and Engineering. The director of engineering immediately assigned two design engineers to the problem. The plan they came up with was to use a higher grade of plastic in the valve body which would not break down into iron oxide. On January 21, with Haleck personnel from the home office in attendance, a pilot run was scheduled to inspect the new higher grade parts being used in the drain valve. On January 15, six days prior to the test, a memo was sent to Broden, the plant manager at Lima, Ohio, where the pilot run was to take place. In it the national marketing director, Walter Swenson, issued a warning that the pilot run must succeed. First-hand information had been received that the quality control director from Haleck was furious with the purchasing director for releasing future production schedules showing approximately one-half of the drain valve business going to RAKCO. The quality control director thought this was poor business when 30,000 valves from RAKCO had been rejected. Swenson emphasized in his memo to Broden that everything at the pilot run must be pretested in order to prevent RAKCO from losing the Haleck account.

On January 21, the pilot run was held as scheduled. Twenty-five valves were built and tested. The testing procedure consisted of operating the valves at 50, 75, 100, and 150 pounds of pressure per square inch. The valves operated with no discernible noise. After the successful pilot run, it was obvious that higher grade materials should be incorporated by RAKCO into the assembly specifications. Porter indicated to representatives from Haleck that he would present the solution to the director of engineering within the next couple of days. Representatives from Haleck seemed satisfied, and their spokesman stated that as soon as agreement was reached with the engineering director, they would release the 30,000 valves. However, he stipulated that RAKCO must send over two quality control people to sort the good valves from bad and that RAKCO must take cost responsibility for 50 percent of the rework on the rejected valves. RAKCO agreed to these stipulations. Forty percent of the valves were found to have the noise problem, and the total cost to RAKCO came to about $75,000.

The Quality Control Department initiated an engineering change authorization form which modified the specifications to include the higher grade material at a cost of fifteen cents per thousand units. The Engineering and Marketing departments signed off on the engineering change notice and everything seemed to be in order.

Further Complications

Three months later, Peter Boorstein, the general manager of Haleck, called Vaughan Askew, the vice-president of marketing for RAKCO, to say that two different, but essentially similar, problems had arisen in actual customer use of products with valves from RAKCO. The first instance involved a housewife in Troy, Ohio, who complained about her dishwasher making funny noises. The other involved the wife of one of their own employees in Mt. Sterling, Kentucky, who had a complaint about her dishwasher not sounding right. A very direct and terse comment was sent to the vice-president of marketing for RAKCO from the quality control director of Haleck stating that the noise problem must be solved immediately or RAKCO would be cut off completely as a supplier. Acting quickly, Askew brought the problem to the attention of the division president, the vice-president and general manager, the director of engineering, and the director of quality control. He directed that the two field returns be sent to R & D at headquarters for analysis. Here it was ascertained that, although each valve was using the upgraded material in the noise diffuser, the diffusers were put in backwards and thus were not able to do the job properly. This very small, human error almost led to the cancellation of $500,000 in annual sales for RAKCO because their credibility regarding quality control was in serious doubt due to the sensitivity of a customer brought about by an earlier related problem.

PROBLEM SITUATION—GARAGE DOOR OPENER

A third problem involving quality concerned RAKCO's relationship with United Products. The product in question was an electromechanical garage door opener control. The problem first surfaced in February of 1984 when several thousand assemblies arrived at the customer's receiving dock and were marked unusable upon inspection. What was wrong was that the bracket which connects the electrical coil with the mechanical control parts was bent. The bent bracket was quickly diagnosed to have been damaged by shipping. It appeared that during transit the parts were jostled enough to ruin the assemblies. The quality control manager for United Products advised his plant manager of the problem and then proceeded to call the quality control manager, Mike Plummer, at RAKCO's Logan, Utah, plant. The problem was explained and Plummer assured him that he would look into the problem. Plummer then relayed the information to the facilities plant manager and to the sales representative who was assigned to United Products.

Description of the Problem

On March 21, Gerald Ludwig, the plant manager at Logan, wrote a memo asking the Engineering Department for a complete and detailed examination of the packaging material used in packing the garage door opener controls. Ludwig suggested that a thin layer of cardboard be inserted between layers instead of putting each layer on top of the previous layer with no protection for the bottom layers. In the meantime, the quantity received by United Products, 23,640 units in all, was held up pending reject responsibility assignment and adequate disposition. In the meantime, Plummer and Will Coluci, the sales representative responsible for United Products, flew to the customer's facility to examine the damaged parts. Upon arrival the quality control manager inspected the units on a per carton basis using one unit per layer as representative sample. The quality control manager inspected 236 cartons each containing 100 units and found 16 percent of the units damaged beyond reasonable limits.

It was agreed that the damaged units would be reworked and reshipped at no charge to the customer. Representatives from United Products requested that RAKCO give serious consideration to using a polyfoam material in future packaging of the garage door opener controls. It was noted that RAKCO's main competitor for United Products' business was already using this polyfoam material with outstanding results. Coluci said that a feasibility study would be initiated at once regarding this matter.

Back at RAKCO headquarters in Fort Wayne, Coluci set up a meeting with Engineering to discuss the packaging problem. Answers were sought for such questions as why the controls were being bent, how they were being bent, and the cost of polyfoam material versus present packaging methods as well as the critical effect on customer satisfaction. At the meeting it was noted that the current price per unit was $2.75. It was estimated that Johnson Controls, RAKCO's major competitor, was selling its product at about $2.72 per unit. There was, therefore, at least some per unit price margin to play with in the solution of the problem since United rated RAKCO as having superior quality. Ed Williams, the chief design engineer, said that one possible idea to be explored was a one-quarter-inch diameter hole in the bracket that may lessen the strength of the upper part of the bracket. This idea came from specifications on the print drawings for another customer. Upon research of the other customer's specifications it was noted that RAKCO could use the same punching and forming die for both customers. Thus, there would be no increase in tooling costs and, in fact, a possible savings from one less operation.

Another idea that was brought up for discussion was the allowable deviation on the print of plus or minus two degrees pitch on the upper plate of the bracket. If the pitch was eighty-eight degrees instead of a true ninety degrees as the customer required,

then it might be assumed that even slight jostling of an eighty-eight degree pitch bracket would bring the bracket out of specifications and prone to a higher rejection rate than would otherwise be normal. Also, it was decided to obtain quotes from several manufacturers of polyfoam packaging material to determine the economic feasibility of using that type of material for the packaging of the garage door opener.

Solution of the Problem

The consensus of those present for the meeting was that the bent bracket problem was not, as first thought, solely related to packaging and shipping. Regardless, the amount of customer dissatisfaction dictated a quick solution to the problem. The first consideration investigated was the punched hole theory. The die used for production was pulled and the part used to punch the upper hole on the bracket was removed and fifty sample units were run. The fifty units then were taken by a quality control technician who used a manually controlled pressure device to measure the strength of the fifty test units compared to the present design. The results of the test did indeed indicate that the unpunched brackets were considerably more sturdy than the punched brackets. The amount of the difference was significant (about 25 percent in total). The results of the test were documented and sent on to Ludwig, Plummer, and Coluci.

The next consideration reviewed was the degree of pitch allowed on the print. Coluci and Pete Domenici, the chief design engineer, came to the plant to discuss the pitch problem with Ludwig, the manufacturing engineering manager and the production superintendent. Coluci asked the plant representatives their opinion of the feasibility of reducing the specifications on the print from plus or minus two degrees to plus or minus one degree. The plant superintendent said that the steel presently on hand was being bought at plus or minus fifteen thousandths of an inch, a fairly low quality steel. In order to change the pitch specifications on the print, the steel used for the bracket must be upgraded. After explaining the problem, the manufacturing engineering manager agreed that the steel must be upgraded to plus or minus seven thousandths of an inch. The engineering manager admitted that he didn't know how much of a price increase was involved, but that the purchasing agent responsible for steel buying would certainly know. The plant superintendent was of the opinion that with steel of plus or minus seven thousandths of an inch tolerance, manufacturing could hold to plus or minus one degree with a better than average confidence level. A slight upgrading in the die would have to take place, but this would be a minor cost.

With this information, Coluci contacted the purchasing agent in charge of buying steel and asked him the price difference for steel of plus or minus seven thousandths of an inch compared with the present steel requirements. The purchasing agent said the difference was roughly fifty dollars per roll. Next, Coluci called the cost accounting department to see what the difference of fifty dollars per roll would translate into per unit. The cost accounting manager stated that the difference would be about one and a half cents per unit. With the gross margin being about 22 percent, Coluci concluded that the price difference between the two steel grades was minor compared to the possibility of losing a large part of the garage door opener business to the competition. With the director of engineering's concurrence, Coluci talked to the purchasing agent about getting samples of this higher grade steel so that sample pieces could be fabricated for evaluation before a final decision was made. The purchasing agent said that the samples would be delivered to sales in about four days.

Customer Relations

The final consideration centered on customer satisfaction. It was noted that United Prod-

ucts did about $3.5 million worth of business yearly with RAKCO in three different product lines. The least significant product was the overhead garage door control. It was agreed by everyone that the customer was entitled to good quality products, and, since United Products' business was growing at a rapid rate, RAKCO should do everything in its power to please United Products by solving the bent bracket problem. The discussion adjourned to await the results of samples using the higher grade steel.

Meanwhile, at the RAKCO's manufacturing facility in Logan, Utah, the die used in making the bracket for United Products was moved from the production area to the tool-and-die room for modification. Since the die was progressive (multistaged) it was rather a minor job to remove one of the stages and modify it to the specifications for United Products. The die was taken back to the production area to await the arrival of the upgraded steel. Three days later, the sales engineer from the supplying steel company delivered a twenty-foot piece of steel with a tolerance level of seven thousandths of an inch. The quality control manager, production superintendent, and manager of plant engineering went out to the production area and ran the twenty-foot piece of steel through the press. The pieces fabricated were then taken to the quality control lab for measurement. The pitch in the pieces varied from plus .48 degrees to minus .89 degrees. This meant that the criterion of plus or minus one degree could indeed be met with the upgraded steel.

The results of the test run were made known to the plant manager who in turn called Coluci. Then Coluci called the engineering manager and formally requested that an engineering change notice be processed to indicate that the steel required for the bracket for United Products' garage door opener be plus or minus seven thousandths of an inch tolerance, the degree of pitch allowed be changed from plus or minus two degrees to plus or minus one degree, and that the print specify the removal of a punched hole for United Products. The engineering manager agreed and said he would get the change process started immediately.

Meanwhile, the purchasing agent for RAKCO was contacting several manufacturers of polyfoam material to get samples and cost estimates. The purchasing agent set up appointments with four different vendors. The manufacturing engineer manager and the divisional quality control manager were invited to the sales presentation. The purchasing agent stated at the start of each meeting with the various vendors that a three-foot-by-three-foot polyfoam sheet was needed and that three layers of sheets per box would be used. The first consideration was whether the vendor could supply three-by-three plies and what was the difference in price between individually cut pieces and rolls of three-feet-wide foam material. Out of the four vendors, two were able to meet the three-by-three requirement, and the cost was relatively close at thirty-one cents and thirty-four cents per unit respectively. Both vendors were instructed to send fifty-piece samples for evaluation.

The samples, when received, were tested for practicality and application of the foam material. The material was cut into three-by-three sheets and inserted in the bottom and top layers and between the three layers of product in a box containing 150 pieces with 50 pieces per layer. Both vendor's samples did this job adequately. The boxes were dropped from a height of ten feet to study the sturdiness of the foam material. The

higher priced material seemed to be the better of the two, although both samples were indeed an improvement over the present system. The engineering manager wrote a report to the purchasing agent that indicated the higher priced sample did the better job. The purchasing agent then contacted the vendor and contracted to buy one year's supply of their foam material per sample standards. The vendor was given three weeks lead time for the initial order of 750 pieces. The purchasing agent then contacted the divisional engineering manager and the cost accounting manager to tell them of the changes. The engineering manager stated that the engineering change would be initiated to modify the prints. The cost accounting manager said that he would put through a costing change to reflect the extra cost of foam material.

When told of the developments, Coluci decided that it was time to contact the customer on the various changes that had taken place to correct the bent bracket problem. A meeting was set up at United Products' manufacturing facility the following week. At the meeting Coluci told United Products management of the changes: polyfoam material would be used to package the parts; a higher grade steel would be used for the bracket; and the bracket would have additional strength because of the absence of an unnecessary hole in the bracket. United Products' reaction to these changes was extremely positive and the previous customer relationship was restored.

Four

Price

FASHION–PLUS CLOTHING COMPANY

FIRST NATIONAL BANK OF FERNWOOD

BIG SKY OF MONTANA, INC.

19

Fashion-Plus Clothing Company *

The Fashion-Plus Clothing Company (FPCC) is a large, well-known, national manufacturer of high-quality fashion clothing. FPCC produces a wide line of clothing for both men and women. Industry sources agree that FPCC has a fine reputation as a leader in the fashion clothing industry.

FPCC has just developed the plans for a new line of Hawaiian beachware. These high-quality, stylish shirts are made from a new type of fabric that will resist fading with repeated washing. Company officials agree that the quality of the new line of Fashion-Plus shirts compares favorably with the offerings of other clothing manufacturers.

FPCC is considering distributing the line of shirts through a variety of retail outlets. For example, FPCC sponsors a national franchise system of retail clothing stores called "Dude's Duds." These stores will carry the new line of Hawaiian beach shirts under the Fashion-Plus label. Also, FPCC plans to approach several hundred independent retail clothing stores concerning their adoption of the new line of shirts. FPCC plans on offering large independent retailers an opportunity to buy the shirts under their own private labels. If a retailer does not select this option, the shirts could be sold to the store under the Fashion-Plus label. Other distribution channels are also being investigated.

* This case was developed by Jon M. Hawes, the University of Akron. Used by permission.

Several of FPCC's competitors have recently introduced similar lines of clothing. Market research has found that the shirts were selling at retail stores for the following prices:

Retail Selling Price	Number of Times Observed
$14.00	2
$15.00	7
$16.00	5
$17.00	3

FPCC is trying to determine what price it should charge for its shirts. They realize that most men's clothing stores apply about a 40% initial markup on the retail selling price of their goods.

FPCC also knows approximately how much it costs to produce the new shirts. The data are shown below:

Cloth	$2.20	per shirt
Buttons	.05	per shirt
Thread	.05	per shirt
Direct labor	20	minutes per shirt
Shipping weight	2	pounds per packaged shirt

FPCC also knows that it will incur a basic marketing cost of about $300,000 the first year in order to introduce the new line of shirts if a penetration-type pricing policy is used. They would incur a basic marketing cost of $340,000 if a skimming-type policy is employed.

Being a large company, FPCC has fifteen production facilities strategically located throughout the U.S. Last year, the average round trip distance from the FPCC production facility to the purchaser of FPCC goods was 225 miles. FPCC plans to produce and distribute its new line of shirts at each of its fifteen facilities.

FPCC is traded on the NYSE. The annual report for last year showed that FPCC incurred the following:

Managerial salaries	$ 1,500,000
Rent and utilities expense	1,200,000
Transportation costs (1,250,000 miles)	750,000
Depreciation on plant and equipment	1,300,000
Other overhead	2,000,000
Direct labor costs (2,000,000 hours)	8,000,000
Total company sales	$45,000,000
Average order size	1,000 pounds

Fashion-Plus has hired the Kurt Behrens Market Research Corporation to develop a sales forecast for the new line of shirts. Behrens' company has an outstanding reputation for its work in the field of new product sales forecasting. Mr. Behrens has become personally involved in the project. His research showed that if a skimming-type pricing policy were used, Fashion-Plus could expect to sell approximately 110,000 to 130,000 shirts. Behrens predicts that if a penetration-type pricing policy is employed, FPCC could expect to sell approximately 130,000 to 150,000 shirts.

Assume that Bill Morris was unexpectedly called out of town and he has asked you to prepare the analysis and written report on the feasibility of the project and then to make a recommendation for the pricing strategy he should use. At a minimum, your analysis should include a cost analysis (variable cost per shirt, fixed cost allocation for the line, and total cost per shirt), a break-even analysis in units and dollars, a determination of the manufacturer's price and suggested retail price, and a statement as to expected profit the company can derive from the new line.

20

First National Bank of
Fernwood *

Since assuming the presidency of First National three years ago, Steve Myers has instituted an aggressive marketing program entitled "First Deal." The program, the major
benefits of which are summarized in Exhibit
1, has met with overwhelming success by
attracting and holding retail customers. Myers reported to the Board of Directors at their
regular monthly meeting in August 1982 on
the success of the program. Some of the ex-
cerpts from this report are as follows:

When you talk about banking in Fernwood we
must keep in mind that we are competing with
the banks in downtown Chicago that have national and international reputations. While we
have two fairly large manufacturing plants located within our borders, the substantial part of our
population of approximately 50,000 is made up of
families where one or perhaps two members work
in other parts of the Chicago area. . . . Since May
of 1979 when we started "First Deal," a total of
950 new customers have been added and 1,500
existing customers have converted to the new
program. At the present time we have 2,450
"First-Deal" customers compared to a total of
1,810 individual checking account customers in
1979 when the program started.

At the conclusion of his presentation, Myers asked for questions. Paul Zimmer, chairman of the board, stated that while we have
grown in checking account customers, we
have done it by "giving away the store."
Earnings have dropped by over 40 percent
and we have had to add to our staff and buy

* This case was prepared by H. Robert Dodge.

a new computer. Mark Bokesch, another director, asked whether it was possible to
make cutbacks and still retain a substantial
number of customers.

Sensing that the mood of the board was to
increase income from the First-Deal program, Myers made the motion that an analysis be made of First-Deal customers with the
view toward increasing net income return.
The motion was seconded, and it was unani-
mously passed to proceed with the investigation.

ANALYSIS OF FIRST–DEAL
CUSTOMERS

To find out what kind of customer has been
attracted by the First-Deal program, Myers
assigned Mark Pollard, vice-president of administrative services, the job of analyzing
the accounts of First-Deal customers. Myers
thought it best to start the project by classi-
fying First-Deal customers in terms of account size (average checking account balance) for the last six months (see Exhibit 2).
From this he was able to conclude the following:

1. Most of the First-Deal customers have
   small average balances. Approximately
   six out of every ten First-Deal customers
   (1,445 out of 2,450) have an average balance of less than $400. The average in-
   vestable balance (amount of money bank
   management expects to be available from

153

Exhibit 1. First-Deal Package

No monthly service charge on checking account
Free checks
Free checkbook balancing
MasterCard with no annual fee
No service charge on cashiers checks, money orders, or drafts
Substantially reduced safe deposit box fees
Cash Reserve—automatic transfer from savings to checking ($200 minimum)

this type of account for other uses) is $220.

2. Sixteen percent, or 392 customers, have an average balance between $400 and $600. The average investable balance is $412.

3. Fourteen percent, or 343 customers, have an average balance between $600 and $1,000 with an investable balance of $634.

4. Eleven percent, or 270 customers, have an average balance of $1,000 or more and an investable balance of $1,305.

Pollard, when discussing with Myers, what he had uncovered in this preliminary analysis' expressed the opinion that the basic problem rested with those customers having less than a $400 average balance in their respective checking accounts. It appeared that the majority of customers attracted by First Deal were far from keeping enough money in their account. To further the study, Myers

and Pollard reached agreement on several assumptions regarding the generation of income:

1. We can earn 7 percent on investable collected checking account balances.

2. We can earn 2 percent on savings accounts over the rate that we are paying the customer.

3. We can earn a profit of 1 percent on installment loans.

4. We can earn 1 percent per month on MasterCard balances.

5. We can earn 1 percent per month on Cash Reserve balances.

6. We can expect a savings account to average $125.

7. We can expect an installment loan to have a balance of $1,000 and be spread out over a three-year payback period.

Exhibit 2. Classification of First-Deal Accounts

	Average Balance			
Number	Under $400	$400 to $600	$600 to $1,000	$1,000 or More
Checking Accounts	1,445	392	343	270
Savings Accounts	924	276	264	208
Loans	462	137	144	113
MasterCard Accounts	1,113	290	298	235
Cash Reserve Accounts	925	176	154	122

8. We can expect an active MasterCard account to have an average balance of $200.

9. We can expect an active Cash Reserve account to have an average balance of $250.

Reviewing the information contained in Exhibit 3 before meeting again with Myers and the board of directors, Pollard concluded that something had to be done about the large number of customer balances below $400. He figured that if those accounts below $400 returned the same gain per account as those between $400 and $600, the increase in monthly profits would be $4,092, or about 91 percent. Even more staggering would be the elevation of all those accounts below $600 to the return for those between $600 and $1,000. Such a result would increase monthly profits from $4,503 to $15,064, or more than three times the profit.

PROPOSED CHANGES IN FIRST DEAL PACKAGE

After presentation of the Pollard report, the board, speaking almost as one voice, felt that some sort of charge must be applied to First-Deal customers with average balances below $400. A substantial number of board members felt that some sort of fee should also be applied to those with balances between $400 and $600. It was decided that a special meeting would be held in two weeks, on September 28. At this meeting Pollard was to have as much additional information as was possible ready for the board to use in making its decision on membership fees for First Deal.

In preparation for the board meeting, Pollard surveyed First-Deal customers and developed the information contained in Exhibits 4 and 5. He concluded that there was little difference between the four classifications in the use of services of the bank. The one big difference was in terms of investable bal-

Exhibit 3. Computation of Potential Income From First-Deal Customers, Monthly Basis

	Average Balance			
Source Revenue	Under $400	$400 to $600	$600 to $1,000	$1,000 or More
Investable Balance—Checking	$1,855	$ 942	$1,269	$2,056
Savings Account	193	145	330	520
Loans	1,540	457	460	942
MasterCard	2,226	580	596	470
Cash Reserve	2,313	440	385	305
Total Revenue	$8,127	$2,564	$3,540	$4,293
Costs				
Checking Account	$6,127	$ 899	$1,201	$1,260
Savings Account	101	58	113	140
Loan	385	120	120	201
MasterCard	1,010	315	381	213
Cash Reserve	925	176	154	122
Total Costs	$8,548	$1,568	$1,969	$1,936
Net Income	($421)	$996	$1,571	$2,357
Net Income/Account	($.29)	$2.54	$4.58	$8.73

ance. About nine out of every ten will utilize at least three services while about six out of every ten will utilize at least four services. The service with the greatest utilization is MasterCard.

In summarizing the situation to Myers, he said that he would like to affix a fee that would allow the bank to balance the loss of customers with increased profits from those remaining. With the help of Myers, he proposed several alternatives. The first was to charge a flat fee of $3.00 for accounts below $400. The second was a flat fee of $2.00 for accounts below $600. His third alternative was a charge of fifteen cents a check for accounts below $400 and ten cents a check for accounts from $400 to $600.

Additionally, he made the assumptions shown in Exhibit 6 regarding the loss of customers and customers moving up to the next higher category in average balance. While he felt that there would be some differences between the alternatives, he thought the differences would be slight.

Exhibit 4. Utilization of First-Deal Package

	Average			Percent Active Utilization					
Average 6 mo. Balance	Investable Balance	Number Checks	Number Deposits	Cash Reserve	Master-Card	Loan	Savings	C.D.	Safe Deposit Box
Under $400	$220	22	3.7	64	77	32	64	12	32
$400 to $600	412	28	3.6	58	84	42	74	12	19
$600 to $1,000	634	26	3.6	45	74	35	68	16	26
$1,000 or more	1,385	23	3.2	45	87	42	77	16	35

Exhibit 5. Number of Services Utilized by First-Deal Customers

6 mo. Average Balance	One *	Two	Three	Four	Five	Six
Less than $400	—	6	32	26	23	13
$400 to 600	—	13	26	19	29	13
$600 to 1,000	—	6	32	36	19	7
$1,000 or more	2	7	16	29	39	7

* Checking account utilization only.

Exhibit 6. Probability of Events Given an Alternative

	Loss of Customers Alternative			Customers Increasing Balance Alternative		
Description of Situation	1st	2nd	3rd	1st	2nd	3rd
Worst case (10%)	50%	45%	50%	0%	4%	2%
Less than normal (20%)	40	38	45	5	6	4
Normal expectation (40%)	30	34	40	8	10	8
More than normal (20%)	20	30	35	10	15	12
Optimistic (10%)	15	25	25	20	20	15

21

Big Sky of Montana, Inc.*

Karen Tracy could feel the pressure on her as she sat at her desk late that April afternoon. Two weeks from today she would be called on to present her recommendations concerning next year's winter-season pricing policies for Big Sky of Montana, Inc.—room rates for the resort's accommodation facilities as well as decisions in the skiing and food service areas. The presentation would be made to a top management team from the parent company, Boyne USA, which operated out of Michigan.

"As sales and public relations manager, Karen, your accuracy in decision making is extremely important," her boss had said in his usual tone. "Because we spend most of our time in Michigan, we'll need a well-based and involved opinion."

It'll be the shortest two weeks of my life, she thought.

BACKGROUND: BIG SKY AND BOYNE USA

Big Sky of Montana, Inc. was a medium-sized destination resort located in southwestern Montana, forty-five miles south of Bozeman and forty-three miles north of the west entrance to Yellowstone National Park.[1] Big Sky was conceived in the early 1970s and had begun operation in November 1974.

* This case was written by Anne Senausky and Professor James E. Nelson, University of Colorado at Denver. Copyright © 1978 by the Endowment and Research Foundation at Montana State University.

[1] Destination resorts are characterized by on-the-hill lodging and eating facilities, a national market, and national advertising.

The 11,000-acre, 2,000-bed resort was separated into two main areas: Meadow Village and Mountain Village. Meadow Village (elevation 6,300 feet) was located two miles east of the resort's main entrance on U.S. 191 and seven miles from the ski area. Meadow Village had an 800-bed capacity in the form of four condominium complexes (ranging from studios to three-bedroom units) and a forty-room hostel for economy lodging. Additional facilities included an eighteen-hole golf course, six tennis courts, a restaurant, post office, a convention center with meeting space for up to 200 people, and a small lodge serving as a pro shop for the golf course in the summer and for cross-country skiing in the winter.

Mountain Village (elevation 7,500 feet), located at the base of the ski area was the center of winter activity. In this complex was the 204-room Huntley Lodge offering hotel accommodations, three condominium complexes (unit size ranged from studio to three-bedroom), and an 88-room hostel for a total of 1,200 beds. The Mountain Mall was also located here, next to Huntley Lodge and within a five-minute walk of two of the three condominium complexes in Mountain Village. It housed ticket sales, an equipment rental shop, a skiers' cafeteria, two large meeting rooms for a maximum of 700 persons (regularly used as sack lunch areas for skiers), two offices, a ski school desk, and a ski patrol room—all of which were operated by Boyne. Also in this building were a delicatessen, drug store/gift shop, sporting goods store/rental shop, restaurant, outdoor-clothing store, jewelry shop, T-shirt shop,

157

two bars, and a child day-care center. Each of these independent operations held leases, due to expire in one to three years.

The closest airport to Big Sky was located just outside Bozeman. It was served by Northwest Orient and Frontier Airlines with connections to other major airlines out of Denver and Salt Lake City. Greyhound and Amtrak also operated bus and train service into Bozeman. Yellowstone Park Lines provided Big Sky with three buses daily to and from the airport and Bozeman bus station (cost was $4.40 one way, $8.40 round trip), as well as an hourly shuttle around the two Big Sky villages. Avis, Hertz, National, and Budget offered car-rental service in Bozeman with a drop-off service available at Big Sky.

In July 1976 Boyne USA, a privately owned, Michigan-based operation purchased Huntley Lodge, Mountain Mall, the ski lifts and terrain, the golf course, and the tennis courts for approximately $8 million. The company subsequently invested an additional $3 million in Big Sky. Boyne also owned and operated four Michigan ski resorts.

Big Sky's top management consisted of a lodge manager (in charge of operations within Huntley Lodge), a sales and public relations manager (Karen), a food and beverage manager, and an area manager (overseeing operations external to the lodge, including the mall and all recreational facilities). These four positions were occupied by persons trained with the parent company; a fifth manager, the comptroller, had worked for pre-Boyne ownership.

Business figures were reported to the company's home office on a daily basis, and major decisions concerning Big Sky operations were discussed and approved by "Michigan." Boyne's top management visited Big Sky an average of five times annually, and all major decisions, such as pricing and advertising, were approved by the parent company for all operations.

THE SKIING

Big Sky's winter season usually began in late November and continued until the middle of April, with a yearly snowfall of approximately 450 inches. The area had eighteen slopes between elevations of 7,500 and 9,900 feet. Terrain breakdown was as follows: 25 percent novice, 55 percent intermediate, and 20 percent advanced. (Although opinions varied, industry guidelines recommended a terrain breakdown of 20 percent, 60 percent, and 20 percent for novice, intermediate, and advanced skiers, respectively.) The longest run was approximately three miles in length; temperatures (highs) ranged from 15 to 30 degrees Fahrenheit throughout the season.

Lift facilities at Big Sky included two double chairlifts, a triple chair, and a four-passenger gondola. Lift capacity was estimated at 4,000 skiers per day. This figure was considered adequate by the area manager, at least until the 1980–81 season.

Karen felt that the facilities, snow conditions, and grooming compared favorably with those of other destination resorts of the Rockies. "In fact, our only real drawback right now," she thought, "is our position in the national market. We need more skiers who are sold on Big Sky. And that is in the making."

THE CONSUMERS

Karen knew from previous dealings that Big Sky, like most destination areas, attracted three distinct skier segments: local day skiers (living within driving distance and not utilizing lodging in the area); individual destination skiers (living out of state and using accommodations in the Big Sky area); and groups of destination skiers (clubs, professional organizations, and so on).

The first category was typically comprised of Montana residents, with a relatively small number from Wyoming and Idaho. (Distances from selected population centers to Big Sky appear in Exhibit 1.) A 1973 study of four Montana ski areas, performed by the advertising unit of the Montana Department

Exhibit 1. Distances From Selected Population Centers to Big Sky

Population centers in proximity to Big Sky (distance and population)

City	Distance from Big Sky (miles)	Population (U.S. 1970 Census)
Bozeman, Montana	45	18,670
Butte, Montana	126	23,368
Helena, Montana	144	22,730
Billings, Montana	174	61,581
Great Falls, Montana	225	60,091
Missoula, Montana	243	29,497
Pocatello, Idaho	186	40,036
Idaho Falls, Idaho	148	35,776

Approximate distance of selected major U.S. population centers to Big Sky (in air miles)

City	Distance to Big Sky*
Chicago	1275
Minneapolis	975
Fargo	750
Salt Lake City	375
Dallas	1500
Houston	1725
Los Angeles	975
San Francisco	925
New York	2025
Atlanta	1950
New Orleans	1750
Denver	750

* Per-passenger air fare can be approximated at 20 cents per mile (round trip, coach rates).

of Highways, characterized Montana skiers as:

1. In their early twenties and male (60 percent),
2. Living within seventy-five miles of a ski area,
3. From a household with two skiers in it,
4. Averaging $13,000 in household income,
5. An intermediate- to advanced-ability skier,
6. Skiing five hours per ski day, twenty days per season locally,
7. Skiing four days away from local areas,
8. Taking no lessons in the past five years.

Karen was also aware that a significant number of day skiers, particularly on the weekends, were college students.

Destination, or nonresident skiers, were labeled in the same study as typically:

1. At least in their mid-twenties and male (55 percent),
2. Living in a household of three or more skiers,

3. Averaging near $19,000 in household income,

4. More likely to be an intermediate skier,

5. Spending about six hours per day skiing,

6. Skiing eleven to fourteen days per season with three to eight days away from home,

7. Taking ski school lessons.

Through data taken from reservation records, Karen learned that individual destination skiers accounted for half of last year's usage based on skier days.[2] Geographic segments were approximately as follows:

Upper Midwest (Minnesota, Michigan, North Dakota)	30%
Florida	20%
California	17%
Washington, Oregon, Montana	15%
Texas, Oklahoma	8%
Other	10%

Reservation records indicated that the average length of stay for individual destination skiers was six to seven days.

The individual destination skier was most likely to buy a lodging/lift package; 30 percent made commitments for these advertised packages when making reservations for 1977–78. Even though there was no discount involved in this manner of buying lift tickets, Karen knew that it was fairly popular because it saved the purchaser a trip to the ticket window every morning. Approximately half of the individual business came through travel agents, who received a 10 percent commission.

The third skier segment, the destination group, accounted for a substantial 20 percent of Big Sky's skier-day usage. The larger portion of the group business came through medical and other professional organizations that held meetings at the resort, as this was a way to combine business with pleasure. These groups were typically comprised of couples and individuals between the ages of thirty and fifty. Ski clubs made up the remainder, with a number coming from Flori-

[2] A skier day is defined as one skier using the facility for any part of one day of operation.

da, Texas, and Georgia. During the 1977–78 season, Big Sky drew thirty ski clubs with membership averaging fifty-five skiers. The average length of stay for all group destination skiers was about four to five days.

A portion of these group bookings were made through travel agents but the majority were made directly with Karen. The coordinator of the professional meetings or the president of the ski club typically contacted the Big Sky sales office to make initial reservation dates, negotiate prices, and work out the details of the stay.

THE COMPETITION

In Karen's mind, Big Sky faced two types of competition, that for local day skiers and that for out-of-state (i.e., destination) skiers.

Bridger Bowl was virtually the only area competing for local day skiers. Bridger was a "no-frills," nonprofit, smaller ski area located some sixteen miles northeast of Bozeman. It received the majority of local skiers, including students at Montana State University, which is located in Bozeman. The area was labeled as having terrain more difficult than that of Big Sky and thus was more appealing to the local expert skiers. However, it also had much longer lift lines and had recently lost some of its weekend business to Big Sky.

Karen had found through experience that most Bridger skiers usually "tried" Big Sky once or twice a season. Season passes for the two areas were mutually honored (by charging the half-day rate for an all-day ticket), and Big Sky occasionally ran newspaper ads offering discounts on lifts to obtain more Bozeman business.

Big Sky considered its competition for out-of-state skiers to be mainly the destination resorts of Colorado, Utah, and Wyoming. (Selected data on competing resorts appear in Exhibit 2.) Because Big Sky was smaller and newer than the majority of these areas, Karen reasoned, it was necessary to follow an aggressive strategy aimed at increasing its national market share.

Exhibit 2. Competitors' 1977–78 Package Plan Rates,[1] Number of Lifts, and Lift Rates

	Lodge double (2) [2]	Two-bedroom condo (4)	Three-bedroom condo (6)	Number of lifts	Daily lift rates
Aspen, CO	$242	$242	$220	19	$13
Steamboat, CO	230	230	198	15	12
Jackson, WY	230	242	210	5	14
Vail, CO	230	242	220	15	14
Snowbird, UT	208	none	none	6	11
Bridger Bowl, MT	(no lodging available at Bridger Bowl)				

[1] Package plan rates are per person and include seven nights lodging and six lift tickets (high-season rates).
[2] Number in parentheses denotes occupancy of unit on which price is based.

PRESENT POLICIES

Lift rates

It was common knowledge that there existed some local resentment concerning Big Sky's lift rate policy. Although comparable to rates at Vail or Aspen, the price of an all-day lift ticket was $4 higher than the ticket offered at Bridger Bowl. In an attempt to alleviate this situation, management at Big Sky instituted a $9 "chair pass" for the 1977–78 season, entitling the holder to unlimited use of the three chairs, plus two rides per day on the gondola, to be taken between specified time periods. Because the gondola served primarily intermediate terrain, it was reasoned that the chair pass would appeal to the local, more expert skier. A triple chair serving the bowl area was located at the top of the gondola; two rides on the gondola would allow those skiers to take ample advantage of the advanced terrain up there. Otherwise, all advanced terrain was served by another chair.

However, Karen believed that if Big Sky was to establish itself as a successful, nationally prominent destination area, the attitudes and opinions of all skiers must be carefully weighed. Throughout the season she had made a special effort to grasp the general feeling toward rates. A $12 ticket, she discovered, was thought to be very reasonable by destination skiers, primarily because Big Sky was predominantly an intermediate area and the average destination skier was of intermediate ability, and also because Big Sky was noted for its relative lack of lift lines, giving the skier more actual skiing time for the money. "Perhaps we should keep the price the same," she thought. "We do need more business. Other destination areas are likely to raise their prices and we should look good in comparison."

Also discussed was the possible abolition of the $9 chair pass. The question in Karen's mind was whether its elimination would severely hurt local business or would instead sell an all-lift $12 ticket to the skier who had previously bought only a chair pass. The issue was compounded by an unknown number of destination skiers who also opted for the cheaper chair pass.

Season pass pricing was also an issue. Prices for the 1977–78 all-lift season pass had remained the same as last year's, but a season chair pass had been introduced that was the counterpart of the daily chairlift pass. Karen did not like the number of season chair passes purchased in relation to the number of all-lift passes and considered recommending its abolition as well as an increase in the price of the all-lift pass. "I'm going to have to think this one out carefully," she thought, "because skiing accounted for about 40 percent of our total revenue this past season. I'll have to be able to justify my decision not only to Michigan but also to the Forest Service."

Price changes were not solely at the discretion of Big Sky management. As was the case with most larger Western ski areas, the U.S. government owned part of the land on which Big Sky operated. Control of this land was the responsibility of the U.S. Forest Service, which annually approved all lift pricing policies. For the 1976–77 ski season, Forest Service action had kept most lift-rate increases to the national inflation rate. For the 1977–78 season, larger price increases were allowed for ski areas that had competing areas nearby; Big Sky was considered to be such an area. No one knew what the Forest Service position would be for the upcoming 1978–79 season.

To help Karen in her decision, an assistant had prepared a summary of lift rates and usage for the past two seasons (Exhibit 3).

Room rates

Room-rate pricing was particularly important because lodging accounted for about one-third of the past season's total revenue. It was also difficult because of the variety of accommodations (Exhibit 4) and the difficulty in accurately forecasting next season's demand. For example, the season of 1976–77 had been unique in that a good portion of the Rockies was without snow for the initial months of the winter, including Christmas. Big Sky was fortunate in receiving as much snow as it had, and consequently many groups and individuals who were originally headed for Vail or Aspen booked in with Big Sky.

Pricing for the 1977–78 season had been determined on the premise that there would be a good amount of repeat business. This came true in part, but not as much as had been hoped. Occupancy experience had also been summarized for the past two seasons to help Karen make her final decision (Exhibit 5).

As was customary in the hospitality industry, January was a slow period, and it was necessary to price accordingly. Low-season pricing was extremely important because many groups took advantage of the lower rates. In addition, groups were often offered discounts in the neighborhood of 10 percent. Considering this, Karen could not price too high, with the risk of losing individual destination skiers, nor too low, such that an unacceptably low profit would be made from group business in this period.

Food service

Under some discussion was the feasibility of converting all destination skiers to the American Plan; each guest in Huntley Lodge would be placed on a package that included three meals daily in a Big Sky–controlled facility. There was a feeling both for and against this idea. The parent company had been successfully utilizing this plan for years at its destination areas in northern Michigan. Extending the policy to Big Sky should find similar success.

Karen was not so sure. For one thing, the Michigan resorts were primarily self-contained and alternative eateries were few. For another, the whole idea of extending standardized policies from Michigan to Montana was suspect. As an example, Karen painfully recalled a day in January when Big Sky "tried on" another successful Michigan policy of accepting only cash or check payments for lift tickets. Reactions of credit card–carrying skiers could be described as ranging from annoyed to irate.

If an American Plan were proposed for next year, it would likely include both the Huntley Lodge dining room and Lookout Cafeteria. Less clear, however, were prices to be charged. There certainly would have to be

Exhibit 3.   Summary of Lift Rates and Usage, Two Seasons

1977–78 lift rates and usage summary (136 days operation)

Ticket	Consumer cost	Skier days [1]	Number season passes sold
Adult all-day, all-lift	$12	53,400	
Adult all-day chair	9	20,200	
Adult half-day	8	9,400	
Child all-day, all-lift	8	8,500	
Child all-day chair	5	3,700	
Child half-day	6	1,200	
Hotel passes [2]	12/day	23,400	
Complimentary	0	1,100	
Adult all-lift season pass	220	4,300	140
Adult chair season pass	135	4,200	165
Child all-lift season pass	130	590	30
Child chair season pass	75	340	15
Employee all-lift season pass	100	3,000	91
Employee chair season pass	35	1,100	37

1976–77 lift rates and usage summary (122 days operation)

Ticket	Consumer cost	Skier days	Number season passes sold
Adult all-day	$10	52,500	
Adult half-day	6.50	9,000	
Child all-day	6	10,400	
Child half-day	4	1,400	
Hotel passes [2]	10/day	30,500	
Complimentary	0	480	
Adult season pass	220	4,200	84
Child season pass	130	300	15
Employee season pass	100	2,300	70

[1] A skier day is defined as one skier using the facility for any part of one day of operation.

[2] Hotel passes refer to those included in the lodging/lift packages.

consideration for both adults and children and for the two independently operated eating places in Mountain Mall (see Exhibit 6 for an identification of eating places in the Big Sky area). Beyond these considerations, there was little other than an expectation of a profit to guide Karen in her analysis.

THE TELEPHONE CALL

"Profits in the food area might be hard to come by," Karen thought. "Last year it appears we lost money on everything we sold" (see Exhibit 7). Just then the telephone rang. It was Rick Thompson, her counterpart at Boyne Mountain Lodge in Michigan. "How are your pricing recommendations coming?" he asked. "I'm about done with mine and thought we should compare notes."

"Good idea, Rick—only I'm just getting started out here. Do you have any hot ideas?"

"Only one," he responded. "I just got off the

Exhibit 4. Room Rates at Selected Sites

Nightly room rates,[1] 1977–78

	Low-season range	High-season range	Maximum occupancy
Huntley Lodge			
Standard	$ 42–62	$ 50–70	4
Loft	52–92	60–100	6
Stillwater Condo			
Studio	40–60	45–65	4
One-bedroom	55–75	60–80	4
Bedroom w/ loft	80–100	90–110	6
Deer Lodge Condo			
One-bedroom	74–84	80–90	4
Two-bedroom	93–103	100–110	6
Three-bed- room	112–122	120–130	8
Hill Condo			
Studio	30–40	35–45	4
Studio w/loft	50–70	55–75	6

Nightly room rates, 1976–77

	Low-season range	High-season range	Maximum occupancy
Huntley Lodge			
Standard	$ 32–47	$ 35–50	4
Loft	47–67	50–70	6
Stillwater Condo			
Studio	39–54	37–52	4
One-bedroom	52–62	50–60	4
Bedroom w/ loft	60–80	65–85	6
Deer Lodge Condo			
One-bedroom	51–66	55–70	4
Two-bedroom	74–94	80–100	6
Three-bed- room	93–123	100–130	8
Hill Condo			
Studio	28–43	30–45	4
Studio w/loft	42–62	45–65	6

[1] Rates determined by number of persons in room or condominium unit and do not include lift tickets. Maximums for each rate range apply at maximum occupancy.

Exhibit 5. Occupancy Experience at Big Sky

1977–78 Lodge-condominium occupancy (in room-nights [1])

	December (26 days operation)	January	February	March	April (8 days operation)
Huntley Lodge	1830	2250	3650	4650	438
Condominiums [2]	775	930	1350	100	90

1976–77 Lodge-condominium occupancy (in room-nights)

	December (16 days operation)	January	February	March	April (16 days operation)
Huntley Lodge	1700	3080	4525	·4300	1525
Condominiums [3]	600	1000	1600	1650	480

Lodge-condominium occupancy (in person-nights [4])

December 1977 (1976)	January 1978 (1977)	February 1978 (1977)	March 1978 (1977)	April 1978 (1977)
7850 (6775)	9200 (13,000)	13,150 (17,225)	17,900 (17,500)	1450 (4725)

[1] A room-night is defined as one room (or condominium) rented for one night. Lodging experience is based on 124 days of operation for 1977–78, while Exhibit 3 shows the skiing facilities operating 136 days. Both numbers are correct.

[2] Big Sky had ninety-two condominiums available during the 1977–78 season.

[3] Big Sky had eighty-five condominiums available during the 1976–77 season.

[4] A person-night refers to one person using the facility for one night.

phone with a guy in Denver. He told me all of the major Colorado areas are upping their lift prices one or two dollars next year."

"Is that right, Rick? Are you sure?"

"Well, you know nobody knows for sure what's going to happen, but I think it's pretty good information. He heard it from his sister-in-law who works in Vail. I think he said she read it in the local paper or something."

"That doesn't seem like very solid information," said Karen. "Let me know if you hear anything more, will you?"

"Certainly. You know, we really should compare our recommendations before we stick our necks out too far on this pricing thing. Can you call me later in the week?" he asked.

"Sure, I'll talk to you the day after tomorrow; I should be about done by then. Anything else?"

"Nope—gotta run. Talk to you then. Bye," and he was gone.

"At least I've got some information," Karen thought, "and a new deadline!"

Exhibit 6. Eating Places in the Big Sky Area

Establishment	Type of service	Meals served	Current prices	Seating	Location
Lodge dining room *	A la carte	Breakfast Lunch Dinner	$ 2–5 2–5 7–15	250	Huntley Lodge
Steak House *	Steak/lobster	Dinner only	$ 6–12	150	Huntley Lodge
Fondue Stube *	Fondue	Dinner only	$ 6–10	25	Huntley Lodge
Ore House **	A la carte	Lunch Dinner	$0.80–4 5–12	150	Mountain Mall
Ernie's Deli **	Deli/restaurant	Breakfast Lunch	$ 1–3 2–5	25	Mountain Mall
Lookout Cafeteria *	Cafeteria	Breakfast Lunch Dinner	$1.50–3 2–4 3–6	175	Mountain Mall
Yellow Mule **	A la carte	Breakfast Lunch Dinner	$ 2–4 2–5 4–8	75	Meadow Village
Buck's T–4 **	Road house restaurant/bar	Dinner only	$ 2–9	60	Gallatin Canyon (2 miles south of Big Sky entrance)
Karst Ranch **	Road house restaurant/bar	Breakfast Lunch Dinner	$ 2–4 2–5 3–8	50	Gallatin Canyon (7 miles north of Big Sky entrance)
Corral **	Road house restaurant/bar	Breakfast Lunch Dinner	$ 2–4 2–4 3–5	30	Gallatin Canyon (5 miles south of Big Sky entrance)

* Owned and operated by Big Sky of Montana, Inc.
** Independently operated.

Exhibit 7. Ski Season Income Data (%)

	Skiing	Lodging	Food and beverage
Revenue	100.0	100.0	100.0
Cost of sales			
Merchandise	0.0	0.0	30.0
Labor	15.0	15.9	19.7
Maintenance	3.1	5.2	2.4
Supplies	1.5	4.8	5.9
Miscellaneous	2.3	0.6	0.6
Operating expenses	66.2	66.4	66.7
Net profit (loss) before taxes	11.9	7.1	(25.2)

Five

Promotion

FRANK W. HORNER, LTD.

MORTON SALT

TEXAS GRAPE GROWERS ASSOCIATION

QUICK MEAL FOOD SYSTEMS, INC.

TOMMY'S TOYS AND THINGS

SANDWELL PAPER COMPANY

COMPUTING SYSTEMS, LTD.

WESTINGHOUSE ELECTRIC CORPORATION

FOOD DYNAMICS

22

Frank W. Horner, Ltd.*

In April 1978, Peter McLoughlin, marketing manager for over-the-counter (OTC) products at Frank W. Horner, Ltd., of Montreal, was planning his 1978–79 communications strategy for Fevertest, with the assistance of Robert Kyba of the market research department. Described by McLoughlin as "our first real consumer-type promotion," Fevertest consisted of a thin plastic strip which, when applied to the forehead, indicated whether or not an individual had a fever. Between early November 1977 and the end of March 1978, factory shipments amounted to 317,000 units. McLoughlin and Kyba wondered whether they could improve on this level of sales by investing in television advertising, an approach which had not been used during the initial promotional campaign.

COMPANY BACKGROUND

Frank W. Horner, Ltd., was founded in 1912 by a nephew of Andrew Wyeth, the artist. By 1977, sales in Canada had reached $15 million. An additional $5 million in export sales were handled by the international division of Carter Wallace N.S. Horner distributed a variety of ethical and OTC pharmaceutical products [1] to 4,000 pharmacies across Canada through a sales force of 65 persons.

* This case was prepared by John A. Quelch of the Harvard Business School. Copyright © 1978 by The University of Western Ontario. Reproduced by permission.

[1] Ethical products are usually available to the consumer only on prescription whereas OTC products, as the name implies, may be purchased over the counter by the consumer without a prescription.

Only 10 percent of sales volume was distributed through wholesalers. The product line included antacids (Diovol), antinauseants (Gravol), analgesics (Atasol), and tonic (Maltlevol). Prior to 1973, dollar sales of ethical products exceeded those of OTC products. However, by 1977 approximately 65 percent of Horner's dollar volume was derived from OTC products.

THE PRODUCT CONCEPT

An individual's temperature is commonly measured orally, though rectal temperature is a closer measure of body or core temperature. There is usually a 3-degree centigrade difference between oral temperature and skin temperature measured on the forehead. A further complication, irrespective of method of temperature measurement, is that there is no absolute figure for normal temperature. Normal temperatures vary among individuals. In addition, an individual's body temperature may vary as much as one-half degree centigrade during the course of the day. Despite these variations, doctors generally agree that a temperature of 38°C or more indicates a definite fever.

In 1976, Horner executives were investigating acquisition of the Canadian distribution rights to a new type of fever indicator developed by Eurand, the Italian subsidiary of NCR. The indicator consisted of a thin strip which, when applied to the forehead for 15 seconds, showed an N if the person's temperature was normal, and an NF if the person had a fever. The strip contained microencapsulated liquid crystals which changed color with changes in temperature. The temperature at which each color change occurred, and the sequence of color changes, were invariable. The microencapsulation process, on which North American patents had been acquired by NCR in 1969, shielded the liquid crystals from contamination and provided both greater reliability and longer effective life. The temperatures at which particular color changes occurred are illustrated in Exhibit 1.

Horner executives learned that the accuracy of the indicator could be jeopardized if it was soaked in water or alcohol, if it was not allowed to cool for 30 seconds between uses, or if it was not applied to a clean dry forehead. The indicator could not be used reliably after sunbathing or strenuous exercise, since the normal temperature relationship between forehead and mouth would be interrupted. In addition, usage on children under two years was not recommended because of the immaturity of the body's thermal regulating systems.

PRELIMINARY RESEARCH

Despite the questionable accuracy of the indicator, both in general and under special circumstances, Horner executives decided to undertake the program of technical and market research outlined in Exhibit 2. The main highlights of the program were as follows.

Consumer Group (May 1976)

On the basis of a focus group interview with 15 consumers in Quebec, women were found to be more interested in the product concept than men. The main concerns expressed related to the product's accuracy and its ability to sustain its effectiveness despite long periods of nonuse. Nevertheless, 12 of the consumers stated that they would buy the product if it were on sale at a pharmacy for a price between $1.75 and $2.00. Because consumers commented that the product appeared fragile and easy to mislay, Horner executives decided that product packaging would be important to provide protection and to convey an impression of quality to support a $2.00 price level.

Exhibit 1. Temperature—Color Change Relationship

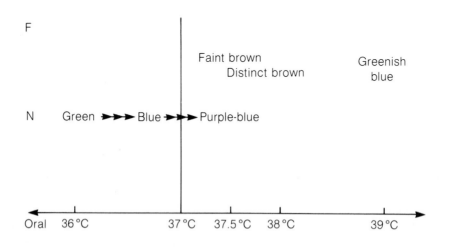

Source: Company records.

Exhibit 2. Summary of Technical and Market Research Program

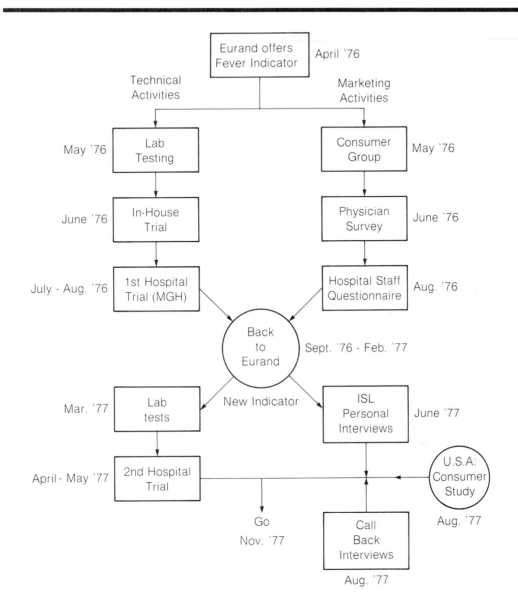

Source: Company records.

Physician Survey (June 1976)

Horner was not seriously interested in selling the product to physicians but, as an ethical drug company, was concerned that the prod-

uct should not detract from the company's reputation with the medical profession if introduced. The physicians reacted positively to the product as a means of readily establishing if a patient had a temperature above

38°C. Positive reactions increased after the physicians tried the product. In the view of several of the group, the product's ease of usage made it appropriate for the many consumers who did not know how to use a thermometer correctly.

First Hospital Trial (August 1976)

The indicator supplied by Eurand was tested in Horner laboratories and in-house by Horner employees. Next, a field trial was conducted involving the staff of Montreal General Hospital. Fifty nurses were asked to measure patient temperatures with both the fever indicator and a thermometer. In replying to a staff questionnaire, they were somewhat negative regarding the product's accuracy, reporting that the indicator showed an F at a variety of temperatures between 37°C and 38°C. In addition, the indicator was not regarded as a time-saving device. Although a glass thermometer took twice as long to register a patient's temperature, the nurse could attend to other duties while the reading was being taken, whereas the fever indicator required the nurse to hold it in position. Some nurses also perceived a hygiene problem in using the same indicator on several patients. In summary, 38 percent of nurses surveyed agreed that the accuracy of the indicator made it suitable for hospital use. Thirty percent stated that they had experienced difficulty using the product. Sixty-six percent believed that a fever-screening device could play a useful role in hospitals, particularly in chronic care and pediatric wards.

Second Hospital Trial (April 1977)

Following the initial trial, Horner asked Eurand to supply a more accurate product. A second batch of improved fever indicators was used in another hospital trial at Montreal General. The second version of the product proved to be more sensitive, indicating an F at only 37.6°C or 37.7°C, rather than across a range of temperatures between 37°C and 38°C. Acceptance of Fevertest as a useful

fever screening device by members of the hospital staff increased significantly beyond the level recorded in the first hospital survey.

Consumer Survey (June 1977)

A survey was conducted with three groups: 50 English-speaking mothers with children of 2 to 10 years; 50 French-speaking mothers with children of 2 to 10 years; 100 members of the general public, half male, half female.[2] Each subject was first shown a point-of-sale display for the product. Next, each subject was invited to open a product package and read about the product. Finally, each subject was asked to try the product. After each stage, consumer reactions to the product were elicited and interest in ownership of the product was measured. Consumers reacted favorably toward the ease with which the product could be used, particularly when taking the temperatures of children. Favorable comments regarding the speed with which the indicator registered increased significantly after consumers tried the product. The unbreakable nature of the product also prompted favorable comment. Negative reactions centered on the questionable accuracy of the indicator and the fact that it did not provide numerical temperature values. Exhibit 3 presents the percentages of each sample subgroup either very or fairly interested in the ownership of a fever indicator after each of the three stages of inquiry, and, in addition, the percentages prepared to pay $1.75 on the spot for the indicator.

The consumer survey also established that 85 percent of the sample had no difficulty comprehending the product concept, and 89 percent did not find the concept difficult to believe. However, the survey results indicated that some consumers did not realize that

[2] Among approximately 7 million Canadian households, there were 1,340,000 English-speaking households with children 2 to 10 years old, and 360,000 similar French-speaking households. There were an additional 900,000 households with children 11 to 15 years old.

Exhibit 3. Percentages of Consumers Interested in Ownership of Fever Indicator

	Total sample N = 200	Mothers with children 2 to 10 years			General public N = 100
		Total N = 100	English N = 50	French N = 50	
After seeing point-of-sale display	53	69	74	64	37
After opening package and reading concept	65	79	64	94	49
After testing product	72	84	76	92	58
Immediate purchase at $1.75	45	68	42	94	21

Source: ISL Consumer Survey, June 1977.

the product was reusable. As a result, this characteristic was highlighted in subsequent point-of-sale material. A substantial majority of consumers in the sample selected Fevertest from among several names as being most appropriate for the product.

Finally, Horner executives had information from a French company which had been selling the microencapsulated fever indicator since the end of 1976 at a price close to $2.00 each. Sales results indicated that close to 1 million units would be sold during the first year in France, a country of approximately 20 million households. On the basis of this evidence and domestic consumer research, Horner executives decided to launch the fever indicator under the brand name Fevertest. The product was packaged in a blue plastic wallet with the comprehensive usage instructions reproduced in Exhibit 4.

INITIAL COMMUNICATIONS STRATEGY

Fevertest was launched early in November 1977, to coincide with the cold and flu season. The product was distributed through the Horner sales force at a price of $1.35 to pharmacies. A retail price of about $2.00 was recommended, thereby giving the pharmacy a margin of 33 percent. Details of the price and cost structure for Fevertest are presented in Exhibit 5. Due to the uniqueness of the product, the sales forecast of 500,000 units between November and April 1978 was regarded as somewhat speculative. This figure represented sales of 458 cases of two dozen units per sales territory. Because of production capacity constraints, a maximum allocation of 120 cases per territory was available in November.

The communications budget for the product launch is summarized in Exhibit 6. An automatic shipment for one case of two dozen Fevertests was sent to the most important 3,100 to 5,000 pharmacy accounts across Canada.[3] The pharmacies were invoiced on a 90-day payment basis for $32.40 each. Accompanying each case was a free Fevertest strip to be used by the pharmacist as a demonstrator, and a letter explaining the product concept, emphasizing the space efficiency of the product, and indicating the manner in which the case could be used as a display device. Executives believed that drugstores would be receptive to the automatic shipment because of the novelty of the product together with Horner's long-standing reputation for distributing quality salable products.

[3] Horner's reputation for successful new product introductions was such that most pharmacies were prepared to receive and merchandise a case of Fevertest shipped automatically from the factory rather than in response to an order.

Exhibit 4. Usage Instructions for Fevertest

How to use.

Hold FEVERTEST strip by the clear ends, and apply to a clean, *dry* forehead, mat (dull) side against the skin. Keep in place for 15 seconds (even though results may appear in just 5 seconds). Liquid Crystals react best indoors between 18 – 30° C (65° – 86° F). Do not use immediately after sunbathing or exposure to extreme heat. Do not wash FEVERTEST strip with any substance.

How to read.

N—normal temperature
NF (brownish F)—transition phase
NF (green/blue F)—definite fever
The transition phase indicates either: 1) the onset of a fever
or 2) a high forehead temperature.
If a distinct F appears and you'd like a more precise reading, use a glass thermometer.

Note.

In children under 2 years of age, the body's thermal regulating system may still be immature. Therefore, it is preferable to use a glass thermometer for very young children.

How to store.

After each use, return FEVERTEST to its package and store away from sunlight, dampness and heat. Do not wash FEVERTEST strip with any substance.
Properly cared for, your FEVERTEST strip may be used thousands of times.

The case was designed in the form of a display which could be shelved in the thermometer section of the drugstore or placed on the dispensary counter where the pharmacist could discuss and demonstrate the product. The second approach was also believed likely to result in less theft. In addition to the display, point-of-sale posters for doors, windows, and cash registers were distributed to the 3,100 pharmacies. Total point-of-sale promotion costs were $20,000.

As part of the sell-in effort, Horner offered a cooperative advertising allowance of $15 to those stores that purchased 10 cases of Fevertests. It was estimated that about 650 stores might take advantage of this offer, for a total promotion expense of approximately $10,000. Trade advertising involved a full-

Exhibit 5. Fevertest Cost and Price Structure

Selling price per case ($1.35 each)	$32.40
Cost of goods	12.53
Gross margin	19.87
Distribution, marketing, and administrative cost allocation	2.59
Sales commission (4% of selling price)	1.30
Available for communications budget and profit	15.98

Source: Company records.

Exhibit 6. Communications Budget for Fevertest Launch

Unit objectives	500,000
Dollar objectives (at $1.35 each)	$675,000
Communications Budget	
Public relations	$ 15,000
Promotion to physicians	10,000
Journal advertising	8,000
Consumer print advertising	75,000
Point-of-sale displays	18,000
Selling sheets	2,000
Case allowances for cooperative advertising	10,000
Television advertising (January 1978)	18,000
Total	156,000

Source: Company records.

page insertion in *Drug Merchandising* and *Le Pharmacien* (combined circulation of 12,000) at a cost of $8,000. A sample Fevertest was affixed to the advertisement in each copy of the magazine to facilitate trial among readers.

Consumer advertising included a full-page four-color advertisement in the December 1977 and January 1978 issues of *Reader's Digest* (circulation 1,256,000), *Selection* (31,000), *Homemakers* (1,232,000) and *Madame Au Foyer* (268,000). One-third page advertisements were inserted in the Views on Value section of *Reader's Digest/Selection* in February, March, and April, and in the Product Idea Unit section of *Homemakers/Madame Au Foyer* in March, April, and May. Total costs for the advertising campaign were $75,000.

At a cost of $10,000, a Fevertest sample was mailed to 12,500 doctors. The accompanying product description emphasized that the product was not intended to replace the thermometer but to act as a screening device. It was suggested that patients might check their temperatures more often with a Fevertest and that, as a result, some unnecessary calls to physicians might be eliminated.

Public relations kits tailored to different media were mailed to all radio stations, television stations, daily newspapers, women's editors, and medical journals. Once again, a free sample was included for demonstration purposes. The cost of 278 public relations mailings was $8,000. Other expenses associated with the public relations drive amounted to $7,000. The public relations material aroused such immediate interest that some announcements were made in the media before initial distribution of the product had been completed.

COMPETITION

Some druggists perceived Fevertest to be in competition with the glass thermometer. However, Horner executives believed that the calibrated thermometer would be used after the Fevertest if the indicator showed positive. Consumer research indicated that 84 percent of consumers would follow up an indication of fever on the Fevertest with a thermometer reading. Thus, they viewed the glass thermometer and the Fevertest as complementary rather than as substitutes. Horner estimated the 1977 glass thermometer market (rectal and oral thermometers) at 4.4 million units. Of these, 2.6 million with a manufacturer's value of $3.25 million and a retail value of $6.5 million were sold to consumers. The remaining 1.8 million thermometers were supplied to hospitals and other health care organizations.

Similar products to Fevertest were on sale in the United States, including Clinitemp, Fever Tester, and Fever Meter. These products were manufactured by small companies and sold at retail prices between $1.95 and $2.49. None of these indicators was microencapsulated. Despite the consequent accuracy and reliability problems, one of the products was calibrated in degrees and purported to provide an exact temperature reading. Promotional material for these indicators included appeals such as "space-age concept," "hospital tested," "every member of the family can carry one," and "keep one at home, one in your car, one in your vacation first-aid kit." In all cases, the target market appeared to be mothers with children.

McLoughlin and Kyba were uncertain whether the manufacturers of these fever indicators would attempt to distribute in Canada and, if so, what channels they would use. Too small to afford a direct sales approach, the competing companies could attempt to use drug wholesalers to distribute to pharmacies. Alternatively, they might try to reach the consumer through mass merchandisers and supermarkets rather than through drugstores. The costs of new packaging and display materials to meet bilingual requirements were thought unlikely to be a sufficient deterrent to entry. McLoughlin and Kyba were concerned about such potential competition, because the poorer quality of the competing indicators might reduce the credibility of the product concept and, therefore, adversely affect Fevertest sales. To differentiate Fevertest on the basis of microencapsulation would, it was believed, pose a difficult communications task. The threat of competition was highlighted early in 1978, when reports were received that a calibrated fever indicator, Stik Temp, was being distributed through drug wholesalers in British Columbia. Nevertheless, company estimates indicated that Fevertest held 95 percent of the Canadian fever indicator market.

TELEVISION ADVERTISING

Horner executives were sufficiently satisfied with sales volume during the product launch that they became interested in the possibility of using television to promote Fevertest. Television advertising held an advantage over radio and print advertising in that Fevertest could be demonstrated as part of the commercial. At the same time, Horner had little experience in consumer advertising, and there was a fear that any money spent in television advertising would benefit similarly named competitive products as much as Fevertest and might, in addition, attract further competition into the market.

Consequently, Horner decided to conduct several experiments testing the effectiveness of television advertising in selected markets. During the period January 2–29, 1978, Horner spent $17,650 for advertising time on three Vancouver television stations with the goal of targeting women 18 years or older. The following tabulation shows the number of WRPs (women rating points)[4] achieved and the distribution of cost on a biweekly basis:

	Weekly WRPs	Average weekly cost	Cost per rating point	Total cost
January 2–13	113	$4735	$41.90	$ 9,470
January 16–29	102	4090	40.10	8,190
				$17,650

Weekly case sales for Fevertest during the introductory period both in total and for three major markets are presented in Exhibit 7. The results indicate that Vancouver sales were at an average level of 40 cases a week prior to the advertising effort. During the

[4] Weekly WRPs represent the percentage of women aged 18 to 49 in the Vancouver market who would be reached at least once by the television advertising during one week multiplied by the average number of times (frequency) each such woman would be exposed to the advertising during the week.

Exhibit 7. Fevertest Weekly Case Sales, 1977–78

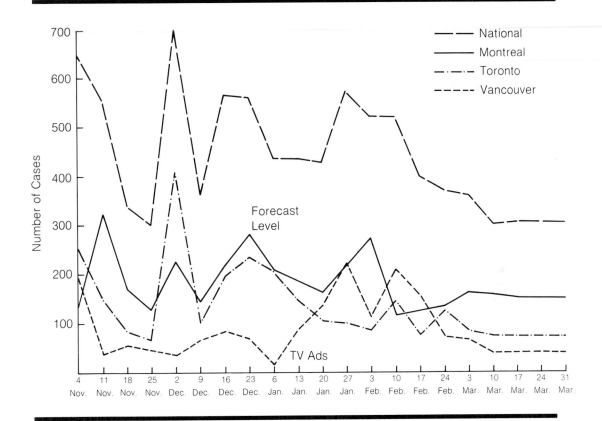

eight-week period after the campaign start-ed, approximately 1,150 cases were sold, but by March 10, sales out of the Vancouver de-pot had returned to the preadvertising level. Horner executives saw no reason not to attri-bute the sales increase to television advertis-ing since Montreal and Toronto sales ap-peared to taper off during the same period.

At the end of January, a comparative test of Fevertest awareness was conducted in Vancouver and Calgary. An awareness level of 77 percent was recorded in Vancouver, and 45 percent in Calgary. Among Vancou-ver consumers, 73 percent cited television commercials as their source of information, while 16 percent cited drugstores. The corre-sponding figures in Calgary, where no televi-sion advertising had been conducted, were 24 percent and 30 percent.

THE 1978–79 COMMUNICATIONS STRATEGY

Before they could formulate the communica-tions strategy for Fevertest, McLoughlin and Kyba were faced with the problem of whether or not to broaden distribution of the product beyond pharmacies. Supermarkets, for example, were thought likely to be inter-ested in Fevertest because of its high margin per square foot in relation to other products. Though Horner had no experience selling to supermarkets, moving into this channel could forestall potential competition and generate substantial sales volume. There was concern, however, about the effects of such a move on Horner's reputation with its phar-macy accounts and the degree to which they would withdraw support from Fevertest, particularly if supermarkets sold the product at a lower price. Furthermore, some Horner executives believed that the supermarkets might promote Fevertest as a novelty or gimmick item, thereby detracting from the desired image of usefulness and excellence of quality.

Sales forecasts suggested that 500,000 Fevertests would be sold in 1978–79 if the company continued to restrict sales to pharmacies. Depending upon the size of the communications budget, Horner executives believed that as many as 1,500,000 Fevertests might be sold to the general public if distribution was broadened.

The distribution issue prompted Horner executives to wonder whether the original target market of mothers with young children should be broadened. The institutional market presented an additional opportunity to generate increased sales volume. It was believed that widespread usage of Fevertests in hospitals could be used by Horner to distinguish Fevertest from competing indicators when promoting the product to consumers.

In light of decisions regarding target market and message strategies, Horner executives recognized that the level and allocation of the communications budget would soon have to be finalized. In addition to the range of promotional activities in which Horner had invested during the 1977–78 year, four additional options were available:

Television Advertising

The Horner advertising agency advised that an advertising objective of at least 100 WRPs was necessary for Fevertest. Exhibit 8 indicates the weekly cost of meeting this objective in 18 markets over 100,000 population. While the cost of year-long advertising in all of these markets was prohibitive, some executives believed that short flights of advertising in selected markets (similar to the Vancouver test) might prove to be a profitable investment. For example, one proposal was made to schedule three four-week flights in all 18 markets at a cost of $400,000.

Cooperative Advertising

If a store purchased a minimum of 10 cases and featured Fevertest in its advertising, Horner was prepared to offer a cooperative advertising allowance of $1 per case. Horner executives estimated that 2000 stores might purchase 10 cases and that half of these might take up the offer for a promotional cost of $10,000.

Tie-in Promotion

Information about Fevertest could be disseminated either on or inside the package of another Horner product at no additional cost. McLoughlin was considering such a tie-in promotion with Atasol, a Horner analgesic.

Point-of-Sale Displays

At a cost of $20,000, one thousand motorized units to be used as counter displays could be produced. The unit would play a videotape showing how a consumer should use a Fevertest, and would be offered to pharmacies or other outlets as an attention-getting device. An additional $10,000 would be needed for accompanying point-of-sale material, including mirrors attached to the case displays to enable potential purchasers to see the color changes occurring when they applied the sample Fevertest to their foreheads.

Within the coming week, McLoughlin and Kyba had to finalize the Fevertest communications strategy for the 1978–79 year beginning June 1.

Exhibit 8. Projected Fevertest Television Cost, 1978

Commercial Length:	30 Seconds					
Weekly Weight:	100 Women Rating Point (WRPs)					
Markets:	Population 100,000 plus					
	WRP weekly objective	Spill-in	Original WRP weekly	Weekly cost ($)	Weekly reach (%)	Average weekly frequency
St. John's/Corner Brook	100	0	100	560.00	63	1.6
Halifax/Sydney	100	0	100	1,290.00	63	1.6
Saint John/Moncton	100	0	100	600.00	63	1.6
Chicoutimi/Jonquière	100	0	100	235.00	65	1.5
Montreal (English)	40	0	40	2,460.00	23	1.7
Montreal (French)	60	0	60	2,544.00	37	1.6
Quebec City	100	0	100	1,420.00	64	1.6
Kitchener	100	59	41	885.60	53	1.9
London	100	40	60	996.00	54	1.9
Ottawa (English)	80	0	80	1,792.00	48	1.7
Ottawa (French)	20	0	20	253.00	10	2.0
Sudbury	100	0	100	685.00	64	1.6
Thunder Bay	100	0	100	245.00	59	1.7
Toronto/Hamilton	100	0	100	8,500.00	55	1.8
Winnipeg	100	0	100	1,620.00	59	1.7
Regina	100	0	100	545.00	64	1.6
Saskatoon	100	0	100	555.00	64	1.6
Calgary	100	0	100	1,450.00	59	1.7
Edmonton	100	0	100	1,800.00	59	1.7
Vancouver/Victoria	100	0	100	4,160.00	58	1.7
				32,595.60		
	Plus 15% reserve for rate increases:			4,889.34		
				37,484.94		

Source: W.R. Kitching Associates Limited.

23

Morton Salt *

George Tate strolled down Michigan Avenue on a warm spring afternoon in Chicago. He had spent the entire morning with Morton Salt's advertising agency, reviewing the company's past promotions and discussing possible plans for the upcoming fiscal year, which would begin on July 1. As he walked, he pondered the problems facing the company, particularly with regard to table salt, traditionally Morton Salt's major product.

WHEN IT RAINS, IT POURS

In the early part of the twentieth century, consumers bought salt in brown paper bags, which had been put up by a grocer from bulk salt he had purchased in barrels. The salt business was keenly competitive, and no firm had been able to gain significant consumer demand or a price advantage. Morton's product was exactly like that of its competition.

If Morton Salt could be differentiated in some way, however, it could improve consumer demand, and thus improve profit margins. By 1920, it developed an innovative way to keep salt from caking or hardening from moisture, and introduced a moisture-proof, two-pound cylindrical package with

an aluminum spout for easier pouring. With these improvements, Morton embarked upon a modest advertising program, utilizing primarily women's magazines. "When It Rains, It Pours" was adopted as a slogan for the advertisement, and was also printed on the package.

The idea of branding and advertising was a new one in the salt market, but it seemed to work, as Morton's sales and market share grew. With this increased degree of control over consumer demand, Morton began to gradually increase prices until its packaged salt sold for double that of any competitor (10¢ per package, compared to 5¢ for unbranded bags).

NO SALT SALTS LIKE MORTON SALT SALTS

Since Morton's product and package improvements were unprotected by patents, competitors were quick to imitate. As a result, some consumer resistance to the price differential began to affect Morton Salt sales. At this point, therefore, Morton needed another innovation.

Because of its leadership in the salt industry, Morton was approached by health authorities and medical organizations who had discovered that an insufficient amount of iodine in the body was a cause of goiter (an enlargement of the thyroid gland, often visible as a swelling in the lower part of the front of the neck). Since salt was a universally used food product, these authorities suggested that Morton take the lead in adding

---

* Morton, the Umbrella Girl design, When it rains it pours, Morton Lite Salt, Sugar Cure, Tender Quick, Nature's Seasons and Dough-It-Yourself are registered trademarks of Morton-Norwich Products, Inc.

Copyright © 1980 by Nancy Stephens and Richard F. Beltramini. Used by permission. Distributed by the Intercollegiate Case Clearing House, Soldiers Field, Boston, Mass. 02163. All rights reserved to the contributors. Printed in the U.S.A.

180

iodine to their salt, in a ratio of 1 part iodine to 5,000 parts salt, for goiter prevention.

Iodized salt was introduced in the early 1920s with advertising support, and by 1926 Morton's iodized salt was outselling plain salt. It was able to continue its market leadership and brand preference for many years, maintaining a premium price.

However, in the early 1960s Morton saw its sales and market share slipping again as competitors had matched product innovations, and had engaged in price-cutting tactics. In addition, consumer lifestyles had changed to produce a declining demand for salt. More people were eating away from home, and more prepared, presalted foods were being consumed at home.

Morton expanded its advertising to focus on the 30–40 age group (then found to consume 75 percent of all salt sold), and reemphasized the company's early innovations in the salt market. Magazines, television, and radio carried the message "No Salt Salts Like Morton Salt Salts" to this target audience. In 1968 Morton was able to enjoy the largest market share of any year in the decade.

THE NEXT BEST THING TO THE REAL THING

By the late 1960s, Morton had also expanded its product offerings beyond table salt. Company divisions had been established to produce prepared foods, chemicals, and agricultural goods, partially as a result of the 1969 merger with Norwich Pharmacal Company.

Further growth depended upon properly defining the firm's business position. As consumers had changed, Morton was no longer just in the "salt business"; it was in the "seasonings business."

In 1970, after extensive product and market research, Morton introduced a new consumer product, Salt Substitute. Morton Salt Substitute was initially available in two varieties, regular and seasoned. It was composed of potassium chloride, and had already been in limited use by people on medically supervised, low-sodium diets.

The introduction of Salt Substitute as a consumer product was supported by a $242,000 advertising campaign which emphasized taste rather than the product's medical uses. "The Next Best Thing to the Real Thing" was chosen as the slogan, and appeared in magazine and newspaper advertisements. Further, a 10¢-off coupon was featured to stimulate trial purchase of the innovative product. By the end of the decade, Morton's sales achieved higher levels than all other salt brands combined.

MORTON, THE SALT YOU'VE BEEN PASSING FOR GENERATIONS

The decade of the 1970s brought increasing attention and concern among Americans about the potential relationship between the use of salt and certain diseases. Medical researchers observed that when certain patients suffering from hypertension or high blood pressure were fed a diet severely restricted in sodium, their blood pressure decreased. Few researchers were willing to state categorically that sodium *caused* hypertension, but some troubling questions were posed.

Several years later, the U.S. Senate Select Committee on Nutrition and Human Needs responded to concerns about salt usage by including it in a set of Dietary Goals for the United States. One of the stated goals was that salt consumption be reduced to approximately five grams per day from the average of ten or twelve grams normally ingested. Such a goal might be achieved, some suggested, by eliminating most highly salted processed foods and condiments, and by eliminating salt added at the table.

Health concerns about salt intake did not escape Morton management, and in 1973 (well ahead of the U.S. Senate Committee recommendations) Morton Lite Salt was introduced to consumers. Lite Salt was the first iodized salt mixture with the taste of regular salt, but with only half the sodium. Unlike Salt Substitute which was not positioned directly against regular salt, Lite Salt was expected to cannibalize Morton's regular salt to some extent. This was not a major concern to Morton management, however, since Lite was seen as "the salt of the future." [1] A $1 million advertising campaign, largely in television, accompanied the roll-out of Lite Salt.

During the 1970s Morton tested several other new seasoning products including Butter Buds, Sugar Cure, Tender Quick, and Nature's Seasons. Some of these products were reasonably successful and remained on the

market, while others were withdrawn due to insufficient sales.

To supplement Morton's fluctuating advertising budgets during this period (see Exhibits 1, 2, and 3), several sales promotion programs were employed. The first attempt was a set of four porcelain mugs offered for $2 plus a spout seal from a 26–ounce table salt package. Each mug featured a different Morton girl from the four periods of the company's history.

In 1975, another sales promotion program was developed to provide additional uses for

[1] "Morton Lite ties into 'RD' special insert." *Advertising Age,* October 29, 1973.

Exhibit 1. Blue Package Media History

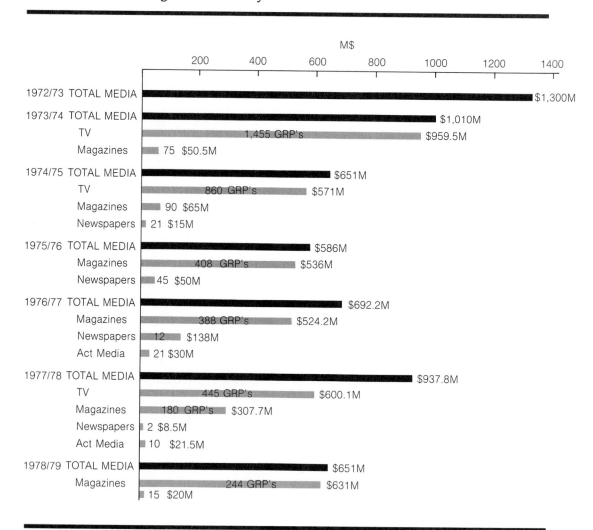

Exhibit 2. Salt Substitute Media History

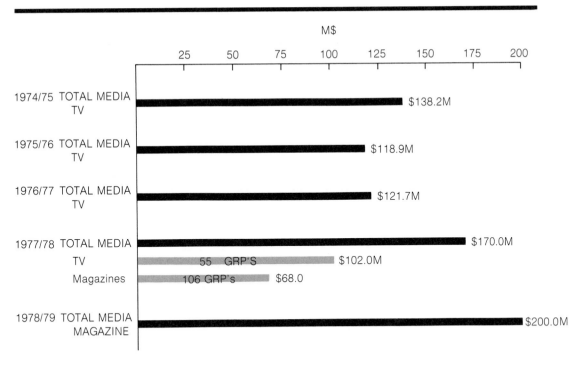

salt. Morton introduced salt sculpture (a mixture of flour, water, and salt) for holiday decorations. Film strips were offered to elementary schools, and a ten-minute film was sent to television stations, explaining salt sculpture. Print advertising in women's magazines offered Morton's "Dough It Yourself" Handbook for $1.

The promotions for salt sculpture ran during the Christmas season, and were continued during Easter and the Fourth of July for two years. By 1977, company executives estimated that 700,000 "Dough It Yourself" handbooks had been sold, and distribution was expanded to craft stores as well.

Despite a series of successful consumer and trade promotions, 26–ounce table salt could not sustain the company. "It's a strong cash producer," commented Morton's president in 1977, "but not a growth market." [2]

[2] "Morton pours more ad dollars into image-building bid." *Advertising Age,* August 8, 1977.

At the same time, management recognized that table salt could not be abandoned completely, for, although it represented only 5 percent of tonnage sales, it produced at least 35 percent of dollar sales.

Therefore, it was decided in 1977 to continue the sales promotion for Morton 26–ounce table salt. To capitalize on Americans' increased interest in geneology, Morton sponsored a "Visit the Land of Your Ancestors" sweepstakes. Also featured were mailed kits which contained recipes from the homelands of Americans of current and past generations. The sweepstakes was tied in with the advertising theme, "Morton, the salt you've been passing for generations." Morton table salt maintained its number-one position among table salts in 1977 with an all-time high market share.

A third promotion (in addition to the salt sculpture and sweepstakes promotions) was begun in 1978. Special salt packages with labels from four past container designs

Exhibit 3.   Lite Salt Media History

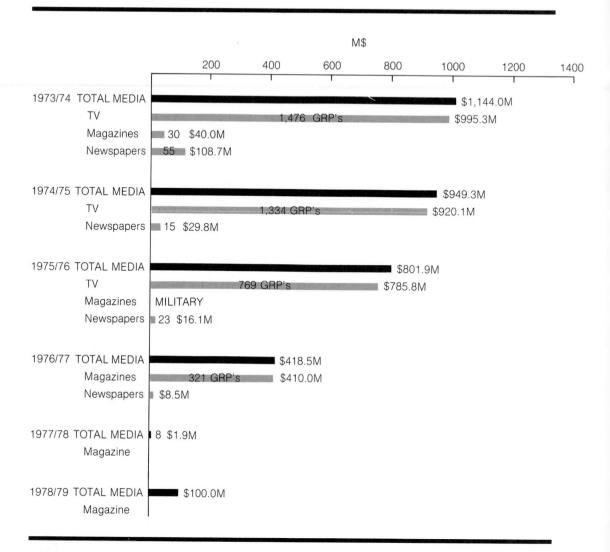

(1914, 1921, 1933, and 1941) were featured in retail stores. Consumers were urged through media advertising to collect the entire "Keepsake Collection." These innovations in sales promotion were another solution to the perennial problem of maintaining brand preference for a parity product.

SUMMARY

As George Tate opened his office door, marked Director of Communications, he realized that some important decisions now faced Morton Salt. Salt Substitute and Lite Salt were leading the market in their respective product categories, and Nature's Seasons was growing in sales as well. Regular table salt seemed to be doing well as a result of the sales promotions, although the medical concerns of the 1970s were not expected to fade.

It seemed to Tate that innovations in product development, in packaging, and in sales promotion had always solved past problems. However, he was now concerned with an advertising innovation as a remedy.

24

Texas Grape Growers Association *

When people think of where wine is produced in the United States, California and perhaps New York quickly come to mind. Rarely does anyone think of Texas. Although this was not always true. Texas has not been a major producer of wine since Prohibition. However, beginning in the mid-1970s several individuals and a few universities began efforts to redevelop a wine industry in Texas. Initial successes caused some people to believe that one day Texas might challenge California for the dominant position in the domestic wine market.

In 1975 and 1976 a small group of the Texas grape growers and agricultural experts from the University of Texas and from Texas A & M began to organize in order to share information and work toward common goals. On March 1, 1977, a meeting was held in Austin, and the Texas Grape Growers Association (TGGA) was officially formed. Since its inception, the TGGA's membership has increased to approximately 175.

Several years after the founding of the TGGA a number of the members of the Association felt that the time was ripe for the TGGA to begin to advertise and promote Texas wines to consumers. They suggested that it was logical for the Association not to attempt to move on a national basis initially, but rather to begin by advertising their

wines exclusively within the state of Texas. Although funds for such advertising were presently nonexistent, it was suggested that some important objectives could be accomplished by carefully budgeting a modest advertising appropriation. The first and foremost question in examining the suggestion that the TGGA launch a generic Texas wines advertising campaign was what constituted an appropriate level of investment during the first fiscal year of such a campaign.

EARLY HISTORY OF WINE PRODUCTION IN TEXAS

Growing grapes in Texas for wine production dates back more than three centuries. Around 1662 the Franciscan Fathers in Texas planted vineyards to produce wines for religious ceremonies and medication. Their grapevines were originally brought from Spain and Mexico. Spanish settlers in Texas also planted vineyards near El Paso, and in the 1800s German immigrants started vineyards in the hill country of central Texas.

During the late 1800s Texas vineyards played an important role in wine history. At that time, Thomas Volney Munson, considered the father of the Texas wine industry, was searching for grapes adaptable to the southern United States. Munson experimented with the Vitis Vinifera grape, the variety used in many of the best European wines. Munson succeeded in crossing this grape with native Texas varieties. He also

* This case prepared by Ronald J. Faber and Tom O'Guinn. From Patti and Murphey, *Cases in Advertising and Promotion Management.* Copyright © 1983 by John Wiley & Sons. Used by permission.

managed to develop hardier, more disease-resistant plants. These hardy hybrid vines made Munson famous.

In the 1880s much of Europe's vineyards were ravaged by a disease called phylloxera. Munson helped to save some of these vineyards by shipping thousands of his disease-resistant root-stock vines to Europe. For his effort, Munson was awarded the French Legion of Honor.

By the early 1900s Texas had become the third largest grape-producing state in the United States, with 25 wineries operating across a wide section of the state. Not only did Texas vineyards produce large quantities of grapes, they also produced high-quality wines. Among other international awards, a Texas wine won top honors at the 1890 World's Fair. However, all wine production in Texas ceased in 1920 with the enactment of Prohibition. When wine became illegal, grape growing in Texas virtually disappeared.

In 1933, with the repeal of Prohibition, many states, most notably California, quickly began growing grapes for wine once again. However, this was not the case in Texas. Wine production remained relatively dormant in the state until the early 1970s.

RECENT DEVELOPMENTS

In the late 1960s the demand for grapes in the United States far exceeded the supply. Grape growers enjoyed boom years when there were simply not enough grapes to satisfy demand. Prices rose rapidly and profits were very good. All across the nation farmers tried to cash in on the scarcity. In Texas, enterprising farmers rushed to plant vines. Unfortunately, the boom ended, prices fell, and many of the novice growers found grape production to be an exercise in frustration. A few, however, persisted.

These survivors were scattered across the state. The most successful of these growers were concentrated in west Texas. Fungal diseases such as Pierce's disease and cotton-root rot limited production in all but north,

northwest, and west Texas. The air in these western regions is so dry that fungal infections of the vines are rare. In addition, the soil in west Texas is particularly good for grape production; it is permeable and has good drainage. It is, in fact, very similar to the grape-growing soils of France.

Through the use of drip irrigation west Texas growers found an efficient means of watering their vineyards. Drip irrigation, a process in which water is slowly dripped from plastic pipes, is not only an efficient means of conservation, but a means by which salt can be leached from the normally saline west Texas soil as well. The growing season, although earlier in the year, was thought by many experts to be more desirable than those of California or New York. Birds and hail were the most serious threats to production in west Texas. They have not, however, proved to be insurmountable problems. Nets have been used to frustrate hungry birds and natural topographical barriers have been used to prevent or minimize hail damage. Late rainfalls do, however, preclude raisin production.

In 1975 there were only 25 acres of Texas land being used for grape production. A few years later there were over 1,000. This growth has not come exclusively from the private sector.

The University of Texas system, which is an important member of TGGA, owns approximately 2.5 million acres of west Texas land. The university lands had for years been exploited for their rich oil reserves. Since the land's utility from oil production is finite, the university has sought alternative uses. After walnuts, almonds, olives, kiwi, jojoba, and pecans were tried, grapes were planted. UT viticulturists and winemakers have produced some very good experimental wines. It appeared the university was primarily interested in demonstrating the commercial feasibility of such an operation and then leasing its vineyards to a large commercial winery. Both Gallo and Paul Masson have expressed interest. The university estimated that it had

40,000 to 60,000 acres suited to the growing of grapes.

Other TGGA members' vineyards and wineries had also been expanding rapidly in an attempt to take advantage of steadily increased demand. For example, the vineyards of the La Buena Vida Winery will triple in acreage by 1986. Such growth is closer to the rule than the exception. As acreage increases, so does wine production.

For example, the Fall Creek Winery produced 1,100 gallons of wine in 1980 compared with only 600 in 1979. La Buena Vida estimated 1981 production at 7,000 cases or approximately 17,000 gallons compared with only 600 cases or approximately 1,400 gallons in 1978. La Buena Vida officials estimated 1985 production to be 15,000 cases or approximately 38,000 gallons. Total statewide production for 1981 was estimated to be 50,000 gallons or approximately 21,000 cases.

It generally takes grape vines five to seven years from the time they are planted until they are capable of producing a crop suitable for wine production. Wines produced before vine maturation lead to poor quality wines. Yet, while the vineyard owners are waiting for their vines to mature, they are losing money. This situation can result in considerable pressure to produce a wine "long before its time" just to stay in business. These pressures were sometimes too powerful to resist and some premature Texas wines have been released on the market.

In some cases this situation has resulted in Texas wines gaining a bad reputation. However, most Texas wines were produced from vines that were six to ten years old and thus capable of producing good-quality wines. The growers learned from their experience and the quality of Texas wines had improved in recent years. Also, there were indications that success may be just around the corner for many Texas growers. One vintner produced a gold medal wine at the 1979 Eastern Wine Competition. Many wine and food critics have found several Texas wines to be truly competitive with similarly priced California and French wines.

It had been only recently that Texas wines became available in retail outlets. They could, however, be found in only a few restaurants, some liquor stores, and a few specialty stores such as wine and cheese shops around the state. It was almost impossible to find Texas wines in grocery or convenience stores. For example, in Austin, the state capital, Texas wines could be found in only a few liquor stores, three or four wine and cheese shops, and one restaurant. As production increased, the Texas grape growers and wineries were well aware of the need to expand the number of distribution outlets in which their product was available.

TRENDS IN U.S. WINE CONSUMPTION

The year 1980 was a landmark year for wines in the United States. For the first time in history, consumption of wine exceeded that of liquor (465 million gallons of wine compared with 450 million gallons of distilled spirits). Additionally, wine consumption expenditures topped the $4 billion mark for the first time. Wine consumption has been on the upswing in the United States for many years; the industry has grown steadily every year since 1962. During the decade from 1970 through 1979, consumption increased 71.6% (see Exhibit 1). The increase in dollar expenditures during this period was even more phenomenal, showing an increase of 173.6%.

Most industry experts forecasted that wine consumption in the United States will continue to enjoy healthy growth during the 1980s despite the fact that prices should continue to rise. *Impact,* a wine industry newsletter, predicted that wine consumption will show a 6 to 10% per year increase in the coming years. Other industry sources projected an average annual growth rate of 6% through 1985. The *Wine Marketing Handbook* predicted that total U.S. wine sales will increase from 154.4 million cases in 1979 to an estimated 209.3 million cases in 1984.

Exhibit 1.   Changes in U.S. Wine Consumption From 1970 to 1979

Year	Gallons Consumed (in millions)	Adult per Capita Consumption (gallons)	Consumer Expenditures (in millions)
1979	439.1	2.94	$3,998
1978	418.0	2.83	3,621
1977	389.7	2.69	3,128
1976	371.8	2.59	2,919
1975	361.6	2.58	2,685
1974	341.8	2.49	2,453
1973	337.8	2.51	2,270
1972	326.9	2.49	2,020
1971	295.7	2.37	1,755
1970	255.9	2.09	1,461

Most experts believe that projected increases for the 1980s will occur not because of any significant increase in the number of people drinking wine, but, rather, because of an increase in the frequency of wine drinking among current consumers. Although the per capita consumption rate in the United States has more than doubled in 20 years, it has not yet begun to approach the rate of many other countries (see Exhibit 2).

Wines may be divided into four different classifications: table wine, dessert wine, champagne and sparkling wines, and vermouth. Table wine accounted for three-fourths (74.6%) of all wine consumed in the United States. Between 1970 and 1979, the number of cases of table wine consumed in the United States increased 156% (from 45 million cases in 1970 to 115.2 million cases in 1979). Projections indicated that by 1984 consumption of table wine will increase to 171.2 million cases. This was good news for Texas grape growers since almost all the wines produced in Texas were table wines.

The market for table wine in Texas had grown even faster than the national rate. In

Exhibit 2.   Approximate Per Capita Consumption of Wine in the United States and Selected European Countries

Country	Per Capita Consumption (in gallons)
France	27.2
Italy	25.2
Spain	19.4
Switzerland	12.8
Greece	11.6
Hungary	9.4
Yugoslavia	7.8
West Germany	6.6
United States	2.0

Source: The Wine Marketing Handbook, 1980.

1979 Texas moved from eighth largest consuming state to the fifth largest. Only California, New York, Florida, and Illinois had greater sales of table wines than Texas (see Exhibit 3). However, while Texas accounted for 3.9% of all sales of table wines, this was less than what might be expected on the basis of its population (5.5% of total United States population). Nonetheless, as wine production in Texas expands and more local wineries are started, the increase in wine consumption in Texas should escalate. Gretchen Glasscock, one of the pioneers of the Texas wine industry, stated, "Research has proved that wherever there is a local winery, wine consumption soars."

As the quality and reputation of domestic table wines have improved, so has consumption. In 1981 less than 25% of table wines consumed in the United States were imported. In recent years all of the major importing countries, with the exception of Italy, have reported a decrease in United States table wine sales. Exhibit 4 indicates the origin of table wines consumed in the United States in 1979.

The type of table wine consumed in the United States underwent a drastic change during the twenty-year period 1960–1980. In 1960, red wines represented the vast majority of table wine consumed. However, as can be seen in Exhibit 5, by 1980 over half of the table wine purchased was white wine. Some wine marketers believe that this change may be due more to a preference for chilled wine than just a preference for white wine. The change toward white wines, for whatever reason, was viewed as advantageous to Texas growers since they have been much more successful in producing quality white wines than red wines.

Along with color, table wines are also categorized by price. The cheapest wines, costing $2 or less for a 750-ml bottle in 1978–1979, were referred to as jug wines. These inexpensive wines represented about half of all table wines sold in the United States in 1979 (see Exhibit 6). There was, however, a growing trend toward the more expensive, premium table wines. Indications were that this was not due simply to inflation, but also to a growing sophistication among American wine drinkers.

Most of the Texas winemakers were interested in selling mid-premium level wines at $3 to $5 per bottle. They believed that this

Exhibit 3. Top Ten States in Table Wine Consumption in 1979

State	Cases Sold	Percent of U.S. Cases Sold
California	28,266,040	24.5
New York	11,537,336	10.0
Florida	5,892,834	5.1
Illinois	5,125,769	4.4
Texas	4,438,524	3.9
New Jersey	4,412,842	3.8
Pennsylvania	4,350,487	3.8
Michigan	4,014,262	3.5
Massachusetts	3,712,212	3.2
Ohio	3,483,502	3.0
Total top ten	75,233,808	65.2
U.S. total	115,216,641	100.0

Source: The Wine Marketing Handbook, 1980.

Exhibit 4.   1979 U.S. Table Wine Consumption by Country of Origination

Country	Gallons Consumed (in millions)	Percent
Italy	43.2	12.3
France	12.9	3.7
Germany	11.7	3.3
Other foreign countries	13.4	3.8
Total imported wines	81.2	23.1
California	246.1	70.0
New York	18.0	5.1
Other states	6.3	1.8
Total domestic wines	270.4	76.9
Total	351.6	100.0

Source: *The Wine Marketing Handbook*, 1980.

was the best market at which to aim since people were moving toward the higher priced wines, and they believed Texas wine quality was competitive in this range.

Cost considerations generally prevented a Texas wine priced much lower than $3 per bottle. While most industry experts felt that very high-priced Texas wines would experience a problem with extremely tough competition, the $3 and $5 per bottle pricing strategy had the advantage of simultaneously encouraging initial purchases and legitimizing the product. It was inexpensive enough to try, but at the same time expensive enough to be good.

WINE CONSUMERS

Sixty-nine percent of all American adults drank some form of alcoholic beverage, and almost all of these people at least occasionally drank wine. Wine consumption tended to be heavier among the younger, better-educated, and wealthier segments of the population. According to a *Newsweek* report, "Spirits

Exhibit 5.   Percent of Market Share for Different Colors of Table Wines

Color	1960 (percent)	1970 (percent)	1980 (percent)
Red	73	50	26
White	17	24	54
Rose	10	26	20

Source: *Ad Age*, April 20, 1981.

Exhibit 6. 1978–1979 Percent of Sales for Table Wines by Price Classification

Class	Price Range	1978 (percent)	1979 (percent)
Low (jug)	under $2.00	51.7	50.1
Lower mid	$2.00–$2.75	26.7	26.9
Middle	$2.76–$4.25	12.6	13.3
Upper mid	$4.26–$5.75	5.9	6.4
Upper	over $5.75	3.1	3.3
		100.0	100.0

Source: *The Wine Marketing Handbook*, 1980.

of '79," 52% of U.S. wine consumers were between 25 and 49 years old: almost half (49%) had at least attended college, and 48% had household incomes of $20,000 or more.

Other studies indicated that women were a particularly important target market. A study of *Glamour* magazine's working women readers revealed that a majority (72%) preferred wine over other alcoholic beverages. They cited taste, fewer calories, and cost as the major reasons for this preference.

A study of *Family Circle* readers found that in 83% of the households polled, women chose the brand of table wine purchased at least some of the time. However 80% of these women also said that a man in their household was a "very" or "somewhat important" source of information about wine.

Other research reported in the *Wine Marketing Handbook* indicated that women played a large role in determining how much to spend on wine. Among the respondents, 37.5% said the woman had a greater role in this decision, 38.5% said it was equally decided; and 24% said that the man in the household usually had a greater influence in this decision.

While most people purchased wine for their own use, or to entertain guests, buying wine as a gift had become very popular. Wine was most commonly given as a house gift, although many people gave wine for Christmas or birthdays. The influence of holiday entertaining and gifts can be seen in the sales increase during the last quarter of the typical year (see Exhibit 7).

The vast majority of wine consumed in the state of Texas was consumed in the state's larger metropolitan areas. Approximately 80% of sales came from either Dallas-Fort Worth, Houston, San Antonio, or El Paso. San Antonio and El Paso taken together accounted for 15% of sales; 34.5% came from Dallas-Fort Worth; and Houston accounted for 30.5% of wine sales in Texas.

In addition to residing in a metropolitan area, the average wine consumer in Texas was young, most often between the ages of 21 and 40. Along most dimensions, the wine consumers of Texas appeared quite similar to the national profile.

LEGAL ISSUES

Texas is composed of both "wet" and "dry" areas. In dry areas, located primarily in east and west Texas, it is against the law to sell alcoholic beverages. Most often county lines define these areas. In a few instances, however, there are wet/dry divisions within one county; for example, Dallas County contains wet and dry precincts. Thus, people who live in a dry area who wish to purchase wine might need only to cross the street or they

Exhibit 7. U.S. Table Wine Sales by Month in 1979

Month	Cases Sold	Percent
January	8,641,248	7.5
February	8,295,598	7.2
March	9,102,115	7.9
April	11,060,798	9.6
May	8,526,031	7.4
June	8,986,898	7.8
July	8,871,681	7.7
August	8,180,382	7.1
September	7,373,865	6.4
October	10,023,848	8.7
November	11,521,664	10.0
December	14,632,513	12.7
Total	115,216,641	100.0

Source: *The Wine Marketing Handbook,* 1980.

might have to travel a considerable distance to make a purchase. This situation created obvious distribution and advertising problems.

Several of the Texas wineries were located in dry areas. Although it was completely legal to make the wine, it was illegal to sell it within these dry areas. This eliminated one possible channel of distribution: direct sales. The tasting rooms of wineries were often the site of substantial sales and had traditionally been a very profitable distribution channel to consumers.

In an effort to eliminate some of the inequity between wineries operating in wet versus dry areas, the TGGA had successfully lobbied the state legislature into enacting laws which allowed a vintner operating in a dry area to sell his first 25,000 gallons directly to retailers. Up until the enactment of the revised laws, all vintners were required by law to sell to a wholesaler. The new law also allowed wineries located in wet areas to sell some wine directly from their tasting rooms with all remaining wine having to go through a wholesaler. While the TGGA was

encouraged by this success in getting the legislature to remove the inequity between wet and dry areas, they realized that several other legislative issues could determine the likelihood of success for the Texas wine industry. Of major concern was the need for legislative assistance during the industry's formative period. On several occasions local wineries in other states had been the object of fierce price competition from the major California wineries; the Californians had not been willing to relinquish even small local markets without a fight. For example, when a million gallon winery was built in Arkansas, price competition by California growers nearly forced it to close. It was only through the enactment of protective state tariffs that the local winery was able to survive. Several TGGA members believed that similar laws would be needed in Texas.

ADVERTISING AND PROMOTION

The TGGA had never sponsored any advertising. Further, while a few individual growers had published their own newsletters, none had attempted to engage in media advertising. As the industry began to be revitalized in Texas, many newspapers and magazines in the state had run stories on Texas wines. While this publicity was helpful, it was unlikely to be sufficient for the successful promotion of Texas wine. The members of TGGA realized that they should consider using advertising and sales promotion to stimulate sales of Texas wines. As was stated earlier, the TGGA felt that their first goal should be to concentrate on the Texas market and then, when production was sufficient, to move into the national market.

Since none of the Texas growers was large enough to engage in a large-scale advertising or promotional campaign on its own, the best approach seemed to be to band together to promote Texas wines in a generic approach. However, there was considerable disagreement among members of the TGGA as to how this could best be accomplished. One of the first considerations was to whom advertising and promotions should be directed.

One group that needed to be reached through advertising and sales promotion was retailers. In 1980 there were 7,246 wine retail outlets in Texas. Approximately 1,700 of these were located in Houston. Dallas-Fort Worth and surrounding areas contained 1,020 package stores selling wines and 544 stores were located in the San Antonio area (Bexar County). These retailers needed to be convinced that it would be worthwhile for them to devote limited shelf space to stock Texas wines. Additionally, these retailers could play an important part in helping to promote Texas wines to the consumer. For example, research on readers of *Family Circle* magazine found that women rated retail stores as an important source of information concerning wine. Fifty percent rated store displays as being "very" or "somewhat" important, and 47% stated that store sales personnel were at least a "somewhat important"

source. The only other sources receiving a greater or equal number of positive ratings were friends and relatives and television commercials.

The retailers themselves believed that the wine companies could be helpful in educating the consumer. In a survey of liquor stores, owners and managers were asked what were the most useful services provided by wine companies. Wine information (28%) and displays (26%) were the most frequently mentioned services. Some of the Texas grape growers, therefore, felt that advertising and promotion should center on the retailer outlets and utilize these stores' personnel to help educate consumers about Texas wines.

Another possible target market was, of course, the consumer. While the first consumer objective would be to make them aware of Texas wines, altering attitudes was also essential. Wine had traditionally been linked to the sophisticate; it was thought to be a sign of culture. Identification with the state of Texas had, however, not always enjoyed that same connotation. The problem of image was one with which Texas winemakers and the TGGA would have to contend. Even though Texas had within its borders three of the nation's 10 largest cities, many Texas vintners still feared that their product would be tied to the image of the Wild West, a place known more for its not-so-smooth whiskey and beer than for fine wines.

Some people were also likely to view Texas wines as a novelty and not something to be taken seriously. Several growers noted that Texas wines had done very well in blind taste tests, but when people were told that the wines were from Texas, their interest seemed to wane. It was, therefore, crucial to convince potential consumers that high-quality wines could, and did, come from Texas.

The members of the TGGA were divided on how best to reach consumers and how any limited advertising appropriation should be used. Some argued that they should forgo advertising and concentrate solely on consumer sales promotions. These promotions could be of two types. First, attractive displays could be set up in liquor stores and supermarkets. These displays would stress the high quality of Texas wines. An attractive, medium-sized in-store display would cost in the $8 to $12 per display range. The second type of consumer promotion could use tasting booths at state fairs and other large gatherings. These would encourage people to taste Texas wines and learn firsthand of their quality.

The growers who favored consumer advertising argued that the sales promotion approach would miss a large segment of potential consumers and would do little to overcome their image problem. They stressed that media advertising was the best method of promoting Texas wines.

A major drawback to consumer advertising was the fear that the TGGA's message would get lost in the huge amount of wine advertising. Budgets for advertising wine had been growing at phenomenal rates. In 1979, $136.6 million was spent on wine ad-

vertising. This was more than twice the amount spent just two years earlier. On the average, the industry had been spending just over $.31 on advertising per gallon of wine sold. Gallo alone, the industry leader, spent over $20 million in 1979, with over 75% of it going to network television. Although these were national figures and the TGGA planned to concentrate on just Texas, any potential advertising campaign might still look very small when compared with their competitors.

Two characteristics stand out in terms of wine advertising. First, the majority of wine advertising was placed in the broadcast media. Over 75% of all wine advertising dollars in 1979 was spent on television and an additional 8.3% went to radio. Exhibit 8 presents a breakdown of wine advertising by media.

Second, wine advertising was heavily concentrated during the last quarter of the calendar year. Over half of all the advertising dollars invested went for ads during the holiday period. Exhibit 9 presents a breakdown of magazine advertising expenditures by month in 1979.

Exhibit 8. Wine Advertising Expenditures by Media in 1979

Media	Millions of Dollars	Percent
Magazine	17.0	12.5
Newspaper	4.9	3.6
Outdoor	.1	—
Total print	220.0	16.1
Spot TV	36.6	26.8
Network TV	66.7	48.8
Spot radio	10.1	7.4
Network radio	1.2	.9
Total broadcast	114.6	83.9
Grand total	136.6	100.0

Source: *The Wine Marketing Handbook*, 1980.

**Exhibit 9. Magazine Advertising Expenditures
by Vintners by Month in 1979**

Month	Thousands of Dollars	Percent
January	425.8	2.5
February	238.5	1.4
March	425.8	2.5
April	1,396.7	8.2
May	1,618.1	9.5
June	1,039.0	6.1
July	647.2	3.8
August	408.8	2.4
September	1,124.2	6.6
October	3,372.5	19.8
November	3,491.7	20.5
December	2,844.4	16.7

Source: *The Wine Marketing Handbook,* 1980.

25

Quick Meal Food Systems, Inc.*

INTRODUCTION

Quick Meal Food Systems, Inc. (QM), based in Rocky Mount, North Carolina, opened its doors in 1960. Wilbur Smith, who opened the restaurant, quickly sold his interest for $20,000. As of October 21, 1976, the company owned 328 restaurants and licensed 625. In the summer of 1977 QM had 1,000 stores in operation, both privately and company owned. The 1,000th unit was opened in the summer of 1977 in Davenport, Iowa. The units were directed from the main headquarters in Rocky Mount, North Carolina. QM grossed $214 million in sales in 1977 and $6.4 million in profits. This was a 2.9 percent profit on sales compared with McDonald's profit, which was almost 10 percent for that same year. In 1978 QM expanded to 1,056 stores.

According to *Food Systems News* (August–September, 1977) QM operated in about 70 percent of the U.S. and several foreign countries including El Salvador, Guatemala, and Japan (Exhibit 1). The company's growth had been outstanding. It was the 25th largest food operation in the U.S. at that time. The U.S. Armed Forces was the number one food

* This case was prepared by Michael V. Laric, University of Connecticut, with the intention of providing a basis for class discussion rather than illustrating either effective or ineffective management of a business situation. Reprinted with permission from *Application of Decision Sciences in Organizations: A Case Approach* by Joseph C. Latona and K. Mark Weaver with the cooperation of the Decision Sciences Institute (formerly the American Institute for Decision Sciences), Atlanta, Georgia, 1980.

operation. Financial data for 1976 is given in Exhibits 2 and 3.

QM and its subsidiaries operated, licensed, and serviced limited-menu, self-service restaurants under the name QM. The QM menu featured popular-priced food, including hamburgers, cheeseburgers, roast beef sandwiches, fish sandwiches, french fried potatoes, apple turnovers, milk shakes and soft drinks.

The Specialty Foods Division processed a varied line of frozen meat and seafood entrees, specialty products, and portion-controlled meat products, which were sold to supermarket chains for home consumption and to institutional distributors.

BACKGROUND

QM was still independent although many competitors, notably Burger King, Jack-in-the-Box, and Taco Bell, were not. QM's major problem has been capital shortage for growth purposes.

The current president and chief executive officer, Jack A. Laughery, age 43, was a tough executive who learned the business the hard way. According to *Fortune* (July 17, 1978, p. 16), "Laughery joined a restaurant chain called Sandy's in 1960, and learned the business from the griddle up, flipping hamburgers in St. Paul. He became a vice-president of QM when Sandy's merged with the larger chain in 1972. Since becoming C.E.O. three years ago, Laughery has extricated QM

Exhibit 1. Quick Meal Food Systems, Inc. Geographical Distribution *

	Company Stores	Licensee Stores		Company Stores	Licensee Stores
AREA 1			**AREA 4**		
Massachusetts	5	0	North Dakota	0	7
Connecticut	17	0	South Dakota	0	0
New York	16	1	Minnesota	1	27
New Jersey	0	8	Wisconsin	0	29
Pennsylvania	19	21	Michigan	23	2
Delaware	22	0	Ohio	4	4
Maryland	3	3	Indiana	0	10
West Virginia	1	1	Illinois	30	39
Virginia	18	62	Iowa	24	18
Washington, D.C.	1	0	Missouri	12	8
AREA 2			Kansas	6	28
North Carolina	57	142	Oklahoma	5	8
South Carolina	21	70	Arkansas	6	0
AREA 3			Texas	0	1
Kentucky	11	1	Arizona	0	10
Tennessee	1	35			
Georgia	62	22			
Florida	5	23			
Alabama	5	49			
Mississippi	0	10			
Louisiana	0	1			

* Company also has stores in El Salvador (4), Guatemala (1), and Japan (1).

from some unprofitable lines of business and has started opening more restaurants in better locations. But to keep growing he needs capital—and that means merger."

QM almost succeeded in trying to merge with Pet, Inc., a $100 million deal. But IC Industries stepped in, and Pet's president and chairman acceded to a $350 million merger. QM was left on the sidelines with just a promise that "good faith" negotiations would continue.

QM's goals were "to provide an above average return to shareholders and to be certain that along with growth . . . close and caring relationships" were maintained.

To maintain growth, QM merged with Sandy's, a midwest fast-food chain of 200 units in 1972 and opened units on Interstate 95 in northeastern U.S. in 1974. They had not been successful in penetrating the western United States with their units. (A list of other acquisitions appears in Exhibit 4.) QM had four distribution centers located in Atlanta, Georgia; Independence, Missouri; Mason City, Iowa; and Quakertown, Pennsylvania. QM's products were manufactured by their own factories and the Gol-Pak Company. They were distributed to four areas of the U.S.: (1) the Northeast; (2) North and South Carolina; (3) the Southeast; and (4) the Midwest. (Refer to Exhibit 1 for the exact configuration.)

QM'S ORGANIZATION

The QM organization was led by 21 vice-presidents directing over 20,000 employees

Exhibit 2. Quick Meal Food Systems, Inc.
Consolidated Balance Sheet October 31, 1976 ($000 omitted)

ASSETS	1976	1975
Current assets:		
Cash	$ 6,557	$ 4,282
Receivables (net)	5,342	5,017
Inventories [1]	9,687	9,689
Deferred tax benefits	290	466
Prepayments	1,151	1,066
Total current assets	$23,027	$20,520
Net property, etc. [2]	32,625	28,703
Assets leased	3,902	4,372
Investments	— [3]	1,390
Noncurrent receivables	2,274	1,518
Goodwill and intangibles	4,620	4,918
Deferred charges, etc.	369	494
Total assets	$66,817	$61,915

LIABILITIES and STOCKHOLDERS' EQUITY		
Current liabilities:		
Notes, etc., payable	$ 2,312	$ 2,415
Accounts payable	9,473	8,505
Closed stores cost [4]	410	611
Income taxes	1,940	1,747
Total current liabilities	$14,135	$13,278
Long-term debt	19,251	20,045
Deferred income taxes	1,787	1,364
Deferred income	261	388
Minority interest	205	172
Closed stores cost [4]	2,148	1,877
Stockholders' equity:		
Common stock [5]	$ 1,714	$ 1,714
Capital surplus	12,100	12,098
Retained earnings	15,387	11,168
Reacquired stock [6]	(171)	(189)
Total stockholders' equity	$29,030	$24,791
Total Liabilities and Stockholders' Equity	$66,817	$61,915

[1] Lower cost (fifo) or market.

[2] Depreciation and amortization: 1976, $16,115; 1975, $12,965.

[3] Investment in and advances to a 50 percent owned partnership, at equity in net assets.

[4] Estimated future cost of closed stores.

[5] 3,428,390 no-par shares.

[6] Shares at cost: 1976, 45,616; 1975, 50,466.

Exhibit 3. Quick Meal Food Systems, Inc.
Selected Financial Data October 31, 1976 ($000 omitted)

	1976	1975
Sales and revenues	$ 188,051	$ 162,907
Cost of sales	98,668	84,650
Selling, etc. expenses	78,527	69,982
Closed store expenses, prov	828	2,308
Income taxes	3,942	1,298
Income continuing operation	4,219	1,540
Earnings, common shares	1.25	0.46
Interest, net	1,867	3,130
Discontinued operations:		
Operating loss	—	26
Disposal loss	—	416
Net income [1]	4,219	1,098
Earnings, common shares	1.25	0.33
Year end shares	3,382,774	3,377,924

[1] After $4,452,916 (1975, $3,960,457) depreciation and amortization.

throughout the system. Next in line were the area executives who supervised regional managers. The regional managers supervised district managers. A district manager directed from five to seven stores and coached the managers in the district.

The store managers were expected to achieve predetermined goals and keep area and corporate staff informed of problems requiring their attention in the district. The store managers also had to plan and execute programs to improve sales, quality of foods, and service. The manager was typically responsible for from 15 to 50 employees and achieving sales and profit goals. He or she also coordinated activities relating to shifts, meeting food standards, unit communications, accident prevention, customer and community relations, and overall operations.

The assistant manager reported to and assisted the unit manager. He or she supervised from 3 to 15 employees and handled recruiting and training of personnel, food production, scheduling, and other tasks necessary to maintain operation of each QM unit.

QM OPENS A NEW STORE

In the fall of 1977 QM's executives were looking into opening a new restaurant next to the campus of the University of Connecticut. The University had over 16,000 students, approximately half of which attended the summer session. The University, located in the town of Storrs, Connecticut, had a population of close to 20,000 people. The per capita income for 1977 was $5,756 with the household income at $19,570 for 1977. The second largest employer in town (after the University with 4,400 employees) was the Mansfield Training School (1,100 employees), a facility for the mentally retarded. Unemployment in 1976 was around 3.5 percent or roughly half the national average. Retail sales (available by county) were $208 million for 1975. Food sales accounted for 30 percent of the above.

**Exhibit 4. Subsidiaries and Facilities Maintained by
Quick Meal Food Systems, Inc. (As of October 1976)** [1]

Restaurant Division:

Annapolis, MD
Atlanta, GA
Glastonbury, CT
Kewanee, IL

Mechanicsburg, PA
Rocky Mount, NC
Southfield, MI

Equipment Division:

Kewanee, IL

Rocky Mount, NC

Food Processing & Distribution Division:

Atlanta, GA
Independence, MO
Mason City, IA
Secaucus, NJ

Oneida, NY
Quakertown, PA
Rocky Mount, NC

Fast-Food Division:

Fast Foodmakers, Inc. (Acquired 1969)
Hardee's Restaurants, Inc. (Acquired 1967)

Specialty Foods Division:

Golden Shore Seafoods, Inc. (Acquired 1967)
New Orleans Shrimp Co., Inc. (Acquired 1968)
Gol-Pak Corp. (Acquired 1969)

---

[1] Based on *Moody's Industrial Manual*, p. 1583.

Competition existing in fast-food chains included a McDonald's restaurant (7.5 miles away) and another one, which was to open for the fall 1978 semester, about 5 miles away. Several restaurants were available within a two-mile radius from the campus and included two student cafeterias, two luncheonettes, two pizza places, a steak house (about 2.5 miles away), and a restaurant.

QM executives preferred a site which would be adjacent to the campus. The only one available was an underground storage area. QM decided to rent it and began renovating the chosen site with a tentative opening in the fall of 1978 (prior to the beginning of classes at the University). Several data collection efforts were underway to try to assess the existing sales potential and the best ways to build up future sales.

MARKETING RESEARCH DATA FOR NEW RESTAURANTS

Exhibit 5 portrays the local media that was available, categorized into local radio stations and local print media. The advertising rates for each medium and some information about circulation are included. Manager Gary Scutti hired a marketing student to survey the local student population. A copy of the survey questionnaire is presented in Exhibit 6.

The highlights of the brief survey can be summarized as follows: The survey was distributed to 135 students randomly selected. A total of 101 students, consisting of 58 males and 43 females, completed the questionnaires. Sixty persons owned automobiles and kept them on campus. Most were full-time students occasionally working part time. Twenty-two percent had a steady part-time job, earning from $26–40 per week.

Exhibit 5. Quick Meal Food Systems, Inc.
Local Media Available in the Area for Proposed New Restaurant

RADIO STATIONS AVAILABLE IN THE AREA *

	WCCC, Hartford	WHCN, Hartford	WTIC, Hartford
Dial position:	1290 AM 106.9 FM	106 FM	1080 AM 96.5 FM
Power: (watts)	500 AM 50,000 FM	50,000	15,000 FM 50,000 AM
Period of operation:	24 hrs FM, Day AM	24 hrs	Both 24 hrs
Broadcast format:	Both album-oriented rock	Album-oriented rock	FM-Top 40 Hits AM-Adult contemporary
Sample rates:	1 time–$25.75 6 ″ –25.75 12 ″ –25.00	$13–$22.00 depending on frequency and time of day	FM 2 p.m.–midnight, 6 × $20; 6 a.m.–2 p.m., 6 × $15; midnight–6 a.m., 6 × $9; AM 6–10 a.m. and 3–7 p.m., 1–12 spots/week, $140; Midday 10–3 p.m., 12 × $85; 8–12 p.m., 12 × $60

	WDRC, Hartford	WXLS, Willimantic	WILI, Willimantic
Dial position:	1360 AM 102.9 FM	98.3 FM	1400 AM
Power: (watts)	5000 AM 15,000 FM	5000	1000 daytime, 250 nights
Period of operation:	24 hrs	24 hrs	24 hrs
Broadcast format:	AM-Top 40 FM-Album-oriented rock	Popular Music	Progressive rock, news on the hour
Sample rates:	$55/minute 5:30–10 a.m. Midday, 10 a.m.–8 p.m. $50; Rest of night– $44	$10.00/60 seconds	Approx. $8/60 seconds depending on the frequency of the broadcast
Circulation:	Monday–Friday	6 days, Monday–Saturday	Daily, mornings
Circulation breakdown:	10,000 distributed on campus, 180 off campus (20,000 readers), AM	10,400 distributed in 15 towns, 5 around Willimantic	Central, Conn. to New Haven to Danielson, Conn. to Mass. line
Page size:	5 column page, 12–16 pp.	8 columns, 18 pp.	7 column page, 90 pp.
Printing method:	Offset	Offset	Offset
Rates per column inch:	$2.05 up to 13″ $1.95 13″–31″ $1.85 31″–54″ $1.75 54″–full page	$2.40	NA
Telephone:	429–9384	423–8466	429–9339

Exhibit 5. (continued)

	Stafford Springs Reminder	Gold Mine Shopper (Free)	Broadcasters Shoppers Guide
Circulation:	Weekly, Tuesday	Weekly, Tuesday AM	Weekly
Circulation breakdown:	10,500 in Stafford Springs, Stafford, Tolland, Conn. (not Storrs)	21,700 distributed in 20 towns around Willimantic	28,000 distributed in Willimantic 16 towns
Page size:	4 columns, 8½″ × 11″ page	4 columns, 30–32 pp.	16 columns, 34–36 pp.
Printing method:	Offset	Offset	Offset
Rates per column inch:	NA	$1.75	$2.00
Telephone:	684–4205	423–8466	456–2211

* WHUS, University of Connecticut, Storrs, Connecticut, operates 24 hours a day but does not accept commercial advertising.

Pizza seemed to be preferred by 40 percent of the participants, while 25 percent preferred hamburgers. Twenty-three percent of the students preferred to eat grinders and 13 percent enjoyed eating club sandwiches. None seemed to like hot dogs, part of QM's menu.

When students were asked to rank existing restaurants, 40 percent selected Kathy John's as their first choice while 24 percent chose Subway as their first choice. Both were traditional, full-service restaurants, rather than quick-food outlets.

All the students surveyed preferred FM music on the radio to other media. The station most preferred (and listened to) was WDRC in Hartford (20 percent). Second were both WCCC and WHCN Hartford, each with 17 percent of the samples. Following a close third was WTIC in Hartford with 16 percent. WPLR in New Haven (not listed on Exhibit 5) took fourth place with 10 percent. Five percent listened to WWYZ, a Hartford-Waterbury station, and four students listened to WAQY in Springfield, Massachusetts. WHUS, the local campus radio, was selected by three persons. Unfortunately, this station did not handle commercial broadcasts, although they did engage in sponsorships and public service announcements for the student population.

Students were asked to identify any other newspapers read besides the *Connecticut Daily Campus* (CDC) which is heavily read by all students. Forty-eight percent of the students read the *Hartford Courant* and 15 percent read *The Wall Street Journal,* a required source for some economics and business courses. Fourteen percent read *The New York Times* and 7 percent read the *New York Daily News.*

When students were asked if they had ever eaten at QM before, a majority (73 percent) answered yes. Sixty-one percent of those who had eaten there said that the food was not as good as other fast-food competitors (such as McDonald's and Burger King). Twenty-eight percent of those who ate at QM previously said it was better than competitors. Thirteen percent felt that only McDonald's was better, whereas Burger King was not as good.

It was also determined from the survey that 47 percent preferred that QM operate between the hours of 10 a.m. and 3 a.m. Some 25 percent of the respondents preferred it stay open until midnight, while 19 percent indicated their desire to see it open 24 hours a day. It was noted by some that QM could stay open until midnight on weekdays, and later on weekends; for example, until 2 or 3 a.m.

Finally, students were asked for the qualities they were most interested in when patronizing a QM. Many were looking for fast service, fresh and high-quality food at low

**Exhibit 6.   Quick Meal Food Systems, Inc.
Survey Questionnaire for Area of Proposed New Restaurant**

MARKET SURVEY

Hi, I am doing a survey which will determine how the new restraurant near campus can serve your needs. It will only take 2–3 minutes of your time.

Age: ___   SEX: M   F   DORM: _____ _____

1. Do you have a car on campus?   ___ Yes ___ No

2. Are you employed presently?   ___ Yes ___ No

3. Range of weekly take-home pay: (circle)
    a. Less than $10.00   c. $26.00–$40.00
    b. $11.00–$25.00   d. $41.00 or greater

4. What type of food do you prefer? (check)
    a. Pizza ___   b. Grinder ___   c. Hamburger ___
    d. Club Sandwich ___   e. Hot Dog ___

5. If you were out on Saturday night and were hungry, where would you prefer to eat?
    (Rank 1 for the first choice to 5 as last choice)
    Kathy John's ___   Subway ___   Hardee's ___   Paul's Pizza ___   Husky's ___

6. What radio station do you listen to the most frequently? (check)
    a. WHUS Storrs ___   d. WCCC Hartford ___   g. Other ___
    b. WILI Willimantic ___   e. WHCN Hartford ___
    c. WDRC Hartford ___   f. WTIC Hartford ___

7. What other newspaper publication (other than CDC) do you read? _____
    _____

8. Have you ever eaten at a QM restaurant before?   Yes ___ No ___
    If so, what did you like about it? _____
    Was QM better than McDonald's   Yes ___ No ___
    Was QM better than Burger King?   Yes ___ No ___

9. What time would you prefer QM to be open? (check)
    a. 10 a.m.–10 p.m. ___   b. 10 a.m.–3 a.m. ___   c. 10 a.m.–12 p.m. ___
    d. 24 hours daily ___   e. Other times _____

10. What are you most interested in when patronizing QM?

                                                                        Thank You.

---

prices, convenience, room to sit, good social atmosphere, and even cute waitresses!

THE PROBLEM

The newly appointed manager had to propose a specific operating budget for the first two years of operations. Specifically, Mr. Scutti had to propose a media plan and publicity campaigns for the new store. He was not certain whether the data he had available was sufficient and requested the regional manager's help in constructing forecasts and operating plans for the first year.

26

Tommy's Toys and Things *

Tommy was uneasy; everything was just too quiet. He liked to work in his office off the main display area of his downtown store. He enjoyed the sounds of people, especially children, talking and laughing. He liked to hear motors running, horns blowing; he just took pleasure in the atmosphere of pleasurable work. Usually his stores sounded like miniature playgrounds. He thought better when there was activity around; if there was ever a time when he needed to think better, it was now. He had two days left to make the most important decision of his business life. Unfortunately, those whose advice he sought were in complete disagreement. Even his own attorney, a young man who didn't know the background of the operation, was unwilling to prescribe a response pattern. Even his advice was contradictory. And, as he kept reminding Tommy, he didn't have to live with the decision full time; that was Tommy's job!

Tommy's Toys and Things, his business, had received a letter of complaint from the Federal Trade Commission more than a week ago. Although he was not engaged in major interstate commerce, he could not deny that his business did affect such trade in the Southeast. The letter of complaint allows the receiver two patterns of response—voluntary and nonvoluntary. Granted only ten days to respond if he wished to admit the error of his ways, he did not have much longer to deliberate. Unfortunately, his problem was com-

plicated by corporate history, present financial concerns, and the nature of the commission's continual concern about advertising directed at children. Determined to decide before returning home, he turned again to the materials on his desk.

BACKGROUND

Tommy's family had always been involved in retail sales. For five generations they were the backbone of their communities, the general storekeepers. Wherever the Tomisons settled, a new store opened. They established a solid reputation for quality, service, and honesty. During hard times, they allowed their regular customers ready credit. They apparently became almost institutions in most of the communities in which they were located. But Tommy's father, from whom he inherited the business, was not satisfied with the relatively low-key family tradition. And world and national events conspired to assist him.

Tommy's father had assumed management and eventually absolute ownership of several family operations during World War II. Because so many of the younger people in the family had to leave the local areas for military service, his father acquired the operations of three of his brothers and two cousins. Before the end of the war, he had eight stores. All were located in the Southeast, many close to rapidly growing military bases such as Fort Bragg, Fort Gordon, and Fort Benning.

The Tomisons' Markets had always had a good-sized toy section. His father discovered

* This case was prepared by Marian Huttenstine of The University of Alabama. From J. Barry Mason and Morris L. Mayer, *Modern Retailing*, rev. ed. Copyright © 1981 Business Publications, Inc. Reprinted with permission.

that the need to occupy leisure time was an acute problem in the military towns, and he happily responded. After the war ended, larger chain stores and supermarkets began to spread throughout the area. Tomisons stocked more and more of the leisure-time products: games, toys, recreational gear. Ultimately, he decided to move into the leisure activity market exclusively. In the process, he closed three operations and moved the locations of several others. Because of the change in products, he also changed the name to its present one. Naturally these changes did not occur without significant changes in marketing, advertising, and promotional strategy.

Tommy never did know the actual story, but during the early 60s his father was cited by the FTC for unfair business practices. According to the cease and desist order on file, the problem was probably based on errors in advertising and/or promotion. There is some indication that double billing requests to a local radio station for a series of cooperative advertisements with a national supplier may have been part of the problem. During this period, Tommy's Toys and Things bought out several smaller craft and hobby shops and made serious inroads into the market of a major competitor. At any rate, whether the FTC began the earlier investigation on a consumer complaint or a competitor's challenge, the business was placed under a rather strict cease and desist order. One of the terms required periodic reports of all advertising placed during a ten-year period; the period expired only last year.

Because of this continuing reporting and compliance problem, Tommy and his father discussed the possibility of a change in the total structure of the business. They planned, in effect, to create a new corporation with Tommy as owner and CEO. Unfortunately, Tommy's father had to step down sooner than expected because of failing health; in the process, the corporate changes were never finalized.

Because the regulatory agencies (under revised powers granted in 1976) may exact more severe penalties for lack of compliance (i.e. repeat offenses), the earlier problem compounds the concern of the moment. Additionally, because of the history of filing copies of all advertisements, the recent problem, if it is really a violation, will appear more deliberate.

Finally, aside from the question of lack of compliance is the financial issue. Any challenge or failure to comply with the requested discover information will cost both time and money. The current economic climate has badly bruised the entire leisure-time market. The margin between profit and loss has become too narrow to allow for an extended legal battle. At the same time, any penalty assessed, should the business be found in violation, will also exact a heavy drain on the corporate finances.

IMMEDIATE PROBLEM

Tommy is fairly certain that the practices under question might come from a recent series of advertisements. With the market slowdown, he deliberately used some appeals and techniques that he had been avoiding. Built on the theme "vacation at home," each one features a female commentator wearing an athletic uniform. The first uses the actual product, a water-activated form of dodgeball. The advertisement uses a stock piece of equipment for the demonstration, but the hose that attaches has a special high-pressure nozzle. The additional pressure, of course, makes the ball more active than it would be under usual household pressure conditions.

The second and third advertisements also show the products in use. One is a commercial form of the old "follow the leader" game, but the stunts and tricks are specially created obstacles, which are placed in the yard. The announcer talks about the training and general conditioning value of the game and strenuous outdoor activity. The other advertisement shows a group of children playing in a park. The game, apparently a pickup softball game, results in an argument.

One child hits another with the bat. The announcer says that "Children will be children, but when they play with athletic equipment made of 'duraflexmore,' no one gets hurt."

PRELIMINARY DECISION

Tommy must first decide, in good faith, whether these advertisements do constitute an unfair or deceptive trade practice. He knows that the FTC is quite concerned about the way children perceive advertisements. Although these advertisements were not aimed primarily at children, he knows that the major purchases will be those stimulated by children. He also knows that the commission concern has not changed during the rather lengthy hearings before passage of the FTC Improvements Act of 1980.

Tommy's major concerns at the moment, however, have to do with general endorsement and demonstration standards. The usual checklist of guidelines is not very comforting:

1. Endorser must make reasonable inquiry into truthfulness of claim.
2. Testimonial must be typical of ordinary consumer experience.
3. Endorsement must be based on true belief in properties of the product.
4. Endorser must be qualified by education or experience to make statement.

1. Consumer is entitled to see what he is told he is seeing.
2. Consumer is entitled to see what he believes he is seeing.
3. Demonstration must actually prove something.
4. Demonstration must be such that if replicated would cause no harm or injury.

27

Sandwell Paper Company *

In the early part of 1975, George Murphy, Sandwell Paper Company's Bakersfield branch manager, undertook a careful study of his operation. The study was in keeping with his philosophy of having an alert, informed management, and it dealt with both the managerial and sales aspects of the distribution center.

COMPANY BACKGROUND

The Sandwell Paper Company, a large paper wholesaler, originated in Omaha, Nebraska, in the 1890s. During its early years, the firm was involved mainly in sales and distribution to final users and bought its paper from other wholesalers. However, as sales grew, the Sandwells soon began a warehouse operation of their own. The product line was quite diversified and included both printing (fine) and industrial (wrapping) grades of paper. Paper merchants carrying both product lines became known as dual distributors. To meet the rapid growth of markets on the West Coast, the company established several divisions in that area. Murphy's operation was the Bakersfield branch of the Los Angeles division. There were two other California divisions located at San Diego and San Francisco.

Murphy was quite pleased with the decentralized profit center arrangement of Sandwell and the independence it afforded

him. He felt that the challenge of earning a satisfactory rate of return on investment for the branch provided sales incentive for his organization.

George Murphy was in his early 50s and had been in paper sales work for the past 25 years. He had graduated in business administration from the University of Southern California in 1944 and had gained sales and management experience with two other firms (a paper manufacturer and another paper wholesaler) before joining Sandwell in 1966.

The Bakersfield sales force under Murphy consisted of three salespeople of fine paper and two of industrial paper. The division had formerly prepared its salespeople in a special sales trainee program that had consisted of daily classroom instruction in products and methods of selling. The instruction involved lectures, cases, and role playing. Regular written homework was required of all trainees. However, because of the company's high turnover of sales personnel, Murphy had terminated this formal method of training. The new method required sales trainees to work at various warehouse jobs, thereby learning firsthand about the products and problems of the business.

According to Murphy, about one-third of his time was spent dealing with problems of warehousing, accounting, and credit extension, and about two-thirds with sales meetings, forecasting, quota setting, and actual selling to his own accounts.

* This case is reproduced with the permission of its author, Dr. Stuart U. Rich, Professor of Marketing, and Director, Forest Industries Management Center, College of Business Administration, University of Oregon, Eugene, Oregon.

PRODUCT LINE

Sandwell Paper had always been a dual house supplying both printing (fine) and industrial (wrapping) paper goods. In addition to traditional paper goods, the company also stocked plastics and other nonpaper items to promote unitized selling.

The objective of unitized or packaged selling was to enable the salesperson to supply all customer needs, thereby simplifying customer ordering and billing and maximizing selling efficiency. Sandwell had been concentrating its unitized sales effort in the meat market and custodial service or janitorial supply areas.

The Sandwell paper product line was divided into two sections—printing and industrial. The fine (printing) paper line (Exhibit 1) represented the more specialized and profitable of the two sections. Printing grades had the best gross trading margin for the Bakersfield branch. Printers did not want to maintain large inventories, yet they wanted quick delivery on the many grades listed in their sample books. They were willing to pay a premium to wholesalers for maintaining

inventories of wide ranges of grade sizes, weights, and colors. In the printing paper field, Sandwell Paper was a franchised distributor for Medallion Paper Company, a large recognized manufacturer of printing paper. In areas serviced by more than one wholesaler, Sandwell had exclusive sales of the Medallion paper line. As a result of handling the complete line, ordering and inventory problems were minimized. Uniform quality could be depended on. Although competitive price inroads were being made on some of Medallion's grades, Murphy and other company managers had elected to continue to carry the line since Medallion's trade name commanded such recognition of excellence.

The Sandwell industrial paper line consisted of those paper goods utilized by manufacturers in making wrapping or in transporting their products. Exhibit 2 lists those items carried by the branch. Industrial grades were characterized by volume selling and price competition, and these grades greatly overtaxed warehouse space. Murphy indicated that industrial sales out of stock were 72 per-

Exhibit 1. Printing Grade Categories

Categories	Percent Sales	Categories	Percent Sales
Bond—Ledger	40	Book—Cover	20
Bond		Book	
Ledger		Cover	
Flat writing		Envelopes	
Safety papers		Specialty	20
Mimeograph		Announcements	
Duplicator		Thin papers	
Index—Bristol	20	Gummed	
Index			
Bristol			
Blotting			
Boards			
Cardboards			
Cut cards			
Tags			
Information			

Exhibit 2. Industrial Grade Categories

Categories	Percentage of Sales
Bags (cellophane, bakery, grocery, department)	20
Industrial (towels, tissue, wrap, lumber wrap)	21
Packing (filter, wadding, corrugated)	3
Waxes, glassine, parchment	6
Boxes, cases, board	7
Food containers, plates, napkins	20
Twine, ribbon, tape	14
Sanitary tissues	9

cent and that direct mill shipments (orders taken by the wholesaler) were 28 percent. Also, because of Sandwell's policy of selling its customers unitized service, many other nonpaper items were carried in stock. Goods such as cleaning fluid, floor wax and waxing machines, light bulbs, and polyfilm and plastic containers were coupled with paper goods to make up unitized or packaged sales to meat markets, building custodial firms, and other user groups.

George Murphy also commented that the branch's inventory turnover rate was 5 to 6 times per year, while the national average for dual houses was 4.5 times.

NATURE OF SALES ACTIVITIES

According to Murphy, Sandwell Paper divided its customer market into three parts—printing, industrial, and resale (retail). The resale market consisted mainly of retail grocery stores and variety stores. The majority of paper wholesalers did not sell directly to this market but let the regular grocery and dry goods wholesaler serve it. Murphy felt that this was a growing market and wanted his salespeople to spend more time developing it.

In 1974 company sales to each market segment were as follows: printing, 13 percent; industrial, 62 percent; resale, 25 percent. The same items might be sold to all three customer types. The market segments differen-

tiated the customer, not the type of paper commodity.

Murphy continually had to make decisions on the performance of his salespeople, market trends, price changes, and quotas. He gleaned much of this information from month-old sales invoices, informal talks with salespeople, and quick calls to the divisional sales manager.

In 1975 the Los Angeles division decided to reevaluate its present sales position and effectiveness. As illustrated by Exhibit 3, the sales volume had continued to expand, while the gross trading margin had declined. In 1973 both gross margin and net profit were below the industry average (Exhibit 4). The problems observed by the division, according to Murphy, were present on the branch level and had in part caused the present study to be done. The pricing in the industrial grades had become very competitive, and warehouse space was critical. Murphy felt that expansion of the warehouse was not economically feasible because of the low profit margin in industrial grades.

Despite the apparent downturn in trading margin, the number of accounts in the sales area was increasing. Murphy noted that customers were continually calling in orders and requests for service even though branch salespeople were constantly on the go, many times calling in their orders instead of dropping them off at the warehouse (as they had once done).

Exhibit 3. Company Trend in Sales and Gross Margin

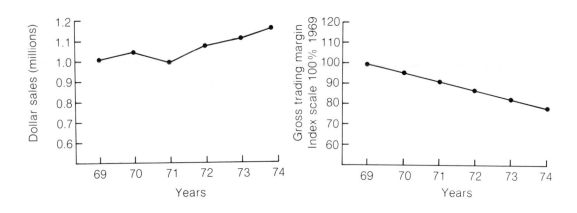

Each salesperson had an established monthly draw (salary). The draw was an advance in anticipation of the coming month's sales. The sales quota was set in profit dollars—that is, dollars above item and operating costs. The salesperson had to cover the draw for the month. Because the draw was a minimal amount, once the draw was covered the salesperson could keep 15 percent of each additional dollar of profit dollar sales.

George Murphy pointed to the schedules of his salespeople, "They've got as many calls crammed into a day as possible," he said. "They really use their effective selling time (i.e., time with the buyer)." Murphy pointed out that certain aspects of paper sell-

ing, especially in selling printing grades, were highly technical in nature. Printers could put an inexperienced salesperson on the spot.

Murphy discussed what he felt was very important in selling—talking to the person who was responsible for the buying. He also pointed out that those who used the paper could help influence the buyer.

As was noted earlier, industrial grades had become quite competitive. Murphy stated that competitors often engaged in price cutting to secure new customers. However, it had been Sandwell's policy to maintain their price against competitive inroads and defend their position by supplying "quality service

**Exhibit 4. Gross Margin and Profit Performance, 1973
(figures represent percentages)**

	Industry Average (NPTA)		Sandwell	
	Warehouse	Direct	Warehouse	Direct
Gross trading margin	22.3	8.5	20.1	8.1
Total expense	19.7	6.5	18.1	7.0
Net profit (before tax) as percent of sales	2.6	2.0	2.0	1.1

Source: National Paper Trade Association, Paper Merchant Performance, 1973.

and goodwill." This policy was still upheld, with the exception of some large-volume competitive goods like toweling and freezer wrap.

New product items were continually being added to the product line, two or three items quarterly. The division headquarters had tried to encourage sales of new items by organizing sales contests. These attempts had been partially successful. Some salespeople had immediate success with a new item, whereas others were unable to move it. With the next new item the success situation might be reversed.

George Murphy decided that the best way to study the selling techniques of his salespeople was to have Phil Edwards, a sales promotion staff member from the Los Angeles division headquarters, accompany the salespeople on calls. Phil had planned on making such a tour for general information and could combine the two projects.

PRINTER SELLING

Mason Printers was a medium-size printing account specializing in offset and letterpress printing. The business was located on Eleventh Street just off the main business section of Bakersfield. Bud Williams, who had been with Sandwell for three years, was precise in his call schedule and arrived at the shop at 10:30 each Thursday morning. While walking to the shop, Bud discussed the account with Phil Edwards.

BUD: Roy Mason is a real artist. When a job is running smooth he is as agreeable as all get out. Other times—look out. Sometimes he's out and I waste time just sitting out front waiting for him. He knows I'll be here, so he sometimes leaves an order or note for me. He's the fellow that buys and I sell him Medallion paper on price, quality, and press runability.

EDWARDS: I hear Mason's shop is one of only two in town that has a multisection offset press in operation.

BUD: I know they were making some expensive additions. I try to keep up on the technical stuff, but it's really complicated. Sometimes Roy starts

in on what's wrong with an order of paper we sent and I just can't defend it at all.

The two arrive at the shop and go in. Roy Mason is in the front office (the print shop is in the rear) and makes a gesture of setting his watch at Bud's approach.

BUD: Good morning, Roy.

ROY: Right on time.

BUD: Roy, this is Phil Edwards of our L.A. sales staff. They've sent him over to visit some of our good customers.

EDWARDS: Pleased to meet you, Roy.

BUD: What's up for today, Roy?

ROY: Oh, things are okay. That offset grade you sent over for our regular Smith Company job is going all right. I wish you fellows hadn't run out of that light pink coated cover we always use.

BUD (with "Well, so long as it's going through the press okay" relieved look): Have you got enough of your other stock grades to keep you through the week? Maybe I should check inventory. I know how you like to keep the bare minimum in there.

ROY: We're all set. We have a special job to do for the city. I got out the sample books and we picked out this grade and color (shows sample). They'd like it with this textured finish. How do you think that will reproduce on the offset press?

BUD: Perfect reproduction! Medallion always runs good.

ROY: I thought it'd be okay, but Ed, my pressman, didn't like the look of it.

BUD: I think it'll be all right. The mill rep is in town so I'll check with him and let you know.

ROY: Okay, but I'll be in and out all afternoon.

BUD: Say—you know that 26-pound letterpress grade you've been buying from Mentons (another wholesaler)?

ROY: Yes?

BUD: Well, we've got the same color and weight made by Simplin at 5 percent off because the sheet didn't pass the mill quality control specifications. The jobs you use that grade for don't demand quality, so you could use up this off-quality stuff and make yourself a good margin.

ROY: Do you think it will give Ed any trouble on the press? You know he gets pretty angry when a sheet picks, lints, or is so porous that the vehicle (ink solvent) carries the pigment into the sheet.

BUD: It shouldn't give you any trouble.

ROY: All right, we'll order it from you this month.

Glancing quickly at his watch, Bud saw he was going to be late for his call at Fan Fair Super Market.

. . . you know, with this new press we just put in, we're trying to compete for some big accounts. I've got some notes and questions here; maybe we could go over some of them.

BUD: I'll tell you what, Roy, the Simplin rep will be here till next Tuesday. Maybe he and I could get in here Monday morning and talk about your plans.

ROY: Okay, fine by me.

A call from the press room ends the discussion. Roy bids good-bye and Bud and Edwards leave. They walk quickly to the car.

BUD: I'm a little late for Fan Fair. Even though they're a small outfit, their school supplies section really sells the paper. Did you want me to drop you at the office?

EDWARDS: Yes, I've got to meet with Jane Austin (one of two industrial account salespeople) after lunch.

The two drive off.

INDUSTRIAL SELLING

Jane Austin stopped by the office (adjacent to the warehouse) and picked up Edwards. Jane had been selling at the branch for about a year. She started work, as did most prospective Sandwell salespeople, in the warehouse. After four months' time she had moved to the office order desk, where orders were called in by customers and salespeople. This procedure had been used to prepare Jane for field selling.

Edwards got into the car, and Jane drove out of the parking area.

EDWARDS: Where are we headed?

JANE: Sun Fair Market. I've got to check with the meat department manager. I think he left an item off his order list. And if he runs out of board trays on a weekend, we'll be sure to get the blame for

it. This unitized selling puts a lot of pressure on the salespeople.

EDWARDS: I can't think of a quicker way to lose a market customer than to have him come up short of wrapping film or trays on a busy weekend. What calls do you regularly make on Thursday?

JANE: Well, last year, when I started out, Thursday afternoons were for my three big department store accounts. Ted Richards and I . . . you remember Ted, he's the rep for Thall's Specialty Bag Company . . . we used to spend a lot of time with store managers laying out the designs for their store merchandise bags. Things have really picked up this year, though, I'll make about eight calls this afternoon, it's a real clockwork schedule. In a way it helps, because people know when you'll be in and they plan on it.

They arrive at the market and walk to the meat department. The man behind the counter waves and points in the direction of the cutting area.

JANE: Jack must be doing some cutting.

They turn the corner and see Jack Wilson.

JACK: What in the world are you doing here today?

JANE: Want to double-check your order for the weekend. You don't have any meat trays down.

JACK: Sure I do! Let's see.

Jack looks at the order sheet developed by Sandwell and Sun Fair executives for ease of ordering.

JACK: Well, I'll be . . .! Guess I don't. Boy, that would have finished us.

JANE: Jack, this is Phil Edwards, one of our staff salespeople from L.A.

EDWARDS: Pleased to meet you, Jack.

JACK: The same.

JANE: Say, Jack, remember you asked me why we didn't carry the new polyvinyl wrap for chicken? Well, I received a sales bulletin from the division office, and not only do we carry it but the price is below that of the film you're buying now.

JACK: That's a good one. You guys sell so much you don't have time to find out everything you're selling. Next time we'll switch over to that new wrap. I hope it "breathes" good and lets the tissue gases escape. We had 50 chickens spoil last month, you know.

JANE: Don't worry! It won't cause any spoilage.

JACK: Well, I better get to work. Thanks for catching my error.

JANE: Okay, Jack. We'll see you.

The two leave, walk to the car, and drive away.

JANE: Now I'm going up to South Eleventh to call on the manager of the New Towers Building. I'm trying to get him to purchase our new custodial service unit. This unit selling works fine sometimes—like at the market—but other times these people don't want to buy everything from you. Are you going to come in?

EDWARDS: No, Jane, I'll sit here and catch up on my study notes.

JANE: Okay.

She parks the car and goes in to see the manager. Twenty minutes later she returns.

JANE: I don't understand it. I've talked with that fellow about using our service on three separate occasions. He's real interested, listens, asks questions, but when I try to get an order all he says is—I'll check into it. I wish he'd let me know one way or the other.

EDWARDS: Who's next on your call schedule?

JANE: Dairy O, that high-volume hamburger and milkshake outfit. Ed Stenuf is the manager.

EDWARDS: Let's go.

They arrive at the Dairy O and Austin and Edwards go in. Ed Stenuf is out front waiting on customers.

JANE: Hi, Ed.

ED: Hello, Jane.

JANE: Ed, this is Phil Edwards from our L.A. headquarters.

EDWARDS: Good to meet you, Ed. Jane tells me you've got a good business here.

ED: Oh, we're doing pretty good.

JANE: Well, Ed, can we stock up your bag, napkin, and container-cup inventories?

ED: Well, you know, your competition was in yesterday offering prices below yours. So if you people can't match em we'll have to switch over.

JANE: Well, Ed, Sandwell likes to be as competitive as the next guy. We give our customers quality goods with the best service of any other supplier. We keep track of your supplies, and you never have to worry about being short.

ED: I know, Jane, but these fellows are offering a good hard dollar-and-cents deal. Those shake containers go for $12.70 a three-gross box, and they're offering the same for $12.00.

JANE: I'll have to check at the office tomorrow and I'll come out and talk price with you.

ED: Okay, Jane. Excuse me, I've got a customer.

JANE: See you tomorrow Ed.

They walk out to the car.

JANE: There goes some good business. Do you think we can match their price?

EDWARDS: We just can't let everyone who wants a little more business scare us into dropping our prices, after all we've done to stabilize our price level. You better check with George (Murphy) this afternoon and see what develops.

JANE: You bet! Now comes the big push—I call on all my Dairy Queen stores. My big accounts take a lot of time. These little stores don't seem to be worth the time the other fellows give them. Say, it's about 2:30. Did you want to go back to the office?

EDWARDS: Yes, I've got to see George about a warehouse mix-up. Medallion sent out the wrong paper in a carton with proper order labels on it.

Jane drops Edwards off and starts her calls on the Dairy Queen stores.

RESALE SELLING

Edwards had told salesperson Bob Thomas to pick him up before making calls Friday morning. Bob had been with Sandwell for four years, selling mainly industrial goods to resale dealers or retail merchants. Before joining Sandwell Bob had been employed as a salesperson for a grocery products company. He was to meet Edwards at the office at 8:30 A.M.

EDWARDS: Who do we see today?

BOB: I'm after my resale picnic supply outlets (independent retail stores and chain supermarkets). The sales department finally got out the new picnic supplies display rack. I guess there was quite a battle deciding what suppliers would get on it.

EDWARDS: Yes, that's an excellent point-of-sale display.

BOB: Do you think the division is going to make the quota for the salmon-fishing trip?

EDWARDS: The way we're going it'll be close. You guys have got to dig in.

BOB: What about the new bakery bag order I called Murphy about yesterday? There's good profit in those white multisized baked-goods bags. I don't see all the fuss about whether to put them on an open account so they'll have credit till the end of the month.

EDWARDS: We don't know much about that outfit. You know the policy on doubtful accounts. You guys get big orders with these accounts, but the office has to collect them.

BOB: Well, we need orders to make the quota. It doesn't make much difference to me whether they wait till the end of the month to pay.

EDWARDS: Spoken as a true salesperson. Say, George tells me he's got you fellows keeping a list of all the prospective customers you've called on about that new polyvinyl strapping for unitized lumber.

BOB: Yes, I called on the Medford and the Sellers Lumber Companies Monday. Put on a little demonstration for their salespeople. I'm afraid the introduction fell a little flat though I told them that the vinyl was stronger than the steel strapping they're now using to hold their unitized lumber packets together during shipment ... but they started asking some technical questions about strength and shipping and I was having enough trouble getting the band taut and crimped around the lumber unit.

EDWARDS: George said they think this item should be very competitive. The vinyl is 8 to 20 percent cheaper, yet performs as well as steel stripping. It's sure to click.

They arrive at the Careways Market and enter the store. Bob approaches Joe Martin, a buyer for the Careways chain. Introductions are made.

BOB: Say, Joe, it's about time you started stocking up on picnic items.

JOE: How much markup can we expect to get this year?

BOB: Fifteen percent on most.

JOE: How fast did they move last year?

BOB: Stores that got their display racks out near the cash registers, and other good selling points, ordered weekly.

BOB: We've rearranged and substituted some of the items on the rack for maximum sales effect. This year should be the best yet.

JOE: Some of the stuff on the rack we already have in stock from other suppliers. I don't think I'll use the rack. You go ahead and see what we need from the inventory listing and I'll check back with you in a few minutes to see what you have.

Joe walks off. Bob checks inventory figures and writes up an order for various tissue and toweling items.

BOB: Phil, the pricing on these consumer products is really getting ridiculous. With so many distributors handling them at such low margins, we'll all be out of business. Every day someone is cutting the price, or a manufacturer is handling the account direct or something!

EDWARDS: Yes. Pricing on those high-volume consumer items is a problem.

The two return to Joe Martin.

JOE: Let's see what you came up with. Yes, that's about right. The toweling, and napkins stay about the same. Send eight cartons of plates, instead of six. Same for the cold cups. Oh, and we won't need any of the plastic knives. They aren't used as much as the forks and spoons.

BOB: All right, Joe. We'll have this order delivered tomorrow.

JOE: Good. So long.

As they leave the store and walk to the car, Bob wonders how he can change Joe's mind on installing some display racks.

BOB: I'll get that rack in there. I'll get back to see him Monday for a little chat. I've got lots of accounts to call on, but I have a flexible schedule, so I can put in a little extra selling effort when I think it's worthwhile.

EDWARDS: A few racks in that Careways chain would really up sales.

BOB: I'll say. I'm going to Smith Company. Did you want to go up there too?

EDWARDS: Well, if you could drop me off at the office on your way up there it would be convenient for me. I'm supposed to see George at 11 o'clock.

BOB: Okay, fine.

Back at the office, Phil Edwards talked with George Murphy about the weaknesses of the three salespeople and how additional sales training could remedy the problems.

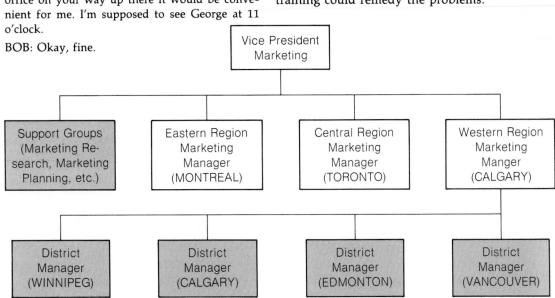

28

*Computing Systems Ltd.**

"**B**ob doesn't appear to be too happy. He isn't making money, because he isn't selling. His own self-image is . . . well, he likes to spend money. He likes nice clothes, a nice car, and a nice house, that kind of thing, but he can't afford to live that way." These thoughts passed through Mike Hagen's mind in February 1980, as he reviewed once again the possible courses of action in dealing with one of his salespeople, Bob Nichols. Mike Hagen was the district manager in Winnipeg, Manitoba, for Computing Systems Ltd., a major full-line computer manufacturer. Mike had become increasingly concerned about Bob's performance in the last year. While the other salespeople in the district were having a very successful year, it had become quite clear to Mike that Bob was not even going to achieve his quota. Bob was thus hindering the district in its drive to meet its goals.

THE COMPANY

Computing Systems Ltd. was the Canadian subsidiary of Computing Systems, Inc., a major multinational manufacturer of a wide range of computers and peripheral equipment. The Computing Systems product lines were in direct competition with some of the computer lines of other major computer manufacturers.

The head office of Computing Systems was located in Toronto. The vice-president

of marketing, who was located in the Toronto head office, oversaw all the firm's marketing activities. Reporting were the various marketing staff groups and three regional marketing managers who coordinated the marketing activities in the Western, Central, and Eastern regions. The Winnipeg office was located in the Western Region, and Mike Hagen reported to the Western Region marketing manager in Calgary. A partial organization chart of the Computing Systems marketing organization is shown in Exhibit 1.

THE WINNIPEG DISTRICT

Mike Hagen had two groups of people reporting to him in the Winnipeg District. Three sales representatives reported directly to him. There were also 10 programmer analysts who reported to him through the district systems manager. A partial organization chart of the Winnipeg Branch is shown in Exhibit 2.

The programmer analysts in each district were responsible for providing systems support to the firm's customers. Many of the programmer analysts worked exclusively with one customer, while the others acted essentially as systems consultants for several of the firm's smaller customers. The programmer analysts were often involved in the presales evaluation of a customer's systems requirements. In this capacity, one or more systems analysts formed a team with one of the district's sales representatives, and together they evaluated the customer's needs and developed a proposed system that they

* Prepared by Adrian B. Ryans of The University of Western Ontario. Copyright © 1983 by The University of Western Ontario, reproduced by permission.

Exhibit 1. Partial Organization Chart of Computing Systems Marketing Department

Exhibit 2. Organization of the Winnipeg District

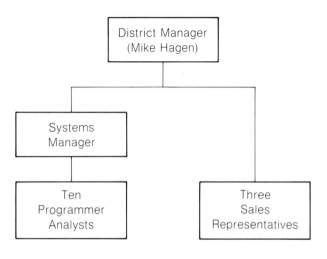

felt would satisfy these needs. Programmer analysts were compensated on a salary basis, with raises dependent on job performance.

SALES ACTIVITIES

When asked to describe and comment on the sales job in the computer business, Mike Hagen said:

The sales job is broken down into prospecting, qualifying prospects; planning the sales campaign, and all those activities related to closing. Now prospecting, generally speaking, is taken rather lightly by the sales reps, and I think that is a big mistake. It's a very, very difficult activity and it is closely related to qualifying—they dovetail very closely together. We're in the stage of the computer business where there is enough activity out there that you don't have to create demand. We qualify a prospect by asking, "Are you going to make a computer buying decision within the next six to twelve months?" If not, we just keep in touch. We don't really have time to say to a prospect, "Well, why don't you think of making this new application or why don't you think of buying that new equipment?" We may go in and try to develop a need if we see an area where a company could computerize, and then make a proposition and try and get their interest. But if they are not immediately interested, we forget it, because we really don't have the time or the resources to do it. So, the key thing in any salesperson's success is to have a big prospect list, because you don't get'em all. And the key thing with the prospect list is how well they are qualified. Will the person buy from us? Are we talking to the right person? Are they going to make the decision in the time frame they say? Timing is particularly important. If you peak out in your sales campaign to a prospect too early, you know your competitor is going to pick up the dice. It is very competitive. So the qualifying aspect is whether you are talking to the right person, will they make the decision, and do they have the guts to be the internal salesperson—the person to carry the ball for you in getting others in the company, the boss and so on, to agree to the purchase. All those questions in any sales campaign are very key because the next steps cost a lot of money in terms of time and resources. So once you get the customers to the point where you can say they are a qualified prospect, you can assume they will make a decision within a reasonable period of time. We have to restrict our dealings to qualified prospects because a person has got to make quota in the 12-month period. That's because, unfortunately, we work on a 12-month planning horizon.

Planning is probably one of the things that most sales-oriented people do worst. They respond to immediate conversations, interactions, and stimuli. The difficult thing is to say, "Well, when are you going to do this? What are you going to do if? What are your contingency plans?" And so on. It's an easy thing really for a manager to get salespeople to put together a plan in terms of putting it down on paper and saying this is what I am going to do. The hard part is to get them to do it, and to discipline themselves to do it when they say they are going to do it. And then to constantly ask the customer for the order, to go through trial closes to get objections. You see, in a sense, the qualifying process in our business never really ends, you never get to that point unless you have the order. So you are constantly asking questions and directing your campaign to further substantiate your qualifications. With one key order we got here in Winnipeg, for example, we didn't qualify until a week before we got the order. We didn't really consider them a prospect until we got very close to the order, because we hadn't been able to get to the top people.

The point at which the systems representative comes in depends on the level of gear. We sell computers anywhere from a $1,000 per month to $100,000 per month. Selling covers such a wide range of activities and such a wide range of customer prospect situations, that you might sell a small computer without ever getting a systems person in. You just go in and you say, "You want to computerize your payroll? No problem, we have just the package for you. It will do a super job for you. Sign here." Generally speaking, customers don't know their own needs well enough to evaluate anything properly anyway, so that after you sell it, anything that you can give them is a hell of a lot better than what they currently have. So if you know a little bit about receivables and payables you don't need a systems person, but you might bring in one or two people to impress the customer. When you get into, say, a large system, you need a host of technical people, not just in systems but in specialized areas of systems, such as data base management, communications, and operations management. With a large system you may have five or six computer operations raising hell, and you've got to coordinate that as a basic management function. When you only have a little main frame, you have a much simpler problem. You have only one person, so it's not really a coordination problem. Thus, the systems support that a salesperson needs varies dramatically from one situation to the next.

Each salesperson in Computing Systems was assigned an annual sales quota. The company used a "top-down" approach in developing sales quotas. Each year the marketing group in Toronto analyzed the anticipated levels of activity in the Canadian economy, the previous years' sales, the trends in the computer industry, etc., to develop a reasonable sales forecast for the following year. This forecast was then broken down into sales quotas for the individual districts, and these quotas were communicated to the district managers. It was then the responsibility of the district managers to develop quotas for the individual salespeople. Mike Hagen felt that this method resulted in salespeople receiving reasonable, attainable quotas. In fact, Mike said that if he asked any of his salespeople what was a reasonable quota for the next year, they usually gave him a figure higher than the quota he would assign them.

Salespeople were compensated largely on a commission basis, receiving a commission on each sale related to the profitability of the sale to the company. Generally, total compensation was highly correlated with quota achievement.

THE GROWTH OF THE WINNIPEG OFFICE

Mike Hagen had joined Computing Systems after graduating with an M.B.A. degree from an eastern university in 1976. Mike had spent his first few months with the company in its sales training course in Toronto. On completion of the course he had become a sales representative in Toronto. After one year with Computing Systems, Mike had been transferred to Winnipeg as a sales representative. Initially, he was the only sales representative in Winnipeg, and he reported to the district manager in the Calgary office. In September 1977, two additional experienced salespeople, Jill Cooper and Nick Johnston, were hired from outside the computer business and joined the Winnipeg office. In 1977, Mike met his sales quota, and in 1978, he was one of the top Computing Systems salespeople in Canada. In June 1978, Winnipeg became a separate district, and a district manager was appointed. The district manager then reported directly to the Western Region marketing manager in Calgary. About six months after moving to Winnipeg, the district manager was promoted and left Winnipeg, and in January 1979, Mike Hagen was promoted to district manager. Mike felt the decision to promote him to district manager had been a difficult one for the company, since he was relatively inexperienced, having only been employed by Computing Systems for two and one-half years. Mike thus felt he had a lot to prove in his new job, and he was anxious to prove that he could do a superior job as district manager.

Shortly before Mike Hagen became District Manager, Bob Nichols was transferred to Winnipeg from Vancouver. Bob Nichols had joined the company directly after graduating from college with a B.Sc. in 1974. Bob spent his initial six months with the company in a training program for systems analysts. After completing the training program in November 1974, Bob became a systems representative in the Vancouver office. He progressed well in the job, and in 1975 he received a President's Award for his outstanding performance as a systems representative. Even though he had spent very little time as a systems representative, Bob's superiors considered him one of the most promising systems people in Canada. The following year Bob requested a move from systems to sales. Bob entered the company's basic sales training program and received part of his training in Toronto, and, in fact, for a couple of months he and Mike worked in the same office in Toronto. Bob's switch into sales was motivated largely by his desire for the higher compensation a successful sales representative could earn. A few of Bob's friends from his undergraduate days, who had been quite successful financially, were also living in Vancouver, and the group of young couples led an active social life. Bob thought that a salesperson's compensation would allow him to lead that type of life.

Within a few months of beginning work as a sales representative, one of Bob's customers purchased a major system, one of the largest systems ever installed by Computing Systems in Canada. The sale of this system was the culmination of a major selling job by Bob and a couple of his superiors in the Vancouver office. Largely as a result of being credited with this sale, Bob won a second President's Award in 1977 for his performance as a sales representative. Bob did not have such a successful year in 1978. In the first nine months of 1978 Bob did not meet his quota, although his performance was considered acceptable. In September 1978, Bob was transferred to Winnipeg because company management felt the change of environment might result in improved sales performance. Although Mike saw very little of Bob and his wife socially after they moved to Winnipeg, he gathered from his conversations with Bob that they were adjusting reasonably well to their new life.

MIKE HAGEN AS DISTRICT MANAGER

When Mike Hagen assumed the job of district manager in January 1979 he had four salespeople reporting to him. His first year in the new job was reasonably successful, and the Winnipeg office made quota at a time when several other districts did not.

The quota achievements for the four salespeople in the Winnipeg District for 1978 and 1979 are shown in Exhibit 3. In late 1979, Tony Webb, whose performance had been satisfactory in 1978 but marginal in 1979, was transferred to the Vancouver office. The performance of Jill Cooper and Nick Johnston both showed a significant improvement between 1978 and 1979. In 1979, they were both among the top Computing Systems salespeople in Canada.

Bob, in his short period in Winnipeg in 1978, had not met his quota, which was not surprising, since it took a few months to develop a list of prospects. However, his performance was again marginal in 1979. As Mike Hagen reviewed Bob's performance record and prospect list in February 1980, it appeared very likely to him that Bob would not make his quota again in 1980. From his previous discussions with Bob about his performance, he knew that Bob realized this too, although Bob would probably not openly admit it. Bob seemed uneasy that he, the senior salesperson in the office, was performing much worse than other, less experienced salespeople.

Exhibit 3. Sales Performance as a Percent of Quota— Winnipeg District

| Salespeople | Percentage of Achievement Quota | |
	1978	1979
Tony Webb	100	81 [a]
Jill Cooper	105	195
Nick Johnston	53	205
Bob Nichols	55 [a]	63

[a] Quota prorated for the period in Winnipeg.

Mike felt that he had developed a good business relationship with Bob in their 18 months together in the Winnipeg office. Shortly after becoming manager Mike had assisted Bob in landing a major order. The order had required a lot of internal selling within Computing Systems, and Mike had spent many hours convincing Computer Systems personnel that the deal he and Bob had worked out with the customer was a good one for Computing Systems. Mike felt that Bob realized that he would not have been able to do the internal selling job himself, and thus, he felt he had gained Bob's respect for his skill and efforts.

THE SITUATION IN FEBRUARY 1980

As he reviewed the situation in February 1980, Mike Hagen felt there were at least four possible courses of action he could take. The first alternative was simply to ask Bob for his resignation. Mike was personally not very happy with this alternative, since he knew there were several other Computing Systems salespeople in other districts performing less satisfactorily than Bob. However, Bob's performance was inconsistent with Mike's goals for the Winnipeg district. He had also broached the subject of Bob's performance with the Western Region marketing manager, and he felt his attitude and the attitude of other people in senior management was that Bob was worth saving.

The second alternative was transferring Bob to another district as a sales representative. This was probably the easiest course of action.

The third alternative was for Mike to spend additional time with Bob trying to improve his sales performance. Mike had spent a large amount of time the previous year accompanying Bob and each of the other salespeople on sales calls and critiquing their selling methods. Mike felt that Bob did an excellent job right up to the point of actually trying to close the sale. In Mike's words, "Bob doesn't have that killer instinct—to go for the throat—the real pressure that you

have to exert to get some orders—the real pushing hard, brass-knuckled approach that is sometimes absolutely necessary to get an order." Mike also felt that Bob did not handle risk well, and often seemed to want to "give away" the systems when he got close to the sale. Mike also believed that Bob was not very effective in doing the internal selling that had to be done inside Computing Systems. Since the computer systems packages were often customized to an individual customer's needs, the computer salesperson had to convince Computing Systems management that the deal they were proposing to the customer was also profitable from Computing Systems' viewpoint. Mike felt Bob had a very difficult time handling the two sets of conflicting demands.

Mike also knew that one of Bob's goals was eventually to move into sales management, but in Computing Systems a necessary condition for promotion into sales management was a good selling record. For this reason he felt he should consider making further efforts to develop Bob in the sales area. He wondered, however, where he would be able to find additional time to spend with Bob without neglecting the other salespeople and, even if he did spend the time, whether he would be successful.

The final alternative was to try to change Bob's career path from sales back into systems. Mike had checked with senior management about any suitable openings for Bob in other offices in Canada in a systems capacity, but there were none. Thus, any move would have to be made within the Calgary office. Mike thought he might be able to persuade Bob to accept a position as a senior systems analyst, but he knew that it would be a difficult switch for Bob to accept. The salary as a senior systems analyst would be comparable to Bob's total compensation in 1979. However, had he made quota in 1979, his total compensation as a salesperson would have been about 50 percent higher than the amount he could earn as a systems analyst. The switch also had other potential problems: Mike felt his systems manager would deeply resent having to take on a "loser" from sales. The personalities of Bob and the systems manager were different, and this was also likely to be an area of further conflict. Furthermore, Mike did not feel he could discuss this alternative with the systems manager before making the decision, since he felt the systems manager would attempt to prevent the change. Mike also felt some of the systems staff would resent a salesperson moving into a senior systems position in the office. If it hadn't been for all these potential problems, Mike felt that Bob would probably do an outstanding job as a senior systems analyst.

As he weighed the pros and cons of the different alternatives in his mind, Mike wondered if there were any other alternatives he had overlooked. He was also concerned about how he should reveal his decision to Bob and to what extent he should involve the Western Region marketing manager and other senior company personnel. Mike knew he had to come to a decision quickly, since he was flying to Calgary in three days to see the Western Region marketing manager. He wanted to tell his superior what course of action he planned to follow and to get his approval.

29

Westinghouse Electric Corporation: Overhead Distribution Transformer Division *

Bob Ray, the marketing manager for the Overhead Distribution Transformer Division (OHDT) of Westinghouse Electric Corporation, was concerned about his field sales engineers. It had been four years since OHDT had initiated any sort of formal training program directed at the field sales force. Company information revealed that the sales force had an annual turnover of ten percent. His concern for newer salespersons' depth of training was paralleled by his conviction that the veteran sales engineers would benefit from more exposure to product knowledge, especially in light of recent innovations. Interpretation of direct and indirect feedback revealed that both groups were reaching for more depth in product knowledge.

THE WESTINGHOUSE ELECTRIC CORPORATION

Westinghouse was the world's oldest and

second largest manufacturer of electrical apparatus and appliances. Founded by inventor George Westinghouse in 1886, the corporation marketed some 300,000 variations of about 8,000 highly diversified basic products ranging from a simple piece of copper wire to a complex commercial nuclear power plant. The firm employed over 145,000 men and women in laboratories, manufacturing plants, sales offices, and distribution centers from coast to coast and around the world. Over 1,800 of its scientists and engineers were actively engaged in research and development activities. The corporation had more than 160,000 stockholders.

Because of its size and the diversity required to serve a variety of markets, Westinghouse was organized into four companies operating within the corporation. The companies were: Power Systems; Industry and Defense; Consumer Products; and Broadcasting, Learning and Leisure Time.

Each company was headed by a president, who had full responsibility for designing, building, and selling the company's products and services throughout the world. Each company had its own staff of specialists in certain fields. It also could draw on corporate resources for additional specialized support in fields such as marketing, manufacturing,

* This case was prepared by Norman A.P. Govoni, Babson College, Richard R. Still, Florida International University, and Kent Mitchell, University of Georgia, with the intention of providing a basis for class discussion rather than illustrating either effective or ineffective management of a business situation. Reprinted with permission from *Application of Decision Sciences in Organizations: A Case Approach* by Joseph C. Latona and K. Mark Weaver with the cooperation of the Decision Sciences Institute (formerly the American Institute for Decision Sciences), Atlanta, Georgia, 1980.

engineering, design, research, personnel and public affairs, finance, and law.

The basic organizational unit of the company was the division, each with its own line of products and services. Each division, in turn, was grouped with a number of other divisions with related products and services, such as major appliances, construction products, or power generation equipment.

Combined sales before taxes were $5.1 billion. The Power Systems Company was the leading contributor to income after taxes with a 43 percent contribution. The Power Systems Company was divided into two main areas: the Power Generation Group and the Transmission and Distribution Division located in Athens, Georgia.

OVERHEAD DISTRIBUTION TRANSFORMER DIVISION (OHDT)

OHDT considered itself first in facilities, developments, and service; and rightfully so, for it had led the nation in overhead distribution transformer sales since 1971 with a fairly consistent market share of about 23 percent. Industry sales were projected to be nearly $900 million by the early 1980s.

Since 1958, all Westinghouse overhead distribution transformers were designed and manufactured in the Athens plant. The previous manufacturing site was in Sharon, Pennsylvania. OHDT was particularly proud of its engineering leadership. In the past few years, Westinghouse had expanded its staff and facility in a time when others were cutting back. Bob Ray was instrumental in making this crucial marketing decision and was later honored with the Corporation's highest award, "The Order of Merit," an award given to three employees each year. In the capacity over demand ratio, the company had been 131 percent, 85 percent, and 88 percent respectively, for the past three years.

COMPETITION

Westinghouse had been recognized for several decades as the primary innovator in the distribution transformer industry. Four other companies, each of which had active R & D facilities, were considered major innovators: General Electric, RTE, Allis-Chalmers, and McGraw-Edison. Other strong companies among the 29 national competitors were Wagner, Kuhlman, and Colt.

The Westinghouse product was generally ranked tops in its field, representing true value for dollar investment. Some competitors, though, had been successful in promoting a less expensive product.

THE CUSTOMER AND PRICING

The electric utility companies were the consumers for distribution transformers, and they were divided into three major classes: investor-owned utilities, rural electric cooperatives, and municipalities. There were approximately 300 investor-owned utilities which accounted for about 80 percent of consumption. The co-ops and municipalities numbered about 920 and 2,000, respectively, and together accounted for the remaining 20 percent. With the increasing migration of families and industries to metropolitan outskirts, the co-ops were expected to represent a considerably larger share of consumption in the years to come. There were about 33 million overhead distribution transformers across the nation. Sales in this market represented about 60 percent changeouts (i.e., replacements in an area where power consumption had increased) and 40 percent new development units.

In pricing, the major utilities negotiated year-long purchasing commitments during November-December of each year. Fierce price competition was prevalent among the investor-owned utilities and large discounts off list prices were normally expected. Pricing for the co-ops and municipalities was more stable with smaller discounts from list being offered. The method of negotiation was small orders throughout the year for the smaller utilities and the sealed bid method for the publicly-owned companies.

PROMOTION

Westinghouse advertised its electrical transmission, generation, and distribution equipment in leading electrical trade journals. Additionally, it was a member of the National Electrical Manufacturers Association (NEMA), which set standards for the industry. NEMA issued monthly reports to its members which included total market volume and member market share information. Distribution was by a field sales force selling direct to customers.

MARKETING MANAGEMENT

The marketing department of OHDT consisted of a marketing manager, a marketing services manager, and four area sales managers who were assisted by a staff of their own. The sales areas were divided geographically. Almost all personnel in the marketing department had an engineering background, which was considered a must in this complex field. The department had ultimate responsibility for success of its product. They were particularly proud that Westinghouse had been number one in market share of transformer sales each year since 1971.

The marketing department had been located in Athens since 1968, when it moved down from Sharon, Pennsylvania. Exhibit 1 shows where the marketing department fitted into the organization of the Athens firm.

THE FIELD SALES FORCE

Overhead distribution transformers were sold through two of the four Westinghouse companies: the Power Systems company and the Industry and Defense company. Each company had its own sales network, as shown in Exhibit 2.

There were over 300 Westinghouse corporate field sales engineers, district managers, and zone managers located throughout the country handling OHDT accounts. In addition to being loaded with OHDT products, the salespeople were responsible for other Westinghouse utility products. For example, they represented the Electrical Relay Division, Circuit Breaker Division, and the Electric Meter Division, each of which was managed through other corporate channels. The field sales engineers, in serving several product divisions, reported to district managers for product loading.

The area sales managers and their staffs (of OHDT) served the field sales engineers by taking and expediting product orders, answering product questions, and collecting feedback. Additionally, they traveled into the field to hold training seminars and to assist salespeople on important sales. Bob Ray often got involved in following through with especially important customers.

TRAINING A FIELD SALES ENGINEER

Westinghouse sales engineers were required to have a Bachelor of Science in Engineering. When brought into the corporation, the new recruit was first sent to Pittsburgh for a basic three-week orientation to the Westinghouse company. The recruit was then assigned to a corporate "graduate studies program" which lasted from three to twelve months, depending on his or her skills. Upon completion, he or she was assigned to the field as an assistant sales engineer to serve a training tenure which lasted anywhere from six to twenty-four months, again depending on individual requirements. During this period, the person would travel for a two-week period visiting the various manufacturing plants he or she would later serve. Each plant gave the future salesperson a two-day training and orientation seminar. Ideally, the sales engineers were supposed to return to these parent manufacturing divisions annually for refresher training. Additionally, they would attend district or zone training seminars held by representatives of the parent divisions.

A sales engineer, depending on experience and length of service to Westinghouse, drew a base salary averaging about $35,000 a year, not including bonus. The number of calls and the type of customer was established

Exhibit 1. Westinghouse Electric Corporation Marketing Department—Athens, Georgia

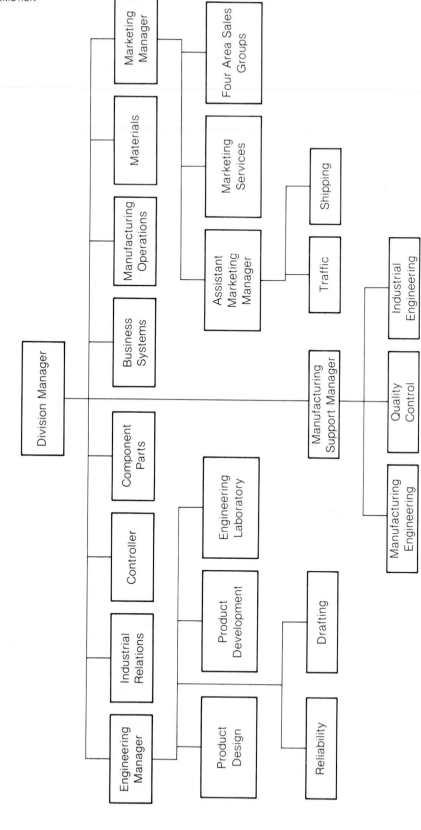

Exhibit 2. Westinghouse Electric Corporation Sales Organization Chart

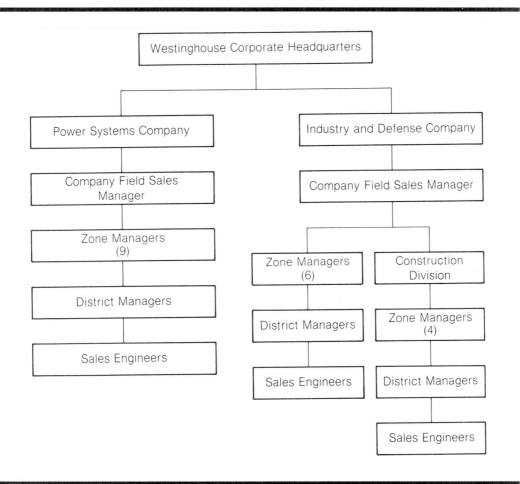

according to ability, experience, and product loading. It took, on the average, about $500,000 worth of sales to support a sales engineer in the field.

THOUGHTS OF AN OHDT AREA SALES MANAGER

Marvin Jones was one of the four area sales managers for the OHDT division. Prior to his present assignment, he was a field sales engineer for over 12 years. Reflecting on his days in the field, he remembered quite well the difficulties involved in attending training

seminars held by the various divisions. Salespeople recognized that training was essential, that effective selling required sound training, and that a person's potential (not to mention the quota) really could not be realized without training. However, getting a salesperson to a training seminar was a difficult task, because when there was a sale to be made, there wasn't time for training. The training, as important as it was, would have to wait. At least this was the common thing when attendance at refresher training was more or less left to the individual sales engineer.

THE NEED TO TRAIN

Bob Ray was very concerned about the field sales force's depth of knowledge about overhead distribution transformers, especially in light of fairly recent innovations (a trend which would be expected to continue). He knew Westinghouse had become the leading producer of transformers, but he attributed this more to excellent engineering, excessive demand, and the expertise of his department. As questions were coming in to the area sales managers at a slightly higher than normal rate, he pinpointed the problem to training. He also knew that the economy might be expected to take a slight decline. With the growing threat that demand might slacken in the months to come, he felt that competition would really start getting rough. In addition, he realized that an unprepared sales force might not fare so well when the time came to give more indepth and high-quality sales presentations. And it had been a while since Athens had initiated a formal training program. The previous program, which was considered a success, consisted of a campaign to inform the sales force about the overhead distribution transformer, and, as a gimmick, miniature transformer parts were sent to the salespeople. Unfortunately, a salesperson's time was an extremely valuable commodity, and Bob Ray knew it. Training in any organization was one of the most difficult tasks to pull off effectively, even when the trainees were geographically close to management; but the Westinghouse field sales force, scattered across the nation, was another matter. Making the training task even more burdensome was the fact that these sales engineers had more than just the OHDT account to worry about. It was realized that Athens would have to compete for both time and attention.

FROM IDEAS TO ACTION

With the facts on the table, Bob Ray called on Larry Deal, who headed Marketing Services, and his assistant, Glynn Hodges, who at that time was involved with marketing communications. Hodges was sent to Pittsburgh a few times to work jointly with Earl Swartz, the corporate contact to the ad agency used by Westinghouse. By June, Hodges had the layout completed for the proposed solution to the training problem—a training campaign to be called "The Problem Solvers." Bob Ray liked it. It was estimated that the campaign would ultimately cost about $20,000 representing a large slice of the OHDT marketing budget. Exhibit 3 gives an idea of the estimated costs.

ABOUT "THE PROBLEM SOLVERS" CAMPAIGN

An overview of "The Problem Solvers" appears in Exhibit 4, which contains the following: background, program objectives, program implementation, elements of the program (Stages 1 and 2), and a summary of elements and timing.

To catch the salesperson's attention, the proposed campaign would consist of expensive and eye-catching adult games which emphasized puzzle problems. The games would cost from $4–$5 each; a good example was a three-dimensional tic-tac-toe game made of three clear plastic decks mounted on top of each other. Each player was represented by either clear blue or yellow marbles about an inch in diameter each. The game could be won horizontally, vertically, or diagonally.

Along with the mailing of each game would be a cover letter and an information bulletin emphasizing a particular feature of the overhead distribution transformer. As the salesperson read each information bulletin, he or she would fill in "clues" to a master crossword puzzle. When the mailings were completed, the salesperson would send in the completed crossword puzzle and picture of himself or herself (along with the rest of the family if desired) to the marketing department in Athens. Athens would have the picture made into a jigsaw puzzle and return it to the participant a few weeks later.

**Exhibit 3. Westinghouse Overhead Distribution Transformers
"The Problem Solvers"—Promotion**

General

This document summarizes various elements of the "Problem Solver" promotion. The costs are based on quotations from suppliers who have seen initially prepared layouts.

Puzzles

Five puzzles will be purchased directly from supplier by Westinghouse.

Shipping Boxes for Puzzles

Four hundred each of five different size boxes plus one 6-by-6-inch envelope (for crossword puzzle and brochure mailing), each to be printed in two colors using the same "Problem Solver" design. (Suggestion: each box to have a different color on the design.)
Delivery time: six weeks from receipt of order.
Cost: including converting boxes, design preparation, color plates and printing—$2,500

Crossword Puzzle

To be completed by salesperson and submitted with photo to get personalized jigsaw puzzle prize.
Timing: Six weeks from receipt of words and clues from Westinghouse. Puzzles to be printed in simple 4-page format and inserted in envelope along with cover letter and brochure.
Cost: $800

Jigsaw Puzzle

One 11-by-14-inch puzzle will be sent to every salesperson submitting photo along with completed crossword puzzle. Photos will be held and sent in bulk to puzzle manufacturer, who will then send completed puzzle directly to each salesperson along with the original photo.
Timing: four weeks delivery from receipt of photographs.
Cost: $1,300

Cover Letters

Total of five (one for each puzzle mailing), 400 copies of each.
Cost: including artwork for masthead, copy editing, typesetting, and printing $600

Brochures

One brochure will accompany each of the five puzzle mailings. Each brochure will focus on one aspect of the overhead transformers. The cover will have a full color cover of the puzzle being sent; inside pages will be black and white and use existing line art.
Cost: including photos, typesetting, tissue layout and key art, copy editing, and production supervision for five 20-page booklets $12,000
Total Cost: up to $20,000

THE MARKETING SERVICES DIVISION— A SPECIAL PROJECT

Larry Deal's Marketing Services Division had been assigned the responsibility of supporting the ad agency by providing the technical information necessary for turning "The Problem Solvers" idea into a manageable campaign. Brian Kennedy, assigned to marketing communications, and assistant Jody Unsler had been asked to design the instruction brochures and crossword puzzle. Also, coordination with Earl Swartz had resulted in the initial selection of a container for the

Exhibit 4. Westinghouse Overhead Distribution Transformers: An Overview of "The Problem Solvers"

Background

The total market for overhead distribution transformers is very good. For Westinghouse, it is excellent.

While Athens is producing at full capacity and the current problem is meeting demand, there still remain several conditions with which Athens must cope if it is to achieve its long-range potential:

1. Many Westinghouse and agent salespeople do not understand the advantages of Westinghouse transformers.

2. There are competitors who manufacture and sell transformers at a cheaper price. These transformers are inferior to those at Westinghouse. The Westinghouse story, which must be communicated through sales personnel to customers, is a *value* story.

3. The present sales boom cannot be expected to continue indefinitely, and the sales force must be prepared to conduct tougher, more effective sales presentations.

Program Objectives

The object of this program is to make Westinghouse and agent sales personnel more effective representatives for Athens by showing them why Westinghouse is the value leader and by giving them the information and tools needed to make more effective presentations.

By accomplishing these objectives, the sales representatives will become more confident of their abilities—and the Westinghouse line. This growing confidence will, in turn, create even greater success.

Program Implementation

This is a two-stage program. The Stage 1 phase, the most important, is directed to the Westinghouse sales force and includes: an explanation of the program, a summary of the transformer market (and the profit contribution made by Westinghouse transformers), and detailed instruction on transformers (using the theme, "The Problem Solvers") along with unique mailings.

The Stage 2 phase is the person-to-person contact between salespeople and customers. Having been effectively indoctrinated into the advantages of Westinghouse transformers, the salespeople are now supplied with effective sales presentation material, which will make contact between sales representatives and customers more productive for the Athens division.

Elements of Program—*Stage 1*

1. Cover letter No. 1 from Mr. Meierkord (general manager, OHDT) or Mr. Ray spelling out the theme "The Problem Solvers," and the purpose of the program.

2. Instruction brochure No. 1 on Cover and Bushing Assembly along with puzzle.

3. Cover letter No. 2 from Meierkord or Ray.

4. Instruction brochure No. 2 on Tank Assembly along with puzzle.

5. Cover letter No. 3 from Meierkord or Ray.

6. Instruction brochure on Core & Coil Assembly along with puzzle.

7. Cover letter No. 4 from Meierkord or Ray. Letter to state that crossword puzzle answers are found in instruction booklet. If salesperson returns completed crossword puzzle along with any photograph of his or her choice, Athens will return a custom-made jigsaw puzzle made out of the photo.

8. Instruction brochure No. 4 on CSP (completely self-protected transformer) features along with crossword puzzle. Crossword puzzle will contain such clues as:
   CSP Transformers (OUTLAST) conventional types by 60 percent.
   CSP arresters (LOWER) discharge voltage on high surge currents.
   After overload trips breaker, breaker can be reset to (TEN) percent more capacity.

Exhibit 4.   (continued)

Elements of Program—*Stage 2*

After salespeople have studied the four bulletins, they are now better prepared to make more effective presentations to their customers. To help them in their calls, they will be furnished with the following:

1. Cover letter (No. 5) again from Meierkord or Ray, reiterating the profitability of transformers, that they are great "Problem Solvers," and that the salespeople (the ultimate "Problem Solvers") are now well prepared to communicate to their customers why Westinghouse transformers are truly the tops in the field. Cover letter will dwell on the importance of customer presentations, preparation, and follow-through.

2. Flip chart presentation entitled "Westinghouse Distribution Transformers: 'The Problem Solver.' " The presentation will summarize the most important "Features/Functions/Benefits" from the four technical bulletins. The presentation will be designed in a horizontal format so that the pages are adaptable for photographic slide or strip film reproduction.

3. Customer booklet to be prepared using same text and artwork from the presentation flip chart. Booklet will be left with the customer as a reminder of what was presented and as a source document for later reference.

4. Capabilities brochure, about to be produced, can be an added ingredient to the presentation. While it emphasizes Athens' manufacturing capability—as opposed to the engineering emphasis of the presentation—the booklet is prestigious and will reflect Westinghouse distribution transformers as being a value line.

   If not used as part of the presentation, the capabilities brochure would make an impressive mailing to the customer along with a "thank you" letter for listening to the presentation.

Summary—Elements and Timing

Stage 1

First Mailing:	Cover Letter No. 1 (Program Summary)
	Bulletin No. 1 Cover and Bushing
	Puzzle No. 1 (Adult Game)
	Master Crossword Puzzle
Second Mailing:	Cover Letter No. 2
	Bulletin No. 2 Tank Assembly
(Two months later)	Puzzle No. 2
Third Mailing:	Cover Letter No. 3
	Bulletin No. 3 Core and Coil Assembly
(Two months later)	Puzzle No. 3
Fourth Mailing:	Cover Letter No. 4
	Bulletin No. 4 CSP Features
(Two months later)	Puzzle No. 4

Stage 2

Fifth Mailing:	Cover Letter No. 5 (Customer Presentations)
	Flip Chart Presentation
(Two months later)	Presentation Summary for Customer
	Athens Capability Brochure
	Puzzle No. 5

adult games. The container was a cardboard box with a design of jigsaw puzzle parts; each part had a letter on it with the total spelling being "The Problem Solvers." Kennedy put in some long hours working on the instruction brochures. In explaining the various components of the transformer, he had decided to set a conversational sales presentation scene between a Westinghouse salesperson and a purchasing agent. The salesperson, who was "Mr. Problem Solver" or "Ms. Problem Solver," was smoothly answering the questions asked by a purchasing agent, who was appropriately labeled "Mr. A. Gent" or "Ms. A. Lady."

EARLY NOVEMBER

One morning in early November, Bob Ray was relaxing at his desk sipping a cup of coffee. He was thinking about "The Problem Solvers" campaign. Things were moving along pretty well. At the present rate he would be able to meet the January 15 target date for the first mailing. He knew $20,000 was a lot of money for OHDT to spend on a training campaign of this type, but he was confident in the overall idea and felt it was the best way to reach such a broad and isolated target. However, a few decisions remained. There was some question about the two-month interval between each of the five mailings. He definitely wanted the sales force ready for November–December when the big utilities would negotiate year-long contracts for the following year. In a way he wanted the campaign to last a good while, as it represented a big chunk of the budget, but he wondered whether the field sales force's attention would be held over such a period. Another thought entered his mind about the effectiveness of the campaign's feedback mechanism. He remembered Glynn Hodges said he anticipated a 65 percent response. Another point that was undefined in the campaign was what stand OHDT should take on the future newcomers to the field sales force. Since the previous campaign, the new people learned through OJT (on-the-job-training) and sales materials, as well as picking up what they could from OHDT bulletins. However, this provided only short-range coverage and would break down in the long run, or when making sales got tough. This had been one of the factors contributing to the present situation.

With those thoughts in mind, Bob Ray decided to call a division head meeting that afternoon.

30

Food Dynamics *

Food Dynamics Inc. was born in 1976 when Bob Galvin, Bob Beaudry, and Florence Busch decided to strike out on their own, leaving a large New England food brokerage firm where they had been star salespeople. Within 30 days, they'd signed on seven product lines—which meant a total of $8,000 a month in commissions.

Their move, though, presented them with an important question: How could they keep top salespeople from eventually leaving their new company? If Food Dynamics was going to grow, the three partners knew they'd have to give their salespeople a reason to stay.

At first, there were no employees to worry about losing. Galvin, Beaudry, and Busch, representing their manufacturers' food lines, traveled around New England with their sample cases; they called mainly on buyers from hospitals, restaurants, schools, and food distribution companies. Since they put any profits into building up Food Dynamics's image, they ran a lean operation.

"I remember when Beaudry and I first began going down to Connecticut for overnight stays," Galvin recalls. "One of us would check into a motel room and the other would sneak up later. It worked out fine until one night we got the room only to find a single bed." Then, he remembers with a laugh, "we learned just how close a partnership we had."

After two years, the partners decided they were ready to expand. They wanted to hire

* Source: From Eileen B. Brill, "Making Sales People into Entrepreneurs," *INC.* July 1982, p. 87. Used with permission.

individuals who were not just good salespeople, but would also become almost as loyal to the company as they themselves were. All three believed that the best salespeople were entrepreneurs at heart who wanted a sense of participation in the business as well as a paycheck. One way to inspire loyalty, they felt, was to give the people they hired a stake in the company by tying commissions to the salesperson's contribution to overall profits.

According to Michael King, a vice-president of the National Food Brokers Association, most food brokers pay their salespeople on a salary basis, with a bonus arrangement. The problem then, says Galvin, "is that there is really no accountability. Salespeople may know how much they do in sales, but they have no idea what their contribution is to the profitability of the company."

So when Galvin, Beaudry, and Busch hired their first seasoned professional, John Vaillancourt, they decided to offer a compensation plan that would give him a stake in the company's growth and to use this plan as a prototype when it came to compensating future employees.

Under the system set up by Food Dynamics's owners, a salesperson would not only develop sales in a territory, but would also take charge of maximizing the territory's profitability for the firm, in return for a portion of the profits earned. Vaillancourt, for example, took total responsibility for the North Country market of Maine, New Hampshire, and Vermont. Food Dynamics, which specializes in providing food for restaurants, hospitals, and schools, among other institutions, had barely penetrated the three northern states and hoped Vaillancourt could increase its sales there to distributors and large-scale consumers.

Vaillancourt received a salary, plus a quarterly bonus based on a careful calculation of the profits he brought in from his area. The owners issued regular reports, advising Vaillancourt of the direct expenses that Food Dynamics had paid out for his salary and expenses. They also added in indirect expenses, figured as a percentage of the cost of maintaining the company's Wellesley, Mass., headquarters and its sales and service staff. After all expenses were subtracted from total sales for the territory, Vaillancourt then received an agreed-upon percentage of the profit.

Vaillancourt found the system gave him incentive to develop his territory—and an equally strong incentive to stay with Food Dynamics once he had developed it. "They treat my territory like another branch of the company," he says. "I've been given a great deal of autonomy, but when I need help the company is right there beside me."

"By making our salespeople responsible for their costs," says Galvin, "we make them more conscious of what's involved in the day-to-day running of our operation. People tend to think that items such as typewriter ribbons don't cost anything. Our financial reports also show the cyclical nature of the business—that we rely on the third and fourth quarters to carry us through the slower half." Moreover, tying bonuses directly to profits conserves Food Dynamics's cash flow in unprofitable periods.

Food Dynamics now had 3 key salespeople—out of a total staff of 19—managing portions of New England. The share of the firm's overhead and sales-support costs that each salesperson must cover varies, depending on the owner's assessment of his territory's potential. Once a year, each of these salespeople meets with the owners to discuss the projected revenues the company can expect from his territory. Expenses are also estimated for the coming year, and the differ-

ence represents the profit likely to be shared with the salesperson.

The company had to work closely with its salespeople in adjusting the profit-based compensation system to the firm's changing needs. Occasionally the company decides to invest in expanding its influence in a given territory; initially there may be no profits for the salesperson to share. That happened when Food Dynamics first hired Vaillancourt to develop the North Country. The solution: an agreement that for the first few pay periods, Food Dynamics's headquarters budget would absorb some of the expenses that would normally have been charged against Vaillancourt's territory.

Finding a compensation system that gave salespeople a stake in the company was a major step for the three partners, but they also recognized that they needed to go beyond dollars and cents if they were going to hang on to their top performers. "At some point," says Galvin, "salary becomes a moot question. More money is not always the way to secure a salesperson's loyalty."

Thus the partners structured the company so that salespeople in the field could count on a maximum of support and personal attention from the three owners. As additional salespeople were hired, each was assigned to the partner who knew the territory best and who could offer the most expert help whenever it was needed. Several times a year, for example, Beaudry visits Vaillancourt's territory to make special presentations to local distributors. And at trade shows at least one partner always works side by side with Food Dynamics's salespeople.

Constant telephone contact is the rule. "When we talk with our salespeople by phone, often three to four times a day, they don't feel that we're checking up on them," Galvin says. "Usually we discuss things like 'How can we increase distribution here?' or 'What's the quickest way to ship a product?' There are no mandates sent down from a central office."

The three partners have placed a great deal of emphasis on developing the skills and knowledge of their salespeople. They send them on trips to manufacturing plants to get a firsthand view of how products are made, and encourage direct contacts between salespeople and the manufacturers whose lines they represent—considered a risky tactic in the food brokerage business, since good salespeople often use their connections with manufacturers to launch their own firms. "We have faith in our ability to pick the right people," says Galvin. "In six years, we've lost only one line through a salesperson's leaving the company—and that salesperson came into our company with three lines."

The results of Food Dynamics's approach to managing salespeople have been financial success and team spirit. Only one salesperson has resigned in the company's history. Today annual sales are $30 million, and 22 top food manufacturers are represented.

"I guess the possibility that we could lose a key salesperson always exists, but I don't lose any sleep over it," Galvin says. "We feel pretty confident that our salespeople enjoy their work, are motivated, and have little reason to move someplace else."

Six

Distribution: Marketing Channels and Institutions

NATIONAL ENERGY DEVICES, INC.

THOMPSON RESPIRATION PRODUCTS, INC.

GOODBUY SUPERMARKET

CHRISTIAN'S

31

*National Energy Devices, Inc.**

ESTABLISHING A DISTRIBUTION NETWORK

Mr. Joseph Howard, founder and president of National Energy Devices, Inc., had recently reviewed his firm's sales records for the past six months and had come to the conclusion that the very future of his fledgling enterprise was in jeopardy unless something could be done quickly to increase sales to the residential market. Although the volume of the firm's product sold to commercial users was considered "satisfactory" by Mr. Howard, sales to individual homeowners had failed to achieve even the most modest of his expectations.

National Energy Devices, Inc., (NED) located in Hartford, Connecticut, marketed its product to both commercial and residential customers with the heavier emphasis being placed on the individual homeowner. While Mr. Howard recognized the potential that existed within the commercial market (businesses, apartment complexes, shopping centers, etc.), he felt that the key to the success of his new venture lay in NED making a major impact within the residential homeowner market.

Joseph Howard, a combustion engineer by training, had served as a consultant in the area of energy efficiency and conservation for a period of twelve years prior to starting National Energy Devices. Among his clients

* This case is from Norman Govoni, S.P. Jeanette; and H.N. Deneault, *Cases in Marketing.* Copyright © 1983 John Wiley & Sons. Reprinted with permission.

had been utility companies, oil refineries, paper mills, a plastics manufacturer and a steamship line. He specialized in helping his clients develop improved methods for drawing maximum amounts of heat into their boilers while using minimum amounts of fuel in the process. This was accomplished through various applications of the technology associated with metering manganese, a combustion catalytic material, into the furnace along with the fuel mix in order to achieve a hotter and more efficient burn.

It was his on-going work in this area that led Mr. Howard to consider various ways to transfer this technology from large industrial furnaces to smaller industrial and residential furnaces. This required identifying a chemical that could be used in microscopic quantities, was less expensive to use and would eliminate the constant maintenance of equipment which had been previously found to be necessary. Following a long period of trial and error, he found that platinum was the only material that met all the criteria. After two years of research and an investment of approximately $55,000, Mr. Howard successfully developed a device that was capable of producing substantial fuel savings for its users. The FuelSaver (the name given the new product by Howard's wife) was made of Lexan, a highly heat resistant and virtually unbreakable material. The device served as the vehicle for introducing platinum into a furnace's combustion process.

Liquid fuels such as gasoline, home heating fuel, diesel fuel and heavy industrial fuel are made up primarily of hydrogen and carbon. As such, fuel is commonly referred to as hydrocarbons. The combustion process is the means of igniting fuel so that the chemical composition of the hydrogen and carbon will break down. The hydrogen (H) will attach itself to oxygen (O_2) from the air and become water vapor (H_2O). The carbon (C) will attach itself to oxygen in a two-step process, first becoming carbon monoxide (CO) and then carbon dioxide (CO_2). These processes, the breakdown of the hydrocarbon, the formation of water vapor, the formation of carbon monoxide and the formation of carbon dioxide are heat releasing processes, and, as such, heat is produced in an oil-burning system.

Under normal conditions, fuel does not release all its available heat. The FuelSaver was designed to meter microscopic quantities of platinum into the combustion chamber of a furnace through the air-intake side of the burner fan. When the platinum was drawn into the combustion chamber, it came into contact with the hydrocarbons and a higher percentage of the fuel was burned. This process resulted in the release of more heat with a reduction of fuel consumption.

The FuelSaver was actually a simple-looking parabolic dome containing a single tube that ran between the apex of the FuelSaver and the fan on the oil burner. A petcock allowed a steady stream of air to enter the device, filter through a liquid solution within the parabaloid which contained the chemical catalyst, and travel through the connecting hose into the fan housing to be breathed into the fuel stream. The FuelSaver operated in a manner very similar to that of a catalytic converter in an automobile. The chemistries of the two were almost identical. The major difference was in the way the FuelSaver burned up the unburnt hydrocarbon in the combustion chamber where the extra heat was beneficial, whereas the catalytic converted burned the unburnt hydrocarbons after they had already left the engine.

Beyond this, the FuelSaver was effective in reducing carbon deposits, thus allowing more heat to penetrate the walls of the furnace. Since carbon or soot possesses a considerable insulating capability, when deposits build up, less heat penetrates the walls of the boiler and more heat is lost up the stack. In addition, because the FuelSaver allowed fuel to be burned more efficiently in the furnace, smaller quantities of gases and acids escaped as pollutants into the atmosphere.

After considerable testing and experimentation, Mr. Howard determined that his new device was ready to market. Consequently, he started National Energy Devices one year ago in order to manufacture and sell the FuelSaver to both commercial and residential users.

The FuelSaver and the platinum solution could be produced for a fraction of the retail cost for the materials. Mr. Howard had subcontracted the manufacture of the Lexan dome to a plastics company. These domes were ordered in quantities of 100 at a cost of $32 per unit. Upon receiving the domes from the supplier, Mr. Howard would complete the manufacturing process by adding the necessary tubing and valves followed by packaging. The entire process took approximately 15 minutes per unit with extra parts costing approximately $5. The platinum solution was prepared separately and sold in 3-gallon containers. Although platinum was an extremely expensive material, the FuelSaver device required only microscopic quantities diluted in water, thus making its use economically feasible. Allowing for fluctuations in the price of platinum, the per gallon cost of the solution generally averaged around $6. The retail price of the FuelSaver was $495 including the first three gallons of platinum solution. The unit held three gallons of solution which in most cases would last the entire heating season. Full refunds were offered for units returned within a 30-day period following purchase if the customer wasn't satisfied. NED estimated that, under normal conditions, the FuelSaver would pay for itself during the first heating season following purchase.

The installation of the FuelSaver took approximately one-half hour and had to be performed by a licensed oil burner service person. This was a critical procedure since improper installation would cause the device to fail to function at all. There was a float within the FuelSaver that required precise adjustment as did a needle valve used to control air flow. National Energy Devices preferred to have the customer's oil burner service person perform the installation under the supervision of a NED field representative. In this way the NED field person could familiarize the oil burner service person with the FuelSaver and its function, thus helping to avoid problems that might occur later on. Many service people tended to be bothered when the burners they serviced had additional unfamiliar equipment installed. Installation of the FuelSaver by the customer's oil burner person generally represented an additional cost to the consumer of between $25 and $35. National Energy Devices manufactured only one size unit since the FuelSaver could work on any boiler regardless of its size.

The energy saving business, while still in its embryonic stage of development, promised to become an extremely large and lucrative industry. Unfortunately, a number of devices were already being produced and sold without having been properly screened and tested. Very little regulation existed within this field and, as a result, many entrepreneurs quickly entered the industry with ineffective products which caused a high degree of skepticism in the marketplace among potential distributors and users. Brookhaven Laboratories was an independent testing laboratory which had been established for the purpose of testing energy-saving devices of all types for the federal government. The lab was sponsored by the government and firms were able to have their products tested at this facility at no cost. It was not, however, mandatory for manufacturers to have their products tested. Due to the high influx of firms into this industry, Brookhaven was experiencing an 8 to 10 month backlog on product testing. Mr. Howard had recently contacted Brookhaven for an application form.

Mr. Howard felt his major competition came from those firms that were also engaged in the sale of oil burner fuel-reduction/efficiency-oriented devices. Although there were a number of companies which marketed products of this type, Mr. Howard considered three particular firms, Energy Technology, Fuel Reduction Engineering, and Resource Instruments, Inc., to be the most formidable competitors. Another firm, Vapor Technology, Inc. (VTI), had emerged onto the scene with considerable fanfare about one year prior to NED's incorporation. Vapor Technology had aggressively advertised its energy-saving device as being capable of producing "up to 40% increases in combustion efficiencies." As a result of the firm's substantial advertising and promotional efforts, it was reported that VTI achieved sales of approximately 15,000 units during its first 6 months of operations.

VTI's device was alleged to produce a "catalyst gas" which, upon injection into the burner's combustion system, would "drastically reduce the amount of fuel expended while materially increasing the amount of the heat generated." As a result of numerous complaints, VTI's advertising claims became the subject of a Federal Trade Commission investigation. Subsequently, the FTC found the firm guilty of having engaged in false and misleading advertising practices and levied a cease-and-desist order against VTI along with a substantial fine. Specifically, the investigation revealed that VTI's device did not produce a "catalyst gas," did not "drastically reduce the amount of fuel expended," nor did it materially "increase the amount of heat generated." In fact, the VTI product was found to consist of nothing more than a clumsy water injection device of no real value. The investigation of VTI and subsequent outcome became an issue of wide public interest. Many newspapers covered the investigation and gave it front page coverage, running headlines such as "Fraud

Uncovered in Fuel Saving Industry" and "Energy Saving Device Proves a Costly Gimmick." The impact of the VTI case on the entire industry was immediate with public skepticism reaching its highest level. VTI eventually went out of business.

In addition to competing against firms producing similar units, NED also competed, on an indirect basis, with firms marketing items designed to aid the consumer in reducing energy costs. Such firms included manufacturers of wood burning stoves, insulation firms, manufacturers of stack dampers and heat exchangers, as well as manufacturers of solar equipment.

National Energy Devices had not engaged in any formal advertising program for its new product for essentially two reasons: (1) a general lack of funds since the product's development had expended the majority of Mr. Howard's savings and efforts to induce additional investors and attempts to procure a business loan had not been successful, and (2) it was Mr. Howard's contention that the best way to enter the industry was through a direct selling effort as opposed to what he viewed as the high costs associated with an advertising campaign.

The firm's sales force consisted of Mr. Howard and two full-time salespersons. Mr. Howard took responsibility for prospecting the commercial market and assigned the two salespeople to the residential market. One of the salespersons called directly on homeowners while the other was responsible for establishing distribution from within the industry through oil dealers and oil burner service companies. Mr. Howard felt that, under this arrangement, demand could be created in two ways. First, if an oil dealer could be interested in the product, then all of that dealer's clients would become sales prospects since the dealer would "push" the FuelSaver to them. Second, if a dealer didn't carry the NED product, a sale could still be made to the homeowner through direct contact with the NED salesperson. In time, Mr. Howard believed that oil companies that did not carry the FuelSaver would begin to notice that

many of their customers had had FuelSavers installed. This, he felt, would lead to an eventual interest on the part of the oil companies and additional dealerships could then be established.

After one year of operation the company had sold only 80 FuelSavers. Of these, 50 were sold to Scott Realty of Bridgeport, Connecticut, at a price of $200 per unit in exchange for using them as a referral for testimonial purposes. Ten units had been sold to local businesses with the remaining 20 sold to individual homeowners along the Connecticut coast.

National Energy Devices had not experienced much success in developing distributors for their products from within the industry. Oil burner service companies and oil dealers alike seemed to shy away from NED's advances for a variety of reasons including bad experiences through previous dealings with other competitors, product skepticism, lack of independent test results, and general unfamiliarity with the technology involved with the FuelSaver. All seemed to be concerned with their reputations and present business. According to Mr. Howard, residential homeowners appeared uninterested in the FuelSaver for many of the same reasons. He felt that, since the VTI publicity, many people assumed that the FuelSaver was the same type of product and sales were suffering for that reason. Also, a few prospects had fallen through since they felt the 30-day return policy to be of marginal use because they were looking to purchase during the off-season (summer months), a time when product performance would be difficult to measure.

Mr. Howard was unsure as to his alternatives. He wondered whether he should close the business or sell his Eastman Kodak stock (approximate market value of $15,000) in order to try to keep the business alive or he wondered what measures he might take to increase company sales. He had also thought there might be a possibility of entering into a licensing agreement with a large chain operation such as Sears or Wards; however, he felt that active pursuit of these alternatives might consume too much of his time and take him away from his business at a point when his constant attention was required. He knew he had a good product, but he didn't know how to convince consumers of it. Yet, with so much attention being paid to energy-saving devices and measures, he did not want to give up at this point. He was at a loss as to what course of action to take.

32

*Thompson Respiration Products, Inc.**

Victor Higgins, executive vice-president for Thompson Respiration Products, Inc. (TRP), sat thinking at his desk late one Friday in April 1982. "We're making progress," he said to himself. "Getting Metro to sign finally gets us into the Chicago Market ... and with a good dealer at that." "Metro," of course, was Metropolitan Medical Products, a large Chicago retailer of medical equipment and supplies for home use. "Now, if we could just do the same in Minneapolis and Atlanta," he continued.

However, getting at least one dealer in each of these cities to sign a TRP Dealer Agreement seemed remote right now. One reason was the sizeable groundwork required—Higgins simply lacked the time to review operations at the well over 100 dealers currently operating in the two cities. Another was TRP's lack of dealer-oriented sales information that went beyond the technical specification sheet for each product and the company's price list. Still another concerned two conditions in the Dealer Agreement itself—prospective dealers sometimes balked at agreeing to sell no products manufactured by TRP's competitors and differed with TRP in interpretations of the "best efforts" clause. (The clause required the dealer to maintain adequate inventories of TRP prod-

ucts, contact four prospective new customers or physicians or respiration therapists per month, respond promptly to sales inquiries, and represent TRP at appropriate conventions where it exhibited.)

"Still," Higgins concluded, "we signed Metro in spite of these reasons, and 21 others across the country. That's about all anyone could expect—after all, we've only been trying to develop a dealer network for a year or so."

THE PORTABLE RESPIRATOR INDUSTRY

The portable respirator industry began in the early 1950s when polio stricken patients who lacked control of muscles necessary for breathing began to leave treatment centers. They returned home with hospital-style iron lungs or fiber glass chest shells, both being large chambers that regularly introduced a vacuum about the patient's chest. The vacuum caused the chest to expand and, thus, the lungs to fill with air. However, both devices confined patients to a prone or semiprone position in a bed.

By the late 1950s, TRP had developed a portable turbine blower powered by an electric motor and battery. When connected to a mouthpiece via plastic tubing, the blower would inflate a patient's lungs on demand. Patients could now leave their beds for several hours at a time and realize limited mobility in a wheelchair. By the early 1970s,

* This case was written by Professors James E. Nelson, University of Colorado and William R. Wooldridge, University of Massachusetts. Some data is disguised. © 1983 by the Business Research Division, College of Business and Administration and the Graduate School of Business Administration, University of Colorado.

TRP had developed a line of more sophisticated turbine respirators in terms of monitoring and capability for adjustment to individual patient needs.

At about the same time, applications began to shift from polio patients to victims of other diseases or of spinal cord injuries, the latter group existing primarily as a result of automobile accidents. Better emergency medical service, quicker evacuation to spinal cord injury centers, and more proficient treatment meant that people who formerly would have died now lived and went on to lead meaningful lives. Because of patients' frequently younger ages, they strongly desired wheelchair mobility. Respiration therapists obliged by recommending a Thompson respirator for home use or, if unaware of Thompson, recommending a Puritan-Bennett or other machine instead.

Instead of a turbine, Puritan-Bennett machines used a bellows design to force air into the patient's lungs. The machines were widely used in hospitals but seemed poorly suited for home use. For one thing, Puritan-Bennett machines used a compressor pump or pressurized air to drive the bellows, much more cumbersome than Thompson's electric motor. Puritan-Bennett machines also cost approximately 50% more than a comparable Thompson unit and were relatively large and immobile. On the other hand, Puritan-Bennett machines were viewed by physicians and respiration therapists as industry standards.

By the middle 1970s, TRP had developed a piston and cylinder design (similar in principle to the bellows) and placed it on the market. The product lacked the sophistication of the Puritan-Bennett machines but was reliable, portable, and much simpler to adjust and operate. It also maintained TRP's traditional cost advantage. Another firm, Life Products, began its operations in 1976 by producing a similar design. A third competitor, Lifecare Services, had begun operations somewhat earlier.

Puritan-Bennett

Puritan-Bennett was a large, growing, and financially sound manufacturer of respiration equipment for medical and aviation applications. Its headquarters were located in Kansas City, Missouri. However, the firm staffed over 40 sales, service, and warehouse operations in the U.S., Canada, United Kingdom, and France. Sales for 1981 exceeded $100 million while employment was just over 2,000 people. Sales for its Medical Equipment Group (respirators, related equipment, and accessories, service and parts) likely exceeded $40 million for 1981; however, Higgins could obtain data only for the period 1977–1980 (see Exhibit 1). Puritan-Bennett usually sold its respirators through a system of independent, durable medical equipment dealers. However, its sales offices did sell directly to identified "house accounts" and often competed with dealers by selling slower moving products to all accounts. According to industry sources, Puritan-Bennett sales were slightly more than three-fourths of all respirator sales to hospitals in 1981.

However, these same sources expected Puritan-Bennett's share to diminish during the 1980s because of the aggressive marketing efforts of three other manufacturers of hospital-style respirators: Bear Medical Systems, Inc., J. H. Emerson; and Siemens-Elema. The latter firm was expected to grow the most rapidly, despite its quite recent entry into the U.S. market (its headquarters were in Sweden) and a list price of over $16,000 for its basic model.

Life Products

Life Products directly competed with TRP for the portable respirator market. Life Products had begun operations in 1976 when David Smith, a TRP employee, left to start his own business. Smith had located his plant in Boulder, Colorado, less than a mile from TRP headquarters.

He began almost immediately to set up a dealer network and by early 1982 had secured over 40 independent dealers located in large metropolitan areas. Smith had made a strong effort to sign only large, well-man-

Exhibit 1. Puritan-Bennett Medical Equipment Group Sales

Item	1977	1978	1979	1980
Domestic Sales				
Model MA–1				
Units	1,460	875	600	500
$(millions)	8.5	4.9	3.5	3.1
Model MA–2				
Units	—	935	900	1,100
$(millions)	—	6.0	6.1	7.8
Foreign Sales				
Units	250	300	500	565
$(millions)	1.5	1.8	3.1	3.6
IPPB Equipment $(millions)	6.0	6.5	6.7	7.0
Parts, Service, Accessories				
$(millions)	10.0	11.7	13.1	13.5
Overhaul $(millions)	2.0	3.0	2.5	2.5
Total $(millions)	28.0	34.0	35.0	37.5

Source: *Wall Street Transcript.*

aged durable medical equipment dealers. Dealer representatives were required to complete Life Products' service training school, held each month in Boulder. Life Products sold its products to dealers (in contrast to TRP, which both sold and rented products to consumers and to dealers). Dealers received a 20 to 25 percent discount off suggested retail price on most products.

As of April 1982, Life Products offered two respirator models (the LP3 and LP4) and a limited number of accessories (such as mouthpieces and plastic tubing) to its dealers. Suggested retail prices for the two respirator models were approximately $3,900 and $4,800. Suggested rental rates were approximately $400 and $500 per month. Life Products also allowed Lifecare Services to manufacture a respirator similar to the LP3 under license.

At the end of 1981, Smith was quite pleased with his firm's performance. During Life Products' brief history, it had passed TRP in sales and now ceased to see the firm as a serious threat, at least according to one company executive:

We really aren't in competition with Thompson. They're after the stagnant market and we're after a growing market. We see new applications and ultimately the hospital market as our niche. I doubt if Thompson will even be around in a few years. As for Lifecare, their prices are much lower than ours but you don't get the service. With them you get the basic product, but nothing else. With us, you get a complete medical care service. That's the big difference.

Lifecare Services, Inc.

In contrast to the preceding firms, Lifecare Services, Inc., earned much less of its revenues from medical equipment manufacturing and much more from medical equipment distributing. The firm primarily resold products purchased from other manufacturers, operating out of its headquarters in Boulder as well as from its sixteen field offices (Exhibit 2). All offices were stocked with backup parts and an inventory of respirators. All were staffed with trained service technicians under Lifecare's employ.

Lifecare did manufacture a few accessories not readily available from other manufacturers. These items complemented the pur-

Exhibit 2. Lifecare Services, Inc., Field Offices

Augusta, GA	Houston, TX
Baltimore, MD	Los Angeles, CA
Boston, MA	New York, NY
Chicago, IL	Oakland, CA
Cleveland, OH	Omaha, NB
Denver, CO	Phoenix, AR
Detroit, MI	Seattle, WA
Grand Rapids, MI *	St. Paul, MN

* Suboffice
Source: Trade Literature.

chased products and, in the company's words, served to "give the customer a complete respiratory service." Under a licensing agreement between Lifecare and Life Products, the firm manufactured a respirator similar to the LP3 and marketed it under the Lifecare name. The unit rented for approximately $175 per month. While Lifecare continued to service the few remaining Thompson units it still had in the field, it no longer carried the Thompson line.

Lifecare rented rather than sold its equipment. The firm maintained that this gave patients more flexibility in the event of recovery or death and lowered patients' monthly costs.

THOMPSON RESPIRATION PRODUCTS, INC.

TRP currently employed thirteen people, nine in production and four in management. It conducted operations in a modern, attractive building (leased) in an industrial park. The building contained about 6,000 square feet of space, split 75/25 for production/ management purposes. Production operations were essentially job-shop in nature: skilled technicians assembled each unit by hand on work benches, making frequent quality control tests and subsequent adjustments. Production lots usually ranged from 10 to 75 units per model and probably averaged around 40. Normal production capacity was about 600 units per year.

Product Line

TRP currently sold seven respirator models plus a large number of accessories. All respirator models were portable but differed considerably in terms of style, design, performance specifications, and attendant features (see Exhibit 3). Four models were styled as metal boxes with an impressive array of knobs, dials, indicator lights, and switches. Three were styled as less imposing, "overnighter" suitcases with less prominently displayed controls and indicators. (Exhibit 4 describes the specifications of the product.)

Four of the models were designed as *pressure machines,* using a turbine pump that provided a constant, usually positive, pressure. Patients were provided intermittent access to this pressure as breaths per minute. However, one model, the MV Multivent, could provide either a constant positive or a constant negative pressure (i.e., a vacuum, necessary to operate chest shells, iron lungs, and body wraps). No other portable respirator on the market could produce a negative pressure. Three of the models were designed as *volume machines,* using a piston pump that produced intermittent, constant volumes of pressurized air as breaths per minute. Actual volumes were prescribed by each patient's

Exhibit 3. TRP Respirators

Model *	Style	Design	Volume (cc)	Pressure (cm H₂0)
M3000	metal box	volume	300–3000	+10 to +65
MV Multivent	metal box	pressure (positive or negative)	NA	−70 to +80
Minilung M15	suitcase	volume	200–1500	+5 to +65
Minilung M25 Assist (also available without the assist feature)	suitcase	volume	600–2500	+5 to +65
Bantam GS	suitcase	pressure (positive)	NA	+15 to +45
Compact CS	metal box	pressure (positive)	NA	+15 to +45
Compact C	metal box	pressure (positive)	NA	+15 to +45

Model	Breaths per minute	Weight (lbs.)	Size (ft.)	Features
M3000	6 to 30	39	0.85	sigh, four alarms, automatic switchover from AC to battery
MV Multivent	8 to 24	41	1.05	positive or negative pressure, four alarms, AC only
Minilung M15	8 to 22	24	0.70	three alarms, automatic switchover from AC to battery
Minilung M25 Assist (also available without the assist feature)	5 to 20	24	0.70	assist, sigh, three alarms, automatic switchover from AC to battery
Bantam GS	6 to 24	19	0.75	sigh, six alarms, automatic switchover from AC to battery
Compact CS	8 to 24	25	0.72	sigh, six alarms, automatic switchover from AC to battery
Compact C	6 to 24	19	0.50	sigh, four alarms, automatic switchover from AC to battery

* Five other models considered obsolete by TRP could be supplied if necessary.

NA=not applicable.

Source: Company sales specification sheets.

physician based on lung capacity. Pressures depended on the breathing method used (mouthpiece, trach, chest shell, and others) and on the patient's activity level. Breaths per minute also depended on the patient's activity level.

Models came with several features. The newest was an assist feature (currently available on the Minilung M25 but soon to be of-fered also on the M3000) that allowed the patient alone to "command" additional breaths without having someone change the dialed breath rate. The sigh feature gave patients a sigh, either automatically or on demand. Depending on the model, up to six alarms were available to indicate: a patient's call, unacceptable low pressure, unacceptable high pressure, low battery voltage/power failure, failure to

Exhibit 4.   The M3000 Minilung

* The M3000 is a planned performance product designed to meet breathing needs. It is a significant step in the ongoing effort of a company which pioneered the advancement of portable respiratory equipment.

* This portable volume ventilator sets high standards for flexibility of operation and versatility in use. The M3000 has gained its successful reputation as a result of satisfactory usage in hospitals, for transport, in rehabilitation efforts and in home care. This model grew out of expressed needs of users for characteristics which offer performance PLUS. It is engineered to enable the user to have something more than just mechanical breathing.

* Breathing patterns can be comfortably varied with the use of a SIGH, which can be obtained either automatically or manually.

* Remote pressure sensing in the proximal airway provides for more accurate set up of the ventilator pressure alarms.

* AC–DC operation of the M3000 is accomplished with ease because automatic switch-over is provided on AC power failure, first to external battery, then to internal battery.

---

cycle, and the need to replace motor brushes. All models but the MV Multivent also offered automatic switchover from alternating current to either an internal or an external battery (or both) in the event of a power failure. Batteries provided for 18 to 40 hours of operation, depending on usage.

Higgins felt that TRP's respirators were superior to those of Life Products. Most TRP models allowed pressure monitoring in the airway itself rather than in the machine, providing more accurate measurement. TRP's suitcase style models often were strongly preferred by patients, especially the polio patients who had known no others. TRP's volume models offered easier volume adjustments and all TRP models offered more alarms. On the other hand, he knew that TRP had recently experienced some product reliability problems of an irritating—not life threatening—nature. Further, he knew that Life Products had beaten TRP to the market with the assist feature (the idea for which had come from a Puritan-Bennett machine).

TRP's line of accessories was more extensive than that of Life Products. TRP offered the following for separate sale: alarms, call switches, battery cables, chest shells, mouthpieces, plastic tubing, pneumobelts and bladders (equipment for still another breathing method that utilized intermittent pressure on a patient's diaphragm), and other items. Lifecare Services offered many similar items.

Distribution

Shortly after joining TRP, Higgins had decided to switch from selling and renting products directly to patients to selling and renting products to dealers. While it meant lower margins, less control, and more infrequent communication with patients, the change had several advantages. It allowed TRP to shift inventory from the factory to the dealer, generating cash more quickly. It provided for local representation in market areas, allowing patients greater feelings of security and TRP more aggressive sales efforts. It shifted burdensome paperwork (required by insurance companies and state and federal agencies to effect payment) from TRP to the dealer. It also reduced other TRP administrative activities in accounting, customer relations, and sales.

TRP derived about half of its 1981 revenue of $3.0 million directly from patients and about half from the dealer network. By April 1982, the firm had twenty-two dealers (see Exhibit 5) with three accounting for over 60 percent of TRP dealer revenues. Two of the three serviced TRP products as did two of the

Exhibit 5. TRP Dealer Locations

Bakersfield, CA	Salt Lake City, UT
Baltimore, MD	San Diego, CA
Birmingham, AL	San Francisco, CA
Chicago, IL	Seattle, WA
Cleveland, OH	Springfield, OH
Fort Wayne, IN	Tampa, FL
Greenville, NC	Tucson, AZ
Indianapolis, IN	Washington, DC
Newark, NJ	Montreal, Canada
Oklahoma City, OK	Toronto, Canada
Pittsburgh, PA	

Source: Company records.

smaller dealers; the rest preferred to let the factory take care of repairs. TRP conducted occasional training sessions for dealer repair personnel but distances were great and turnover in the position high, making such sessions costly. Most dealers requested air shipment of respirators, in quantities of 1 or 2 units.

Price

TRP maintained a comprehensive price list for its entire product line. (Exhibit 6 reproduces part of the current list.) Each respirator model carried both a suggested retail selling price and a suggested retail rental rate. (TRP also applied these rates when it dealt directly with patients.) The list also presented two net purchase prices for each model along with an alternative rental rate that TRP charged to dealers. About 40% of the 300 respirator units TRP shipped to dealers in 1981 went out on a rental basis. The comparable figure for the 165 units sent directly to consumers was 90%. Net purchase prices allowed an approximate 7% discount for orders of three or more units of each model. Higgins had initiated this policy early last year with the aim of encouraging dealers to order in larger quantities. To date one dealer had taken advantage of this discount.

Exhibit 6. Current TRP Respirator Price List

Model	Suggested Retail: Rent/Month	Price	Dealer Rent/Month	Dealer Price 1–2	3 or more
M3000	$380	$6000	$290	$4500	$4185
MV Multivent	270	4300	210	3225	3000
Minilung M15	250	3950	190	2960	2750
Minilung M25	250	3950	190	2960	2750
Bantam GS	230	3600	175	2700	2510
Compact CS	230	3600	175	2700	2510
Compact C	200	3150	155	2360	2195

Source: Company sales specification sheets.

Current policy called for TRP to earn a gross margin of approximately 35% on the dealer price for 1–2 units. All prices included shipping charges by United Parcel Service (UPS); purchasers requesting more expensive transportation service paid the difference between actual costs incurred and the UPS charge. Terms were net 30 days with a 1½% service charge added to past due accounts. Prices were last changed in late 1981.

CONSUMERS

Two types of patients used respirators, depending on whether the need followed from disease or from injury. Diseases such as polio, sleep apnea, chronic obstructive pulmonary disease, and muscular dystrophy annually left about 1900 victims unable to breathe without a respirator. Injury to the spinal cord above the fifth vertebra caused a similar result for about 300 people per year. Except for polio, incidences of the diseases and injury were growing at about 3% per year. Most patients kept one respirator at bedside and another mounted on a wheelchair. However, Higgins did know of one individual who kept eight Bantam B models (provided by a local polio foundation, now defunct) in his closet. Except for polio patients, life expectancies were about five years. Higgins estimated the total number of patients using a home respirator in 1981 at

polio	3000
other diseases	6500
spinal cord injury	1000

Almost all patients were under a physician's care as well as that of a more immediate nurse or attendant (frequently a relative). About 95% paid for their equipment through insurance benefits or foundation monies. About 90% rented their equipment. Almost all patients and their nurses or attendants had received instruction in equipment operation from respiration therapists employed by medical centers or by dealers of durable medical equipment.

The majority of patients were poor. Virtually none were gainfully employed and all had seen their savings and other assets diminished to varying degrees by treatment costs. Some had experienced a divorce. Slightly more patients were male than female. About 75% lived in their homes with the rest split between hospitals, nursing homes, and other institutions.

Apart from patients, Higgins thought that hospitals might be considered a logical new market for TRP to enter. Many of the larger and some of the smaller general hospitals might be convinced to purchase one portable respirator (like the M3000) for emergency and other use with injury patients. Such a machine would be much cheaper to purchase than a large Puritan-Bennett and would allow easier patient trips to testing areas, x-ray, surgery, and the like. Even easier to convince should be the fourteen regional spinal cord injury centers located across the country (Exhibit 7). Other medical centers that specialized in treatment of pulmonary diseases should also be prime targets. Somewhat less promising but more numerous

Exhibit 7. Regional Spinal Cord Injury Centers

Birmingham, AL	Houston, TX
Boston, MA	Miami, FL
Chicago, IL	New York, NY
Columbia, MO	Philadelphia, PA
Downey, CA	Phoenix, AZ
Englewood, CO	San Jose, CA
Fishersville, VA	Seattle, WA

would be public and private schools that trained physicians and respiration therapists. Higgins estimated the numbers of these institutions at:

general hospitals (100 beds or more)	3800
general hospitals (fewer than 100 beds)	3200
spinal cord injury centers	14
pulmonary disease treatment centers	100
medical schools	180
respiration therapy schools	250

DEALERS

Dealers supplying homecare medical products (as distinct from dealers supplying hospitals and medical centers) showed a great deal of diversity. Some were little more than small areas in local drugstores that rented canes, walkers, and wheelchairs in addition to selling supplies like surgical stockings and colostomy bags. Others carried nearly everything needed for home nursing care—renting everything from canes to hospital beds and selling supplies from bed pads to bottled oxygen. Still others specialized in products and supplies for only certain types of patients.

In this latter category, Higgins had identified dealers of oxygen and oxygen-related equipment as the best fit among existing dealers. These dealers serviced victims of emphysema, bronchitis, asthma, and other respiratory ailments, a growing market that Higgins estimated was about ten times greater than that for respirators. A typical dealer had begun perhaps ten years ago selling bottled oxygen (obtained from a welding supply wholesaler) and renting rather crude metering equipment to patients at home under the care of a registered nurse. The same dealer today now rented and serviced oxygen concentrators (a recently developed device that extracts oxygen from the air), liquid oxygen equipment and liquid oxygen, and much more sophisticated oxygen equipment and oxygen to patients cared for by themselves or by relatives.

Most dealers maintained a fleet of radio dispatched trucks to deliver products to their customers. Better dealers promised 24 hour service and kept delivery personnel and a respiration therapist on call 24 hours a day. Dealers usually employed several respiration therapists who would set up equipment, instruct patients and attendants on equipment operation, and provide routine and emergency service. Dealers often expected the therapists to function as a salesforce. The therapists would call on physicians and other respiration therapists at hospitals and medical centers, on discharge planners at hospitals, and on organizations such as muscular dystrophy associations, spinal cord injury associations, and visiting nurse associations.

Dealers usually bought their inventories of durable equipment and supplies directly from manufacturers. They usually received a 20 to 25 percent discount off suggested list prices to consumers and hospitals. Only in rare instances might dealers instead lease equipment from a manufacturer. Dealers aimed for a payback of one year or less, meaning that most products began to contribute to profit and overhead after 12 months of rental. Most products lasted physically for upwards of ten years but technologically for only five to six: every dealer's warehouse contained idle but perfectly suitable equipment that had been superseded by models demanded by patients, their physicians, or their attendants.

Most dealers were independently owned and operated, with annual sales ranging between $5 and $10 million. However, a number had recently been acquired by one of several parent organizations that were regional or national in scope. Such chains usually consisted of from 10 to 30 retail operations located in separated market areas. However, the largest, Abbey Medical, had begun operations in 1924 and now consisted of over 70 local dealers. Higgins estimated 1981 sales for the chain (which was itself acquired by American Hospital Supply Corporation in April 1981) at over $60 million. In general, chains maintained a low corporate visibility and provided their dealers with working capital, employee benefit programs, operating advice, and some centralized purchasing. Higgins thought that chain organizations might grow more rapidly over the next ten years.

THE ISSUES

Higgins looked at his watch. It was 5:30 and really time to leave. "Still," he thought, "I should jot down what I see to be the immediate issues before I go—that way I won't be tempted to think about them over the weekend." He took a pen and wrote the following:

1. Should TRP continue to rent respirators to dealers?

2. Should TRP protect each dealer's territory (and how big should a territory be)?

3. Should TRP require dealers to stock no competing equipment?

4. How many dealers should TRP eventually have? Where?

5. What sales information should be assembled in order to attract high quality dealers?

6. What should be done about the "best efforts" clause?

As he reread the list, Higgins considered that there probably were still other short-term oriented questions he might have missed. Monday would be soon enough to consider them all.

Until then, he was free to think about broader, more strategic issues. Some reflections on the nature of the target market, a statement of marketing objectives, and TRP's possible entry into the hospital market would occupy the weekend. Decisions on these topics would form a substantial part of TRP's strategic marketing plan, a document Higgins hoped to have for the beginning of the next fiscal year in July. "At least I can rule out one option," Higgins thought as he put on his coat. That was an idea to use independent sales representatives to sell TRP products on commission: a recently completed two-month search for such an organization had come up empty. "Like my stomach," he thought, as he went out the door.

33

Goodbuy Supermarket *

The Goodbuy supermarket in Oakdale, Michigan, occupies 42,000 square feet of the total of 79,000 square feet available in its shopping center locale. Store hours are from 8 A.M. to 11 P.M., seven days a week (township statutes prohibit 24-hour operation).

Approximately a year before the Oakdale Goodbuy supermarket opened, however, a research team from the Grand Markets Corporation (Goodbuy's parent company) was gathering information on economic, demographic, social, and competitive characteristics of the area in order to answer questions such as these:

1. In terms of area ethnic composition, what facilities (such as a delicatessen or liquor store) and product lines should be represented in the new Goodbuy outlet?

2. In terms of the geographic distribution of various ethnic and economic groups, what media should be used to promote these facilities and product lines?

3. Based on an understanding of facilities offered and products carried by competitive stores in the new outlet's trading area, and consumer attitudes toward these competitive outlets, how might Goodbuy's marketing mix (i.e., products stocked, services offered, prices charged, promotional appeals, etc.) be planned to fill competitive gaps?

4. Based on all of the foregoing considerations, how much business could the

* From Philip Ward Burton and R. Sandhusen, *Cases in Advertising,* Copyright © 1981 John Wiley & Sons. Reprinted with permission.

new store expect to do in an average week?

5. What effect would the sales volume generated by this new outlet have on the sales volume of other Goodbuy outlets in the area?

Following are some of the key findings of this research effort, all of which affected, directly or indirectly, the advertising planning effort.

POPULATION TRENDS

According to census figures, more than 150,000 people live within eight minutes of the proposed Oakdale Goodbuy, with practically no population growth shown during the previous five years.

In terms of distances that these people would have to travel to get to the proposed Goodbuy, the population breakdown was as follows:

Minutes from Proposed Goodbuy	Population	Population, Cumulative
0–2	8,200	8,200
2–4	36,500	44,700
4–6	61,100	105,800
6–8	52,000	157,800

ETHNIC COMPOSITION

The ethnic breakdown of the population located within eight minutes' travel time of the proposed new outlet was as follows: black, 20 percent; Italian, 16 percent; Spanish, 10 percent; Jewish, 8 percent; Polish, 7 percent; other, 39 percent.

However, when this ethnic breakdown was considered in terms of traveling distances from the proposed new Goodbuy, a different picture emerged:

1. Forty-seven percent of the population residing within four minutes of the new Goodbuy outlet were of Italian descent.

2. Of the 38,500 blacks residing within the overall eight-minute traveling area, 35,700 lived between four and eight minutes from the proposed new outlet and accounted for roughly one-third of the total population in this zone.

3. Of the 16,000 people of Spanish descent living within the overall eight-minute area, nearly 75 percent, or 12,000, resided in the four-to-eight minute zone and accounted for 10 percent of the total population in that zone.

4. While only 13,800 (8 percent) of the total population of the eight-minute zone were Jewish, 80 percent of this total lived within four minutes of the proposed new outlet.

For an example of an advertisement with an ethnic slant, see Exhibit 1.

INCOME

The research team also discovered that the median family income in the overall eight-minute zone—$13,500—was slightly above the norm for the entire state. However, because of sharp variations among different groups within this area, income was examined in depth on a town-by-town basis. Following are some of the more significant results of this study.

Royal Park (predominantly Spanish descent)	$ 8,900
Harpur Village (predominantly black)	12,200
East Rapids (predominantly Italian)	17,600
Oakdale Hills (predominantly Jewish)	18,800

COMPETITIVE FACTORS

This investigation focused on both qualitative considerations (i.e., consumers' perceptions of various competitors) and quantitative considerations (sales volume, share of market of various competitors). Among the key findings:

Sales Volume

Following is a summary of sales volume totals among the higher-volume supermarkets in the proposed Goodbuy's eight-minute primary trading zone.

Store	Sales Volume (Weekly)
Oakdale A & P	$250–275,000
Fernwood Shopwell	200–250,000
Grubtown	175–200,000
Harpur Village A & P	130–150,000
Royal Park Shopwell	125,000
Foodfair	100,000

Among these six competitors, the closest to the proposed Goodbuy location (one minute) was the Oakdale A & P. The other five stores on this list were located in outlying areas of the proposed Goodbuy trading area, between six and eight minutes away. And since these five large stores were located in the same two-minute time band, the researchers concluded that there was a strong likelihood that they would act as trading area "cut-offs," shortstopping Goodbuy's customers from beyond the six-minute circumference. Thus, while the typical Goodbuy outlet got between 20 and 30 percent of its business from the area beyond the eight-minute circumference, it was felt that the Oakdale Goodbuy was likely to get in the neighborhood of only 10 percent.

In addition to the above-mentioned "Big Six" competitors, the research team also developed the following information on 48 smaller competitors in the eight-minute area.

Store name and location

Weekly sales

Sales/square feet

Number of cash registers

Type of meat trays (foam vs. clear)

Produce (pre-pack vs. loose)

256

Exhibit 1. Advertisement with Ethnic Slant

Prices effective Sunday, October 10 thru Saturday, October 16

So that we may serve all our customers, we reserve the right to limit sales of any item. Items offered for sale not available in case lots. Certain items not available where prohibited by law.
Items and prices valid only at Pathmark Supermarkets. Not responsible for typographical errors. Some pictures shown in this circular are for design purposes and do not necessarily represent items on sale.

Hormel Imported Polish Cooked Ham
Freshly sliced ¼-lb. 59¢

Hebrew National Griddle Franks
Kosher lb. $1.49

Hillshire Farm Polska Kielbasa
lb. $1.49

Cold Cuts
- **Pastrami** Lean (By the Chunk) (Sliced on Request) lb. $1.49
- **Corned Beef** Chef Mark Cooked (Freshly Sliced) ¼-lb. 65¢
- **Hard Salami** Hormel Burgermeister (Freshly Sliced) ¼-lb. 59¢
- **Chicken Roll** (Freshly Sliced) ½-lb. $1.09
- **Wunderbar** Wide Bologna (Freshly Sliced) Artificial Casing ½-lb. 59¢

Cheese & Salads
- **Fresh Salad** Potato Salad, Macaroni Salad or Cole Slaw lb. 49¢
- **Kraft Swiss** Casino Domestic ½-lb. 99¢
- **Wine Cheddar** Cheese ½-lb. 89¢
- **Dak Danish** Harvarti Cheese ½-lb. 99¢
- **Provolone** Domestic Cheese ½-lb. 89¢

Seafood
(Fresh Fish Available Wed. thru Friday)
- **Fresh Cod Fillet** lb. $1.59
- **Fresh Whiting** Pan Ready lb. 99¢
- **Clams** Casino or Stuffed Clams Cyrstal Bay - Frozen - 12 oz. pkg. 89¢
- **Frozen Smelts** Highliner Eviscerated 1-lb. pkg. 79¢
- **Sea Trout** Fresh Pan Ready lb. $1.39

Deli (service vs. self-service)

Seafood (fresh or frozen)

Bakery (in-store vs. vendor)

Sunday—open or closed

General appearance

Liquor department

Pharmacy

Among these 48 smaller competitors, the researchers took note of DiFranco's in East Rapids, approximately two minutes away from the proposed Goodbuy. With only 6,000 square feet of selling space, the store was doing between $74,000 and $90,000 per week. Also, according to the research findings, DiFranco's had built up a loyal clientele among middle- and upper-income groups, and had attained and maintained an excellent reputation for quality and service. As compared to customers at other outlets (including the nearby Oakdale A & P, which presented a generally "seedy" appearance), the DiFranco customer would probably be least likely to transfer to the new Goodbuy. Neither the DiFranco nor the Oakdale A & P outlet featured in-store baked goods or an in-store pharmacy, and the DiFranco outlet had no liquor department—all planned for the new Goodbuy.

SALES VOLUME PROJECTIONS

Based on the above research findings, plus historical data on the experience of other Goodbuy outlets, the research team projected the following figures pertaining to potential sales at the new Goodbuy outlet, and the impact these sales would have on other Goodbuy outlets within, or just beyond, the eight-minute trading zone.

Oakdale Goodbuy

At the end of its first year's operation, the Oakdale outlet should be doing approximately $300,000 per week in sales, more than any of their competitors in the eight-minute primary trading zone.

Impact on Area Goodbuys

The researchers estimated that the new Goodbuy would drain the following sales volumes from other Goodbuy outlets in its general trading area: (1) Harpur Village Goodbuy—between $5,000 and $10,000 per week, (2) Smoky Rapids Goodbuy—between $15,000 and $20,000 per week, (3) Unity Goodbuy—between $5,000 and $8,000 per week. On the average, this sales volume loss represented about 8 percent of the total volume generated by each of these outlets.

For all of these Goodbuy outlets, however, the researchers concluded that a significant portion of the lost business could be regained with aggressive promotion programs. This was especially true in the case of the Smoky Rapids outlet, which was situated in the center of a densely populated area.

34

Christian's *

BACKGROUND

In the spring semester of 1984 four seniors at the University of Virginia were trying to decide whether they should invest in Christian's Restaurant, a small eating establishment located several miles from the university's campus in Charlottesville, Va.

The four students—Jeff Curry, Dean Salpini, Art Scibelli, and Gordon Shanks— were all business majors who had become involved with Christian's as the result of a management course entitled "Entrepreneurship," in which they were enrolled. The objective of this course was to "set up a new company that is completely researched in all phases of the business (location, services, finance, etc.) and submit the written business plan for evaluation." The four students had decided to work together on the project at the beginning of the semester, and had quickly begun investigating potential business ventures in the Charlottesville area.

The group's first idea centered on the opening of a seafood restaurant. Art believed that a restaurant offering the same product as a local chain of seafood houses near his home in northern Virginia could prove highly successful in Charlottesville. These restaurants offered fresh seafood for relatively moderate prices in a family-type atmosphere, and also featured several "all you can

eat" items. Art had gotten in touch with one of the owner-founders of the chain, Mr. Easby-Smyth, and the group had gone to northern Virginia to meet with him and discuss their idea.

The meeting with Easby-Smyth had produced two conclusions: Charlottesville was probably too small a market to support the size restaurant the group had originally considered, and the money involved would make the project unfeasible for the group. Easby-Smyth had informed them that the cost of building and outfitting a seafood house of 6,000 square feet would be approximately $300,000. The group had no desire to enter into an investment of this magnitude and were also aware of the great difficulty they were sure to encounter in trying to raise the capital for such a venture.

The students still felt a smaller seafood restaurant might be successful in Charlottesville and began searching for a suitable building for their restaurant. Ideally they hoped to find a restaurant that was selling out and could easily be converted for their purposes. Then news of the Happy Clam reached them.

The Happy Clam was a new seafood restaurant opening on Route 29 North, the main highway leading from Charlottesville. One visit to the new restaurant confirmed that not only was it located in the general area the group had hoped to locate in, but was also offering the same basic product mix as they had hoped to offer. In addition, the restaurant's owner had already successfully opened an identical seafood house in nearby Fredericksburg, Va.

* This case was prepared by Jeff Curry, Dean Salpini, Art Scibelli, and Gordon Shanks under the supervision of Professors Thomas L. Wheelen and Moustafa H. Abdelsamad. Copyright © 1984 by T.L. Wheelen and M.H. Abdelsamad. It also appears in *Strategic Management and Business Policy,* by Thomas L. Wheelen and J. Hunger, Addison-Wesley Publishing Co., 1986.

258

Up to this point, there had been no restaurant similar to the one the students had conceived of in the area. Now they were faced with a direct competitor of proven success in the seafood business. At this point, as the students reconsidered their strategy, Art visited a local realtor and found out about Christian's.

Christian's was a small restaurant specializing in sandwiches for lunch and specialty dishes for dinner (see dinner menu, Exhibit 1). It was being sold as an ongoing business

to include the name Christian's. The students met with the realtor handling the sale, William Page, who arranged a meeting with Christian's owners.

Peter and Mary Tarpey, a young couple from the New York area, were the owners of Christian's along with a University of Virginia professor who acted as a silent partner. The students met with Page and the Tarpeys as arranged on a Wednesday afternoon in Christian's to answer each others' questions and discuss the possible purchase.

Exhibit 1. Dinner Menu

SOUPS
French Onion $1.50
Cream of asparagus $1.25
Vegetable $1.00
Split pea or lentil $1.00

WINES
By the glass $1.25
½ Liter $3.25
Full liter $5.75
Champagne cocktail $1.25

ENTRÉES (SERVED WITH SALAD AND BREAD)
Beef Bazzare — $4.25
Marinated beef, onions & green peppers broiled and served on rice
Broccoli Casserole — $3.25
Broccoli, tomatoes, onions, and eggs topped with cheese
Lobster Scampi — $4.25
Langostinos broiled in herb butter and served on rice
Syrian Chicken — $3.85
Marinated Chicken in pita bread with lettuce and tomatoes
Sausage Lasagne — $4.25
An Italian dish that speaks for itself!
Omelet Special — $3.95
Large dinner omelet filled with pepperoni and provolone cheese
Crêpes — $3.75
Chicken Divan or Sauteed Mushrooms

DESSERTS
Ginger Sherbet $.75
Homemade Pecan Pie $1.00
Cheesecake $1.25
Carrot Cake $1.25

Coffee or Tea $.35
Soft Drinks $.50
Beer $.75

Mary Tarpey first showed the group a handwritten profit-and-loss statement for the period from June 13, 1983, to October 31, 1983 (see Exhibit 2). She explained that some of the expenses were direct payments to the banks and were being written off as business expenses like car payments and a life insurance policy, and need not be incurred by a new owner. She also showed the students monthly sale figures for the period of January 1983 to October 1983, as verified by a local CPA firm (see Exhibit 3), as well as a list of assets owned by Christian's (see Exhibit 4).

The Tarpeys defined their target market as "Young Professional." By this, they meant

Exhibit 2.   Christian's Profit and Loss Statement
June 13, 1983—October 31, 1983 [a]

Sales	$100,000.00
Cost of sales	
Beer and wine	2,688.30
Food	29,189.60
Total	31,877.90
Gross Profit	68,122.10
Operating expenses	
Paper	1,079.88
Insurance	
Store	600.00
Car	150.00
Health	460.00
Workmen's compensation	950.00
Employment commission	360.00
Laundry, linen	483.25
Licenses	250.00
Sales tax (state)	4,000.00
Repairs maintenance	250.00
Rent	2,500.00
Rubbish removal–city	448.50
Salaries and wages	20,000.00
Payroll taxes	6,000.00
Utilities	4,000.00
Loan payment	1,150.00
Equipment payments	1,150.00
Life insurance	625.00
Car payment	1,095.00
Maintenance	950.00
Lease dishwasher	448.50
Advertising	2,750.00
Business association dues and expenses	450.00
Administrative salaries	5,000.00
Total	55,150.13
Income before taxes	12,971.97

a This was a handwritten statement provided by the owners.

Exhibit 3. Monthly Sales Figures, January 1983–October 1983

BROWN AND JONES COMPANY CERTIFIED PUBLIC ACCOUNTANTS
CHARLOTTESVILLE, VIRGINIA 22906

January 9, 1984

Peter Tarpey
Christian's, Inc.
1703 Allied Lane
Charlottesville, Virginia 22901

Dear Peter:

As per your request, enclosed are sales figures for Christian's, Inc. for the ten months ending October 1983 as filed on your monthly Virginia sales tax returns.

January 1983	$18,543.30
February 1983	19,085.43
March 1983	18,097.54
April 1983	19,984.20
May 1983	20,422.71
June 1983	21,836.37
July 1983	19,304.76
August 1983	22,231.69
September 1983	20,002.19
October 1983	20,588.86

If you need sales figures for November 1983 and December 1983, you will have to get these amounts from worksheets in your files. Let me know if I can be of further assistance.

Yours truly,

Thomas L. Brown
Certified Public Accountant

TLB/d
P.S.The sales figures for November 1983
are $19,300.00
TLB

---

persons in the 18–35 age group who worked in the area and came to Christian's for the menu variety and quality of food. They stated that these people eat out about 22 times a month for lunch and dinner, and their strategy was to try to have them eat at Christian's five days a month. The Tarpeys also quoted the average lunch check as being $3.76 and the average dinner check amounting to $5.92.

The Tarpeys also answered questions concerning Christian's daily operations and suppliers. One of the important issues raised was that of a transition period. The group hoped to hire an experienced, full-time manager for the restaurant, and the Tarpeys agreed they would stay on for a period of two weeks or so to help train the manager and show him the cost control and portion

Exhibit 4. Additional Information Provided by Thomas L. Brown, September 27, 1983

Attached is a schedule of fixed assets owned by Christian's, Inc., and the estimated market value of each. Since a purchaser of these would have a cost basis for depreciation and useful life different from that of Christian's, Inc., this information is not provided.

21 Tables	$ 525
43 Chairs	430
2 Banquettes	100
6 Church pew benches	120
Small refrigerator	300
Walk-in box	1,500
Ice machine	100
NCR cash register	150
3 toasters	225
Jordan box	250
Fogle refrigerator	1,200
Hobart slicer	1,000
Hobart microwave	1,000
Sandwich box	200
Stainless prep. table	100
Deep fat fryer	75
Steam table	75
Stainless prep. table	125
3 butcher block chef tables	300
Small Hobart slicer	200
3 basin sinks	75
Universal freezer	100
Sears' freezer	75
Stereo system	150
Curtains	100
Pots, pans, flatware, china, glassware	600
Place mats, salt and pepper mills	100
New sign	2,000
Total fixed assets	$ 11,175

Should you desire additional information in this matter, please contact Peter Tarpey and the data will be forthcoming.

control procedures they had used. In addition, the Tarpeys stated that the whole employee staff had expressed their willingness to stay with the restaurant after an ownership change. The group viewed these two factors as distinct assets.

Another important issue was the future plans of the Tarpeys. As it turned out, the Tarpeys would be opening a new restaurant in a shopping center being built three quarters of a mile from Christian's. Peter Tarpey explained that the restaurant was to be more dinner-oriented than Christian's. He described it as an "Irish cafe with French food" that would serve more expensive meals than Christian's and also serve liquor, which Christian's did not feature. Tarpey estimated that by his moving and opening a new restaurant, Christian's might lose at most 5 percent of its customers.

A second meeting was held with the Tarpeys at a later date, during which more of the group's questions were answered. The lease would have to be renegotiated by any new owner in August 1984, which would be substantially higher than the current one. The students had questions about Christian's suppliers and asked to see the restaurant's books, but the Tarpeys wanted some sort of firm commitment on the group's part before giving out more information about Christian's.

The price being asked for Christian's was $57,750 and the students estimated they could put up about $17,500 of their own capital. Since the balance would have to be financed by a loan, Jeff visited several banks to discuss terms. One bank told him they loaned money for a restaurant only if it was going to be family owned and operated. At Sovran Bank, Jeff got a more positive response. The loan officer there stated the bank would loan up to 70 percent of the purchase price, fully collateralized. The interest rate would be 14 or 15 percent.

At this point the group decided to evaluate their objectives and "take stock" of the situation. They hoped to run the restaurant as absentee owners with the full-time manager handling daily operations. Art's immediate plans included law school in September, although he was still unsure which law school he would attend. Dean planned to work in northern Virginia after graduation, and Jeff and Gordon would return to the University of Virginia in the fall to complete their degrees.

The students' families, from whom they hoped to borrow some of the initial equity capital, all had reservations about the venture. Most of the doubt centered on the policy of running the restaurant as absentee owners. The families also wondered if it was wise for the students to make such an investment at this time in their careers when their futures were so undecided.

By now it was March 24, and the students knew a decision had to be made soon. A call to William Page had confirmed the rumor that another party was seriously considering

buying Christian's. The group called a meeting to decide their next move.

At the meeting, the students decided some sort of comprehensive analysis of the information they had gathered was necessary. With the analysis they felt they would be able to reach the best conclusion.

The group decided to break up the information into sections, with Jeff concentrating on the finance, Dean on the marketing, and Gordon and Art on the operations. When they got back together on March 31, one week away, to put all the results together, the decision would have to be made.

MARKET ANALYSIS

Although Mr. Tarpey assured the group of the existence and loyalty of a definite market for Christian's, it was felt that a marketing survey would strengthen the group's understanding of this market. The survey was conducted among 88 people who were customers at competitive restaurants, using the survey form shown in Exhibit 5. The competition was determined from an assessment based on a number of factors including location, clientele, product offering, and Peter Tarpey's estimates. Christian's was not included, however, because the group felt their regular clientele might bias the results in favor of the restaurant.

The survey revealed that most people were aware of Christian's but were not attracted to it. In addition, only 7 percent of those who had eaten at Christian's did so at least five times a month, so their repeat business seemed to be lacking. Of those who ate there regularly, 60 percent seemed to prefer the lunch period, as opposed to the dinner period, which Peter Tarpey had claimed would occur. Analysis of the various factors involved with Christian's showed that location was the most significant problem, with 64 percent of respondents rating it below average. However, a study of traffic flow patterns in Charlottesville around the McIntyre Road area, where Christian's is located, revealed that 20 percent of the entire day's

Exhibit 5.   Marketing Survey

Hello, we are students doing a research study on Christian's restaurant. Could you *please* take a little time to help us to fill out our survey and help make Christian's a better place to eat. Thank you for your cooperation. The key results of the survey are summarized below:

1. Have you ever eaten at Christian's? YES 50%   NO 50%
   If *NO*, have you heard of it? YES 59% If *NO*, no further questions 41%
   If *YES*, how often do you eat there?   Less than 5 times a month 93%
                                                         5 times a month 5%
                                                         More than 5 times a month 2%
2. Which meal do you usually eat at Christian's? Lunch 59%
                                                                      Dinner 32%
                                                                      Both 9%
3. How would you rate Christian's on these factors:

	Poor	*Fair*	*Average*	*Above Avg.*	*Excellent*
Location	29.5%	34%	32%	4.5%	____
Food quality	____	____	23.3%	53.5%	23.3%
Price	4.5%	11%	61.5%	16%	7%
Service	____	14%	48%	33%	5%
Atmosphere	9%	11.4%	41%	34%	4.6%
Menu variety	____	5%	33%	45%	17%
Cleanliness	9.5%	9.5%	36%	33%	12%

4. What is the main reason(s) you eat at Christian's? Answers varied, but were mostly complimentary.
5. How did you hear about Christian's? *TV* 2%; *Radio* 12%; *Newspaper ads* 10.6%; *Friends* 58%; *Drove by* 5.8%; *Other* (please specify) 11.6%
6. Would you like to see the following at Christian's?

	YES	NO
More vegetarian dishes	44%	56%
More seafood	81%	19%
More take-out variety	48%	52%
Live entertainment	19%	81%

7. An informal survey of age was conducted.

traffic passed Christian's between 11:00 and 2:00 p.m. Price and service seemed to be average and comparable to that of other restaurants in most respondents' minds.

The most significant factors in a person's decision to eat at Christian's were the menu variety and food quality. Most diners named specific food items as their main reason for coming. This also accounted for Christian's major form of advertising, which seemed to be word-of-mouth from satisfied customers. As far as changes in Christian's were concerned, most respondents favored adding seafood to the menu (81 percent), whereas the same percentage felt live entertainment would be a mistake.

One of the problems that might confront the group was the introduction of the Tarpeys' new restaurant down the street. Since the Tarpeys had already developed a loyal clientele, the group was afraid of losing them to the new restaurant, although Peter Tarpey assured them that only 5 percent of the market would be affected. According to the survey, the figure to determine those customers that would be lost through a change in management was approximately 6.8 percent, a little higher than Tarpey's estimate.

Although no survey questions directly addressed demographics, respondents were asked to place themselves in one of the three age brackets: 18–35, 35–50, and over 50. Customer age was thought to be important in the decision to purchase Christian's so that the target market could be firmly established. Overall, it was found that 60 percent of those interviewed were between 18 and 35 years of age, while 31 percent fell into the 35–50 bracket. Further analysis showed that 98 percent of those who presently eat at Christian's were within the 18–50 range.

Diners over 50, therefore, figured to be an insignificant part of Christian's target market. Therefore Tarpey's claim of "young professionals" as his primary customers seems to have been supported by these age group data.

As can be seen from Exhibit 6, sales for eating and drinking establishments in 1982 were 10.5 percent above 1981, while total retail sales increased only 6.8 percent for the same period. Households also seemed to be forming at a faster rate than the total population was growing. In addition, the Virginia State Planning Office projections showed that the 20–35-year-old segment had showed disproportionate increases, which could explain the faster formation of households. These same figures also showed that the 25–39-year-old age group would increase 17 percent between 1980 and 1985. In Albemarle County, where Charlottesville is located, this increase would be almost 32 percent.

These growth figures were considered important because of the number of people who drive into Charlottesville's central business district (C.B.D.) from the county who use McIntyre Road as a major artery. The C.B.D. itself was also considered to be important, since a large part of Christian's cli-

Exhibit 6. The Charlottesville Market [a]

Year	Retail sales (in thousands)	Eating and drinking [b] sales (in thousands)	Population (in thousands)	Households [c] (in thousands)
1978	153,995	NA [d]	38.8	13.8
1979	176,731	NA	38.7	14.0
1980	224,588	NA	39	14.2
1981	235,679	17,882	39.1	14.7
1982	251,766	19,753	38.9	14.7

[a] Data provided by Virginia State Planning Service.

[b] Eating and Drinking Places: This is a broad classification that includes any establishment selling prepared food or drink. Caterers, lunch counters, and concession stands are included as well as restaurants.

[c] Households: All people occupying a single housing unit whether related or not. Includes single persons living alone.

[d] NA: not available.

entele came from there. Over $2,000,000 had been privately invested in the downtown since 1982; thus the C.B.D. appeared to be booming. Another important development was the county's move of their executive offices into Lane High School, located down the street from Christian's. This move would increase Christian's target market, since these people seemed to fit the characteristics of their clientele.

ADVERTISING AND PROMOTING

Christian's present advertising program was very sporadic with a yearly expenditure of only $2,750. Tarpey spoke of occasional spots on television that he had used, along with local radio stations and the major newspaper in Charlottesville. However, Dean and the other members of the group felt that the effectiveness of this program was lacking.

OPERATIONS

The students were aware of their lack of experience in the restaurant business, and since the daily operations of Christian's had gone smoothly in the past, they did not plan any significant changes upon taking over.

The entire employee staff had stated they would be willing to remain at Christian's after the ownership change, and Peter and Mary Tarpey agreed they would stay on for a transition period to "show the ropes" to the new manager.

The students had realized early in their involvement with Christian's that they would need to hire a full-time manager for the restaurant were they to purchase it. It was determined that they would want someone with experience in restaurant management from the Charlottesville area. Their realtor had informed them he knew of a man who fit this description and had expressed interest in the opportunity, but the group was unable to get in contact with him before the week ended.

The group planned on putting the manager in charge of general daily operations to include ordering, cost control, hiring, firing, scheduling, and any other operations-related duty. The students planned on doing the bookkeeping themselves. They planned to pay the manager a salary of approximately $12,000, plus a commission based on the bottom line figure. This commission would be approximately 11 percent.

It was determined that the following employees would be needed to operate Christian's:

1 Manager @ $12,000 salary plus commission

3 cooks @ $5.00/hour

1 grillman @ $4.75/hour

2 countermen @ $4.25/hour

2 prep men @ $4.25/hour

2 dishwashers @ $4.25/hour

2 cashiers @ $4.25/hour

12 waitresses @ $1.50/hour plus tips.

Employees were to be allowed free drinks and half-price meals while working.

Under the students' ownership, Christian's would continue to buy its food supplies from institutional food distributors from Richmond, Va., who delivered to Charlottesville. In addition, they would obtain their beer from local distributors and their soft drinks from local bottling companies.

In the past, inventory had turned over approximately once a week. Normal credit terms of suppliers had been net 30 days.

The marketing survey had indicated that Christian's menu was one of its strongest points, so the group planned few changes. The lunch menu featured over 40 sandwiches along with omelets, salads, and chili. The dinner menu featured specialty dishes such as "Beef Bazzare" and "Syrian Chicken" (see Exhibit 1).

In the past, Christian's had varied its dinner menu daily. The students would plan to vary it weekly, and if one combination proved particularly popular, it would be used again at a different time.

Approximately 15 percent of Christian's

gross sales came from beer sales. The restaurant carried mainly premium and foreign beers in keeping with its target market of young professionals.

INVESTMENT

Benefiting from knowledge obtained in a business law course the previous semester, the group decided to establish Christian's as a Subchapter S corporation. This business form was chosen because of the tax advantages and flexibility it would allow the group, since the business would be taxed as a partnership, but would retain the limited liability of a corporation to protect the shareholders. Since income tax rates for individuals in this case are substantially lower than for a corporation, the group felt this form would offer the best return on their investment.

LEASE

At the time of negotiations, Christian's was paying Allied Realty, the owner of the shopping plaza in which the restaurant was located, a base rent of $350.00 per month plus an additional percentage of gross sales (4 percent) not exceeding a total monthly rental of $500.00 per month. However, this lease would expire on August 1, 1984, and a new lease would have to be negotiated by the new purchaser.

The new rent terms would be considerably higher than those for previous owners and would consist of a minimum payment of $600.00 per month or 4 percent of sales, whichever is the higher, not exceeding $750.00 per month. Since Christian's historical monthly sales have averaged approximately $20,000.00, this would mean payments of $750.00 per month. There would be an additional requirement that if gross sales exceeded $60,000 in any quarter, the restaurant would pay 3 percent of sales exceeding this amount.

Fortunately, the group was informed by its realtor, Henry Brasswell, that it might be possible to negotiate a less expensive lease, so that average monthly payments would be between $650 and $700. Because the outcome of such negotiations was uncertain at the time, the group used $750 per month in developing pro forma statements for the business.

INCOME STATEMENTS

An examination of 1983 sales uncovered two major factors that had to be considered in developing pro forma income statements. First, the monthly sales figures supplied by the CPA firm indicated a seasonal fluctuation in sales (see Exhibit 7). The effect of this on the cash flows of the restaurant and its ability to meet its debts had to be determined. Secondly, the revenue growth of this restaurant would be limited by its capacity. Jeff needed to establish how close to capacity the restaurant was currently operating. Lunch and dinner sales should be considered separately. Lunch projections would be based on 260 days a year (52 weeks × 5 days) while dinner would be based on the full 312 days that the restaurant was open. The current owners had already estimated the average check at each meal. The restaurant seated 56 people.

Jeff then took the handwritten income statement provided by Mary Tarpey and attempted to adjust it to get an idea of the expenses that the new management could face. Several of the perquisites the Tarpeys enjoyed had been discussed during the meeting at Christian's. Excessive long-distance calls and the car payments could be eliminated. The new management would have to add the manager's salary and bonus. A 10 percent annual bonus on pretax profits would be offered to motivate the manager to run a tight ship. These expenses had to be separated into variable and fixed expense categories to determine a break-even point. The new estimates were in line with those found in a book entitled *Restaurant Finance*.

Jeff was certain sales in the first year could be maintained at the current level with ef-

Exhibit 7.   Seasonality Index 1983 Sales (100 = 19,945)

Month	Sales	Actual Seasonality
January	$18,543	93
February	19,085	96
March	18,097	91
April	19,984	100
May	20,423	102
June	21,836	109
July	19,304	97
August	22,231	111
September	20,002	100
October	20,589	103
November	19,300	97
December	18,948 [a]	95[a]

[a] Assumed.

fective advertising. Forecasted sales for the second year are based on expanding lunch sales to capacity. Years three through five assume the restaurant will operate at capacity for both lunch and dinner. Increased sales will be achieved through advertising.

THE BANK LOAN

With the income statements prepared, Jeff approached the Sovran Bank to discuss the terms of a loan (see Exhibits 8 and 9). The bank was willing to set the monthly pay-

Exhibit 8.   Pro-forma Income Statements (in thousands) for the Year Ended July 31

	Year			
	2	3	4	5
Net sales				
Lunch	$ 120.0	$ 120.0	$ 120.0	$ 120.0
Dinner	144.0	152.0	152.0	152.0
Total	264.0	272.0	272.0	272.0
Variable expenses (68%)	(180.0)	(185.0)	(185.0)	(185.0)
Operating margin (32%)	84.0	87.0	87.0	87.0
Fixed expenses	(40.8)	(40.9)	(42.4)	(42.4)
Earnings before interest	43.2	46.1	44.6	44.6
Interest	(3.9)	(2.9)	(1.9)	(1.0)
Earnings before bonus (EBB)	39.3	43.2	42.7	43.6
Bonus (0.10 × EBB)	3.9	4.3	4.3	4.4
Taxable Earnings	35.4	38.9	38.4	39.2

Exhibit 9. Balance Sheet (000s)

			Year			
	Initial	1	2	3	4	5
Assets						
Current assets						
Cash and securities	0.30	10.70	20.70	20.70	34.60	27.70
Inventory						
Beer and wine (0.04 month)	0.80	0.80	0.90	0.90	0.90	0.90
Food (0.36/month)	7.20	7.20	7.90	8.20	8.20	8.20
Total current assets	8.30	18.70	29.50	29.80	43.70	36.80
Fixed assets	22.30	22.30	22.30	27.30	27.30	32.30
Accumulated						
Depreciation	0.00	4.40	8.80	13.20	17.60	22.00
Net fixed assets	22.30	17.90	13.50	14.10	9.70	10.30
Intangibles						
Goodwill	35.20	35.20	35.20	35.20	35.20	35.20
Accumulated amortization	0.00	3.52	7.04	10.56	14.08	17.60
Net goodwill	35.20	31.68	28.16	24.64	21.12	17.60
Organization costs	0.50	0.40	0.30	0.20	0.10	0.00
Total assets	66.30	68.68	71.46	68.74	74.62	64.70
Liabilities						
Current Liabilities						
Account payable	7.60	7.60	7.90	8.20	8.20	8.20
Note payable	1.00	0.00	0.00	0.00	0.00	0.00
Total current liabilities	8.60	7.60	7.90	8.20	8.20	8.20
Long-term note	40.25	32.20	24.10	16.10	8.00	0.00
Total liabilities	48.85	39.80	32.00	24.30	16.20	8.20
Equity						
Stock	17.50	17.50	17.50	17.50	17.50	17.50
Retained earnings	0.00	11.38	21.96	26.94	40.92	39.00
Total equity	17.50	28.88	39.46	44.44	58.42	56.50
Total liabilities and equity	66.35	68.68	71.46	68.74	74.62	64.70

ments at a level the cash flows of the restaurants could meet as long as the maturity of the loan did not exceed ten years. It appeared that five years would be an acceptable maturity. This would be monthly payments of approximately $1,000.

The bank would accept 50 percent of the book value (approximately the $11,175 listed as market value by the CPA firm) of the assets as collateral, but demanded that the balance be fully collateralized also.

The loan officer was concerned that the purchase price was too high and that an excessive amount of goodwill would be involved in the new business. He was also concerned that none of the new owners had any experience operating a restaurant. With this in mind, he wanted to know more about the manager and the cook.

EVALUATING THE PURCHASE PRICE

Since several people had expressed concern over the price the owners were asking, the partners wanted to decide the proper value of the restaurant. They agreed this should be based on the present value of the income stream the restaurant could generate. In light of the fact that eight out of ten restaurants fail, the partners selected 25 percent as the hurdle rate that would be used to discount future earnings. The setup costs should not exceed the present value of the income stream. The partners wanted to include the eventual sales price or liquidation value of the restaurant at the end of five years in computing the present value, assuming various levels of sales would establish a proper price range. The setup costs included the $57,750 asking price and $500 organizational expense for legal and accounting fees. Since this was a going concern, they would not have to invest significant additional working capital.

CONCLUDING REMARKS

On March 31, at the final meeting to discuss the prospects of purchasing Christian's, the group members were fully aware of the implications such a decision would have. It was generally agreed that such an endeavor provided potential for optimum managerial skill and experience in the business world; though none of the group members was certain that this was the route he wanted to take. Faced with exams in the coming weeks, time pressure from the realtor, and the knowledge that at least one other party was interested in purchasing Christian's, the group set out to make their decision, which for better or worse, would affect their immediate futures.

The students were informed by the present owners that they must reach a decision quickly since other purchasers are interested in the same business opportunity.

Seven

Marketing Strategies and Comprehensive Programs

MAYTAG COMPANY

DONALDSON COMPANY, INC.

TENNESSEE PEWTER COMPANY

CAMVAC, INC.

GENERAL MOTORS CORPORATION

35

Maytag Company *

The Maytag Company of Newton, Iowa, has maintained an enviable position in the home-laundry market. Despite increased competition, and a price premium charged to consumers of roughly $100 per unit, it has continued to capture a "traditional" 15% share of the washing machine market, and has enjoyed profit margins roughly twice that of competitors. Operating results for the period 1974–1981 are given in Exhibit 1. The largest competitive share growth in laundry equipment has gone to Whirlpool, who, buoyed by the surge of its private-label sales to Sears and by Frigidaire's abandonment of the market, now sells approximately 45% of all home-laundry equipment in the U.S.

Maytag Company backs its premium policy with a product consistently evaluated as superior in quality. The famous lonely Maytag repairman hammers home the theme that the purchase price premium buys lower service costs. But the quality gap appears to be lessening. Arnold Consdorf, editor of the trade journal *Appliance Manufacturer*, noted, "The quality gap that existed five or ten years ago doesn't exist anymore. Model for model, I really don't see much difference as far as premium quality goes." A retailer

notes, "The critical thing is that the rationale to run out and buy a Maytag has declined."

Maytag values highly its retail dealer relationships. A feature of the company's 1979 Annual Report was this assessment:

Among Maytag's more than 10,000 independent retailers are most of the leading merchandisers in North America. While the wide geographic dispersion of so many dealers provides Maytag with outstanding service coverage, it is the mass merchandisers who generate much of the volume that keeps us growing. ...

Historically, Maytag ... sought dealer coverage in each community and thus had product availability, along with service, throughout the U.S. and Canada. [C]hanging ... competition [required] developing quality volume accounts in major markets.

Because selling quality appliances requires well-trained salespersons and outstanding parts and service availability ... Maytag has stopped short of attempting to market its products through self-service "shopping cart" outlets. Nor do we have dealer arrangements with any chains across the board nationally, requiring instead that dealer selection be made in each market by those responsible for generating our market share in that locality.

A natural expansion of Maytag's home-laundry emphasis has been the commercial laundromat business. This business was pioneered in the 1930s when coin meters were attached to Maytag wringer-type washers. Rapid growth of coin-operated laundries occurred in the United States during the late 1950s and early 1960s. Increased competition and soaring energy costs of the 1970s cut deeply into laundromat profits. In 1975

* Copyright © 1982 by Lester A. Neidell; Sources: "The Problems of Being Premium," *Forbes* (May 29, 1978), pp. 56, 57; "A Duel of Giants in the Dishwasher Market," *Business Week* (October 9, 1978), pp. 137–138; Lawrence Ingrassia, "Staid Maytag Puts in Money on Stoves But May Need to Invest Expertise, Too," *The Wall Street Journal* (July 23, 1980), p. 27; "The New Maytag Recipe for Going Into Kitchens," *Business Week* (May 24, 1982), pp. 48, 49; and Maytag Company Annual Reports.

Exhibit 1. Financial Summary for Maytag Company, 1974–1981 (in millions of dollars)

	1974	1975	1976	1977	1978	1979	1980	1981
Net Sales	229	238	275	299	325	369	349	409
Net Income	21.1	25.9	33.1	34.5	36.7	45.3	35.6	37.4

Maytag introduced new energy-efficient machines and a "Home Style" store concept that has rejuvenated this business. More than 1,000 Home Style stores are currently in operation in the United States.

Until recently, Maytag's other major product effort has been dishwashers. Here the leading competitor is Design & Manufacturing, Inc., (D & M), whose "bread and butter" are private-label dishwashers for Sears, other retailers, and other appliance manufacturers. D & M's market share is approximately 45%. Other major dishwasher competitors include General Electric and Hobart Corporation's KitchenAid brand, each with approximately 19% shares. Maytag, who has been making dishwashers since 1966, has generally obtained annual shares in the 4–6% range. The "premium" price-quality segment is dominated by KitchenAid, and despite Maytag's efforts, little recognition of the Maytag name is apparent in the dishwasher business. Maytag's president, Daniel Krumm, admitted in 1978, "We might as well be selling the Jones dishwasher." A revamped 1979 product line provided an increase in sales but it is too soon to tell if the share increase is permanent.

Other product lines include food waste disposers and cooking appliances. Maytag's entry into cooking is being achieved by acquisition. In 1981 the Hardwick Stove Company was purchased for $28 million. Early 1982 saw the introduction of Maytag microwave ovens, produced by the Hardwick subsidiary. In April 1982, Maytag reached agreement with United Technologies to acquire its Jenn-Air subsidiary for an estimated $75 million. Jenn-Air is a producer of indoor barbeque grills and other innovative cooking and kitchen ventilation equipment.

President Krumm, explaining the recent Maytag thrust into kitchen appliances, noted, "Cooking equipment is a mature market, but it is an exciting one because product innovation is changing the traditional way people cook and broadening sales opportunities."

Maytag expects a profitable future:

High inflation has not been especially detrimental to our sales, as consumers seem to buy better-quality goods during inflationary periods. Rising energy costs will play an especially important part in future sales for both home and commercial appliances. The energy-saving Maytag washers and dryers will have potentially large markets as both households and self-service laundries replace the millions of appliances purchased in the 1960s. Home kitchens and laundries will be upgraded, compensating for the slump in new housing construction. The changing composition of the American family, with more women working and subsequent increase in family incomes, will produce a growing demand for labor- and time-saving appliances.

36

Donaldson Company, Inc.*

Donaldson Company, Inc. (DCI), Bloomington, Minn., learned in 1983 that the rules of the industry in which it had been a dominant force worldwide for over sixty years were changing. DCI weathered the Depression, World War II, numerous recessions, and major changes in technology and manufacturing processes while maintaining a steady stream of profits. In 1983, however, it experienced its first loss in 50 years. Sales decreased from $262 million in 1982 to $203.6 million in 1983. Earnings declined from $7.2 million, or $1.40/share in 1982 to a loss of $3.5 million, or -$.68/share in 1983. Chairman of the Board Frank Donaldson II began his annual letter to DCI stockholders in 1983 by saying, "A year ago we said that business was lousy. Well, it got worse. We learned firsthand about a profit *and loss* economy." Although 1984 yielded some improvements over 1983, DCI began a critical look at its worldwide operations, with the goal of returning the company to its previous performance levels.

THE COMPANY

History

In 1915, Frank Donaldson, Sr., the original chairman of the company, invented the first effective air cleaner for internal combustion engines. Air is a necessary ingredient for the combustion process to occur. Prior to this

* This case was prepared by Shannon Shipp. Copyright © 1985 by the Case Development Center, University of Minnesota.

invention, engines were extremely susceptible to "dusting out," or becoming inoperative due to excessive accumulation of dust entering the engine from unfiltered air.

In subsequent years, DCI led the industry in introducing new products, such as oil-washed filters, mufflers, multi-stage air cleaners, and high-tech hydraulic filters. DCI became the world's largest manufacturer of heavy-duty air cleaners and mufflers, and established a worldwide reputation for high-quality, reliable products which were at the leading edge of filtration technology. Facilities grew from 200 square feet of manufacturing space in 1915 in St. Paul, Minn., to more than 3 million square feet of manufacturing and office area worldwide in 1980.

Mission

By 1984, the company had broadly defined its mission as to design, manufacture, and sell proprietary products which "separate something unwanted from something wanted." The company's product line included air cleaners, air filters, mufflers, hydraulic filters, microfiltration equipment for computers, air pollution equipment, and liquid clarifiers. These products were developed, sold, and serviced by the organizational structure appearing in Exhibit 1. According to this exhibit, DCI has a functional organization structure, with the nine worldwide support groups responsible for product development, manufacturing, and administration and finance, while the four business groups are responsible for selling and servicing products to their respective markets. The

Exhibit 1. DCI Organizational Chart (1983)

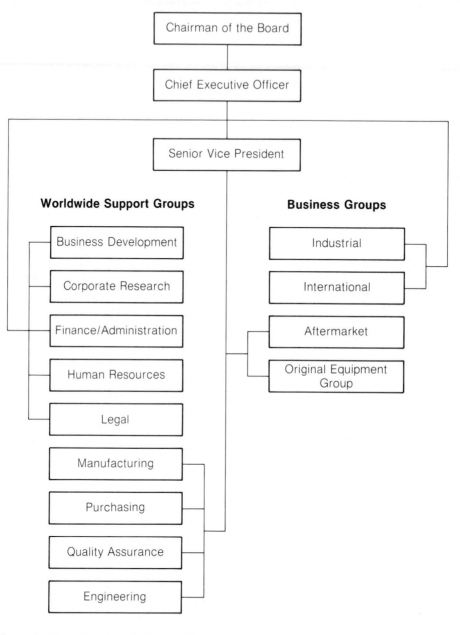

Source: Internal company documents

1980 to 1984 sales of the four major business groups are listed in Exhibit 2. The fifth group listed, Microfiltration and Defense Products (MFD) was a part of the Business Development Group until 1984, when it was spun off to form a new business group.

Exhibit 2. DCI's Four Major Business Groups
1980–84 Annual Sales (In Millions)

	1984	1983	1982	1981	1980
Original Equipment Group	$102.2	63.9	101.3	104.6	101.6
Aftermarket	22.6	17.6	20.5	20.1	17.0
Industrial	32.2	32.0	41.3	37.0	35.0
International	71.2	68.7	81.4	87.0	69.4
MFD	26.0	21.4	17.4	15.1	11.4
TOTAL	$254.2	203.6	261.9	263.8	234.4

Source: DCI 1984 Annual Report.

The 1983–84 Situation

In 1983, a peculiar set of circumstances combined to downgrade DCI's performance. Sales of medium/heavy duty trucks, buses, tractors and combines, construction equipment, and aftermarket replacement elements simultaneously hit five-year or all-time lows. These markets constituted the majority of sales for both the Original Equipment Group (OEG) and International. Although soft demand had been experienced in one or two of these markets before in one year, never had all businesses declined so precipitously in the same year.

Both external and internal causes were proposed to explain the decline of each market. External causes included slow construction and agricultural equipment sales. Construction equipment purchases slowed as major projects accounting for the majority of new equipment purchases, such as the interstate highway system, neared completion. Also, developing nations (especially oil-producing), a major market for construction projects in the 1970s and early 1980s, were curtailing construction, based on declining oil revenues. Caterpillar, DCI's largest customer, experienced a devastating seven-month strike by workers at its U.S. production facilities, that produced the bulk of Caterpillar's heavy-duty mobile equipment. Agricultural equipment sales were slowing because of generally depressed conditions in the agricultural industry, particularly in the United States. Purchases of new equipment by U.S. farmers, squeezed by high fixed costs and low market prices, were at a five-year low. Finally, the strength of the dollar in 1982–84 was making DCI's customers less competitive in foreign markets. This, in turn, affected DCI's sales of replacement parts.

Some of the internal problems included an inability to coordinate customer service to multinational customers, inability to provide accurate cost figures for given production quantities, and, especially for its small customers, "being difficult to buy from." Each of these problems will be explained in greater detail below.

DCI found it difficult to coordinate customer service efforts for those customers with multiple purchasing or production facilities in different countries. Although DCI had offices in all of the countries, such as West Germany, Brazil and Mexico, where high sales potential existed, lack of coordination among the offices caused spotty customer service. For example, customers were known to "shop" for the best prices among DCI offices, since each office was free to set prices according to local conditions. Unfortunately, with its customers willing to look worldwide for the lowest DCI price, different offices were competing against each other for the same business, to the detriment of DCI performance overall.

DCI was also unable to provide accurate

cost figures for production of small amounts of product. This hampered salespeople's efforts to quote prices which would cover DCI's costs and yield profits. For example, set-up costs in switching from producing one product to another were not factored into the cost of production runs. As a result, DCI salespeople were willing to promise delivery of low quantities of products (sometimes as low as one or two units) based on the actual production cost, without taking into account the changeover costs borne by manufacturing small quantities. Order costs, estimated at $35 per order processed, were also not taken into account when salespeople quoted prices for small lots. Lastly, account executives were measured primarily on sales rather than profits, thereby encouraging them to devote less attention to the costs of actually filling an order.

Finally, DCI had a reputation for being "difficult to buy from." Although relationships with its largest customers were strong based on its ability to work with those customers in solving problems, smaller customers complained to salespeople of slow response for engineering drawings and price quotes. They also complained of slow responses to questions about billing or order status. Very small customers (under $25,000 in annual sales) were not vocal with complaints about DCI because they were seldom contacted by DCI representatives.

Although these internal problems existed to an extent in all divisions, it was crucial to DCI's success for OEG to address them promptly. Exhibit 2 shows that OEG is the largest of the four major business groups. OEG also suffered the largest absolute and percentage loss from 1982 to 1983. For DCI to regain its former performance levels, OEG must perform more strongly.

In 1984, DCI's operating results began to return to pre-1983 levels (see Exhibit 3). One reason was a success in the wet filtration area, particularly with high-tech lube filters which were designed to protect mechanical components in high-stress environments. The primary reason, however, was that DCI's worldwide markets, particularly heavy-duty truck, began to return to pre-1983 levels. Because of the external causes listed previously, however, DCI management thought it unlikely that its market opportunities would return to pre-1980 levels. To minimize the effects of the decline in worldwide demand for DCI's products, attention was placed on internal problems that also affected 1983 results. For DCI to return to its steady pattern of consistent growth, those internal problems must be rectified.

ORIGINAL EQUIPMENT GROUP (OEG)

Products and Markets

OEG constitutes the bulk of DCI's traditional businesses, such as heavy-duty trucks, and construction, mining, industrial and agricultural equipment. It sells air and hydraulic filters, acoustical products (mufflers) and replacement elements to manufacturers and end-users of heavy-duty mobile equipment. OEG has not typically sold oil filters, as they are a commodity item and require much higher production runs than OEG traditionally makes. OEG is reviewing its position on producing oil filters as its customers seek a single source for all their filter needs. North America constitutes about one-half of the annual worldwide sales of these products.

CURRENT ORGANIZATIONAL STRUCTURE FOR OEG

OEG is currently organized around the markets it serves. The construction, agriculture, industrial, and truck-bus markets have their own market director and support staff. Each market is headed by a market director, responsible for all planning and administration, as well as maintaining good relations with the largest customers in the market. Each market group has outside salespeople who call directly on customers, as well as inside salespeople responsible for routine orders and customer service. A manager of marketing support includes order entry per-

Exhibit 3. DCI Operating Results (in 000s)

	1984	1983	1982
Net Sales	$254,052	203,608	262,018
Cost of Sales	157,257	131,548	169,816
Gross Earnings	96,795	72,060	92,202
Earnings (loss) before income taxes	20,238	(1,738)	12,805
Income Taxes	10,546	1,800	5,572
Tax Rate	52.1%	—	43.5%
Net Earnings	9,692	(3,358)	7,233
Depreciation	7,694	8,320	8,518
Interest	2,670	2,076	2,345
Financial Position			
Current Assets	97,425	81,668	82,109
Current Liabilities	45,022	32,796	35,574
Current Ratio	2.2	2.5	2.3
Working Capital	52,403	48,872	46,535
Long-term Debt	19,549	21,791	18,752
Shareholder's Equity	90,232	84,880	91,637
Capitalization Ratio	22.1	22.1	21.2
Return on average shareholder's equity	11.1	(4.0)	7.9
Return on average invested capital	9.0	(3.3)	6.4
Property, plant and equipment (gross)	118,663	118,182	114,465
Property, plant and equipment (net)	55,045	59,694	63,739
Total Assets	160,613	148,083	151,160

Source: DCI 1984 Annual Report.

sonnel and clerks and two special projects. The first special project manager coordinated the efforts of the worldwide action teams responsible for gathering information on competitors and customers. The second special project manager developed a marketing program aimed at gaining understanding of small OEs. A chart showing the executive level positions under the market-based organizational structure appears in Exhibit 4.

Within each market, customers were served by size. Large accounts (more than $250,000 in annual sales) were served by market directors or salespeople assigned to that account. Mid-sized customers (between $25,000 and $250,000 in annual sales) were called upon by a salesperson responsible for that territory. Small OEs were served, if at all, by inside salespeople or order-entry personnel in the marketing support services group.

Organization by market area offered a number of advantages to OEG. For example, with a market-based organization, it was easy to track marketwide changes in demand or customer usage characteristics. This helped OEG in product development and allocation of application engineering resources. Furthermore, a market-based organization in OEG mirrored similar organizations in Engineering, which facilitated communication across functional divisions, since marketers and engineers worked on products and programs for the same markets.

Exhibit 4. OEG's Market-based Organizational Structure

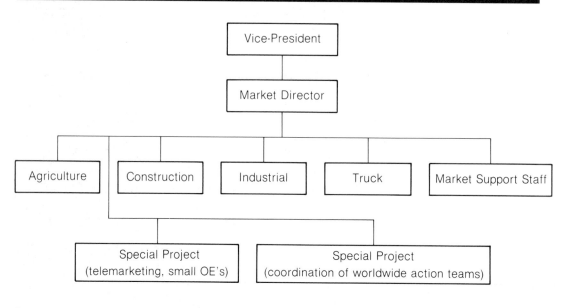

Source: Internal company documents

Organization by market area also had some problems. Some customers straddled markets, making it difficult to assign the costs and profits from serving that customer to a specific market. One large customer, for example, manufactured both agricultural and construction equipment. Instead of having one salesperson from each market area call on the account, one salesperson from the agricultural division maintains customer contract to reduce overlap in customer service. In charging the market areas for the sales, however, agriculture is fully responsible for the salesperson's salary and expenses, while the construction market area enjoys the benefits of the sales to that customer without incurring any selling expenses. Another problem was the occasional inability to coordinate the engineering support for those customers who straddled market areas. Engineers were assigned by market, not customer. If a customer had a problem with applications in two markets, the tasks were assigned to two engineers, even if the actual parts were very similar.

OEG'S POSITION WITHIN DCI

OEG had primary worldwide responsibility to serve manufacturers of mobile heavy equipment. Other divisions within DCI served or competed with those customers. For example, the Aftermarket group sold heavy equipment replacement elements under the Donaldson name through fleet specialists, heavy-duty distributors and other sources. These elements competed with the products sold through manufacturers' dealers supplied by OEG. Engineering, a staff group, was also an important part of OEG's selling function. Engineering helped customers design filters and other products for specific applications. Since OEG's reputation depended on Engineering's service to its customers, this group was important in maintaining close customer relations. The International Division sold OEG's products in markets outside the U.S. Communication between OEG and International was particularly crucial in providing high levels of customer service for multinational customers, as the responsibilities for these customers were split geographically.

OEG'S PROPOSED STRATEGIES FOR REGAINING FORMER PERFORMANCE LEVELS

In 1983, Tom Baden was appointed the new vice-president of OEG. Baden had 35 years experience with the company. He began at DCI as a draftsman while still in college, and over the years held posts in Engineering and Fluid Power (a division later absorbed by the OEG business group) before assuming leadership of OEG. Baden's task was simply stated; he was to return OEG to financial performance levels of the 1975–79 era and establish a base for long-term consistent growth in the markets served by OEG. Baden was also responsible for maintaining and reinforcing DCI's corporate image as a high-quality, high-service provider of state-of-the-art products.

To reach those goals, Baden instituted a year-long strategic development process that involved Finance, Human Resources, Engineering, Manufacturing, International and all units within OEG. Several studies that evaluated markets and identified customer needs provided input for developing strategy. These studies were undertaken with a worldwide focus. Reports were prepared by worldwide action teams, composed of members from DCI offices around the world. These reports and activities were coordinated by a market director at OEG headquarters.

Some of the studies performed included: 1) research on telemarketing and global account management as alternatives to personal selling in reaching customers; 2) in-depth analyses of customers and competitors; and 3) definition of pricing, promotion and distribution policies. These studies and analyses of current OEG operations were the basis for meetings designed to solicit suggestions for changes that would allow OEG to meet the demands of its customers. These meetings included all OEG executives, as well as various functional specialists who presented information from related studies. The schedule of meetings is presented in Exhibit 5. The stated purpose of the meetings was to develop overall marketing strategies and derive specific supporting strategies in promotion (including advertising, trade promotion and

Exhibit 5. Meeting Schedule for the Strategic Development Process

Activity	Week
Preparation/Meetings Within Market Area Groups and Worldwide Action Teams	0
Opening Meetings/All OEG Executives	
—Presentations of Worldwide Action Team Reports	
—Presentation of Market Area Reports	1
Development of Options	2–3
Present/Analyze Options	4
Refine/Reanalyze Options	4–5
Review Alternatives/All OEG Executives	6
Refine/Test Against Resources/Constraints	7–10
Present and Review Final Recommendations—All OEG Executives	11
Prepare Final Recommendations for DCI Executives	12

Source: Internal company documents.

personal selling), organizational design, distribution, pricing and product management. OEG executives used the results of the worldwide action team reports and the analyses of current OEG operations to suggest changes in OEG's marketing policies and organizational structure.

WORLDWIDE ACTION TEAMS REPORTS AND ANALYSES OF CURRENT OPERATIONS

OEG's Customers

OEG had over 600 customers, divided into three groups: large, mid-sized and small.

Large Accounts. OEG's large customers, consisting of 46 accounts and their dealers, constituted more than 90 percent of OEG sales and more than 50 percent of DCI sales. Thirty of these customers were headquartered in the U.S., eight in Europe and eight in Japan. A partial list of these customers appears in Exhibit 6. These customers were all large, and most had sales offices and production facilities in more than one country.

The competitive environment for large original equipment manufacturers (OEs) was undergoing rapid change. Some large OEs, such as Caterpillar, were experiencing increasing competition from non-U.S. manufacturers. Increasing competition from other manufacturers, coupled with the strength of the dollar against other currencies, forced Caterpillar to reduce costs to remain competitive. Caterpillar announced a three-year program beginning in 1983 and terminating in 1985 that required its suppliers to maintain stable prices even though inflation was predicted to increase 22% for that period. In 1984, Ford announced a similar program, that required suppliers to reduce costs by 10 percent per year for the next five years. Other manufacturers were considering similar programs.

The implications for DCI of these announcements were profound. Caterpillar, for example, was DCI's largest single customer, accounting for between 10 and 12 percent of annual revenue. As a result, the squeeze on DCI's margins brought about by Caterpillar's announcement could strongly impact DCI's performance. The emphasis by large customers on cost containment was a major change from the 1960s to the 1970s, which emphasized product performance.

According to meetings among salespeople and account executives, DCI's largest customers had common needs for filtration equipment. At a minimum, large customers desired state-of-the-art products at the lowest possible prices for products meeting specifications. Recent demands by large customers included:

1. just-in-time deliveries; *

* Just-in-time deliveries occur when the supplier and customer have devised a schedule to ensure the next shipment of parts or supplies is delivered when the customer is about to use the last unit from the previous shipment.

Exhibit 6. Some Large Current or Potential Customers for OEG

North America	Europe	Japan
Allis-Chalmers	Daimler-Benz	Hitachi
Caterpillar	IVECO	Isuzu
Champion	Leyland	Komatsu
Clark Equipment	Lister	Kubota
Cummins	Lombardini	Mitsubishi
Detroit Diesel	MAN	Nissan

Source: Internal company documents.

2. long-term fixed source contracts;

3. drop-ship arrangements to customers' dealers and/or manufacturing facilities for OE parts;

4. worldwide availability of product;

5. the OE brand name on the product; and

6. electronic system tie-ins for improved order placement/followup and customer service and support.

These recent demands were concomitant with OE's efforts to consolidate their purchases to achieve stronger positions vis-a-vis their suppliers.

ORIGINAL EQUIPMENT DEALERS

Large customers also perceived sales opportunities for replacement element sales through their distributor networks. In North America, the large OEs had 21,000 outlets, or original equipment dealers (OEDs) through which DCI could sell replacement elements. OEDs represented a different market opportunity for DCI. Traditionally, DCI had sold replacement elements to OEs imprinted with the OE's brand. Once the OE took title to the products, DCI expected the OE to provide the necessary training and support to its distributors through which the products would be sold. Within the past three to five years, OEDs were more actively looking for product lines to improve cash flow and profitability. Part of the impetus for the search for additional products was slow equipment sales. Service parts provided a logical line extension and source of steady cash flow for OEDs. To capitalize on the market in service parts, however, OEDs needed extensive support in terms of sales training, product knowledge, product literature and merchandising. They also needed full lines of filters to service all makes of equipment, not just the lines they represented. To increase their share of the service parts business, (currently at 20 percent, with the remainder held by independent dealers) OEDs would have to rely on greatly increased OE and filter manufacturer support.

Mid-Sized and Small Customers. Smaller OEs (usually under $250,000 in annual purchases) were offered only standard products from the OEG catalog. Custom engineering was rarely provided to these customers, unless they were willing to bear its full cost.

Smaller OEs had different needs than large OEs. In general, they desired state-of-the-art products, but were willing to wait for a large OE to install a new product first. They also desired consistent contact with DCI salespeople to keep abreast of changing filter fair prices (while realizing that they did not have the volumes to command the lowest available prices) and good product quality. Small OEs often requested the DCI name on the filters used in their equipment as a marketing tool, capitalizing on DCI's reputation for high quality among end-users.

Major Competitors

DCI was the traditional heavy-duty mobile equipment market leader. Major competitors included Fleetguard, Fram, Nelson and Mann and Hummel. Other firms, such as Wix, Baldwin, Purolator and AC/Delco competed in certain market segments. In general, all of the competitors were on sound financial footing. Fleetguard and Fram had very healthy parent organizations (Cummins Engine and Allied/Bendix Corporation, respectively). Mann and Hummel and Nelson were healthy from good internal financial management. Research and development costs were generally lower for these organizations than for DCI because they tend to follow DCI's technological breakthroughs.

Each competitor was strong in a particular market or through a particular channel. AC/Delco and Fram, for example, were very strong in the automotive aftermarket, which required good merchandising skills and emphasizes high volume production. Fleetguard promoted directly to end-users. It recently began a program aimed at educating end-users on the total costs of maintaining equipment. To serve users with a variety of filter replacement patterns, it brought out different lines of filters. For users demanding maximum protection because of extended use in high-stress environments, a high-priced filter with high filtration specifications was introduced. For fleet users, or those on scheduled maintenance, a cheaper filter was introduced to provide protection between replacement periods, without providing unused capacity. Mann and Hummel targeted German and Scandinavian manufacturers, particularly at their corporate headquarters, with extensive technical support and high-quality products. Wix and Baldwin were known, particularly in the truck and construction markets, for providing inexpensive replacement elements. All of these manufacturers, except Nelson, offered a full line of air and oil filters. A full line helps both customers and distributors meet all their filter needs through one source.

MARKETING STRATEGIES

Product and Price

DCI was known throughout the industry for its conservative management style. Its strategic moves occurred slowly, based on careful planning. OEG was no exception. OEG preferred serving selected, high-margin markets where customers were beginning to demand higher performance levels than those available from the products currently available. OEG's strengths were its quality design and engineering capabilities. It preferred pursuing markets where those capabilities demanded a price premium. Price-cutting was not a major component of OEG's market strategies.

Distribution

Distribution of OEG's products occurred through two primary channels. The first was directly to OEs, who purchased products for installation on new equipment. DCI's management philosophy and strengths in technology reinforced its position as an "OE house." In some markets, such as heavy-duty trucks and construction equipment, more

than 70 percent of all new units shipped were factory-equipped with DCI products. OEs depended on DCI as a reliable supplier of state-of-the-art products. DCI encouraged its major customers to think of it as their filter and acoustic products design group. DCI's engineers often worked closely with its customers' engineers to design products for special applications or environmental conditions.

The second major channel was for replacement elements. These elements were often packaged and sold under the manufacturer's logo and distributed through its dealer network. OEG provided replacement elements for Caterpillar, International Harvester, J.I. Case, Freightliner, Volvo and several other OEs.

Promotion

OEG products are promoted several ways, including advertising, direct mail, trade shows and promotional literature. A distribution of OEG's promotional expenditures for 1984 appears in Exhibit 7. DCI encourages direct communication between OEG engineers and technicians and their customer counterparts. While this is not reflected in the promotional budget, it is an important

Exhibit 7. Promotional Budget (1984)

Item	Percent of Budget
Advertising	55%
PR	2
Sales Literature	13
Other Sales Materials	1
Advertising Specialties	1
Trade Shows	16
Photography	2
Coop Advertising	4
Audiovisual Materials	1
Other	5
	100%

Source: Internal company documents.

element in OEG's communications with its customers.

Other off-budget promotional expenses include sending OEG engineers to attend professional meetings and guiding customers on tours of the research and testing facility. At professional meetings, engineers talk to customers to detect changing trends in customer demand or areas where DCI's technical expertise can be brought to bear. The engineers also act as informal "good-will ambassadors," reminding customers that OEG is monitoring their concerns. OEG also uses its facility as a selling tool, bringing customers' representatives to corporate headquarters in Bloomington, Minn., for a tour of its engineering and research facilities. As some of the most modern, state-of-the-art filtration research facilities in the world, DCI's headquarters constitute a potent selling tool.

Selling Methods

OEG has traditionally relied on face-to-face selling to provide information to and solicit orders from customers. Two major problems existed with heavy reliance on personal selling. First, it was not cost efficient for OEG to serve mid-sized and small customers unless a standard product already existed to fit the customer's application. Service to these customers was provided primarily by local distributors or through DCI's Aftermarket Group. As a result, OEG's knowledge of these customers' needs was minimal, leading to possible missed market opportunities. Second, for large customers with multiple purchasing and usage sites, it was difficult to coordinate the activities of salespeople assigned to customers geographically. This problem became acute when the customer had purchasing or usage sites overseas, served through the International Division. This meant that salespeoples' activities had to be coordinated across geographic regions as well as across divisions within DCI. Two selling methods, telemarketing and global account management, are being considered as substitutes or supplements to the current selling method.

Telemarketing

Telemarketing involves organized, planned telephone communication between a firm and its customers. Telemarketing ranges from salespeople simply calling prospective customers to set appointments to complex systems with different employees responsible for different parts of selling, such as prospecting or customer service.

One special projects manager explored the feasibility of telemarketing to small OEs. The study's objective was to profile the small OEs to understand their needs. The subjects were small OEs that had purchased OEG products. These firms were questioned about their use of OEG products, needs for additional OEG support, and overall satisfaction with OEG products and services. Four hundred and sixty-one small OEs were contacted during the month-long study, none with more than $25,000 in purchases from OEG the preceding year. Some study results appear in Exhibit 8.

Global Account Management (GAM)

GAM is a method of assigning salespeople to accounts. Sellers use GAM when customers are large, with multiple purchase or use points. Under a GAM system, an account executive is responsible for all the communications between the customer and the seller, including (but not limited to) needs analysis, application engineering, field support, customer service and order processing. Depending on the account size, the executive might have several subordinates provide necessary services. GAM's major advantage is communication coordination. Since all seller and buyer contact is monitored by the account manager, uncoordinated communication is unlikely.

Implementing GAM would involve assigning teams to OEG's largest customers to improve support. Account teams would be composed of salespeople and applications engineers, with the number of people on the account proportional to its annual orders. Each team head, or account manager, would coordinate communications between all cus-

Exhibit 8. Telemarketing Study Results

	Number	Percent of Responses
Quotes	8	2%
Follow-up phone calls	17	4
Literature requests	211	46
Not qualified as customers	58	13
Satisfied customers	102	22
Terminations	5	1
Orders	9	2
Unavailable, not listed, duplicates	51	11
	461	100%

Source: Internal company documents.

tomer buying locations and OEG. Account managers would have worldwide P & L responsibility for their assigned customers. Sales representatives in district offices in other countries would report their customer activities to the lead account executive. Account executives are responsible for the subsidiaries of global customers in their geographic area. Account executives and sales representatives typically have multiple reporting relationships. A sample organizational chart appears in Exhibit 9. The boxes

Exhibit 9. Global Account Management Sample Organizational Chart

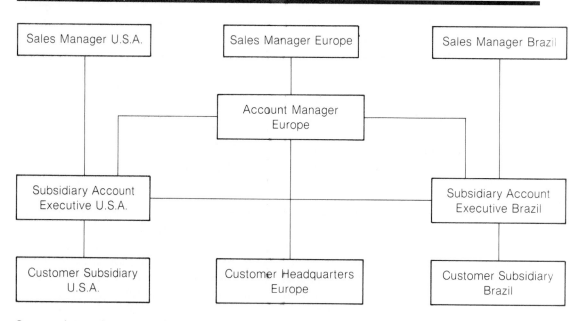

Source: Internal company documents

do not all represent people assigned full time to that account. A brief example may clarify Exhibit 9. The account manager in Europe for Daimler-Benz would report to the Sales Manager in Europe. The Daimler-Benz account manager for Europe might also be a subsidiary account executive for Caterpiller in Europe, reporting to an account manager in the U.S.

MAKING THE DECISION

After attending the worldwide action team and OEG operations presentations, OEG executives split into two groups. Each group prepared a presentation explaining its vision for OEG's future corporate structure and marketing strategy. One group maintained that the current organization structure (see Exhibit 4) would adequately meet the challenges posed by current external and internal problems. The other group proposed a different organizational structure, explained below.

Proposed New OEG Corporate Structure

Based on the results of the strategic development process, the second group made several suggestions to improve OEG's performance. Two suggestions, global account management for large OEs and telemarketing for small customers were key features of the proposed organizational structure.

To incorporate these selling methods into OEG operations, the second group proposed the organizational structure appearing in Exhibit 10 to replace the structure in Exhibit 4. The major difference was the replacement of the market groups (truck, agriculture, industrial and construction) with the large customer and mid-sized and small customer groups. The product/technical group is added to improve communication between engineering and marketing. Although this is a change from the current organizational structure, it is not a basis on which to accept or reject the

Exhibit 10. Proposed Structure—OEG

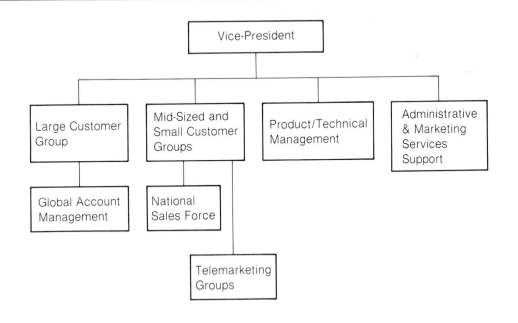

Source: Internal company documents

new structure, since it could be appended to the current structure with little ado.

The suggested organizational structure would offer a number of advantages. Service to multinational customers would be coordinated under a single account manager. Current problems with lack of coordination among DCI offices could be minimized. Small OEs would receive more attention. Although little deviation from standard products would be permitted these customers, they would be contacted more frequently under telemarketing. Service to mid-sized accounts would not change.

The proposed plan has several disadvantages as well. With fewer managers at the market director level, the number of workers each must supervise would increase. For the director of large accounts, that would involve 10 to 13 account managers for 30 to 40 accounts (some managers would be responsible for more than one account). Second, the reporting relationships (see Exhibit 9) grow rather complex under a GAM structure. This can obscure good and poor performance, making it more difficult to reward outstanding performance or detect poor performance. It could also make the salesperson's job more ambiguous as orders come from a variety of bosses. Third, new product development would be centered around applications for specific customers. With all salespeople focusing on specific customers, no one would be charged with maintaining a perspective on the market as a whole. Without a broad perspective on changing market conditions, it would be possible to miss a trend in customer usage characteristics, DCI missing a chance to be technology leader in a new market. Narrow focus on a single customer's needs might also cause the salesperson or applications engineer to miss similar work performed for another account, duplicating effort.

SUMMARY

Baden must choose one of the two organizational structures to present to corporate management. He can, of course, modify the struc-

tures as he deems necessary, but three issues preclude much tinkering with the two structures as presented. First, the strategic development process ensured that all OEG executives, including Baden, had the same information on which to suggest changes in OEG organizational structure. As a result, Baden was not likely to develop a change because he had information unavailable to other executives which made their suggestion untenable. Second, the executives suggesting changes were responsible for implementing the plan. Modifying their approaches too much might lose their commitment to implementing whichever organizational structure was selected. Finally, there was a corporate urgency that something must be done to improve OEG's performance. This required that a decision be made soon on the appropriate organizational structure so that OEG personnel could work on bringing OEG's performance back to previous levels.

Baden is aware that any organizational change inevitably causes staff upheaval, and wants to ensure that the OEG structure chosen will remain in place for a long time. In deciding, he also must remember that the current organizational structure has been successful for many years, and that any changes must be supported by sound reasoning. To help decide, he prepared the following questions to organize his presentation on the appropriate organizational structure to top DCI management.

1. How will customers react to both plans?

2. Which plan comes closest to solving the problems OEG faced in 1983?

3. Other than the alternatives presented, what organizational structures exist to accomplish the same goals?

4. Analyze the major strengths and weaknesses of each alternative. What conclusions can be drawn from the analysis?

5. Assuming the new organizational structure is selected, how should it be implemented?

37

Tennessee Pewter Company *

The Tennessee Pewter Company makes and markets a wide range of pewter tableware and decorative items. Located in Grand Junction, Tennessee, a small town about fifty miles directly east of Memphis, Tennessee Pewter was started about one year ago by Carl Dunn. In thinking about what steps he needed to take for successful development of the firm, Dunn summed up the progress to date in talking to Jack Logan, a consultant from the Center for Industrial Services at the University of Tennessee:

After we got an economic development loan from the government, machinery such as old bronze molds, steel chucks, spinning lathes, and casting equipment were purchased from companies in the New England states and shipped here to Grand Junction. Training of our employees has taken about six months. In the eight months that we have had products for sale, the total volume has been $33,100, or about $4,000 a month. Now that all the problems in production have been solved, we face difficult problems in marketing our products at about twice the present rate to reach $100,000 a year.

THE PEWTER MARKET

With increasing emphasis on Early American history brought on by the Bicentennial, the market for pewter tableware has experienced rapid growth. Today's total market is estimated at $15 million annual sales; imports from England and Europe are a third of the market. Overall growth during the last four years has averaged 10 to 20 percent annually.

Forecasts for the next few years project a doubling of total sales every three or four years, which translates to an average growth rate of 18 to 24 percent.

Data on the pewter market is sketchy, but it is generally conceded that Stieff of Baltimore, Maryland, and International of Meridan, Connecticut, are the two largest firms. Both have grown at a very rapid pace in the last ten years. Stieff, for example, is said to have grown from about $100,000 to between $2.5 and $3 million in ten years. Stieff offers four lines of, what are called in the trade, antique reproductions. The names of these lines are Williamsburg, Stieff, and Sturbridge which are available in polished and satin finishes, and Newport which has an oxidized finish.

International, the next largest company, markets a single line with a satin finish. The third largest company is Foreign Advisory Service located in Princess Anne, Maryland. This firm is an importer of the Royal Holland line. The designs are largely contemporary with either satin or oxidized finishes, although they do have a partial antique reproduction line. The fourth largest company is Woodbury Pewterers of Woodbury, Connecticut, while the fifth largest is Boardman from Wallingford, Connecticut. The sales of these two companies are estimated to range from $400,000 to $600,000, or about one-half those of the third largest firm. Firms selling between $200,000 and $300,000 a year include Queens Art, Trinac, Crown-Revere, Preisner, Empire, and Garden.

---

* This case was prepared by H. Robert Dodge.

A HISTORICAL DESCRIPTION OF PEWTER

Pewter is centuries old. The ancient Chinese, as well as the Japanese, Romans, Greeks, and early Egyptians used pewter in their households and in religious and public ceremonies. As early as the thirteenth century, pewter began to replace wood in the English household. Craftsmanship signifying quality in the making of pewter products has always been highly prized. English guilds set up regulations to enforce the highest level of quality in terms of performance from their membership. To distinguish the products of one craftsman from those of another, pewter was marked. These touch marks, as they were called then, or trademarks, as we know them today, can be traced back to the fourteenth century in England.

In earliest times, the appeal of pewter was its superiority over wooden products. Today it has a charm that no other product can duplicate—a product which is at the same time a collector's item and a useful household item with prestige appeal. Much of pewter's appeal is its basic simplicity of design. Pewter is much like the old saying— "The more things change, the more they remain the same."

Contemporary pewter is defined by the American Pewter Guild as containing:

Tin—92 percent minimum;

Antimony—5 to 7 percent to give it hardness; and

Copper—1 to 3 percent to give it a good finish.

Pewter products are soft and easily dented or scratched; however, instead of detracting from the appeal of pewter this seems to add to it. Among the possible benefits of pewter are:

1. Quality reproductions of authentic antiques (especially by Stieff) have done much to influence the acceptance of pewter by department and jewelry stores as a legitimate and worthy product to stock.

2. Promotion and acceptance of pewter as a superior substitute (rather than silverplate) for the extremely high-priced sterling silver holloware.

3. No maintenance because there is no need to polish pewter. (Fewer and fewer consumers are interested in polishing silverplate.)

4. Pewter is considered to be fashionable among persons regardless of age. Pewter products are considered chic, sophisticated, and beautiful. Pewter has a casual look with its simplicity, is hand-made, and provides a link to our history.

5. The adaptability of pewter in terms of decor is a benefit. Pewter, unlike other forms of tableware, fits any decor—modern, traditional provincial, colonial, or oriental.

6. Pewter has excellent heat and cold retention, making it a good choice for either hot or cold drinks.

PRODUCT LINE

In developing a product line, Tennessee Pewter has retained classical shapes and designs. All forty-two of its items combine the charm of history with a contemporary use that is both varied and functional. The porringer is a good example. A flat-bottomed bowl with steep sides and a side handle, the porringer can be used to hold fruits, vegetables, dips, or appetizers. It may also be used in floral displays or as an ash tray.

Tennessee Pewter products are buffed to give a polished appearance. Further polishing is not necessary and the products do not tarnish. When a product becomes dusty and finger-marked, all that is necessary is a washing in warm soapy water and wiping with a soft cloth. The wear and tear from use will show because pewter is a soft metal; however, the marks of time are considered a contributor to the product's charm. Pewter products should last a lifetime with reasonable care.

The scope of the product line is comparable to Tennessee Pewter's larger competitors. Differences may occur in finish, size, and weight of the individual items.

DISTRIBUTION AND SALES

Tennessee Pewter uses independent sales reps, paying them a 15 percent commission on sales volume produced in contacting primarily department, jewelry, and gift stores. Both Dunn and his assistant manager feel that market representation leaves much to be desired. Only two, possibly three sales reps are doing an adequate job at the present time. No sales rep has been retained to call on the major midwest metropolitan areas such as Chicago, Detroit, Minneapolis, or St. Louis.

The approach taken by Dunn is to contact potential sales reps by phone. The only information he has on a potential rep is from a listing in a directory of sales reps. This is usually limited to the geographical area covered plus the general types of products handled by the sales rep at present.

It is also discouraging to Tennessee Pewter's management that only two accounts now stock what might be considered a representative inventory. One of these is a jewelry store in Virginia, the other is a savings and loan association in South Georgia that uses pewter as a premium in the solicitation of new accounts.

Tennessee has not done any advertising, and the sales promotional literature sent to sales reps consists of sheets of paper with pictures of selected items in black and white. The only copy other than the names and numbers of the individual items is the phrase "immediate delivery." However, this phrase may not be true because Tennessee, plagued by backorders, has not been able to make quick, reliable delivery of complete orders. Not being able to fill an order has already cost Tennessee several large orders.

Pricing is a sensitive matter for Tennessee Pewter. The price list shown in Exhibit 1 was largely arrived at by selectively reducing the prices charged by a major competitor. In other words, if the major competitor had a price of $8.00, Tennessee's price would be pegged lower, perhaps $7.25 or $6.95. Dunn has intimated to his assistant manager that he would like to mark up products 50 percent based on

cost. The 50 percent figure is standard industry practice; however, he does not have a grasp of costs at this point.

OPERATIONS

Located in an old abandoned school building, Tennessee Pewter employs in addition to Carl Dunn, an assistant manager whose main responsibilities have been in production, one part time and three full-time production workers, and a secretary-bookkeeper. The salaries and/or wage rates for these people are as follows:

Carl Dunn	$24,000/year
Assistant Manager	18,000/year
Secretary/Bookkeeper	$4.50/hr.
Full-time production workers	5.20/hr.
Part-time production worker	3.75/hr.

The production facility was planned to allow three trained workers, a spinner, a solderer, and a finisher, to produce 100 pieces per day at an average cost of $4 to $5 each. Cost of the metals to produce each piece is estimated to be 25 percent of the total cost of each piece.

The costs of equipment for the production facility are itemized below. In addition, it was necessary to train the production workers and oversee getting the operation moving smoothly. An experienced supervisor was hired at a cost of $10,500 ($7,500 salary plus expenses of $3,000) for six months. The supervisor was charged with responsibility of setting up the organization and training the solderer and finisher. Additionally, an experienced spinner was hired at $7.50/hour for a period of one year.

Equipment Purchased	
2 Spinning lathes @ $2,500 (used)	$ 5,000
Soldering equipment	1,000
Casting Pot	1,000
3 Buffing lathes and blowers	2,250
Sanding machine	600
Band Saw	600
16 Bronze molds (for handles, etc.)	6,400
40 Steel cheeks	6,000
Buffs, wheels, etc.	500
Total	$23,350
Shipping Costs	$ 5,000

Exhibit 1. Tennessee Pewter Price List

TENNESSEE PEWTER—CONFIDENTIAL PRICE LIST AND ORDER FORM
TENNESSEE PEWTER INC.   Date _____ Order No. _____
Box 278 Grand Junction, Tenn. 38309

Ship To

TERMS 2% 10 days—Net 30 days   _____
Service charge of 1½% per month for accounts over 30 days old.   _____

No.	Item	Qty.	Price *	Total
101	Sugar & Creamer Set		13.75	
102	Sugar & Creamer Set		12.50	
201	Porringer		6.25	
202	Porringer		5.00	
203	Wine Taster		5.00	
204	Baby Cup 8 oz.		8.25	
205	Baby Cup 8 oz.		5.75	
301	Chamber		8.25	
302	Chamber with glass		9.50	
303	Candle with glass		10.75	
304	Candle (Pair)		12.50	
401	Eagle Paper Weight		3.25	
402	Bird Paper Weight		3.25	
403	Open Salt		1.50	
404	Salt Spoon		.60	
501	Vase 7¾"		9.50	
502	Vase 7"		7.50	
503	Vase 5½"		7.00	
601	Butter Dish		9.50	
701	Salt & Pepper		8.50	
702	Salt & Pepper		7.00	
703	Liberty Bell Salt & Pepper		7.00	
704	Cock & Bell Salt & Pepper		7.00	
801	Jigger 2 oz.		2.75	
802	Double Jigger 1 & 2 oz.		4.75	
901	Bread & Butter		4.75	
1001	Snuffer		4.00	
1002	Snuffer		5.75	
1101	Large Mint Julep 16 oz.		8.25	
1102	On-the-rock Cup 16 oz.		5.50	
1103	Water Tumbler 12 oz.		5.50	
1104	Jefferson Cup 9 oz.		4.00	
1201	Stamp Dispenser		8.25	
1701	Bird Dog Stein 18 oz.		15.00	
1702	Stein 18 oz.		13.00	
1401	Bowl 5"		4.50	
1402	Bowl 6"		5.75	
1403	Tray 9½"		8.00	
1501	Goblet 7" 12 oz.		8.75	
1502	Goblet 8½" 12 oz.		8.75	
1503	Martini Glass 5"		6.00	
1601	Napkin Ring		2.50	

* Prices subject to change without notice.

FUTURE PLANS AND GOALS

Tennessee's major goal for the next three to four years was to develop a sound, growing business. After a sound foundation is established, sales should grow at about the industry rate of 20 percent per year. Dunn stated his idea of Tennessee's goals in more detail:

Our goal is a profitable company and one this community can be proud of in terms of reputation. First we have to establish a sound sales network so we can get market penetration. Next, we need to produce a quality product line. A third goal is to do our jobs efficiently. I am afraid I will have to hire more and more people as production increases. Finally, we have to know what products are selling and what are not selling. Originally, I thought a sales volume of $100,000 a year would be adequate. Now I feel we need at least $150,000 in sales every year.

CONSULTING ASSISTANCE

The Center for Industrial Services supplied Tennessee's management with information on sales of pewter, results of interviews with retailers in Memphis handling Tennessee pewter products, and an itemization of plant finished goods inventory. An analysis of sales for the first eight months of operation is shown in Exhibit 2. No data is available on the sales to the jewelry store in Virginia or the savings and loan association in Georgia. It is assumed, however, that a quantity of each of the products listed on the price sheet (Exhibit 1) was ordered.

Visits with retailers who handle Tennessee Pewter products revealed the following:

1. No customer recognition of the name Tennessee Pewter.

2. Many units are too small for most customers and as a result are outsold by their larger editions. This includes the sugar and creamer set, porringer, and vase.

3. Customers are not educated and lack buying knowledge of various pewter products. Consequently, only portions of the line (any manufacturer) sell well. One of

Exhibit 2.   Unit Sales of Pewter *

Description of Item		Units Sold	Description of Item		Units Sold
101	Sugar & Creamer Set	136	702	Salt & Pepper	137
102	Sugar & Creamer Set	62	703	Liberty Bell Salt & Pepper (new)	16
201	Porringer	91	704	Cock & Bell Salt & Pepper (new)	13
202	Porringer	51	801	Jigger (2 oz.)	141
203	Wine Taster	117	802	Double Jigger	139
204	Baby Cup (8 oz.)	203	901	Bread & Butter	76
205	Baby Cup (8 oz.)	179	1001	Snuffer	184
301	Chamber	184	1002	Snuffer	101
302	Chamber (glass)	141	1101	Large Mint Julep	172
303	Candle (glass)	161	1102	On-the-rock Cup (new)	7
304	Candle (pair)	127	1103	Water Tumbler (new)	4
401	Eagle Paper Weight	78	1104	Jefferson Cup (new)	105
402	Bird Paper Weight	86	1201	Stamp Dispenser	109
501	Vase (7¾")	95	1701	Bird Dog Stein (new)	6
502	Vase (7")	87	1702	Stein (new)	2
503	Vase (5½")	53	1401	Bowl (new)	5
601	Butter Dish	217	1402	Bowl (new)	6
701	Salt & Pepper	110	1403	Tray (new)	13

* The large orders to the jewelry store in Virginia and the Savings and Loan Association in Georgia were not included.

the most popular pewter products is the Jefferson cup.

4. There is noticeable interest in traditional products.

5. Pricing of the product from the wholesale standpoint is out of line with existing retail prices. For example, a Jefferson cup normally retails at $12.00. The price quot- ed to a retailer is $4.00. Normally, a retailer will double the cost to arrive at retail price. Thus, it is obvious that prices following industry practice would be too low at retail for Tennessee Pewter.

An inventory of finished products stored in Grand Junction is shown in Exhibit 3.

Exhibit 3. Finished Products Inventory

Item No.		Number of Units	Item No.		Number of Units
101	Sugar & Creamer Set	4	703	Liberty Bell Salt & Pepper (new)	50
102	Sugar & Creamer Set	42	704	Cock & Bell Salt & Pepper (new)	48
201	Porringer	10	801	Jigger 2 oz.	28
202	Porringer	15	802	Double Jigger 1 & 2 oz.	13
203	Wine Tester	10	901	Bread & Butter	16
204	Baby Cup 8 oz.	—	1001	Snuffer	5
205	Baby Cup 8 oz.	2	1002	Snuffer	3
301	Chamber	—	1101	Large Mint Julep 16 oz.	—
302	Chamber with glass	—	1102	On-the-rock Cup 16 oz. (new)	12
303	Candle with glass	2	1103	Water Tumbler 14 oz. (new)	123
304	Candle (Pair)	20	1104	Jefferson Cup 9 oz. (new)	18
401	Eagle Paper Weight	40	1201	Stamp Dispenser	84
402	Bird Paper Weight	8	1701	Bird Dog Stein 18 oz. (new)	17
403	Open Salt (new)	120	1702	Stein 18 oz. (new)	22
404	Salt Spoon (new)	60	1401	Bowl 5" (new)	43
501	Vase (7¾")	—	1402	Bowl 6" (new)	48
502	Vase 7"	6	1403	Tray 99½"	47
503	Vase 5½"	33	1501	Goblet 7" 12 oz.	36
601	Butter Dish	—	1502	Goblet 6½" 12 oz.	36
701	Salt & Pepper	36	1503	Martini Glass 5"	48
702	Salt & Pepper	40	1601	Napkin Ring	60

38

CAMVAC, Inc.*

CAMVAC, Inc., with headquarters in Oak Brook, Illinois, began operation in 1943 as a producer of highly specialized machine tools. Saul Campanic and Raymond Vaccon, cofounders of the company, held several patents on machine tooling, the use of which was vital to the war effort. The history of the company can be divided into three phases. The first phase, from 1943 through the end of the Korean War, saw sales of machine tools grow at a rapid rate. Sales volume in 1955 was $38 million. The second phase from the mid-1950s to 1970, saw the company expand by purchasing small machine tool operations in the Chicago area. Growth slowed in this period with sales reaching $49 million in 1970.

In the last fifteen years sales have more than doubled. Sales in 1985 totaled $111 million with machine tools contributing about $25 million. The principal means of growth for CAMVAC in the third phase has been the purchase of small companies making various types of innovative industrial machinery and equipment. Recent acquisitions include companies making robots, automated cranes, and steel-stripping machines. The typical candidate for acquisition is a firm with a technologically superior product that is experiencing problems in either financing, management, or marketing. The owner of a typical acquisition is usually technically oriented, oftentimes the inventor of the product.

Wayne Mosby, the president and CEO of CAMVAC feels that under the CAMVAC

umbrella good, sound technological innovations can be turned into successful products. A case in point is the Crespi Machine Division that produces steel-stripping machines. Stanley Crespi designed a machine that was capable of precision cutting narrow widths of steel previously obtainable only by flattening wire. However, Crespi lacked working capital and, as he himself admitted, his only interests were in machine design. He knew nothing about management or marketing. Today, as part of CAMVAC, Crespi is able to devote his full efforts to product design while the rest of the operation has been turned over to CAMVAC personnel. As a result sales have increased dramatically and CAMVAC is now marketing a splitting machine that can be set and controlled electronically.

POSSIBLE ACQUISITION

Always on the lookout for new acquisitions, Mosby has come across a company in Crown Point, Indiana, that makes oil reclamation equipment. The owner and inventor of what appears to be an innovative system, Everett Manley, would like to sell his firm, Reclaim Corporation, and retire to Florida. After a visit to the facilities to confirm the potentiality of the firm, Mosby assigned Mark Whitmer, Joan Selig, and Donald White to the task of preparing an acquisition report. All three are administrative assistants reporting directly to the president. Whitmer specializes in manufacturing, Selig's field is marketing, while White considers the financial aspects of the acquisition.

* This case was prepared by H. Robert Dodge.

At a meeting with the three employees, Mosby went over the minimum requirements for an acquisition. Foremost of the requirements is the sales of the firm. The acquired firm must be doing or have the potential of contributing at least 10 percent of the annual sales volume for CAMVAC. Since annual volume for CAMVAC is about $105 million, this means that Reclaim Corporation must have the potential of $11 million in sales. Present sales volume for Reclaim is $3 million.

Next in importance is the profit requirement. Profits before taxes should run between 15 and 20 percent of sales. However, this might be waived for a strong product that does not require large infusions of capital for manufacturing and marketing development.

Potential for growth in both sales and profits is the third most important requirement. Usually CAMVAC will want a product that will show a growth of 20 percent compounded for the next five to ten years, or a doubling of sales every four years or so.

The fourth requirement is the market status of the product. The product must have a strong competitive edge that cannot be readily duplicated by competition. Since CAMVAC does not engage in R & D, the acquired firm must have this capacity or the product should not need technological modifications for at least five years.

RECLAIM CORPORATION AS POTENTIAL ACQUISITION

The report as prepared by Whitmer, Selig, and White was divided up into four sections. The first section dealt with the background of the oil reclamation industry. The second part was a description of the product and the third part dealt with product benefits. The final and fourth part summarized the advantages and disadvantages and suggested options.

Background

The EPA estimates yearly generation of used oil in the United States to be about 1.2 billion gallons. Approximately 520 million gallons are consumed as fuel each year leaving 500 million gallons available for reclamation, burning, and re-refining.

During the 1980s the overall demand for lubricating oil is expected to grow slowly at one percent a year. However, the supply provided by refineries should increase even slower so that it is extremely likely that a potential shortage of virgin lubricating oil will cause prices to increase.

Oil reclamation indefinitely extends the product life of unconsumed oil. The economic advantage of this is that used oil can be reclaimed at about one-half or less the cost of new oil. Also, by removing water and particulate matter from used oil on-site such as is accomplished by the Reclaim machine, the lifetime of production machinery can be extended. As an example, contaminants can cause the lubricating and cooling properties of hydraulic oil to deteriorate which in turn inflicts damage to product machinery.

Another advantage is an environmental one. Oil reclamation on-site avoids both the costs and environmental regulations of oil disposal on-site. The EPA is expected to list used oil as a hazardous waste. Therefore, a company must follow strict rules for transporting, treating, storing, reusing, and disposing of used oil. On-site reclamation avoids the costs associated with off-site disposal and at the same time the complexity of environment regulations. One major problem is that the source of oil cannot shift responsibility for another firm's disposal activities.

Description of Product

There are three different models or types of installations made by Reclaim Corporation. Using a patented process that combines filtration, heat, and vacuum separation, Reclaim Corporation has developed the different types to serve specific needs of customers. Briefly, the patented Reclaim process can be described as the passage of used oil through a 100-mesh strainer to a density heater and on to another filtering unit. Clogging of the filters by contaminants causes an automatic shutdown of the Reclaim process. The next step sees the filtered oil flow into a liquid-gas separation container where a vacuum is maintained. Volatile liquid contaminants such as water evaporate while gaseous contaminants such as air are removed from the oil by a vacuum pump. The remaining oil, now purified, exits the system through a discharge pump.

The smallest Reclaim product is permanently installed on a piece of machinery, allowing the reclamation of oil on a continuous or demand basis. The price of Reclaim 10, as it is called, is from $3,500 to $6,000 depending upon the type of machinery to which it is to be attached.

The next biggest Reclaim product that can be moved from one location to another is the Model 100. The basic Reclaim 100 has a processing rate of 100 gallons per hour with a flow rate of around 600 gallons. The price of this unit is $25,000. The Reclaim Corporation has plans to build a Reclaim 60 that can process 60 gallons per hour with a flow rate of 300 gallons per hour. The cost of this unit is projected at $18,000.

The largest unit built is designed for use by oil reclamation service companies that operate locally in industrial areas. The Reclaim 2000 is attached directly to a truck and costs about $150,000. The throughput of the unit is 2,000 gallons per hour and the processing rate varies between 300 and 500 gallons per hour.

There is some demand to use Reclaim technology in building complex installations at large manufacturing sites. The exact size as well as characteristics and processing capabilities would hinge on customer specification. The role of Reclaim would be in design rather than construction.

Product Benefits

The major benefit from using Reclaim products is in cost savings. Comparing the cost of reclaimed oil to new oil, the minimum savings is 50 percent. With a large volume of oil, one customer reported savings of 80 percent over new oil. Added to this are the savings from not transporting or handling the used oil or risking EPA penalties on disposal.

Another savings is from reducing pollution that can lead to lost time for employees and workmen's compensation. Reclaim products minimize exposure of employees to the used oil, thus reducing the possibility of damage to skin or lungs.

Compared to the common procedure of fluid disposal, there is no downtime, no transport cost, and no need for permits. Also, in sending used fluids off-site there is always the possibility of not getting back the same fluid that was sent out to be cleaned. Among the fluids acceptable to a Reclaim product are lube, cutting, hydraulic, seal, bearing and gear oils. Among those oils that are nonacceptable are any that would explode, have a high acid content, or boil below 300 °F.

Another product benefit is the ease of usage. The Reclaim product employs state-of-the-art technology, yet can be operated with no special training. Tests have shown that the oil is clean and without odor after being processed by a Reclaim product. Contamination and possible harmful effects on skin are eliminated. At the same time, companies have experienced better quality output from machines, longer tool life, less downtime, and reductions in fluid usage of up to 15 percent.

Market Potential and Sales History

There seem to be two markets for the product. One is the accessory or add-on market where the Reclaim product is sold to the firm. The other is the sale of the Reclaim product to oil reclamation service companies. The Reclaim Corporation has only two models that can be sold in the add-on market. If prices of $5,000 for Reclaim 10 and $25,000 for Reclaim 100 were utilized, it would take unit sales of 2,000 Reclaim 10s or 400 Reclaim 100s to attain $10 million in sales.

Over the four years the Reclaim Corporation has been in business, they have never sold more than 50 of either model.

Sales of the truck unit (Reclaim 2000) have been minimal principally because of the relatively high price. In a four-year period only eight 2000s have been sold. Last year three 2000s were sold. An alternative to selling the Reclaim 2000 would be a royalty structure based on number of gallons processed. Suppose a truck-based unit processed 1,000 gallons a day for 200 workdays in the year. If the average price was $1.25/gallon, total revenue would equal $250,000 on a total of 200,000 gallons. A royalty fee of $0.25/gallon would amortize the cost of the Reclaim product over four years.

Oil Reclamation Service

Potentially more profitable but more capital consuming would be the development by CAMVAC of its own oil reclamation service division. The expenses were estimated for each truck operation for a year:

Truck expense ($25,000 for four years)	$ 6,250
Insurance	5,000
Travel expenses (gasoline and oil)	10,000
Maintenance of truck	5,000
License and fees	1,500
Driver salary	24,000
Fringe benefits (25 percent of salary)	6,000
Helper's salary	15,000
Fringe benefits (25 percent of salary)	3,750
Reclaimer Service	
Maintenance	12,000
Filters and other accessories	20,000

Incentive bonuses [1]
Driver 5¢/gallon, first 100,000 gallons, 7½/gallon after that
Helper 2¢/gallon

[1] Fifty percent of the cost of rectifying mistakes will be charged against incentive bonuses to driver and helper.

Evaluation of Reclaim

The manufacturing facilities at Crown Point are far from adequate. It is doubtful whether the necessary volume could be obtained with three shifts a day. Tooling and machinery, what there is, is in excellent condition but not state-of-the-art. To produce the necessary $11 million in sales, capital appropriations of approximately $4 million must be made in addition to increasing the work force by 50 percent and having to find or build additional space.

Production at present is labor-intensive with a cost of goods sold of around 60 percent. To be truly effective and efficient, production needs to be mechanized. This is another reason for the need to add capital machinery and equipment. In addition, the labor force is nonunion. Acquisition by CAMVAC would mean unionization and an increase in average wages of about $5.00/hour ($8.85 to $13.63). This would in turn increase the cost of goods sold to approximately 72 percent of sales if no labor-saving machinery were installed.

For the most part, Reclaim has no direct competition for either equipment or service in on-site reclamation. Only re-refiners who do about 8 percent of the total gallons reclaimed can be considered as competition for service. Usually re-refiners are small firms working in a local area. Competitors selling reclamation equipment are of negligible impact on the potential market. Estimates vary, but it would seem reasonable to assume that no one has more than 1 percent of the market. As a consequence a large proportion of the available used oil is burned as full, discharged (often illegally) into sewers and land fills, or used illegally for wood oiling.

39

General Motors Corporation *

In late 1982, General Motors Corporation launched a long-awaited offensive to establish itself as a leading European automobile producer. Although it had been a resident of Europe ever since 1928, when it acquired control of Vauxhall in the U.K., GM had never succeeded in building a dominant position. In contrast, its main U.S. rival, Ford, had been remarkably successful over the years in Europe. This was especially true since the 1960s, when Ford began to implement a strategy of expanding and geographically integrating its European operations. GM currently ranked sixth in European market share behind (in declining order) Ford, Renault, Fiat, Volkswagen, and Peugeot.

GM planned to use its German company, Adam Opel, to spearhead the expansion program. At the center of the program was the "Corsa"—the first of GM's "world cars" designed and initially launched outside the U.S. and the first GM entry in the critical subcompact market in Europe. The "Corsa" went on sale at the end of 1982 in Spain, Italy, and France, and in 1983 in West Germany and the U.K. Preliminary sales figures seemed to indicate that GM would exceed its target for the car of capturing 2 percent of the European market. This would be a significant contribution to what analysts thought was GM's goal of lifting its current 9 percent share of the European car market

to at least 15 percent by 1988, a market forecast to be 10 million vehicles.

GM'S U.S. HISTORY

General Motors Corporation was created in 1908 by William Durrant through the consolidation of three separate companies: Oldsmobile, Buick, and Chevrolet. From the very beginning, GM started buying component producers—companies like Harrison Radiators and Saginaw Steering that still exist today as separate divisions. However, GM failed to match the success of Ford, and by the early 1920s Ford was ten times the size of GM (which had about 5 percent of the US market). In the 1920s, Ford was also outdistancing its rival by rapidly expanding its overseas operations. In 1923, Alfred P. Sloan took over GM from Durrant and began to reorganize the company.

GM achieved its prominent position by the 1930s through the efforts of Sloan and the mistaken decision of Henry Ford I not to replace his Model T until 1927. In the 1930s both Chrysler and GM managed to pull ahead of Ford in the U.S. market. (William P. Chrysler had left GM to set up his own company after a row with Durrant).

After the hiatus of World War II, the major U.S. producers scrambled to reestablish production and dominant position. U.S. market shares stabilized at approximately 50 percent for GM, 25–27 percent for Ford, and 16–18 percent for Chrysler. This prevailed until the turbulence of the 1970s in which both Ford and Chrysler lost ground to GM and all three lost ground to Japanese imports.

GM'S EUROPEAN OPERATIONS

GM entered the European market shortly after Ford when it acquired Vauxhall in 1928. The next acquisition was the German firm Adam Opel in 1929. But GM's U.S. management gave little direction to the European operations until the mid-1970s. By then, the parent company's management had become increasingly concerned about the poor productivity and profit performance of Vauxhall and the lack of any collaboration between the two European subsidiaries— Vauxhall in the U.K. and Opel in West Germany. Ford, although weaker than GM in the U.S., was markedly stronger in Europe and had made greater progress in its efforts to integrate its U.K. and West German operations.

In 1975, GM made two key organizational decisions. The first was to give responsibility for the car operations of Vauxhall to Opel while all truck operations were to be based in the U.K. using the successful Bedford trademark. The second decision was to set up a separate world headquarters in New York to emphasize the commitment of GM to its global operations.

General Motors had other operations in Europe in addition to those in the U.K. and West Germany. In Greenevilliers, France, GM's subsidiary, AC Delco, employed 2,000 people making fuel pumps, break systems, and distributors for GM and all the French automobile firms. In Strasbourg, France; a similar-size facility made automatic transmissions and carburetors. In 1978, two large projects were started. Harrison/GM France built a radiator and heater plant at Donchery, near Sedan, and a battery plant was set up at Sarreguemines, in Lorraine.

In Antwerp, Belgium, Opel had a major assembly plant building the J-car, which was sold as the "Rekord" and "Cavalier" models for West Germany and the U.K., respective-

ly. Then in early 1979, investments in Spain and Austria were announced to build GM's small car, the "Corsa." The Corsa had its origins in 1977 when GM was first contemplating an integrated European strategy. Ford by that time had demonstrated success in its international operations. It had a strong production base in Brazil, it had displaced GM's dominance in Australia, and Ford of Europe was resoundingly successful. (Indeed, it was the profitability of its European operations that would sustain the company through its U.S. depression of 1982–1983.)

GM's strategic thinking was centered on the world car concept, but Europe had not yet been satisfactorily integrated into that concept. The Corsa (originally the "S-car") was to remedy that failing. It was to be a small car, designed by Opel, and first marketed in Europe. It would subsequently be transferred to the U.S. with a minimum of changes.

GM management expected to find a huge market for the Corsa in southern Europe, where it had only a 4 percent share but where small cars in the same category as the Corsa constituted 40 percent of automobile sales. It estimated that the Corsa would give it an added two percentage points of the European market and 100,000 more unit sales in the fast-growing Spanish market if the Corsa assembly plant were located there.

After preliminary study, three countries were selected for final site evaluation— France, Austria, and Spain. This led to a widely publicized lobbying effort by all three countries to win the jobs. After further study, GM decided in 1978 to place the engine plant at Aspern, Austria, the components plant at Cadiz, Spain, and the $1.5-billion assembly operation for 270,000 units annually at Zaragoza, Spain. The package that GM negotiated with the Spanish government was similar to one previously worked out between Ford and the government for Ford's plant in Valencia. (In fact, GM's negotiating time was considerably shortened by having the Ford plant as a precedent.) The cars went on sale at the end of

1982 in Spain, Italy, and France, and were available in Germany and the U.K. in 1983.

GM'S GLOBAL OPERATIONS

Prior to 1970, GM's major area of operation outside Europe and the U.S. was Australia. GM Holden was established there in 1947 as an integrated car manufacturing operation with major investments made in what had been until then just an assembly operation. This enabled GM Holden to establish a dominant position in the marketplace that lasted until 1975. That year Ford, using the 626 model of Toyo Kogyo (Mazda) called the Ford "Laser," took over the number one position.[1]

In the early 1970s, GM took positions in two Japanese companies—Isuzu, in which it held a 34.5 percent equity stake, and Suzuki, in which it held 5 percent of the equity. These investments were thought to be necessary to the developing GM policy of global sourcing and assembly. In 1981, Bedford announced that it would assemble an Isuzu light van/truck in England. Isuzu also started supplying the gearbox for GM's first world car, the "J-car."

In South Korea, GM announced in 1983 that new models were planned for the 50-percent–owned Daewoo Motor Company that was assembling a version of the Opel "Kadett" called the "Maepsy."

In February 1983, GM and Toyota announced agreement to collaborate in the production of a new small car to replace the aging GM Chevette in the U.S. market. Manufacturing was to be shared between the two companies. Production was initially set at 400,000 units annually but this was later reduced to 200,000 units. The car was to be designed by Toyota, and Toyota was to be

responsible for running the previously mothballed GM plant in Freemont, California. Toyota would thus gain a manufacturing base in the U.S. market.

The advantages of the deal to GM were that it could develop a new small car for the U.S. market quickly and cheaply and get firsthand experience with Japanese automotive design concepts and management techniques. It would also reemploy some of the nearly 100,000 GM workers previously laid off. GM's hope was that by the end of the decade it would have learned enough to build small cars successfully on its own.

The GM–Toyota joint venture provoked a bitterly hostile response from both Chrysler and Ford, and intense scrutiny by the U.S. Federal Trade Commission. (Toyota and Ford had held negotiations over a similar joint venture earlier, but the negotiations had broken down.) The Federal Trade Commission had the power to block the project, but recent policy changes in the U.S. antitrust enforcement agencies made approval a likely prospect.

THE DEVELOPING EUROPEAN COMPETITION

General Motors had always been a strong proponent of free trade. Indeed, its global strategy now depended on the free flow of components internationally and on the ability of GM to execute the various cooperative ventures on which it had embarked. GM's world cars, code named the J, X, and T, were now well established in most of GM's markets and were increasingly using components sourced from around the world. As an example, the Vauxhall Cavalier built in Luton, England, had an engine from Australia, a gearbox from Japan, a radiator from France, and lights from West Germany. These components were not exclusively dedicated to the Cavalier. The Corsa, designed by Opel, had just been launched in Europe and would soon be transferred to the U.S. and Australia, again with parts sourced from outside these areas. GM's joint venture with Toyota in

---

[1] Foreign direct investment in the Australian automobile industry was subject to an 85 percent domestic content rule. This percentage could be offset, however, by exports of components and built-up units from Australia. Thus, for example, Mitsubishi exported its "Lonsdale" to the U.K. and Nissan exported aluminum engine castings to Japan.

California was critical to the company's success in the U.S. small-car market. Suzuki, in which GM held a share, was starting work on another small car for the U.S.

Organizational changes had recently been made to support the evolving global manufacturing strategy. GM was not pleased with its New York worldwide headquarters experience, so in the late 1970s all domestic and international operations were consolidated in Detroit. International operations such as Opel, Bedford Truck, and GM Holden were given divisional status like Chevrolet and Fisher Body.

Some analysts thought that GM's strategy was to identify the optimum level of output for each constituent part, and to make sourcing and output decisions for components and vehicles from Detroit for the world markets. With close links to Japanese and South Korean producers, GM was well prepared to exploit its strategy.

GM in Europe had made no public statement about local content regulations or about the prospective Nissan plant in the U.K. Industry analysts felt that GM had relatively little to fear from Nissan. In 1983, GM was very successful in its two traditional European markets—the U.K. and West Germany—and its new Corsa had made a big impact in Spain and Italy. In short, GM was well prepared for battle in Europe as long as relatively free trade was allowed.

Other principals in the European automobile theater agreed. Jean-Paul Parayre, president of Peugeot S.A., was widely quoted as saying that the major threat to the native European producers came not from the Japanese, but from a war between the two American giants fought across Europe. Already some skirmishes had taken place. In 1983, a fierce discounting battle started in the U.K. and spread across Europe. Ford was generally thought to have started it in a desire to keep the Sierra number one in European sales. The company cut prices to fleet buyers up to 25 percent to match GM's marketing push.

The worry for the Europeans, as well as perhaps for Ford, was that GM—a company that lost nearly $1 billion in Europe in 1980 and 1981—was no longer an also-ran. It looked as though GM finally had the automobile models, the organization, the strategy, and (after its remarkable 1982–1983 recovery in the U.S.) the financial resources to build a position in Europe as strong as that it had long held in the U.S.

Eight

Control of Marketing Activities

CAPREE MANUFACTURING, INC.

GERVAIS–DANONE

40

*Capree Manufacturing, Inc.**

Capree Manufacturing, Inc., located in Columbia, South Carolina, is a manufacturer and marketer of an extensive line of nursery products and related toys. Founded in Trenton, New Jersey, thirty-five years ago by Donald L. Cannon and Wayne S. Preech, the company has grown from one selling only teething rings and rattles to an organization offering a full line of more than 420 items for the nursery and the care of infants and toddlers. Along with its headquarters and plant in Columbia, South Carolina, Capree operates plants in Moultrie, Georgia, and Valdosta, Georgia. The company moved south in 1975 after a bitter strike at their Trenton, New Jersey operation.

Historically, sales had always followed an upward growth pattern (10 to 15 percent a year) until 1981 when sales dropped from $4 million the previous year to approximately $2.5 million. Even more disastrous than the drop in sales was the abrupt drop in profits as a percentage of sales. In 1981, profits after taxes were 8.7 percent of sales; one year later, profits were 5.2 percent of sales.

Donald L. Cannon, Jr., the president of the company, took over the responsibility of running Capree after the death of his father in 1969. Cannon's mother, who holds the title of chairman of the board, is also active in the design of sewn products. Preech, who, along with Cannon, Sr., founded the company, is represented on the board by his son-in-law Justin Willoughby and his attorney Peter Watson.

* This case was prepared by H. Robert Dodge.

Capree markets its entire line of nursery products and related toys under the brand name of "Snoo Cums." Sales reps with assigned geographical areas are the principal means of market representation. Working on a commission basis, sales reps principally call on department stores and specialty stores specializing in products for babies and young children. It is not uncommon for a sales rep to represent competing manufacturers. Orders written by sales reps are shipped direct from Capree to the customer.

Normally, customers for the "Snoo Cums" line of merchandise will visit a central market location such as New York. For the last twenty years, Capree personnel have had a display at seasonal showings in New York. They have also had showings at Atlanta and Dallas in the past few years. All orders obtained at these locations are credited to the appropriate sales rep who has the account in his or her territory.

Cannon as president functions as CEO. Sean Murphy has been sales manager for the last twenty years, and David Collas, the controller, has been with the firm about three years. These three together with Mrs. Cannon, Sr., hold executive meetings every week. At the meeting held during the second week of July (1982), Collas reported that after five months of 1982 it seemed apparent that total sales for the year could be expected to be about $2 million, or about 20 percent less than last year. He also felt that the profit margin would fall to less than 4 percent. Murphy disagreed with Collas's sales projection, stating that the new designs in crib linens and accessories would bolster sales. He believed the new designs had caught the eye of a lot of buyers who are enthusiastic about the line.

Mrs. Cannon, Sr., pointed out that while she disagreed with the decision to go outside the firm and spend $100,000 for new designs, she did feel it was a beautiful, comprehensive line. Donald Cannon, while expressing a personal liking for the new designs, was unswayed by the feelings of Murphy and his mother that the new line would solve all their problems. He pointed out that to date, three weeks after the spring market-showing in New York, Capree had not yet received a single order for the new line. He expressed his belief that small design houses who contract out their manufacturing were taking over the industry. On the West Coast, particularly, design houses completely dominated the business. Their advantages were modern designs that seem to have a high degree of market acceptability; generally better fabrics; and lower prices to the retailer, offering either higher profit potential or the possibility of discounting without significant profit loss. The design houses were also doing a lot of custom work for the large retailers. To find out what was happening, the firm of Driscoll and Perkins was hired to study Capree operations.

DRISCOLL AND PERKINS REPORT

The study by Driscoll and Perkins was basically a series of sales analyses by product, by market territory, and by sales representative. After presentation of the specific findings to the executive committee, Donald Cannon assigned himself, Murphy, and Collas with the task of writing up recommendations to improve their control of sales performance.

Product Categories

For purposes of analysis, some 420 product designations were categorized into nineteen product categories plus a miscellaneous category and a category designated not-on-file. The bases for grouping products were similari-

ties in product use and sale. For example, there were forty different product names for rattles; these comprise only one product category.

The Best and Poorest Sales Performers. Looking at Exhibit 1, we can see that the five best-selling product categories contributed nearly 32 percent of all sales in 1980, or about eight times the volume of the five poorest sales performers (4 percent). In 1981, the relative importance of the "top five" increased to 40 percent while the "bottom five" remained around 4 percent. Also of interest is the fact that all of the "top" product categories are greater in relative importance than the total for the "bottom" five. In fact, a total of seven and eight product categories, respectively, were greater for the two years.

It should be noted that the same five product categories are included for both years. The biggest change was comforters dropping from second to fourth in relative importance (see Exhibit 2).

Adding five more product categories to each group we see that the "top ten" categories contributed almost 50 percent of the sales in 1980 and over 60 percent in 1981 (see Exhibit 3). There is also greater difference in what is included in the listings for the two years.

As for the poorest performers, the relative importance is approximately the same for the two years. However, there are significant differences between the two years in the relative ranking of product categories.

In summary, the "top" sales producers were four times as important as the "poorest" performers in 1980 and five times as important in 1981. When the groups are limited to the "top" and "poorest" five, the membership is the same from year to year. When these groups are expanded to ten, the membership varies from year to year.

Changes 1980 to 1981[1]**.** Overall sales dropped 24 percent or $969,205.93 between 1980 and 1981. The next question is what

[1] No product breakdown available for 1981 Seaboard Marketing Group.

Exhibit 1. Relative Importance of Top Five Product Categories

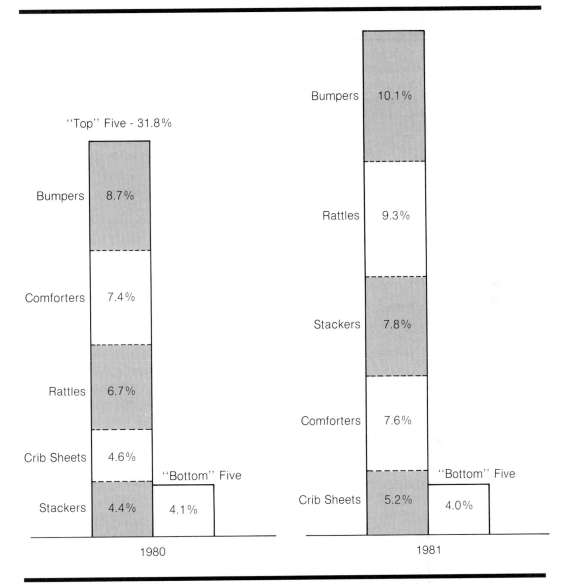

"Top" Five - 31.8%

Bumpers 8.7%

Comforters 7.4%

Rattles 6.7%

Crib Sheets 4.6%

"Bottom" Five

Stackers 4.4% 4.1%

1980

Bumpers 10.1%

Rattles 9.3%

Stackers 7.8%

Comforters 7.6%

"Bottom" Five

Crib Sheets 5.2% 4.0%

1981

happened to the "top five" product categories during this same time frame (see Exhibit 4 for this information).

We can see that four of the five did decrease. Only stackers increased over the time frame. The biggest percentage decrease was recorded by comforters followed by crib sheets and bumpers. None of the categories reached or were greater than that recorded for the overall drop in sales. The total de-crease of almost one-quarter million dollars accounted for one-fourth of the 24 percent decrease. Of the 19 product categories, only three increased in sales: stackers, pillows, and wall hangings.

Sales of the "Top" Products by the Best Sales Reps. If we look at the sales of the five best sales reps judged in terms of sales volume produced in 1980 and 1981, we can see that

Exhibit 2. Five Best and Five Worst Products in Terms of Sales Contribution

1980			1981		
			Top Five Sales Performers		
Bumpers	8.7%		Bumpers	10.1%	
Comforters	7.4		Rattles	9.3	
Rattles	6.7	31.8%	Stackers	7.8	40.0%
Crib Sheets	4.6		Comforters	7.6	
Stackers	4.4		Crib Sheets	5.2	
			Bottom Five Sales Performers		
Wall Hangings *	0.0		Miscellaneous Sewing	0.6%	
Baby Hangers	0.6		Baby Hangers	0.8	
Cumfys	0.6	4.0%	Wall Hangings	0.8	4.1%
Miscellaneous Sewing	0.7		Cumfys	0.8	
Banks	0.9		Banks	1.1	
Teethers & Pacifiers	1.2				

* Sold by only one account—noncommission wholesale ($720).

the "top" products are significant contributors to their sales production. The relative importance of four of the five categories declined in 1981 as sales tumbled. The overall dollar volume was slightly less important in 1981 (see Exhibit 5).

Granted that the top sales reps rely upon the five most important products for a substantial proportion of their respective sales volume, it is not surprising that they tend to be ranked at the top in each of the product categories (see Exhibits 6 and 7).

Relationship to Market Potential. Exhibit 8 relates product category sales to a measure of market potential (e.g., number of households).

Comparing this index against the performance of the top five sales reps, we come to some very significant conclusions (see Exhibit 9). One is that, by and large, the top sales reps do a much better job relative to potential than their less successful counterparts. Another is that every sales rep is below average for at least one product grouping. For example, Cooper is below average for three of the five groupings, but way over for rattles.

To use this information as a control tool, let's use Atkinson as an example. Sales of rattles for this sales rep are far below the average of $3.27 per 1,000 households, in fact, $2.17. Translating this into lost sales, this $2.17 per 1,000 households represents $18,087 in sales volume or about a potential 4.4 percent increase in total sales for 1980. The sales loss from being below average in rattles for the Seaboard Group is $12,459. Adding the two figures together, we find that we could have had over $30,000 more in sales of rattles if our two sales reps would have reached the average for the product category.

Another use that can be made of the data is a year-by-year comparison. In 1981, this figure for bumpers sold by Atkinson fell to $3.21, or $2.13 less. If Atkinson would have maintained the 1980 rate of sales in 1981, sales volume for bumpers would have increased $18,277, or about 7 percent overall.

Exhibit 3. Ten Best and Ten Worst Products in Terms of Sales Contribution

1980   *1981*

Top Ten Sales Performers

1980		1981	
Bumpers		Bumpers	
Comforters		Rattles	
Rattles	31.8%	Stackers	40.0%
Crib Sheets		Comforters	
Stackers		Crib Sheets	
Zip-A-Quilts	4.3%	Safe-Naps	5.2%
Safe-Naps	4.3	Music Boxes and Pillows	4.6
Music Boxes and Pillows	3.2	Diaper Bags	3.8
Carrier Covers	3.0	Carrier Covers	3.6
Dressing Bags	3.0	Gift Sets	3.5
Total	49.6%	Total	60.7%

Bottom Ten Sales Performers

1980		1981	
Wall Hangings *		Miscellaneous Sewing	
Baby Hangers		Baby Hangers	
Cumfys	4.0%	Wall Hangings	4.1%
Miscellaneous Sewing		Cumfys	
Banks		Banks	
Teethers & Pacifiers		Chain Items	1.4%
Pillows	1.3%	Lamps	1.6
Chain Items	1.3	Snuggle Bugs	1.6
Stainless	1.7	Teethers & Pacifiers	1.7
Squeeze Toys	2.1	Bassinet Liners	2.0
Curtains	2.4	Total	12.4%
Total	12.8%		

* Sold by only one account—noncommission wholesale ($720).

Sales Reps

Of the sixteen sales territories in 1980 and the twenty-three in 1981, the best salespersons sell a significant share of the total sales volume. In 1980, the five largest sales territories as measured by sales volume sold 63.4 percent of the total commissioned sales. This

Exhibit 4. Changes in Sales Contribution, Five Best Products

	Changes 1980–1981
Comforters	($100,707.66) or (34.8%)
Crib Sheets	(49,656.46) or (27.1%)
Bumpers	(88,503.24) or (25.5%)
Rattles	(30,302.26) or (11.3%)
Stackers	20,754.45 or 11.7%
Total	($248.415.06) or (25.6%) of Total Drop

Exhibit 5. Sales of Five Best Products by Top Sales Representatives

	Sold by Five Best Sales Reps	
	1980	*1981* *
Bumpers	$203,387.75 — 58.6% **	$134,030.41 — 51.9% **
Comforters	182,342.20 — 61.9	102,613.81 — 52.9
Rattles	143,704.20 — 53.6	137,250.98 — 57.8
Crib Sheets	116,036.60 — 63.3	74,342.25 — 55.6
Stackers	104,681.60 — 59.0	60,285.74 — 30.4
Totals	$753,681.60 — 32.2%	$508,523.19 — 29.7%

* No Product Data on Seaboard Marketing Group.

** Percent of total product sales less miscellaneous merchandise.

same group of sales reps in 1981 sold 62.2 percent of total commissioned sales, or some $542,242 less (see Exhibit 10).

When we include the next five sales reps in order of sales performance, it is seen that their collective contribution is 86.5 percent in 1980 and 91.0 percent in 1981.

Individually, MGD is the only rep showing a relative increase between 1980 and 1981 because of actually selling more in actual sales dollars during 1981.

Poorest Sales Reps. Three sales reps were ranked in the lowest five for both 1980 and 1981. Interestingly enough, the relative importance of the lowest five dropped by one-half in 1981. The importance of the lowest five dropped from 10.2 percent in 1980 to 5.5 percent in 1981. The drop for the next-to-lowest five was from 19.8 percent to 10.5 percent. In dollars, the five poorest sales reps sold $205,965.82 less in 1981. In other words, the poorest got worse in 1981 (see Exhibit 11).

Using Rita Parish as an example, her sales in 1980 as related to population (1,000 households) were as shown in Exhibit 12 for the top five product categories.

Exhibit 6. Rank of Five Best Products By Sales Representatives

	1980				
Sales Rep	Bumpers	Comforters	Rattles	Sheets	Stackers
Seaboard	(2)	17.8% (1)	(3)	(3)	17.6% (1)
Baker, Inc.	16.8% (1)	(2)	15.0% (1)	19.9% (1)	(3)
Atkinson	(3)	(3)		(2)	(2)
Cooper			(2)	(5)	(4)
Lucas	(5)	(5)	(4)	(4)	
MGD	(4)				(5)
Weinstein		(4)			
Lawrence			(5)		

**Exhibit 7. Relative Importance of Top Five Product Categories
for Best Sales Representatives**

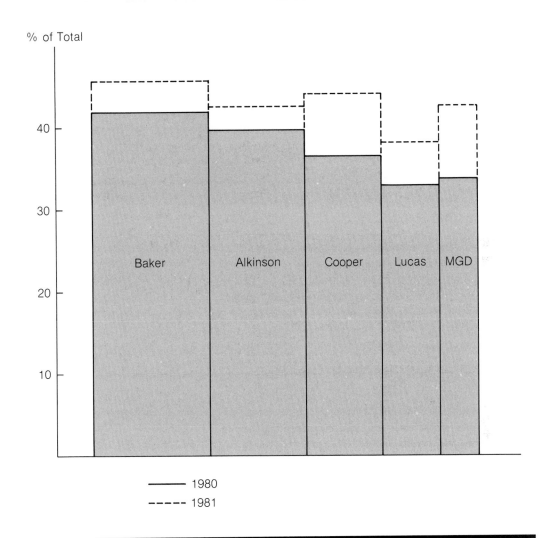

The closest she comes to average is with stackers and the farthest is with bumpers, the number one selling product category. Viewing her as typical, we can say that the low-selling reps do not take advantage of those products where the selling strength of the company is focused. Making the situation even worse, in 1981 she obtained only $0.31/1,000 households in selling bumpers, or less than one-half what she accomplished in 1980. In 1981, she only sold $0.10/1,000 households in selling comforters; this is over a 90 percent drop.

Totaling all the drops in sales/1,000 households for the top five products she could have increased sales by $38,515, or more than doubled her total volume by meeting average sales. Her total for 1981 would have been just over $74,000, or about 29 percent more than 1980.

Exhibit 8.   Product Sales Related to Population Characteristic

_1980_

Product Category	$ Per 1,000 Households
Bumpers	$4.24
Comforters	3.60
Rattles	3.27
Crib Sheets	2.24
Stackers	2.17

Exhibit 9.   Product Sales Related to Population Characteristic for Top Sales Representatives

Sales $'s Per 1,000 Households

Sales Rep	Bumpers	Comforters	Rattles	Sheets	Stackers
Seaboard	5.02	4.54	2.52 *	2.26	2.71
Baker, Inc.	5.30	4.41	3.66	3.33	1.92 *
Atkinson	5.34	5.14	1.10 *	3.56	2.89
Cooper	3.61 *	2.62 *	5.96	1.87 *	2.87
Lucas	4.67	4.28	5.47	2.34	1.94 *

* Below national average.

Exhibit 10.   Highest Ranked Sales Representatives

Top Sales Reps

_1980_			_1981_		
Seaboard	17.8%		Seaboard	20.0	
Baker, Inc.	15.3		Baker, Inc.	13.6	
Atkinson	12.0	$2,156,876.65	Atkinson	10.3	$1,614,634.95
Cooper	9.4		Cooper	9.7	
Lucas	8.9	63.4%	MGD *	8.6	62.2%
MGD	6.5%		Lucas	8.3%	
Weinstein	4.4		Smyth **	6.8	
Lawrence	4.4	$784,964.96	Weinstein	4.7	$748,371.61
Borozin	4.2		Dumas	4.7	
Johnson	3.2	23.1%	Borozin	4.3	28.8%

* Increase in Sales Dollars 1980–1981.

** No Sales for 1980.

Exhibit 11. Lowest Ranked Sales Reps

Parish Muldowney Burley Fashion Sales Co. Bulter	} $349,005.63 10.2%	Monroe Dietz Burley Parish Fashion Sales Co.	} $143,039.81 5.5%
Thomas Johnson Borozin Lawrence Weinstein	} $674,607.51 19.8%	Meger Muldowney Kelley Stowe Constamus	} $271,496.50 10.5%

Product Category Sales for Top Sales Reps. Looking at the best sellers for the "top" sales reps, we can see consistency in the two years. What was the best product category for a sales rep in 1980 continued to be in 1981. The same can be said for the poorest seller with the exception of Baker, Inc. Here cumfys were replaced with miscellaneous sewing items. It is also apparent that the relative importance of the five best selling product categories increased in 1981 as compared with 1980 (see Exhibit 13).

Customers

Eighteen accounts were sorted out on the basis of purchases of $20,000 or more in either 1980 or 1981. Sales to these accounts were $429,593.70 less in 1981 than in 1980. The most significant drop was Discount Retailers, which dropped $166,409.32. Increases were reported for Kiddie Land Operation ($111,277.63), Imports-Latin America ($13,574.93), and Cassidy-Morse Buyers ($19,659.14) (see Exhibit 14).

These top eighteen customers accounted for slightly more than one-third of total sales in 1980 and 1981 (34 and 37 percent). Looking at the top ten customers for both years, we see bumpers, comforters, and zip-a-quilts as the most frequently mentioned products (see Exhibit 15). This is consistent with the findings on leading product categories in terms of total sales (see Exhibit 16).

Exhibit 12. Rita Parish's Sales Related to Population Characteristic, 1980

	Sales/1,000	Below Average
Bumpers	$ 0.64	($3.60)
Comforters	1.55	(2.05)
Rattles	1.57	(1.70)
Crib Sheets	0.10	(2.14)
Stackers	0.45	(1.62)

Exhibit 13. Best Sellers for Top Sales Representatives

1980

Sales Rep	Best Seller	Poorest Seller	Top Five Product Sales
Baker, Inc.	Bumpers	Cumfys	42.0%
Atkinson	Bumpers	Cumfys	40.2
Cooper	Rattles	Misc. Sewing	36.2
Lewis	Rattles	Misc. Sewing	36.0
MGD	Bumpers	Baby Hangers	36.2

*1981 **

Sales Rep	Best Seller	Poorest Seller	Top Five Product Sales
Baker, Inc.	Bumpers	Misc. Sewing	45.5%
Atkinson	Bumpers	Cumfys	42.1
Cooper	Rattles	Misc. Sewing	44.8
MGD	Bumpers	Baby Hangers	43.7
Lewis	Rattles	Misc. Sewing	38.7

* There was no breakdown for the Seaboard Group in 1981, so they were omitted from consideration in both years.

Exhibit 14. Top Customers for 1980, 1981

Top Customers

Customer	1980	1981	
Save-Wise Stores (Nat'l)	$235,144.16	$154,068.18	(1)
Discount Retailers (Nat'l)	206,001.49	39,592.17	(7)
Armed Forces Exchanges (Nat'l)	183,159.84	79,671.13	(5)
Renee Stores (Nat'l)	173,346.00	145,825.20	(2)
Burwell's (Chicago)	135,950.80	114,127.51	(4)
Jackson's (Houston)	75,306.33	20,270.50	(13)
Thaller's (Cleveland)	59,521.54	19,302.05	(14)
McIntosh (Atlanta)	46,164.11	21,829.75	(11)
Watco (Philadelphia)	46,004.82	41,579.80	(6)
Buyers Group	41,544.51	37,158.20	(8)
Wallace's (Birmingham)	38,059.57	28,861.85	(9)
Holm's (Baltimore)	27,990.18	15,267.00	(16)
J.P. Smyth (Cleveland)	25,459.95	16,998.70	(15)
The Downtown Store (Chicago)	21,987.86	11,969.00	(17)
Bean's (Boston)	21,900.48	11,045.20	(18)
Save-Wise Stores (Kiddie Land Operation)	21,520.58	132,798.21	(3)
Imports (Latin America)	8,906.10	22,481.03	(10)
Cassidy-Morse Buyers	1,314.26	20,973.40	(12)
Totals	$1,363,362.58	$933,818.88	

Exhibit 15. Top Customers and Leading Product Category for Each Account

1980

Customer	*Leading Product Category*
Save Wise Stores	Zip-a-Quilt
Discount Retailers	Zip-a-Quilt
Armed Forces	Not-on-File
Renee Stores	Assorted (9279–9634)
Burwell's	Bumpers
Jackson's	Bumpers
Thaller's	Comforters
McIntosh	Comforters
WATCO	Bumpers
Buyers Group	Bumpers

1981

Customer	*Leading Product Category*
Save Wise Stores	Zip-a-Quilt
Discount Retailers	Assorted (9729–9634)
Armed Forces	Zip-a-Quilt
Renee Stores	Bumpers
Burwell's	Not-on-File
Jackson's	Bumpers
Thaller's	Zip-a-Quilt
McIntosh	Bumpers
WATCO	Comforters
Buyers Group	Comforters

Exhibit 16. Breakdown of Total Sales by Product Category

	1980		1981 *	
Music				
Music Boxes & Pillows	$ 129,322.18	3.2%	$ 117,663.81	4.6%
	$ 129,322.18		$ 117,663.81	
Plastic				
Rattles	$ 267,934.96	6.7%	$ 237,632.70	9.3%
Squeeze Toys	85,673.48	2.1	83,837.64	3.3
Chain Items	51,108.10	1.3	35,027.38	1.4
Teethers & Pacifiers	45,935.34	1.2	43,146.10	1.7
	$ 450,651.88	11.3%	$ 399,643.82	15.7%
Purchased				
Shoes, Books, Cups	$ 104,214.36	2.6%	$ 82,648.03	3.2%
Gift Sets	99,827.15	2.5	88,748.76	3.5
Stainless	67,675.80	1.7	48,018.00	1.9
Banks	35,095.77	0.9	27,093.60	1.1
Baby Hangers	23,253.33	0.6	19,620.60	0.8
	$ 330,066.41	8.3%	$ 266,128.99	10.5%

Exhibit 16. (continued)

	1980		1981 *	
Sewing				
Bumpers	$ 346,885.85	8.7%	$ 258,382.61	10.1%
Comforters	294,609.36	7.4	193,901.70	7.6
Crib Sheets	183,224.86	4.6	133,568.14	5.2
Stackers	177,487.65	4.4	198,242.21	7.8
Zip-a-Quilts	173,349.75	4.3	104,127.97	4.1
Safe-Naps	171,547.33	4.3	132,933.51	6.2
Carrier Covers	120,717.65	3.0	92,155.38	3.6
Dressing Bags	120,520.78	3.0	81,035.40	3.2
Diaper Bags	115,247.10	2.9	97,281.83	3.8
Lamps	109,855.90	2.8	40,032.05	1.6
Dust Ruffle	100,653.95	2.5	76,823.90	3.0
Bassinet Liners	96,091.65	2.4	50,378.15	2.0
Snuggle Bugs	95,029.75	2.4	40,910.33	1.6
Canopies	94,609.37	2.4	52,845.14	2.1
Curtains	94,247.94	2.4	47,927.15	1.9
Pillows	51,515.96	1.3	52,148.05	2.0
Miscellaneous Sewing	29,561.01	0.7	15,024.20	0.6
Cumfys	24,057.27	0.6	21,366.79	0.8
Wall Hanging	720.00	0.0	21,096.90	0.8
	$2,339,933.13	60.1%	$1,710,181.41	67.0%
Miscellaneous Mdse. Not-on-File	682,376.19	17.1%	59,475.23	2.2%
Totals	$3,992,349.19		$2,553,093.26	

* Incomplete Product Data on Seaboard Group.

41

Gervais–Danone *

In December 1982, marketing managers in the German ready-made "pudding-with-topping" market wondered how the industry would evolve in the coming year. The past two years had been characterized by a general decline in prices, accompanied by an increase in advertising spending. As a consequence, industry profitability had declined. Moreover, total industry sales had grown by a mere 2 percent in 1982, after having shown two-digit growth rates for many years. All of this seemed to indicate that the industry was headed for its maturity phase.

Industry participants needed to reassess their market share and profitability objectives in the light of these developments. Of all the firms, the moves of Gervais-Danone and Dr. Oetker would be particularly critical for the industry's future. Gervais-Danone was the industry leader with a market share of about 34 percent. Dr. Oetker, a late entrant, had gained market share rapidly at the expense of Gervais-Danone. The moves and countermoves of these two firms had been a major factor in the industry since 1980.

GERMAN PUDDING MARKET

The German pudding market consisted of three major submarkets: pudding powder for preparing homemade pudding; ready-made pudding without a topping, and ready-made

pudding with a topping. Pudding powder was the oldest of the three submarkets and was still the largest in terms of volume (about 270,000 tons). Dr. Oetker had a dominant position in this submarket. Sales of pudding powder had been declining regularly since the introduction of the different types of ready-made pudding, which offered the consumer greater convenience. Ready-made pudding without a topping came in water-based and milk-based varieties. Dr. Oetker dominated the former segment, while Elite had a major share of the latter segment. After a promising start, this submarket stagnated and then declined to a level of about 10,000 tons in 1982.

Pudding-with-topping differed from simple ready-made pudding by being creamier and because it had a topping of whipped cream or sauce. Despite being more than twice as expensive as traditional homemade pudding, this submarket had shown double-digit growth rates with the exception of 1982. Sales of ready-made pudding-with-topping amounted to 68,000 tons in 1982. Gervais-Danone was the leader in this submarket.

COMPETITORS

The pudding-with-topping market was dominated by four national competitors which together accounted for approximately 70 percent of the market: Gervais-Danone, Dr. Oetker, Chambourcy, and Elite. The remainder of the market was shared by approximately 30 local or regional competitors (Exhibit 1).

* This case was prepared by Reinhard Angelmar, associate professor, of INSEAD. It is based in part on the case "Dr. Oetker Fertigdesserts" written by Georg Tacke under the supervision of Professor Hermann Simon of the Universität of Bielefeld. Copyright © 1984 by INSEAD, Fontainebleau, France.

**Exhibit 1. Annual Market Shares and Industry Demand.
Pudding-with-Topping Market (1978–1982)**

	Annual market share (volume) (in percent)					
	Gervais-Danone	Dr. Oetker	Elite	Chambourcy	All other	Industry demand (1000 tons)
1978	46.8	4.8	9.1	19.0	20.3	42
1979	43.2	6.1	10.1	17.0	23.6	52
1980	35.5	11.3	9.2	14.0	30.0	60
1981	34.0	11.8	9.7	14.4	30.1	67
1982	33.9	11.9	10.4	14.2	29.6	68

Gervais-Danone

Gervais-Danone AG, located in Munich, was a wholly owned subsidiary of the French BSN group, Paris. Its 1982 sales of DM 362 million showed an increase of 11 percent relative to 1981, while its profits increased to DM 2 million from 1.1 million. Although the BSN group was active in a number of different product markets (e.g., beer, mineral water, pasta, infant food, and packaging material), Gervais-Danone AG concentrated on dairy products. Its brands in the ready-made pudding, yogurt, and fresh cheese markets gave it the leadership of the German dairy products market with an overall 10 percent share.

All of the Gervais-Danone's pudding-with-topping products were sold under the brand names "Dany + Sahne" and "Dany + Alcohol" with the "Danone family" brand umbrella. The products were offered in a variety of flavors such as chocolate, vanilla, coffee, apricot, and strawberry, but only in one cup size (125 g).

Production took place in Gervais-Danone-owned production units on specialized and highly automatized equipment which could turn out 36,000 cups per hour. The cost per 125 g cup was estimated at DM 0.25 until May 1982. A change in product formulation had subsequently increased the cost to an estimated DM 0.28.

Because pudding-with-topping was produced with fresh milk and cream, cooling trucks were required for transportation to the retailers. Gervais-Danone made direct deliveries to retailers in the areas surrounding the production sites, and to several hundred of its largest customers throughout Germany. It used specialized dairy products wholesalers elsewhere. In the stores, ready-made pudding was displayed in the dairy products section. Gervais-Danone's 150–person sales force was responsible for selling all of the company's products to the retailers. Altogether, the sales force had to carry nine major brands. The average total cost of a salesperson was estimated at DM 85,000. Dany + Sahne was distributed by 89 percent of the German retailers (Exhibit 2).

Although Gervais-Danone had no direct control over the retail price charged for Dany + Sahne, it could influence retail prices by its list price, trade promotions, and other trade conditions. On the average, retail prices were marked up 56 percent above the manufacturer's selling price. The average retail price for Dany + Sahne was 65 pfennigs [1] in 1982 (Exhibit 3).

In the past, Gervais-Danone had attempted to balance expenditures for trade promotions and for consumer advertising. Radio and especially television had been the

[1] One DM (or deutsche mark) has 100 pfennigs.

Exhibit 2. **Distribution Penetration Percentage, Pudding-with-Topping Market (1978–1982)**

	Gervais-Danone	Dr. Oetker	Elite	Chambourcy	All other
1978	84 [a]	49	85	54	70
1979	88	57	86	58	76
1980	89	64	86	63	82
1981	88	65	85	69	84
1982	89	71	86	70	85

[a] The stores which carried Dany + Sahne accounted for 84 percent of the 1978 food sales.

preferred media. Advertising spending for Dany + Sahne amounted to DM 3.6 million in 1982 (Exhibit 4).

Dr. Oetker

To generations of German housewives, the name Dr. Oetker had been synonymous with packaged dessert products, especially baking and pudding powder products. In fact, the Oetker group was a highly diversified concern with interests in shipping, insurance, banking, and other sectors outside the food industry. But packaged food products still accounted for more than 40 percent of the group's total sales of DM 3.2 billion.

The mother company, Dr. August Oetker in Bielefeld, handled the baking and dessert products which were Oetker's traditional areas of strength. Dairy products were a relatively recent addition to its product line. Industry sources estimated Oetker's total 1982 dairy products sales at DM 30 million. Pudding-with-topping and créme fraîche (sour cream which could be used for gourmet cooking) were its two major dairy products. Crème fraîche, a traditional French product, had been introduced to the German market in 1977. Although its sales had grown beyond initial expectations and attracted numerous small competitors, distribution remained spotty and usage was restricted to cooking enthusiasts.

Oetker's puddings-with-topping were sold under the Dr. Oetker family brand umbrella, but with different names. The prod-

Exhibit 3. **Annual Average Retail Prices (DM) Pudding-with-Topping Market (1980–1982)**

	Gervais-Danone	Dr. Oetker	Elite [a]	Chambourcy	All other	Weighted average price
1980	0.70	0.68	0.78	0.67	0.63	0.68
1981	0.66	0.63	0.74	0.63	0.62	0.65
1982	0.65	0.64	0.72	0.61	0.60	0.64

[a] Weighted average of the prices for the 125 g and 250 g cup size.

Exhibit 4. Annual Advertising Expenditures of National Brands (DM 1,000) Pudding-with-Topping Market (1980–1982)

	Gervais-Danone	Dr. Oetker	Elite	Chambourcy	Total
1980	2,700	700	2,400	300	6,100
1981	700	1,000	1,000	1,000	3,700
1982	3,600	1,900	1,200	1,300	8,000

ucts with chocolate, vanilla, walnut, and coffee flavor were marketed under the "Gala" brand name. The fruit-based varieties carried the "Cremilla" brand name, and some other products were marketed under generic names such as "Rotwein Creme" (red wine cream). All products came in the 125 g size.

Oetker had no production facilities of its own for its dairy products. Instead it had agreements with three dairy companies which it had equipped with the machinery necessary for the production of 12,000 cups per hour. Oetker's costs per cup of pudding-with-topping were estimated at DM 0.29.

All of Oetker's dairy products were distributed by specialized dairy products wholesalers to the retail stores. Selling these products to the retailers was the responsibility of Oetker's sales force. The sales force carried the entire line of retail-distributed products or about 200 different products. This made it difficult to obtain sustained support for specific products or product groups. Oetker's pudding-with-topping was distributed by about 71 percent of the German retailers by the end of 1982. On the average, the trade margin for Oetker's pudding-with-topping was similar to that for Dany + Sahne, that is, 56 percent. Slightly more than half of Oetker's consumer advertising effort had gone into television advertising in recent years.

Chambourcy

Chambourcy GmbH of Munich was a wholly owned subsidiary of the Nestle Erzeugnisse GmbH which was part of the German Nestle group. The total 1982 sales of the group in Germany amounted to DM 3.2 billion. Chambourcy concentrated on dairy products, with a line similar to that of Gervais-Danone but lacking fresh cheese. Its 1982 sales were estimated at around DM 100 million.

Chambourcy marketed its pudding-with-topping products under three different brand names. "Wiener Becher" (Viennese Cup) was Chambourcy's counterpart to Dany + Sahne, and had a similar range of flavors. "Mein Lieblingsdessert" (My Favorite Dessert) was a three-layer pudding with fruits. Both of these products were sold under the Chambourcy family umbrella. "Milchpudding mit Sahne" (Milk pudding with cream) was sold as a generic product to the trade. All products came in the 125 g cup size.

Chambourcy had its own production facilities. When necessary, it also used extra capacities from dairy companies. Its twin-cup equipment could turn out 24,000 cups per hour. Production costs per cup were estimated at DM 0.27 per cup.

Chambourcy supplied retailers directly in the areas surrounding its production units and used specialized dairy wholesalers elsewhere. Its sales force carried only dairy products. Chambourcy's puddings-with-topping were present in 70 percent of the German food stores. The total trade margin was similar to that of its competitors. Chambourcy's consumer advertising effort concentrated on radio and television advertising.

Elite

Elite GmbH belonged to the German Unilever concern which had a total 1982 turnover of DM 9.3 billion. Elite concentrated on dairy products. Its sales were estimated at DM 140 million.

Elite's pudding-with-topping products covered a variety of flavors. Although all used the Elite family brand umbrella, they were marketed under different names such as "Puddingtraum" (Pudding Dream), "Schokolust" (Chocolate Desire), "Schokoliebe" (Chocolate Love), and others. In addition to the standard 125 g cup size, the production cost of which was estimated at DM 0.27, Elite also produced some varieties in 250 g cups.

Production and distribution policies were similar to those of Gervais-Danone and Chambourcy. Elite's products were sold to the trade by a sales force which carried the full range of Unilever products. Elite was thought to be highly effective in utilizing Unilever's strengths in other areas, such as margarine, for promoting its pudding products to the trade. Its pudding-with-topping line was carried by 86 percent of all German retailers. Elite's consumer advertising effort concentrated almost exclusively on television.

Other Competitors

The remainder of the market was accounted for by a variety of competitors including generic and private brands of retailers and by many small regional dairy companies. The vast majority of the latter were organized as farmers' cooperatives whose main objective was to market their members' milk, either directly or in transformed form. They typically followed new national brands by bringing out me-too products at lower prices and somewhat lower quality. Their main strengths were their production expertise, short distribution channels, and strong local customer base despite a low advertising intensity. Their production cost per 125 g cup was estimated at DM 0.24.

A few of the regional companies had been making attempts to broaden their geographic reach. Foremost among them was Ehrmann, a privately managed (i.e., not a farmer's co-operative) dairy products company with a strong base in southern Germany and Nordrhein-Westfalen. Its total 1982 sales were estimated at DM 165 million. Despite a national distribution of only 32 percent at the end of 1982, Ehrmann had managed to reach a 8.5 percent market share in the pudding-with-topping market. Ehrmann produced its own high-quality products and distributed them via specialized dairy wholesalers. The production cost per cup for its pudding-with-topping products was estimated at DM 0.27. Its 50–person sales force allowed the company to cover only a limited number of specific retail targets chosen for their high sales.

COMPETITIVE DYNAMICS

The first pudding-with-topping was launched on the German market by Gervais-Danone in 1970. Despite its high price compared to traditional pudding powder, the chocolate-flavored Dany + Sahne was very successful and soon accounted for the bulk of Gervais-Danone's sales and profits.

Gervais-Danone faced no competition until 1975 when Chambourcy and Elite entered the market with a similar product. By that time, Gervais-Danone had already added vanilla and coffee flavor to its line. Yet chocolate was, and still is, the dominant flavor with about 60 percent of sales. Although profit margins were already high, the newcomers attempted to obtain a price premium relative to Gervais-Danone. When this was unsuccessful, they lowered their prices to match the market leader. The newcomers obtained reasonable volumes and expanded the total market. Gervais-Danone responded to the competitive entries by introducing fruit-flavored products under its Dany + Sahne brand.

During 1976, a number of small dairy companies started introducing pudding-with-topping products at prices generally below those of the national brands. All of this competitive activity expanded the total market. It also drove Gervais-Danone's market share down to about 50 percent.

In 1977, Gervais-Danone launched a new variety, three-layer desserts (fruits, pudding, and whipped cream), at a price higher than Dany + Sahne. Although other firms also introduced similar products, this variety never met with consumer success and was eventually abandoned by most competitors including Gervais-Danone. This year also marked the initial entry of Dr. Oetker into the dairy products market with three products: three-layer desserts, crème fraîche, and Cremilla fruit pudding. But these were marginal products. The real entry came during the following year with the launch of Gala, Oetker's chocolate-flavored pudding-with-topping. In order to gain distribution in a market which already had three national and many regional brands, Oetker offered substantial promotions to the trade. The resulting retail prices positioned Oetker approximately 5 percent below the established national brands. Chambourcy's and Elite's prices started drifting down in order to maintain market share.

Gervais-Danone maintained its prices at previous levels. It responded in two ways to the erosion of its market share that resulted from the stronger price competition. First, it increased its advertising spending. Its television commercial, which simulated a blind taste test by a housewife, argued that it was not worthwhile to save a little money by buying a low-priced yet poor-tasting dessert because that product would be rejected by the family. Second, it launched a consumer promotion program designed to maintain customer loyalty.

In 1979, Gervais-Danone introduced Dany + Alcohol, an alcohol-flavored pudding with a whipped cream topping, at a price slightly above that of a Dany + Sahne. Chambourcy, Oetker, and local competitors soon introduced their versions of the same product. This product variety met with satisfactory consumer response. Despite all of these efforts, Gervais-Danone lost 3.6 points in 1979 and was now down to an average 43.2 percent.

During 1980, Gervais-Danone continued to lose market share to Oetker and to the regional competitors whose products sold at significantly lower retail prices. Its share went as low as 32.4 percent during August and September (Exhibit 5). In the fall of 1980, Gervais-Danone inaugurated a new trade promotion program which substantially reduced the trade prices of its products, without actually changing their list prices. As a consequence, their retail prices dropped about 4 percent below those of Oetker (Exhibit 6).

Market share response was immediate: Gervais-Danone's October–November 1980 share increased by almost 6 points to 38 percent, while Oetker's share dropped 2.5 points to below 10 percent. After some hesitation, Oetker responded to the price cut, and by April–May 1981 its retail prices were about 8 percent below those of Gervais-Danone. This drove Gervais-Danone's market share down to 31 percent, while Oetker rebounded to 13 percent.

Gervais-Danone extended its trade promotion program into the summer of 1981. This kept its retail prices at a more or less constant level from October–November 1980 on. Advertising spending was cut to zero starting in December 1980 (Exhibit 7). But when market share continued to decline, a new advertising campaign was launched in the fall of 1981. Simultaneously, trade promotions were cut while list prices were reduced drastically. The net result of the price moves was a further reduction in the manufacturer's price, and a slight decline in Gervais-Danone's retail prices.

Toward the end of 1981, Oetker's trade promotion activities were becoming less intensive. Its retail prices started moving up and were practically at parity with Gervais-Danone's by April 1982. Oetker's market

**Exhibit 5. Bimonthly Average Retail Prices (DM),
Pudding-with-Topping Market (1980–1982)**

Period	Gervais-Danone	Dr. Oetker	Elite [a]	Chambourcy	All other
Dec.–Jan. '80	0.70	0.68	0.76	0.67	0.64
Feb.–March	0.70	0.66	0.76	0.67	0.64
Apr.–May	0.70	0.66	0.76	0.67	0.63
June–July	0.72	0.68	0.80	0.66	0.63
Aug.–Sept.	0.69	0.69	0.80	0.67	0.63
Oct.–Nov.	0.66	0.69	0.78	0.65	0.63
Dec.–Jan. '81	0.66	0.67	0.78	0.65	0.62
Feb.–March	0.67	0.64	0.75	0.64	0.62
Apr.–May	0.67	0.62	0.71	0.63	0.62
June–July	0.67	0.62	0.74	0.63	0.62
Aug.–Sept.	0.66	0.62	0.74	0.63	0.62
Oct.–Nov.	0.65	0.62	0.72	0.60	0.61
Dec.–Jan. '82	0.65	0.65	0.72	0.60	0.60
Feb.–March	0.65	0.62	0.71	0.62	0.59
Apr.–May	0.64	0.64	0.70	0.60	0.59
June–July	0.65	0.65	0.72	0.60	0.59
Aug.–Sept.	0.64	0.64	0.72	0.60	0.60
Oct.–Nov.	0.65	0.65	0.72	0.61	0.61

a Weighted average of prices for the 125 g and 250 g cup size.

share was hovering around 12 percent and Gervais-Danone's around 34 percent.

The new advertising campaign launched by Gervais-Danone in the fall of 1981 emphasized the superior "creaminess" of Dany + Sahne. Consumer taste tests carried out during 1981 showed that the chocolate-flavored Dany + Sahne was preferred more often than either Oetker's Gala or the Elite product. However, only the difference between Dany + Sahne and Elite was statistically significant. A blind product test of Cremilla against the equivalent Dany + Sahne products indicated that consumers preferred Oetker's products (Exhibit 8).

In May 1982, Gervais-Danone modified the composition of Dany + Sahne. The resulting products were preferred by a ratio of approximately 80 to 20 to Oetker's products in blind taste tests. During the rest of 1982, retail prices remained more or less at the same levels as in the spring. One could even observe a slight upward tendency during the October–November period. Except for the months of August and September, Gervais-Danone maintained a high advertising pressure throughout the year. Although Oetker almost doubled its advertising spending compared to 1981, its absolute level reached only slightly more than half that of the market leader.

By the end of the year, Gervais-Danone's market share reached 35 percent for the first time in almost two years. Oetker's share was slightly below 11 percent, or what it had last been about one year ago.

OUTLOOK FOR THE FUTURE

Growth of the total pudding-with-topping market slowed during 1982. This could indicate that the market was entering its maturi-

Exhibit 6. Bimonthly Market Shares (volume) and Industry Sales (million 125 g cups), Pudding-with-Topping Market (1980–1982)

Period	Gervais-Danone	Dr. Oetker	Elite	Chambourcy	All other	Industry sales
Dec.–Jan. '80	37.97	10.53	10.19	14.73	26.58	77.78
Feb.–March	36.48	11.87	9.93	12.91	28.81	80.03
Apr.–May	34.72	13.05	7.70	14.34	30.19	76.17
June–July	33.37	11.44	9.15	14.27	31.82	80.68
Aug.–Sept.	32.35	12.03	9.77	12.88	32.97	76.39
Oct.–Nov.	38.16	9.48	8.03	14.75	29.58	89.14
Dec.–Jan. '81	37.32	10.04	7.66	15.64	29.34	88.94
Feb.–March	35.97	10.76	8.47	14.83	29.97	89.31
Apr.–May	31.69	13.12	10.47	15.10	29.62	89.94
June–July	31.62	12.14	10.64	14.13	31.47	88.96
Aug.–Sept.	33.09	13.06	11.02	12.61	30.22	82.16
Oct.–Nov.	34.33	11.57	10.08	14.09	29.92	93.34
Dec.–Jan. '82	34.22	10.98	8.73	16.47	29.60	91.80
Feb.–March	33.48	12.88	9.84	12.76	31.04	92.00
Apr.–May	34.68	12.25	10.43	12.54	30.10	93.39
June–July	31.44	11.87	10.79	15.90	30.00	90.65
Aug.–Sept.	34.07	12.90	11.07	13.17	28.79	84.19
Oct.–Nov.	35.34	10.87	11.60	14.01	28.19	91.90

ty phase and that future volume growth of individual manufacturers could be obtained only at the expense of competitors. Another explanation for the slowdown in industry growth could be the difficult economic situation in Germany during 1982. GNP had declined by 1.2 percent relative to 1981, and private consumption declined by 2.2 percent (both in real terms).

Consumer surveys suggested that less than 60 percent of the potential consumers had ever tried pudding-with-topping. The comparable figure for yogurt was about 75 percent. Pudding-with-topping consumption was particularly high among consumers who lived in cities with more than 100,000 inhabitants; had a household income between DM 3,000 and DM 4,000; were middle- and higher-level civil servants and employees;

were between 14 and 19 years old. Especially low consumption was found among people who were farmers; members of households with four or more children; and had a household income below DM 1,500. Among the pudding-with-topping consumers, approximately one third could be considered brand loyal, one half switched between "good and popular" brands, and the rest systematically bought the least expensive brand.

The competitors in the pudding-with-topping market needed to reconsider their market share and profitability objectives in the light of future growth prospects of this market. Also they had to anticipate competitive behavior and assess their relative strengths and weaknesses. They would also have to decide which prices and advertising levels would best achieve these objectives.

Exhibit 7. Bimonthly Advertising Expenditure of National Brands (DM 1,000) Pudding-with-Topping Market (1980–1982)

	Gervais-Danone	Dr. Oetker	Elite	Chambourcy
Dec.–Jan. '80	208	35	463	22
Feb.–March	822	130	455	3
Apr.–May	375	190	219	41
June–July	28	98	654	0
Aug.–Sept.	519	245	319	36
Oct.–Nov.	706	10	319	231
Dec.–Jan. '81	0	89	3	351
Feb.–March	0	63	28	700
Apr.–May	0	539	531	19
June–July	0	119	430	0
Aug.–Sept.	365	127	6	8
Oct.–Nov.	361	90	19	8
Dec.–Jan. '82	518	125	0	3
Feb.–March	790	400	544	601
Apr.–May	532	600	647	237
June–July	856	305	2	0
Aug.–Sept.	2	362	1	34
Oct.–Nov.	862	123	0	415

Exhibit 8. Summary of Consumer Product Tests (1981)

Chocolate-Flavored Products

	Blind test			As-marketed test		
	Gervais-Danone	Dr. Oetker	Elite	Gervais-Danone	Dr. Oetker	Elite
First Choice	57%	47%	35%	58%	43%	37%
Second Choice	35%	46%	57%	35%	50%	54%
Both equal	7%	6%	6%	6%	7%	8%
No answer	1%	1%	2%	1%	—	1%

Fruit-Flavored Products (Blind Test)

	Dany Erdbeer	Dany Aprikose	Cremilla Erdbeer	Cremilla Pfirsich
First choice	30%	26%	65%	57%
Second choice	62%	69%	28%	37%
Equal	8%	5%	7%	6%

Nine

Not-For-Profit Marketing

DENVER ART MUSEUM

THE DEEP SOUTH CIVIC CENTER

42

Denver Art Museum *

The Denver Art Museum, the major visual arts institution for the Rocky Mountain region, was founded as an artists' club in 1893. It had no collection and no permanent building. By 1932 it became the official art institution for Denver, but until 1971 the collection was divided among various locations, including an old mansion and a remodeled automobile showroom.

In 1971 the Denver Art Museum's spectacular six-story building was opened. The striking silver-gray structure, designed by Gio Ponti of Milan and James Sudler of Denver, was located near downtown in the city's Civic Center. The opening of that new building marked a significant boost to the visual arts of the area. According to Thomas N. Maytham, who became museum director in 1974, "In the new building, we had a doubled budget, a new board of trustees, quadrupled attendance, and a challenging question: How can we best use this building?"

The answer continued to change, but by most measures the museum had been very successful. The permanent collection numbered 35,000 objects valued at more than $70 million. The major areas in the collection were European Art, American Art, New World (including Pre-Columbian Art), Oriental Art, Native Arts (including American Indian Art), and Contemporary Art. The largest single area in the museum's collection was American Indian Art, which numbered more than 13,000 objects and was among the

* This case was prepared by Professor Patricia Stocker of the University of Denver. Used by permission.

finest assemblages of its type in the world. It had been described as the finest collection of American Indian works in any art museum.

About twenty special circulating exhibitions were also shown at the museum each year. These were usually borrowed from other museums or from private collections. The exhibitions ranged in scope from the well-known Armand Hammer collection of European and American masterpieces and "Masterpieces of French Art" to "Art of the Muppets" and "Secret Splendors of the Chinese Court," a costume collection. (See Exhibit 1). The museum had not been on the tour for such "blockbuster" exhibitions as King Tut or Picasso.

The museum also had a number of educational programs including lectures, tours, films, seminars, dance, mime, music, and other performing arts. These programs were generally planned around the circulating exhibitions or the museum's permanent collection and were designed to increase the visitors' appreciation of the visual arts they were seeing.

BACKGROUND INFORMATION

Although the Denver Art Museum was not strictly a government agency, its assets were held by a Colorado nonprofit educational corporation for the benefit of the public. It served as the official arts agency for the city and county of Denver. (The city and the county were one entity.) The museum was managed by an elected, unpaid board of trustees including civic leaders in the community and those who had special skills

329

Exhibit 1. Attendance at Selected Temporary Exhibitions (six-week showings)

Armand Hammer Collection	152,106
Masterpieces of French Art	56,836
The Art of the Muppets	115,531
Heritage of American Art	22,583
Frederick Remington: The Late Years	35,000
Silver in American Life	30,000

needed by the museum, such as lawyers, advertising agency executives, professional artists, business managers, and others.

Attendance averaged between 500,000 and 600,000 a year (See Exhibit 2), which put it ahead of the Boston, Houston, and Philadelphia art museums. Perhaps more significantly, the museum boasted the highest attendance on a per capita basis of any major art museum in the country. Of the visitors to the Denver Art Museum, about 28 percent came from out of state, another 40 percent came from Colorado but outside of Denver, and the remaining 32 percent from the city and county of Denver. Included in these attendance figures were visits from students as part of gallery tours led by museum guides. The largest community in the Rocky Mountain region, Denver had a population of 500,000, but the population of the metropolitan area was 1,650,000.

The museum was open 40 hours per week, including one evening. It was closed on Mondays. There were 105 employees, about half on the security force and the other half in curatorial and administrative positions.

The Denver Art Museum had traditionally been free to the public. However, admission fees had been charged for major circulating exhibitions. Over the past three years, the museum had collected an average of $160,000 per year in fees for these special exhibitions.

There were about 15,000 museum members, the majority of these family memberships at $30 per family per year. The greatest impetus to membership had been the major exhibitions for which admission fees were charged, because members had been admitted free. Among other membership benefits were 10 percent discounts at the museum on purchases

Exhibit 2. Total Yearly Denver Art Museum Attendance

1972	674,299
1973	527,311
1974	555,058
1975	524,193
1976	527,859
1977	530,000
1978	608,178 *
1979	466,361
1980	598,648
1981	500,000 (preliminary figure)

* The popular Armand Hammer Collection was included this year.

of $5 or more, a monthly newsletter about museum activities, and previews of the nine or ten major traveling exhibitions per year. At each preview showing light refreshments were served free of charge and there was a cash bar. At a few previews an arts celebrity, patron, or collector appeared. A recent example was Baron Thyssen von Bornemiza when a portion of his collection was exhibited.

The museum had been more marketing-oriented than most other art museums, with marketing considerations in terms of exhibitions, educational programs, fund raising, and acquisitions of art objects for the permanent collection. The museum had traditionally been supported financially by local, state, and federal allocations, gifts from private foundations, and museum memberships. The trend had been toward a greater percentage of the budget each year being raised from private sources. To succeed in this change, the museum had instituted a number of innovative funding ideas, such as the successful museum associates program, for which membership was limited to those individuals who contributed at least $1,250 each year in unrestricted funds for museum support. This was in contrast to restricted funds contributed by individuals and others for specific purposes, such as the support of special exhibitions or the purchase of a specific piece of art for the museum's permanent collection. In its solicitation of funds from private foundations, companies, and individuals for those restricted uses, the museum had been successful by demonstrating its relationship to the quality of life in Denver and by including recognition to the donors, such as associating a special exhibition with the sponsoring organization in the publicity about that exhibition.

The museum also had received substantial support from the federal government. In 1981, the museum received about $200,000 from federal sources, including the National Endowment for the Arts, the National Endowment for the Humanities, and the Institute for Museum Services. Much of this support had come as matching grants. Matching grants required the museum to raise $3 for each $1 of the grant. Walter Rosenberry, chairman of the museum's board of trustees, explained that these challenge grants had had a "tremendously stimulating effect" on private contributions.

The museum budget for 1981 was $3.8 million. The city provided about 24 percent of that amount, with state appropriations making up another 10 percent of the total. However, that situation began to change dramatically in 1982.

THE FUNDING CRUNCH

A combination of government cuts, inflation, and changes in tax deductions for private contributions were forcing changes in the museum's funding picture. The total allocation from the state of Colorado and the city and county of Denver was reduced by $320,000, about 25 percent, in 1982. At the same time, federal funds were slated for a 50 percent cut. This meant that the $200,000 received by the museum in 1981 would be reduced to $100,000 for 1982. Museum director Maytham noted that the halving of funds from the National Endowments for the Arts and Humanities could cut back funds for purchase of art works and for traveling exhibitions.

The museum generated about $2.4 million of its operating budget of $3.8 million in 1981 from gifts, grants, memberships, and admission fees at special exhibitions. Changes in federal tax laws for charitable contributions were also expected to reduce revenues for the museum. With the announced budget cuts for 1982, Maytham expected the Denver Art Museum to receive $420,000 less than in 1981. With 10 percent added to the budget for inflation, 1982 expenses were expected to be $380,000 higher than in 1981. This left an $800,000 gap between revenue and expenses.

BRIDGING THE GAP

Museum employees and trustees responded to the cuts by increasing their solicitation of individual, corporate, and foundation gifts. Also planned were cutbacks in the number of traveling exhibitions, with more emphasis on the museum's own permanent collection. Fewer exhibits were to be sent around the state from Denver and fewer exhibitions of international collections would be brought to Denver.

Management planned to expand the museum's retail shop to increase sales and to close a small gallery called the Discovery Gallery used for specialized shows. Maytham estimated that $30,000 a year would be saved on packing, shipping, insurance, staff time, fees to lending institutions, and other costs associated with exhibitions in that small gallery. The space would be given to the shop for expansion.

On a long-range basis, the museum would attempt to establish a substantial endowment through foundation and individual gifts, which would allow the museum more flexibility in meeting inflation and other unpredictable contingencies.

However, the most noticeable action taken by the museum was the institution of an admission fee. For about a decade, the museum had vigorously opposed such a fee, although the city administration and others had proposed the charge as a way to avoid increasing city and state aid to the museum.

Museum officials had debated not only the imposition of a fee but also what form of admission charge would be most effective in terms of generating the greatest revenue with the smallest drop in attendance. Maytham suggested as an alternative to mandatory entrance fees, a "recommended contribution" along with a sign, "Pay what you wish, but you must pay something." This flexible type of admission fee was pioneered by New York's Metropolitan Museum of Art, where it had been used with success since 1971. The Metropolitan had signs suggesting certain donations. Several months after the flexible fee was introduced by the Metropolitan Museum, the Art Institute of Chicago adopted the system, which it continues to use today.

The Denver Art Museum trustees decided to adopt this "recommended" admission fee. Maytham explained that the museum expected to net approximately $340,000 with the new fee. "While we regret that we must institute the fee," he said, "we hope the flexible system will encourage people to come to the museum regardless of their financial means."

"Our two major goals connected with inauguration of the fee are an increase in critically needed revenue and retention of our healthy attendance goals," he continued. Recommended contributions at the Denver Art Museum were $2 for adults and $1 for senior citizens and students. Museum members and children under 12 would be admitted free. There would not be separate charges for special traveling exhibitions, which had previously brought in about $160,000 each year.

Costs of implementing the fee collection were $60,000, which included such items as cash registers and turnstiles, according to Steven Schmidt, the museum's public relations director. He noted that the museum expected to generate a 26 percent increase in memberships in 1982, from about 15,000 to 19,000, in view of the free admission given to museum members.

Schmidt noted that the Denver Art Museum decision relied heavily on the experience at the Metropolitan Museum and Chicago's Art Institute and that the differences in the Denver museum and its audience might make the flexible fee more or less successful. For this reason, he suggested that the imposition of the fee be closely evaluated, and if the flexible fee was not successful, a fixed fee would be considered.

A fixed fee had been avoided by museum officials because of other museums' experiences in instituting such fees. "With a fixed fee, we'd expect a drop in attendance of 20 to 30 percent at first," Schmidt explained, "with rebuilding after that." He noted that education and advance notification might offset some of the drop in attendance.

The drop associated with a fixed fee was

of particular concern in terms of the museum's efforts to attract lower-income visitors. It saw its mission as education, and museum officials worried that attendance might become restricted to middle and upper economic classes.

43

The Deep South Civic Center *

Lafayette, Louisiana, is a city of approximately 90,000 people located in the Arcadian section of Louisiana. Arcadiana comprises most of the southwestern section of Louisiana ranging from Baton Rouge on the east to Lake Charles on the west. Most of the area is rural and populated sparsely by people of French Canadian descent. There are, however, a number of cities and towns ranging from approximately 250,000 people in Baton Rouge to small cities like Thibodaux and New Iberia with populations of 50,000 and 80,000, respectively.

The economy of the area is based on sugarcane, cotton, and rice farming; the fishing and seafood industries; and oil exploration. Some of the finest shrimp, oysters, and crabs come from the waters along the coast of Louisiana. Also many oil companies engage in exploration and production activities along the Louisiana coast and offshore in the Gulf of Mexico.

HISTORY OF THE DEEP SOUTH CIVIC CENTER

When Conceived

In the late 1950s Lafayette's only public gathering facility, the Lafayette Municipal Auditorium, caught fire and burned to the ground. At that time Lafayette was a sleepy town experiencing increasing decay in its

* This case was prepared by Dr. Jeffrey D. Schaffer, University of New Orleans. Used by permission.

downtown area. Some slum areas had developed and the general quality of life in the city suffered from a lack of cultural activity.

The burning of the old auditorium sparked some of the city fathers to begin thinking about what was happening to their downtown area.

The Reasons for a New Civic Center

Shortly after the fire, discussions began in the Lafayette City Council regarding the future of downtown and of Lafayette. Lafayette was headquarters for many of the oil companies' field operations in Louisiana. As a result, a substantial portion of the population were executives of oil companies and their families. The oil industry had experienced substantial growth in Louisiana and new oil leases were being sold by the government on a regular basis. Other cities and towns in Arcadiana had begun to compete for the new field offices that were being developed as a result of the oil industry's growth.

The city fathers recognized that in order to continue to attract the interest of the oil companies to locate their offices in Lafayette, they would have to do something about the decaying environment and lack of cultural and entertainment activities in the city. In addition, there was little in the way of suitable meeting space for civic groups that were made up of the executives, bankers, merchants, and other professionals in Lafayette. These groups, such as Kiwanis and Rotary, had been growing in membership.

Discussion also centered around what appeared to be a growing trend in convention and trade show activities throughout the South. The city fathers felt that the central location of Lafayette, between New Orleans and Houston, would provide opportunities for regional and statewide conventions and trade shows. They hoped this would help promote the overall economy of the city and bring economic benefits to the retail businesses, motels, and restaurants. They discussed the need for facilities that could be used for social events such as weddings and banquets, as well as the need for a sports arena for the local high school basketball games, gymnastics events, and the like.

The Development Process

During the next two years much discussion took place regarding the development of a new civic center that could be designed to fulfill the needs of the community and help to reverse the decline of the downtown area. The area adjacent to the site of the old auditorium had become a full-fledged slum.

The City Council finally decided to take action and design the proposed civic center. To keep the project "within the community" a decision was made to call upon all five of the architectural firms in Lafayette.

The five firms created a consortium and undertook to design a new civic center for Lafayette. The site to be used was that of the old auditorium plus the slum area adjacent to it. If feasible, the city intended to condemn the buildings in the slum area and thereby be in a position to purchase and utilize the land.

Design of the Deep South Civic Center

Working together under a project director chosen from among the five architectural firms and utilizing specialized consultants such as acoustical consultants, theater consultants, and food service consultants from New York and other cities, the architects de-

signed a three-segmented structure comprising an auditorium, an exhibit hall, and an arena. They presented their designs to the City Council nine months after the initial assignment.

Cost of the New Facility

Shortly after the design was completed the City Council passed a proposition accepting the design that the architects had prepared and authorizing a cost estimate to be made for both construction of the civic center and the purchase of the additional land necessary for the site. By late 1963 the costing process was complete and the total amount necessary to develop the facility and purchase the land was $14,800,000.

Financing the Civic Center

After much debate it was decided that the city would finance the development of the new civic center by issuing general revenue bonds for $7,800,000 at 7 percent interest for 15 years and finance the remainder from the city treasury (a surplus of $10,000,000 existed at that time) to be repaid by increasing the utility tax on its citizens.

The proposal was put to a vote in early 1964 and defeated soundly. At that time only property owners were permitted to vote on matters concerning city financing. In 1965 a new ordinance was passed permitting all citizens of the city to vote on all matters and in 1966 a second proposal to build the Deep South Civic Center was put up for a vote. This time it was easily passed and preparations for the condemnation and purchase of the necessary land were begun immediately.

Building the Facility

Construction began in 1968 with a great citywide celebration at the ground-breaking ceremony. Finally, after three years of construction, the new civic center was opened in March 1971.

THE IMAGE OF THE DEEP SOUTH CIVIC CENTER

Early Years

There was considerable excitement and enthusiasm when the new civic center opened in 1971. Great things were expected. However, within two years it became evident that the civic center was in financial trouble. Where operating revenues were expected to cover all operating costs, substantial losses were being incurred. These losses had to be made up from city revenues. The civic center soon became known as the "white elephant" and with help from the local newspaper, public criticism grew.

The initial manager was soon fired, and his replacement, a local Chamber of Commerce executive, continued to experience criticism and growing financial losses.

Current Management

In 1977 George Smith was hired to manage the Deep South Civic Center. George had been in the amusement management business for the past 15 years. His most recent position was manager of the Baton Rouge Municipal Auditorium, a facility of about 8,000 seats. He was quite familiar with the city of Lafayette. Over the years he had watched the development of the Deep South Civic Center, had observed the local criticism grow, and was aware of the financial problems of the facilities.

George felt that to be successful in his new position he had to improve the image of the civic center in the community. He felt that to change local feeling about the civic center he needed to give lots of attention to the local community. He felt that his efforts and that of his staff must be directed toward pleasing the memberships of local organizations and especially the press. He proceeded to set up VIP tours for local people and went out of his way to roll out the red carpet whenever a member of the press came to visit. George and his staff spent a major portion of their time entertaining local dignitaries and trying to find ways to please the local press.

George was also well aware of the civic center's history of substantial financial loss. He had seen from past experience how the Baton Rouge City Council had zeroed in on the annual operating statements of the Baton Rouge Municipal Auditorium and were highly critical of any increase in operating losses. George knew that he had to find a way to achieve operating results better than his predecessors'. Cultural events, conventions, and trade shows were all part of the potential market; unfortunately, they usually paid only minimum fixed rentals. Thus, while they added much in the way of economic and cultural benefit to the city, they were not profitable to the civic center.

The big money was in concerts, especially those that could attract large numbers of people. The usual arrangement for these types of shows (mostly rock, country, and gospel concerts) was one in which the auditorium shared in the gross receipts. Usually 12 percent of the gross take went to the auditorium in the form of rent plus an additional 3 percent as a "box office" advance for selling tickets. With 11,000 seats in the coliseum, a healthy amount of revenue could be generated for a good concert.

It cost no more to set up the space for a concert than it did for a convention or trade show. In fact, it was generally easier because one had to deal only with the concert's manager, who usually was well organized and knew the ropes, as opposed to a multitude of exhibitors for conventions and trade shows. Exhibit 1 shows a comparison of the fixed-rate structure with the potential rates for various levels of concert ticket prices.

MANAGEMENT HIERARCHY

The Commission

The Deep South Civic Center, owned and operated by the city of Lafayette, is organized as a department within the city. The primary difference from other city depart-

Exhibit 1. Comparison of Civic Center Revenue Potential (Coliseum Only)

	Daily revenue potential
Regular fixed rate (convention, trade show, etc.)	$ 1,200
Concert revenue potential (11,000 seats—12% of gross)	
Ticket Price—$4.00	$ 5,300
Ticket Price—$5.00	$ 6,600
Ticket Price—$8.00	$10,600
Ticket Price—$10.00	$13,200

ments is that, by City Council ordinance, a seven-member civic center commission was established. This commission is to act as an independent body and set policy for the civic center in the areas of advertising, promotions, rates, ticket sales, parking, concessions, and catering contracts. The commission is composed of private citizens of the city of Lafayette. The City Council also has seven members.

Each member of the commission is appointed by the entire City Council; candidates can be recommended by one or more council members, or any citizen can petition the council to be considered for membership.

One member of the City Council sits on the commission as a liaison to the council. This person has no voting rights on the commission. The commission serves at the pleasure of the council, and appointments to the commission are for a one-year period.

Structure Within the City

The city of Lafayette is operated through the office of the city manager, the chief operating officer of the city, who is appointed by and reports directly to the City Council. The City Council is composed of six council members elected at large and the mayor. The mayor is primarily a figurehead who serves as a council member and has the same voting power as other council members.

The director of administration and public safety reports to the city manager and is responsible for the Deep South Civic Center. The manager of the Deep South Civic Center reports to the director of administration and public safety and is in turn responsible for the day-to-day operation of the civic center (Exhibit 2).

Responsibility of the Civic Center Manager

The responsibilities of the manager of the civic center include all activities related to the booking and handling of events, sales, administration of the operation, maintenance of the facility, preparation of all operating and capital budgets, and staffing. However, the civic center manager is not directly responsible for food service or concessions. This aspect of the operation is handled through a private operator under contract with the civic center commission. The contract is negotiated and set by the civic center commission. The civic center manager must coordinate with this contractor for the food service and concession needs of the activities booked into the civic center.

The Operating Organization for the Deep South Civic Center

The internal structure of the Deep South

Exhibit 2. Organization of the City of Lafayette Relative to the Civic Center

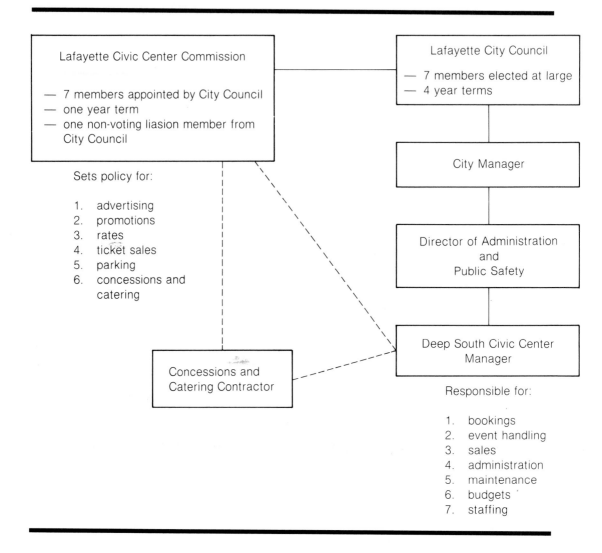

Civic Center is composed of 18 full-time people. The organization consists of the civic center manager, the assistant civic center manager, a box office supervisor, four box office attendants, a parking lot supervisor, two secretaries, a promotions coordinator, and operations superintendent, four lead men, and two laborers (Exhibit 3).

Many other people are needed when events are set up and taken down. These additional part-time employees are drawn when needed from the city of Lafayette's centralized labor pool. They consist of janitors, electricians, engineers, plumbers, carpenters, and general laborers. The civic center is charged for the time of these additional employees based upon rates established by the city Finance Department. These rates include all city overhead and benefits plus an administrative cost factor. The civic center management has no control over the rates charged by the city for tempo-

Exhibit 3. Deep South Center Management Organization

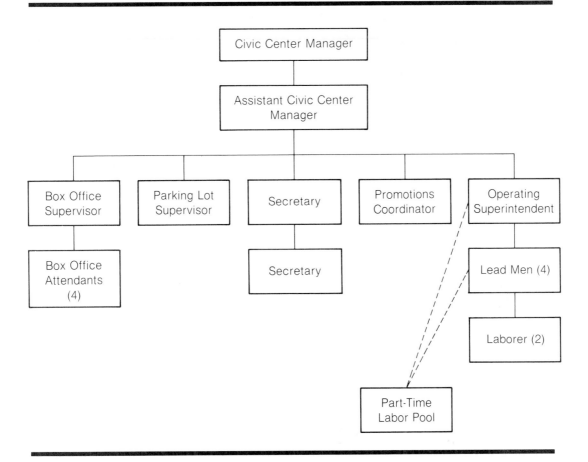

rary labor. The rates charged are substantially higher than that which would have to be paid for comparable part-time help hired directly (Exhibit 4).

The Promotions Coordinator

The position of promotions coordinator was approved as an addition to staff about 10

Exhibit 4. Deep South Civic Center City Labor Pool vs. Market Wage Rates

Jobs	City labor pool rate	Market rate [a]
Janitorial/laborer	$ 8.72/hr.	$ 3.35/hr.
Building maintenance services (electrician, plumber, etc.)	$10.84/hr.	$5.50–7.50/hr.
Grounds maintenance	$10.85/hr.	$ 3.35/hr.

[a] In most instances unskilled minimum wage people are all that would be required. In addition, fringe benefits would be because of the part-time nature of the jobs.

months ago to generate more business for the civic center. According to George Smith, however, little actual sales development has been done yet. Most of the promotion coordinator's time has been spent dealing with local activities and publishing the calendar of events. George Smith said the primary reason for not engaging in more direct selling is that they don't have the four to five additional slide presentations they need as a selling tool. Their one slide presentation, entitled "Booking a Concert," has been shown frequently at local civic club meetings and at city high school presentations.

The Operating Superintendent

The operating superintendent and his four lead men handle the setting up and taking down of booked events. The operating superintendent's responsibility is to decide on the number of extra employees needed and to arrange for them through the city labor pool. The superintendent knows from experience how many and what kinds of people are needed for a particular event.

MARKETING AND SALES

Uses of the Deep South Civic Center

According to George Smith each area of the civic center is used somewhat differently, but there is substantial overlap in some types of use. The breakdown in Exhibit 5 provided by George Smith shows the uses to which the various areas can be put.

Key Markets

"The big money is in booking concerts in our coliseum," according to George Smith. "If we want to maintain a bottom line that won't cause the City Council to get into an uproar, we've got to make sure we book enough concerts during the year to generate the revenue we need. . . . Conventions bring a lot of people to the city, but all we get is the fixed daily rate. With the labor rates we have to pay, it costs us more than we take in. The same is true for operas and symphonies because they get the fixed civic rate.

"Our plan is to try to keep everyone happy. We have to book some conventions and cultural events as well as cater to local civic

Exhibit 5. Key Markets for Deep South Civic Center

Coliseum		Exhibit hall	Auditorium (primarily an entertainment facility)
Ice shows	Conventions	Trade shows—most frequent use	Broadway road shows
Circuses	Political rallies	Banquets	Symphonies
Rodeos	Association meetings	Dinners	Ballets
Concerts	Religious meetings	Dances	Opera
Basketball	Banquets	State testing	Individual artist presentations
Hockey		Bar exam	(concerts)
Wrestling		CPA exam	Beauty pagents
Boxing		Citywide tests	Religious meetings
Trade shows		Weddings	Corporate meetings
Antiques		Proms	
Cars		Council meetings	
Boats		Corporate meetings	
Homes			

groups. But we can't let them get in the way of our concert business." Therefore, Smith conceded, "we try not to commit our facilities to these activities too far in advance because you never know when a concert promoter will call. Yet it's obvious that our greatest source of revenue is the concert business, although I can't say exactly how much it is. We don't keep those kinds of records. ... We are interested in how many days we have the civic center in use. That's what the city council wants to see ... that the facility is being used as many days as possible."

Exhibit 6 summarizes the occupancy and attendance records kept monthly. A listing of events held each month and a breakdown of attendance by area of civic center facility is kept. The amount of ticket sales for each event is also recorded, but sales reflected in these reports do not reflect civic center net revenue; they represent gross ticket sales.

Advertising

Because the Deep South Civic Center, according to George Smith, is in the amusement business, most of the advertising is placed in magazines that are the "Bibles" of the industry. About $3,000 per year goes toward advertising. The budget is reached by adding the cost of placing ads in the periodicals. The periodicals usually are

Talent & Booking Magazine

Meetings & Conventions

Trade Show & Concert Guide (annual issue)

Bill Board Magazine

Special ads are placed in magazines when they make an editorial comment about the city or region. For example, last year *Successful Meetings Magazine* ran an article about Arcadiana, and the Deep South Civic Center took an ad in that issue.

Sales Promotions

"Most of our business comes because we are here," said George Smith. "Our sales promo-

tion is on a day-to-day basis. ... The city doesn't have enough hotel rooms for us to go after the big conventions and our airport is served by only one carrier.

"In addition our meeting rooms are not adequate for most convention groups. We need smaller rooms and more flexibility to be able to satisfy the conventions and meetings that do come.

"What I think we need is a community room for about 400 people or fewer. This room should be flexible so that it can be broken down into smaller rooms. We also need more exhibit space and parking is at a premium. When we have concerts and conventions that draw heavily, we don't have enough room for all the cars, and we have to make arrangements with one of the hotels in the area to use its lot for our overflow. The problem is, we've got nowhere to expand. There is no more land available around our site."

Smith added, "To really make the Deep South Civic Center complete, we want to have an on-site restaurant and a small community theater of about 400 seats. That way, everything will be under one roof. People could have dinner and then see a show without going outside."

Competition

"We really have to work hard to compete with other civic centers and auditoriums in cities throughout southwestern Louisiana. We're all vying for the same concerts, conventions, and trade shows. People in the area who attend these concerts will gladly drive 100 miles or more to see a show.

"We are careful to treat the concert promoters right so they will remember us when they have another show."

BUDGETS AND FINANCIAL REPORTS

Accounting

All accounting for the civic center is done centrally by the city Finance Department. The civic center is required to follow the

Exhibit 6. Deep South Civic Center Summary of Occupancy and Attendance

Month/Year	Coliseum				Auditorium				Exhibit hall				Total complex			
	Attendance	Ticket Sales	Occupancy (days)	(%)	Attendance	Ticket Sales	Occupancy (days)	(%)	Attendance	Ticket Sales	Occupancy (days)	(%)	Attendance	Ticket sales	Occupancy (days)	(%)
July 1980	6,667	$ 45,518	3	10	10,142	$16,122	10	32	3,548	$ 2,459	8	26	20,357	$ 64,098	18	58
August 1980	11,110	63,093	4	13	4,867	8,415	6	19	6,549	4,862	15	48	22,526	76,370	19	61
September 1980	15,458	104,505	7	23	5,550	0	2	7	4,971	1,898	15	50	25,979	106,403	18	60
October 1980	38,910	166,913	17	55	18,037	27,769	11	35	2,328	0	16	52	59,275	194,682	25	81
November 1980	30,648	169,472	10	33	9,334	30,446	14	47	12,162	11,943	19	63	52,144	211,861	24	80
December 1980	18,528	102,180	14	45	10,646	28,269	8	26	5,697	246	15	48	34,871	130,695	23	74
January 1981	40,812	154,290	N/A	N/A	3,434	2,320	N/A	N/A	3,147	5,893	N/A	N/A	47,393	162,503	N/A	N/A
February 1981	8,886	30,808	N/A	N/A	5,525	12,424	N/A	N/A	4,737	0	N/A	N/A	19,148	43,232	N/A	N/A
March 1981	44,351	246,765	N/A	N/A	14,594	42,245	N/A	N/A	4,588	0	N/A	N/A	63,533	289,010	N/A	N/A

budgetary and planning process as pre-scribed by city management.

Monthly Operating Statement

Exhibit 7 is the operating statement of the Deep South Civic Center covering the nine months ending March 1981. A financial statement in this format is prepared month-ly, on a cumulative basis, by the city finance department.

Budget

"When I'm not entertaining someone from the local community or a newspaper representa-tive, I'm working on our budgets." That's the way George Smith described the budgetary process used at the Deep South Civic Center. The actual information required to complete the budget amounted to over 200 pages. The following is a list of the major summary forms and reports included in the budget report.

1. A statement of objectives and activities

**Exhibit 7.   City of Lafayette, Louisiana, Civic Center Fund
Comparative Income Statement for the 9 Months Ended March 13**

	1981	1980
Operating revenue		
Rentals	$186,249	$205,068
Event expenses	57,693	62,383
Advertising	2,600	2,140
Admissions tax	48,840	61,657
Commissions	50,290	52,944
Event profit—city-sponsored	6,775	70
Parking fee	48,938	—
Total operating revenue	401,385	384,262
Less operating expenses before depreciation		
Administrative		
Personal services	249,385	218,350
Utilities and communications	190,768	194,965
Administrative expenses	340,139	565,658
Promotional expenses		
Personal services	38,392	32,623
Sevices and charges	1,591	5,305
Total operating expenses before depreciation	820,275	1,016,901
Operating (loss) before depreciation	(418,890)	(632,639)
Less depreciation	243,178	238,942
Operating (loss)	(662,068)	(871,581)
Nonoperating income		
Supplement from general fund	240,000	375,000
Miscellaneous	4,649	9,181
Interest on investments	849	3,428
Total nonoperating income	245,498	387,609
Net (loss)	$(416,570)	$(483,972)

2. Personnel recap

3. Budget worksheet A

4. Detail of budget request

5. Reason and justification of basic budget request

6. Computerized form #2A

7. Equipment request forms

8. Revenue estimate form

9. Budget request form

10. Revenue estimate income generated

11. Detailed description of each budgetary account

12. Budget recap

13. Supplemental budget request recap

14. Supplemental budget request cover

15. Improvements, maintenance, and capital budget cost request and budget estimates

16. Equipment request recap

17. Reason and justification of supplemental budget requests

18. Justification for additional personnel requests

19. 5 percent decrease budget

20. 5 percent decrease account summary

LOOKING AHEAD

After reviewing all these facts, Smith wondered what specific steps he should now take to ensure the viability and success of the center. There was much to be done, and things had to begin happening.